MICRO MANAGEMENT SCIENCE

Microcomputer Applications of Management Science

MICRO MANAGEMENT SCIENCE
Microcomputer Applications of Management Science

SANG LEE
University of Nebraska–Lincoln
JUNG SHIM
Mississippi State University

wcb
Wm. C. Brown Publishers
Dubuque, Iowa

Book Team
John Stout Executive Editor
Linda M. Galarowicz Editor
Kathy Law Laube Editorial Assistant
Michael E. Warrell Designer
Ann Helling Production Editor
Vicki Krug Permissions Editor

wcb group

Wm. C. Brown Chairman of the Board
Mark C. Falb President and Chief Executive Officer

wcb

Wm. C. Brown Publishers, College Division
Lawrence E. Cremer President
James L. Romig Vice-President, Product Development
David A. Corona Vice-President, Production and Design
E. F. Jogerst Vice-President, Cost Analyst
Bob McLaughlin National Sales Manager
Catherine M. Faduska Director of Marketing Services
Craig S. Marty Director of Marketing Research
Marilyn A. Phelps Manager of Design
Eugenia M. Collins Production Editorial Manager
Mary M. Heller Photo Research Manager

Library of Congress Catalog Card Number: 85–71792

ISBN 0–697–00389–2

Printed in the United States of America

10 9 8 7 6 5 4 3 2 1

To the memory of my brother Sang Jin Lee—S.M.L.

To my parents—J.P.S.

CONTENTS

2 CHAPTER

3 CHAPTER

Break-Even Analysis *31*

CHAPTER

Linear Programming *43*

5 CHAPTER

Linear Programming—Sensitivity Analysis and Integer Problems *73*

CHAPTER

The Transportation Problem *109*

7 CHAPTER

CHAPTER

12 CHAPTER

13 CHAPTER

14 CHAPTER

15 CHAPTER

17 CHAPTER

Computer-Based Simulation *389*

18 CHAPTER

Implementation of Management Science for Productivity Improvement *405*

PREFACE

Management science encompasses a broad spectrum of quantitative and scientific methodologies that are useful in management decision making. For this reason, a course in management science is now a requirement in most business administration programs. Many texts are marketed for this required course, most of them theory oriented.

While most texts intended for use in management science courses are of a strictly theoretical orientation, *Micro Management Science: Microcomputer Applications of Management Science* is unique because it is application oriented. Management science concepts are presented through practical application on the microcomputer, the tool that is revolutionizing management in organizations. A comprehensive management science software program, the *Micro Manager,* accompanies the text and completes the hands-on learning package.

Specific features of the text include the following:

- a comprehensive, readable presentation of the microcomputer-based application of management science.
- well-organized instruction and complete documentation for the *Micro Manager.*
- thorough discussion of current management science topics.
- menu-driven, user-friendly programs for various management science topics. These programs can be used on IBM PCs or compatible computers.
- logical organization of concepts from the fundamental to the abstract.
- a solutions manual presenting the computer answers to all text assignments.

The text is intended primarily for use by undergraduate and graduate students of business administration. However, when used with the *Micro Manager,* it can also be a valuable resource tool for practicing managers or prove to be an indispensable supplement to any management or quantitative course.

In writing this book, we benefited greatly from the suggestions of our colleagues and students. We are especially appreciative of the help of S. O. Kim and J. D. Kim, two microcomputer "wizards" at the University of Nebraska. We also thank Y. Cho, André Everett, J. Im, G. C. Kim, S. H. Lee, Bruce Speck, and Y. Yu for their assistance in polishing the text and the *Micro Manager*. The reviewers were also very helpful: David Burkitt of Emory University; Stuart Nagel of the University of Illinois, Champaign-Urbana; Joelee Oberstone of Pepperdine University; and Jack Thorton of East Carolina University. We are very grateful to our office staff—Joyce Anderson, Cindy LeGrande, and Cathy Jensen—and to Linda Galarowicz, Gretchen Hazen, and Kathy Shields of Wm. C. Brown Publishers. Finally, we would never have completed this text without the support of our families.

CHAPTER 1

Management Science and the Microcomputer

Management science is a discipline of a host of quantitative approaches for management decision making. In this chapter, we will discuss management science, its use of the microcomputer for decision making, and use of the programs contained in the *Micro Manager* software package.

What Is Management Science?

Management science is concerned with the application of quantitative analysis to managerial decision making. Thus, the primary objective of management science is to assist the decision maker in finding the best feasible solution to a decision problem by analyzing available alternatives. Many real-world decision problems are simply too complex to solve by using our hunches or the "art of muddling through." The decision maker uses management science to analyze a problem through quantitative techniques that generate pertinent information about the problem. In other words, management science itself may not be the answer to a given problem, but it certainly sharpens and improves the decision-maker's judgment.

The basic purpose of decision making is to achieve a set of organizational objectives in the most effective way. Thus, some leading authorities on management, such as Herbert A. Simon, a Nobel laureate in 1978, have defined decision making as being synonymous with management. In the process, the role of management science has increased a great deal in organizations.

To improve the rationality in decision making, management science has placed greater emphasis on approaches that generate, synthesize, and summarize pertinent information about the decision environment and the outcomes of alternative courses of action. Consequently, organizations have used management science frequently—not as a black box of solutions, but as a decision-making aid for the decision maker. Also, the aggregate effects of recent advances in management technology, the ever-increasing complexity of environment, and the improved capability of decision makers have greatly influenced the increasing role of management science.

It should be emphasized here that management science does not, and it is not intended to, replace the intuitive decision-making ability of the decision maker. The intuitive ability is based on the experience of the decision maker who has become known for his or her decision-making capabilities, and who has a general awareness of the situation and some personal insights about future outcomes. With or without management science, decision makers usually exercise some degree of personal judgment. Management science, therefore, should be intended to enrich and sharpen the decision-maker's judgment in reaching a final decision.

Again, let us emphasize that the central theme of management science is the application of scientific methodologies to the process of decision making. As such, management science has become an integral part of modern management.

The Role of Management Science

The beginning of management science is unknown. However, the term *management science* or its synonym *operations research* surfaced around the early 1940s. Serious operations research activities originated in the United Kingdom during the early stages of World War II. To discern the most effective military strategies, there was an urgent need for scientific approaches to analyze a multitude of logistics problems. The British, and then the American, military authorities formed various interdisciplinary groups of scientists to perform research on military problems.

After World War II, especially since 1951, operations research has developed rapidly in the United States. Three important factors precipitated this rapid development. First, there was an economic boom following World War II. With the arrival of the industrial boom came continuous mechanization, automation, decentralization of operations, and division of management functions. Such rapid organizational change resulted in complex managerial problems. Many operations researchers, including those management consultants who served in the operations research teams during the war, found these business problems basically the same as the military problems. Thus, application of operations research to managerial decision making became popular.

Second, many operations researchers continued their research after the war. Consequently, some important advancements were made in various operations research techniques. For example, George B. Dantzig, after continuous research, developed the simplex method of linear programming in 1947. By 1950, many important operations research techniques were well developed for practical application, such as linear programming, dynamic programming, queuing theory, and inventory models.

The third factor in the rapid growth of operations research is the staggering analytic power made available by high-speed electronic computers. Complex managerial problems usually require an enormous amount of computation, and the computer revolution has made it possible to apply many sophisticated techniques to practical decision analysis.

Management science has been the most popular synonym of operations research. We shall use the term *management science* in this book since we are basically concerned with scientific approaches to management decision making.

While we recognize the value of systematic analysis for management decision making, we must also accept the fact that management is a human process. Thus, we cannot be *totally* scientific or rational in decision making. As a matter of fact, many empirical studies have shown that the decision maker does not always behave rationally. In reality, the decision maker is quite incapable of making the optimum decision because of the lack of analytical abilities, imperfect information, or the unstable preference structure for the organization.

Herbert A. Simon presented the now-celebrated concept of "bounded rationality." Under this concept, the decision maker strives to be as rational as possible in achieving organizational goals, given his or her limited cognitive abilities and information. The decision maker is not trying to be irrational, but attempts to do his or her best under the circumstances. Thus, the person employs an "approximate" or "intentional" rationality in decision making.

If we accept the notion of bounded rationality, which we must accept as reality, decision making will always be based on human judgment, creativity, and perhaps even courage. Management science should be accepted as a tool to improve the quality of our decision making rather than as a panacea. Therefore, we believe much of the criticism directed toward management science is the result of the unrealistic expectations of decision makers who have used it.

We believe management science plays the following roles in modern organizations:

Management by Multiple Objectives

Management science application is possible only when an organization has a definite set of objectives. Furthermore, managers are faced with multiple, and often conflicting, objectives such as attaining satisfactory levels of return on investment, market share, industrial relations, meeting government regulations, and customer demands.

Management science is essential for putting the purpose-oriented decision-making process into operation in organizations. A number of computer-based interactive approaches have been developed to analyze multiple goals in terms of their priorities, trade-offs, and resolution. Many satisficing approaches for management by multiple objectives have been suggested. In this text we will discuss goal programming for multiple-objective decision making.

Productivity Management

The ultimate purpose of management is to achieve and/or sustain the desired level of productivity. To achieve organizational effectiveness, management should analyze three important factors and their relationships: (1) productivity of human resources; (2) application of modern technologies; and (3) innovative management systems. Management science can be an important tool in integrating the above-mentioned three essential factors to improve productivity.

Management by Ideology and Information

The basic purpose of management is to achieve long-term organizational goals. R. H. Hayes and W. J. Abernathy, management professors at Harvard Business School, suggest that one of the important reasons for the sagging productivity of many organizations in the United States is their emphasis on short-term financial goals, often at the expense of long-term goals. An emerging concept of management is management by ideology and information.

Management by ideology and information emphasizes a stable organizational philosophy at the top level and efficient information-based decision making at the operational level. Under this system, superordinate organizational goals, values, and philosophies are clearly communicated from top to bottom. Based on this stable organizational culture, middle- and lower-level employees are encouraged to operate based on management by information. Thus, the bottom-up communication system is used to develop intermediate operational objectives, such as market share, research and development, human resource development, operational efficiency, and others.

Management by ideology and information, although strictly American in its origin, is closely related to the Japanese style of management. A harmonious integration of two completely different approaches, management by ideology from top down and management by information from bottom up, requires imaginative managers. We believe management science can make an important contribution in this area as an integrated decision support system.

Efficient Materials Management

With the increasing scarcity of critical materials, the efficient materials management is of vital concern to management. Efficient approaches to secure, store, or process materials require systematic analyses. Management science, augmented by computer-based information systems, can be an important asset for such an efficient materials management system.

The Process of Management Science

Every practitioner of management science has his or her own way of doing things. However, there are several major steps that almost everyone agrees are important in management science. We will discuss these phases.

1. Formulate the Problem

One of the most important characteristics of the scientific approach to a decision problem is an insistence on determining exactly what one is trying to do. As an old adage goes, a problem well-put is half-solved. As a matter of fact, identification of the problem is the most difficult part of decision analysis. The management scientist is usually presented with an incomplete list of symptoms rather than a diagnosis. Consequently, the management scientist must obtain additional symptoms before he or she can diagnose (formulate) a problem correctly.

Although decision analysis should begin with the formulation of a problem, this step is a continuous process until a solution is reached. In other words, once an initial formulation of the problem is completed and analysis proceeds, the problem is subjected to continuous modification and refinement.

The problem formulation phase may include the following steps:

- The orientation period for an overall analysis of the organizational goals, culture, and climate.
- Identification of critical decision factors—the decision maker, objectives, constraints, and decision environment.
- Decision alternatives that could give a choice to the decision maker should be thoroughly analyzed.

2. Develop the Model

Model development is the crux of management science application. This phase involves the fine details of the problem. Developing a model requires a comprehensive analysis because the process must uncover the complexities, unique characteristics, and possible uncertainties involved in the problem. Logical expression of such problem characteristics requires a mathematical model to represent the interrelationships among the system elements. Some of these relationships may be expressed by equations, inequalities, or other constraints that impose restrictions on the decision variables. The model must be capable of representing the most relevant and important characteristics of the problem. The systematic analysis is possible only when the relationships among the components and their objective criteria are expressed in a manageable mathematical model.

One more consideration requiring close attention in the model-developing phase is the time horizon for the use of the model. The problem at hand may change drastically in time. Therefore, a continuous updating of the model parameters, their relationships, and the objective criteria is necessary. It is imperative to evaluate the objective criteria continuously, as management goals do change in time with the changing organizational environment.

It is sometimes necessary to modify a model, even when it is perfectly functional, if required data are not available or too costly to obtain. Thus, it may be necessary to go through several cycles of model development and search for data. The search may not always yield the required data, but it often reveals how the model should be modified to use what is available.

3. Solve the Model

Once a management science model is formulated, the next step is to solve it for an optimum alternative. The optimum solution must provide the values for the decision variables that optimize the given decision criterion (or objective). A mathematical model is a simple representation of reality. If the model formulated represents every possible aspect of the problem under analysis, it may be simply too difficult to formulate, manipulate, and solve. On the other hand, if the model is too simple, it may not include all relevant elements of the problem. Thus, the model solution phase may in fact reveal whether the model is or is not appropriate for the problem.

4. Implement the Solution

The true value of management science application is realized when the model solution is actually implemented for the problem on hand. Thus, the model solution should be transformed into a set of policies or operating procedures that will be implemented. The implementation process usually results in an organizational change that causes disturbances to established routines. Because of its importance, we will devote chapter 18 to the implementation process of management science.

Management science has its focal point in the construction and solution of decision models. Therefore, it is characterized by (1) a rational and methodical approach; (2) heavy reliance on quantitative models; and (3) extensive use of the computer. Although the topics of management science can be introduced without the use of the computer, it would be impractical or even totally impossible without the use of the computer to apply management science to real-world problems. Therefore, some knowledge of computers is usually required for applying management science. We believe that there is a definite trend toward a more extensive use of microcomputers for management science. Thus, we are providing a user-friendly, easy-to-use microcomputer software, the *Micro Manager,* to accompany this book.

Modeling in Management Science

A primary purpose of this text is to acquaint you with the modeling of management systems. We will present a variety of specific models throughout this text to provide an exposure to the full range of modeling opportunities in the business environment.

It has been said that life consists of solving problems. Of course, as human beings, we are better at solving most problems than are the animals because we can *think*. We solve important problems by the process of building models. We are image builders by nature, as we recognize our own existence and are capable of visualizing ourselves in various situations. In short, we have imagination and creativity to build models.

A model is an abstract representation of reality. It describes the reality by using only those elements or variables that are important. A very abstract form of model is the mental model. Our mental model of a situation may consist of a few words, feelings, or flashes of images corresponding to those few important aspects of the situation.

A model is much simpler than reality. The power of a model in solving a problem comes precisely from this simplicity that reflects pertinent, important elements for describing the problem at hand. All sorts of models are around us—maps, model airplanes, chemical molecule relations, toys, and mathematical equations.

One way to avoid the problem of confusion or ambiguity in modeling is to employ the language of mathematics in describing our thoughts. For example, if we use x to represent the number of pigs that went to market, then we do not have to count our toes over and over again. When another person looks at the model, the analysis process will not be hindered by any "oink" thoughts or smelly toes.

There are a number of advantages in using mathematical models. First, they are precise, concise, and objective. We cannot misinterpret or receive misunderstanding from them. Second, we can manipulate the models by changing certain components to test possible consequences without actually changing real-world situations, such as increasing the unemployment figure by a million people.

Management science is based on mathematical models and their solutions on computers. One obvious advantage of a model is its simplicity, as we discussed previously. We can test the behavior of a system under various conditions. Thus, the real challenge of management science modeling is to build as simple a model as possible while retaining all pertinent attributes of the system.

In developing a model, we can always rely on the law of natural phenomenon known as the "critical few." This law simply suggests that only a small number of attributes explain the major portion of the system's behavior. For example, several key managers make 80 percent of major decisions, 20 percent of products contribute 80 percent of sales, several employees are responsible for 85 percent of product defects, and the like. In modeling, we must identify those few critical attributes that explain a major part of the system behavior. The art of modeling requires a good working knowledge of management science, experience of building models for real-world problems, and creativity in conceptualizing the complex problem.

Management science models are usually expressed as mathematical relationships in the form of equations or inequalities. For example, we can express our disposable income as follows:

$$DI = GI - (T + D)$$

where DI = disposable income
GI = gross income
T = taxes
D = all other deductions

When we study the behavior of a system, we must analyze a set of components known as *variables.* In our disposable income model shown above, GI, T, and D are good examples of variables. Variables can be classified as follows:

Dependent Variables

The dependent variables, also referred to as criterion variables, are those that reflect the performance level of the system under study. For example, the disposable income level (DI) is a dependent variable. If DI = \$75,000, we can see a reasonably successful person in terms of income. The value of the dependent variable is based on the values taken up by independent variables.

Independent Variables

The independent variables are those whose values are not dependent on other variables. The independent variables can be classified into two types: the decision variables and the exogeneous variables.

Decision Variables

The decision variables are those variables whose values we are trying to determine. For example, let us formulate the gross income model as

$$GI = \$15W,$$

where \$15 = wage rate per hour
W = total working hours per year

In order to earn enough income to secure GI = \$60,000, we can solve for the hours that we must work as

$$60{,}000 = 15W$$
$$W = 4{,}000 \text{ hours.}$$

Exogeneous Variables

The exogeneous variables are those over which we have very little control. In our model, tax rates and deductions are good examples of exogeneous variables.

Parameters

The remaining components of the model are known as the *parameters*. The parameters determine the relationship among the variables. Parameters can be classified as constant or random parameters. The parameters may have a static or constant value. For example, in our disposable income model, the total income and the total hours worked are related to the constant parameter of $15, the hourly wage rate. If the hourly wage rate is not set but depends on the commission for selling different products, it may be a *random parameter*.

The Microcomputer

Recent advances in microelectronics, brought about by large-scale integration (LSI), have made it possible to put a powerful computer into a single, integrated circuit package, i.e., the microcomputer. The microcomputer or personal computer is the product of the fastest-growing segment of the fastest-growing industry the world has ever known. For example, although the microprocessor chip dates only from 1971, it is expected that more than 9 million microcomputers will have been installed in business firms by 1992.

When Apple and Radio Shack began marketing their personal computers in 1977, only a few business managers recognized the implications of the microcomputer for business applications. However, when IBM introduced its personal computer in late 1981, the desktop microcomputer began making a major impact on management decision making. Today, application of microcomputers to the automation of industrial processes (e.g., controlling robots), testing and inspection, and to general management information processing has been widely discussed. However, microcomputers have an enormous potential as a management tool, especially as an economical means to apply management science in organizations. The following characteristics of the microcomputer are important reasons for its great potential on the future application of management science.

Low Cost and Small Size

Because of its low cost and small size, many small organizations and departments of large firms can have their own computing facility. Thus, the manager and staff can obtain firsthand experience in using the computer for information processing and decision making.

User-Friendliness

The microcomputer usually does not inhibit managers because it does not demand the technical knowledge and skills associated with professional programmers. This is the result of a conscious effort to produce software that would not generate "computer phobia." Thus, the decision maker can, with appropriate software support, interact with the microcomputer to obtain decision support.

Improved Software Availability

As the microcomputer has proliferated in business offices, the availability of decision support software packages has become more widespread. A number of advanced mathematical and statistical software packages are now available.

The Widespread Availability of Microcomputers

All types and sizes of organizations are using microcomputers. The low cost and ready availability of these microcomputers are attractive features that will ensure the rapid rate of microcomputer installations in organizations.

Expanding Capabilities

The constant rate of improvement in both speed and storage capacity of the microcomputer makes it a powerful computer. Thus, the microcomputer is now running complex management science models. This is especially true with currently available hard disk memory systems and a new wave of more powerful microcomputers with 32-bit memory chips.

Experimental and Learning Tool

The decision maker can use the microcomputer as a laboratory for trying out new ideas. The dedicated nature of the computer (stand-alone or decentralized to perform specified tasks) means that the organization's central system will not be burdened. Thus, the microcomputer can be a convenient experimental tool for new ideas or a learning tool for understanding complex systems.

All of the above factors clearly indicate that the spread of microcomputers into all levels of organizations is very natural. As a matter of fact, the use of microcomputers has been nothing short of phenomenal. Since the microcomputers are finding their way into managers' offices at such a rapid rate, they have great potential as a cost-effective means of applying management science for decision-making purposes. We believe such potential is already being achieved in a number of organizations. Thus, we need a complete and user-friendly software package for the application of microcomputers to decision making. This text, *Micro Management Science,* serves as the manual for such a package, the *Micro Manager.*

Micro Management Science

Since management science can be effectively applied through the use of microcomputers, it is our prediction that we stand on the threshold of a tremendous breakthrough. Given the unprecedented proliferation of microcomputers and their growing power, it seems quite logical to extrapolate their increased use for decision making in all types of organizations. Improvements in cost, software support, and computational capacity of the microcomputer, along with managers' increasing computer fluency, clearly support the prediction that the time has already arrived for the conversion of most management science programs to microcomputers. We estimate that perhaps 80 percent of existing organizations can perform about 80 percent of their management science application on microcomputers.

As a preparation for this text, your authors conducted a questionnaire survey in the spring of 1983. To determine the extent to which microcomputers are being used as an instructional tool in management science courses, we sent questionnaires to 650 randomly selected members of the American Institute for Decision Sciences. We received back 122 usable questionnaires, a return rate of 18.8 percent.

About 84 percent of the sample respondents indicated that they use computers in their management science related courses. Among these computer users, 37 percent indicated that they use microcomputers for instructional purposes. The current hardware usage breakdown is: Apple—35 percent; IBM—28 percent; Radio Shack—15 percent; and others—22 percent. The microcomputer installation arrangements were: lab—62 percent; faculty office—23 percent; classroom—3 percent; and other—12 percent. About 44 percent of the respondents, who were not using microcomputers at the time of the survey, indicated that they would be purchasing microcomputers for instructional purposes in the near future. Furthermore, the most likely hardware they are planning to purchase is: IBM—42 percent; Apple—13 percent; and others—45 percent.

The survey also revealed several interesting facts. First, a fairly large proportion (38 percent) of the respondents felt that the roles of a large mainframe computer system for management science would decrease dramatically in the future. Second, about 64 percent of the respondents believed that microcomputers would play important roles in teaching or applying management science in the future. Third, the most severe problems associated with the use of microcomputers were: (1) limited access (26 percent); (2) limited software (24 percent); (3) physical facility and security (16 percent); (4) technical maintenance (10 percent); and others. Fourth, the survey indicated a generally negative degree of satisfaction with currently available microcomputer software for management science.

Based on the results of the survey, it appears clear that the microcomputer is becoming an important instructional vehicle for management science. At the same time, there is a definite need to develop a user-friendly, comprehensive, and efficient software package for the microcomputer application of management science. This text and its accompanying software package, the *Micro Manager,* are intended to meet such needs.

Summary

Management science is concerned with the application of a host of scientific methodologies to management decision making. Most real-world problems are complex, usually requiring computer-based analysis. The advent of the microcomputer is changing the way organizations work and make decisions. Thus, it is only natural to use today's powerful, compact, inexpensive, and dedicated microcomputers for management science applications. *Micro Management Science* and the *Micro Manager* are intended to meet this critical need.

References

Churchman, C. W., R. L. Ackoff, and E. L. Arnoff. 1957. *Introduction to operations research*. New York: John Wiley & Sons.

Hillier, F. S., and G. J. Lieberman. 1980. *Introduction to operations research*. 3d ed. San Francisco: Holden-Day.

Lee, S. M. *Introduction to management science*. 1983. Chicago: Dryden.

Lee, S. M., L. J. Moore, and B. W. Taylor. (1985). *Management science*. 2d ed. Dubuque, IA: Wm. C. Brown Co. Publishers.

Lee, S. M., C. Snyder, and M. Gen. 1982. The microcomputer: Experience and implications for the future of multiple criteria decision making. In *Essays and surveys on multiple criteria decision making*, ed. P. Hansen. Berlin: Springer-Verlag.

C H A P T E R 2

The *Micro Manager:* An Overview

The *Micro Manager* software package you are about to use represents the most comprehensive set of management science programs ever developed for the microcomputer. This package includes 21 programs that cover today's most widely used management science tools. Furthermore, the package is extremely easy to use since all of the programs are completely user-friendly.

Even though the *Micro Manager* is not intended for solving large-scale models that should be solved on a mainframe computer, you can solve many smaller problems easily and inexpensively by using the *Micro Manager* on a microcomputer. The *Micro Manager* has two basic purposes. First, it is intended to provide students, managers, and practicing professionals with the basic understanding about when and how to use management science for decision making. Second, you can use the *Micro Manager* either to solve simple management science problems or as a learning/teaching aid.

In this chapter, we will present an overview of the *Micro Manager* in regard to its operating procedures, its equipment requirements, and its program descriptions. Each subsequent chapter dealing with a specific management science topic will provide more in-depth information about the program description, input instructions, and model output.

Figure 2.1 Contents of the *Micro Manager* Package

Contents of The Micro Manager Package

1. Break-Even Analysis
2. Linear Programming I
3. Linear Programming II
4. All Integer Programming
5. Zero One Programming
6. Transportation
7. Assignment
8. Goal Programming
9. Decision Making under Risk
10. Decision Tree
11. Decision Making under Uncertainty
12. Bayes' Decision Rule
13. Shortest Route
14. Minimum Spanning Tree
15. Maximum Flow
16. PERT/CPM
17. Inventory Models
18. Dynamic Programming
19. Queuing Models
20. Markov Analysis
21. Simulation

Figure 2.1 lists the contents of the *Micro Manager* software package. You can use the 21 programs provided in the diskettes to solve many decision problems that are covered most frequently in curricula such as management science, decision science, quantitative methods, operations management, operations research, decision-support systems, and the like. Thus, this package of programs can be a valuable supplement in a number of study areas.

Program Design Philosophy and Characteristics

In the *Micro Manager,* we try to avoid giving any confusing instructions. Thus, we present easy-to-follow input formats and readable output formats. For each management science topic, we employ the most frequently used and understood terminology.

It is virtually impossible to develop a computer program that satisfies everyone's needs. Nevertheless, we have tried to generalize the programs and maintain a consistent structure throughout the package. The end result is a software package that features query-driven and command-driven operating procedures. This special feature helps you to run a program quickly and easily. The section on "Commands Available in the *Micro Manager*" will provide complete information about the commands available throughout the *Micro Manager.*

All programs in the *Micro Manager* are based on either an interactive procedure or batch processing. Thus, all input data are prompted either through query-driven instructions or from the input data file already built in separately in your formatted diskette. In addition, all programs have data-storing capabilities. Thus, you can store any data set entered interactively for future use or modifications. This data-storing capability enables you to modify input data and compare the output with the previous one. For your convenience, we will provide all relevant information about each program in the *Micro Manager* (when you select the "information" option) and also in the appropriate chapter in this text.

All program output will either be shown on the monitor screen or released through a printer. After running the program, you can scroll back and forth to review the input data and the output by issuing the command "LOOK." For more details, refer to the section on "Commands Available in the *Micro Manager.*" You need not worry about preparing the data-input formats for each program because they are formatted automatically inside the program and displayed on the screen in the form of a model, a table, a chart, or other appropriate formats. This is the primary reason for not preparing a separate user's manual for the *Micro Manager.* The *Micro Manager's* major value is its ease of use—its user-friendliness.

Hardware Requirements for the *Micro Manager*

The *Micro Manager* has been developed for application on an IBM personal computer or a variety of IBM-compatible microcomputers. You may use either a color or monochrome monitor.

The *Micro Manager* requires 128K memory to run all of the programs provided in this text. Other hardware requirements are at least one disk drive and an IBM, Epson, or other types of printers (a compressed 132 characters per line printer using the same ASCII codes to involve and revoke—see the IBM-DOS manual). If you have a different printer, utility programs are available from various sources that will make your printer respond like an IBM or Epson printer. Table 2.1 presents a summary of hardware requirements for the *Micro Manager.*

Table 2.1 Equipment requirements for the *Micro Manager*

Basic equipment

- An IBM PC, IBM PC XT, IBM PC AT, or an IBM-Compatible PC
- At least one disk drive (5-¼ inch diskette)
- A color or monochrome monitor capable of displaying program input/output

Optional equipment

- An IBM 80 CPS matrix printer, or
- An Epson MX-80, FX-80, FX-100, RX-80, or
- An NEC spinwriter, Diablo, or other compatible printer
- A formatted blank diskette for data storage

Starting Your *Micro Manager*

The operating procedures for *Micro Manager* are very simple and are thoroughly described in this section. However, before you can run a program, you must follow a certain sequence of operating steps. This sequence of steps is usually called the "start-up" or "booting" procedure for microcomputers. The start-up procedure is described in detail in the IBM-DOS manual or an IBM-compatible microcomputer DOS that you might already have. You need to learn this procedure completely before you access the *Micro Manager*.

System-Setting Procedure

The following procedure is provided only for the users of the *Micro Manager* who have the IBM PC. The user who has an IBM-compatible machine should examine his or her own disk-operating manuals.

Step 1: Insert your DOS diskette (*version 2.0 or 2.1*) into disk drive A and insert the *Micro Manager* into disk drive B. Close the diskette doors.

Step 2: Turn the computer on. If it is already on, press the Ctrl, Alt, and Del keys simultaneously and release them at the same time.

Step 3: Enter

```
A>SYS B:
A>COPY COMMAND.COM B:
```

Step 4: Remove the IBM-DOS and the *Micro Manager* from the disk drives.

Step 5: Insert the *Micro Manager* into disk drive A and enter

```
A>COPY CON:AUTOEXEC.BAT
MANAGER
```

and strike the function key <F6> and the enter key.

The system-setting procedures just described apply to to both the master diskette (Menu 1) and the slave diskette (Menu 2). If you have followed the steps exactly, the *Micro Manager* is now ready to be booted automatically. You can now access any program you want to run.

When Using Drive A for Working Space

Input data cannot be stored on the *Micro Manager* diskettes. The *Micro Manager* will use menu diskettes for working space only. The write–protect notch on the *Micro Manager* diskettes must be uncovered. Using the *Micro Manager* without a write–protect notch can possibly damage the programs. Thus, we advise you not to use drive A as the working space. You can, of course, use this option for solving small-sized problems without storing data.

When Using Drive B as Working Space and Data Storage

You must insert a formatted diskette or data diskette into drive B.

When Using a Hard Disk

You can store data on a hard disk. But, in this case, you have to access the *Micro Manager* by typing

```
A>MANAGER
```

instead of booting automatically. In this manner, you can use the directory for data storage.

Running the *Micro Manager*

- Insert the diskette into drive A (default drive) and push it in slowly. Do not force it in.
- Close the diskette door.
- Turn on the printer (if you have one), the monitor, and then the computer.
- After about 20 seconds, the red light on the diskette drive will glow and the drive will make some clicks and whirs. As soon as the red light is out and the noises stop in about 10 seconds, the screen will display the publisher's logo (wcb) and then the title of the program package will appear.
- All you have to do next is just follow the instructions. The *Micro Manager* will guide you in a very friendly way.

Possible Unhappy Situations After the Booting Procedure

Even after you follow the start-up procedure successfully, some unfortunate situations might occur.

- Situation 1: The book title does not appear on the screen. In this situation, you need to check the diskette, which might be the wrong diskette or a damaged one.
- Situation 2: The red light is still on, which means that the disk drive keeps on spinning.

  In this situation, do not try to take the diskette out of the disk drive and do not turn off the computer. Reboot the diskette by pressing the Ctrl, Alt, and Del keys simultaneously, and then release all the keys simultaneously. If the diskette is still not working, then it is probably damaged.

When You Make Typing Errors

1. If you make a typing error and realize it before striking the enter key, move the cursor back by pressing the backspace key ← and retype the input data according to the instructions.
2. Even if you realize that you made a typing error after you strike the enter key, you do not need to rerun from the beginning of the program since the *Micro Manager* provides a data-correction feature. You can change the input data by using the command "CHANGE". However, there is a limitation—the command "CHANGE" allows you to change only alphanumeric values already typed in. (See the section on "Commands Available in the *Micro Manager*.") When you want to delete or add some data, you may want to first store the current data using the command "STORE" after running the program. Then you can modify the data by using "EDLIN" in the DOS mode or by using a word processor (see the Batch-Input Data instructions on page 22).

After the Program Run

You can take out the diskette whenever you want, as long as the red light is off. Then you can turn off the computer.

Program Selection

The *Micro Manager* software package has two diskettes. Every time you start up Menu 1 or Menu 2, you will see the menus shown below after about 20 seconds. Once the Menu 2 diskette is booted on the drive, you cannot access Menu 1 unless you boot Menu 1. However, you can access Menu 2 from Menu 1. If you would like to exit to DOS, strike the escape key "ESC."

Menu 1 ⇄ Menu 2

```
MICRO MANAGER SOFTWARE

Programs Available From Menu #1

A  Break-Even Analysis          H  Goal Programming
B  Linear Programming I         I  Decision Making Under Risk
C  Linear Programming II        J  Decision Tree
D  All Integer Programming      K  Decision Making Under Uncertainty
E  Zero One Programming         L  Bayes' Decision Rule
F  Transportation               M  Intro Menu #2
G  Assignment                   Esc Exit to DOS

Please enter letter of program desired  ---->
```

```
MICRO  MANAGER  SOFTWARE

Programs Available From Menu #2

A  Shortest Route                    F  Dynamic Programming

B  Maximum Flow                      G  Queuing Models

C  Minimum Spanning Tree             H  Markov Models

D  PERT/CPM                          I  Simulation

E  Inventory Models                  Esc Exit to DOS

Please enter letter of program desired  ----->
```

The next step is to select one of the programs you want to run and strike the corresponding letter key. For example, you should type letter "H" in Menu 2 to access the "Markov Models" program.

Running the *Micro Manager*

In this section, we will discuss the menu for each program in the *Micro Manager,* including specific information about what each program does, the sample problems it solves, and its data-input options. Each program provides the following options, as shown by the Goal-Programming Program:

```
Welcome to Goal Programming


YOUR CHOICE -

Program menu is shown in the box.
Select the program you want.
```

```
Type in option number (1, 2, 3, 4, or ESC) here
```

```
****** PROGRAM MENU ******

1. Information
2. Sample Problem
3. Interactive Input
4. Batch Input (To Read Input Data From File)
ESC - To Return To The Main Menu
```

Information

You will be provided with helpful information when you run a program for the first time just by pressing “1”. This option provides the following three types of information:

```
(1) INFORMATION ABOUT COMMANDS

(2) INFORMATION ABOUT PROGRAM AND BATCH INPUT DATA FORMAT

(3) BOTH (1) AND (2)


Select  a number (1, 2, or 3)
```

The following is the first page of information about Goal Programming when you choose (2).

```
                                                            - PAGE  1 -

<< PURPOSE >>

GOAL PROGRAMMING determines a satisficing solution for a decision-making
problem with multiple objectives.  This program can handle GP problems with up
to 50 decision variables and 40 constraints.  Initial and final tableaus will
be given, in addition to the final solution.

<<  BATCH INPUT DATA FORMAT  >>

Type in the values of the following input data requirements, after creating a
new file.  You may enter as many values as you want in a line, separating them
by commas for alphabetic characters and by commas or blank spaces for numeric
values.  However, the input data must be exactly in the following order:

1. Number of decision variables (maximum 50)
2. Number of constraints (maximum 40)
3. Number of priorities
4. Number of deviational variables in the objective function
5. Type of each constraint:
      For goal constraint type:
         B    :  d- and d+ (minimize d- and/or d+)

                                                        <PgDn> or <Esc>
```

The *Micro Manager* provides you with another convenience here by enabling you either to go forward to the next page (press "PgDn" key) or backward to the previous page (press "PgUp" key).

Sample Problem

A sample problem (an example problem in the appropriate topical chapter) is provided for the purpose of helping the first-time users run the program without any difficulty. The number of sample data sets provided depends on the characteristics of each program.

Data Input

The data input is created in two ways, either by following the query-driven instructions during the program operation or by preparing a data file in your own blank diskette. However, you should keep several key rules in mind for using each type of input option.

Interactive Data-Input Option

Rules:

- Follow instructions exactly as provided.
- Strike the enter key (←┘) to send input data to the computer.
- When you need to input more than one value, each alphanumeric data must be separated by a comma.

Batch-Data File Option

This option is available to those people who use drive B or a hard disk for data storage. Batch-input data can be built on a formatted diskette in two different ways: by using the "STORE" command after the interactive input mode and by using the IBM-DOS command "EDLIN" or a word processor.

Rules:

- Be familiar with the data-input format.
- The format for batch-data input is described in the program diskettes as well as at the end of each topical chapter in this text.
- Enter as many values as you want in a line, separating them by commas for alphabetic characters and either commas or blank spaces for numeric values, after you create a file in your data diskette. However, data input should be in the exact order as provided in each chapter of this text or in the "INFORMATION" option in the diskette.

- Type in your file name when you encounter the following:

```
PROGRAM: Break-Even Analysis

FILE NAME LIST :

GP      .DAT IFL     .$$$ DFL     .$$$ BRK         OFL     .$$$ LP1     .DAT
LP2     .DAT INT1         ZEROONE .DAT TRANS   .DAT ASSIGN

Do not enter temporary system file names [*.$$$].
Enter input file name: BRK
```

Commands Available in the *Micro Manager*

The *Micro Manager* has internal commands that will guide you conveniently and properly throughout the running session of the program. You can issue those commands in either uppercase or lowercase characters, whenever you encounter the prompt (COMMAND →) at the lower right-hand corner of the screen. However, this does not mean that random selection of the commands is allowed independent of the state of the program. In other words, a command is valid only at a proper stage of the running session of the program. When you use an improper command at a certain stage or mistype a command, the *Micro Manager* will lead you to use appropriate commands by issuing the next error message.

```
Wrong command !
Available commands at this stage are listed at the bottom of the screen.
Use the function keys on the left-hand side of the keyboard.

F1 GO    F2 CHANGE F3 RERUN  F4 EXIT                COMMAND ->  PRINT
```

The *Micro Manager* defines the command stage by dividing it into two parts as follows:

1. The first stage—the first part of the running session of the program before the command GO is issued.

```
F1 GO    F2 CHANGE F3 RERUN  F4 EXIT                COMMAND ->
```

2. The second stage—the second part of the running session of the program after the command GO is issued.

```
F1 LOOK  F2 PRINT  F3 STORE  F4 RERUN  F5 EXIT      COMMAND ->
```

You can issue a command by pressing one of the appropriate program function keys, which are located on the left-hand side of your keyboard. All commands available at each stage of the program process will be displayed at the bottom of the screen.

Suppose that you have the following example on the screen while you are running a certain program.

```
F1 GO    F2 CHANGE F3 RERUN  F4 EXIT                    COMMAND ->
```

If you want to change some of the input data entered, just strike the key <F2>.

Command GO

When the input data entered are correct, you can run the program to obtain output by issuing the GO command. This command is available only one time during the running session of a program.

Command CHANGE

As explained earlier, the *Micro Manager* transforms the input data you entered into model formulations, tables, or charts, depending on the program characteristics. If you find any mistakes, you can correct them by using the CHANGE command before you go further.

Command LOOK

You may want to see if your input and output are correct. In this case, you can use the command "LOOK." You can review the whole program session by turning pages back and forth by pressing the "PgDn" or "PgUp" key. This command has two advantages. First, it is very useful for the user who has no printer. Second, it saves printing time and paper, both of which would have been wasted if the output generated contained the wrong data.

Command PRINT

After running the program, you may want to release the screen output to the printer by using the command "PRINT."

Command STORE

As stated earlier, you can store data in your own data diskette by using the DOS command "EDLIN" or word processor before you run the programs. However, this command "STORE" is for storing data sets that are internally created through the interactive process. The main purpose of this command is for future use or modification of data. The command "STORE" is available only after you run the program.

Command RERUN

When you wish to run the same program again, regardless of the stage in the program operation, you may use the command "RERUN."

Command EXIT

When you wish to return to the main menu, regardless of the stage in the program operation, you may use the command "EXIT."

Now we can summarize the *Micro Manager's* commands as follows:

Command	Description
GO	To obtain solutions. Available only after display of input and before output. Available only one time during the operation.
CHANGE	To correct the input data entered. Available only after display of input and before output.
LOOK	To review the whole program running session by turning pages back and forth. Available only after issuing command GO.
PRINT	To have screen output released to the printer. Available only after issuing command GO.
STORE	To store data set. Available only after issuing command GO.
RERUN	To run the same program again. Available at any time.
EXIT	To exit to the main menu. Available at any time.

Program Description

The program description for each program deals with: (1) the types of problems that the program can solve; (2) the types of results that the program generates; and (3) the size of the data set that can be solved.

1. Break-Even Analysis

This program determines the volume at which we break even from an operation by analyzing the relationship among costs, volume, and profit. The output will show you the level of operation in terms of the quantity of products, total dollar amount of transactions, or the percentage of productive capacity. This program can handle almost any size break-even problem.

2. Linear Programming I

This program determines the optimum allocation of scarce resources to achieve the minimum or maximum of a single objective criterion. This program can handle LP problems with up to 50 decision variables and 40 constraints. This program also performs sensitivity analysis.

3. Linear Programming II

The program's function is the same as LPI except for the computational procedure. LPII utilizes the revised simplex method whereas LPI uses the standard simplex method. LPII presents just the final result without giving intermediate solution tableaux. This second version of LP is intended for LP problems with up to 50 decision variables and 40 constraints. This program is faster than LPI. Thus, large-sized problems should be solved by LPII.

4. All-Integer Programming

This program determines the optimum solution to meet the integer requirements of a linear-programming problem by using the branch and bound method. This program is very restrictive and time consuming. Although it can handle problems with up to 10 decision variables and 20 constraints, it is recommended that this program be used to solve smaller-sized problems. During the execution, the program displays the search process starting from level 0 and node 0. The major purpose of this program is to provide you with an idea about how the technique works and how it can be applied to real-world problems.

5. Zero–One Programming

This program determines the optimum solution to the zero or one type of linear-programming problem. It utilizes the implicit enumeration algorithm, which is computationally inefficient. Therefore, this program's capacity is quite limited. It can handle problems with up to 10 decision variables and 10 constraints. The major purpose of this program is to demonstrate how the technique works on the microcomputer.

6. Transportation

This program solves a special type of linear-programming problem by finding either the minimum total transportation cost or the maximum payoff from a distribution problem where items are shipped from a set of sources to a set of destinations. This program can handle problems with up to a 40 × 40 size matrix.

7. Assignment

This program solves another special type of linear-programming problem where the objective is to find the maximum payoff or minimum cost that can be obtained by assigning a set of objects to a set of stations. This program can solve problems with up to a 40 × 40 matrix.

8. Goal Programming

This program determines a satisficing solution for a decision-making problem with multiple objectives. It can handle GP problems with up to 50 decision variables and 40 constraints. Initial and final tableaux will be given, in addition to the final solution.

9. Decision Making under Risk

This program determines the expected payoff or monetary value for each course of action when certain probabilities are given for possible events or states of nature. The output presents the maximum expected monetary value or minimum expected loss of the best course of action. This program can handle problems with up to 20 courses of action and 20 possible states of nature.

10. Decision Tree

This program determines the optimum alternative that should be selected among various paths of a decision tree. It also computes the expected value of the optimum alternative. The program can handle up to 100 nodes in a decision tree.

11. Decision Making under Uncertainty

This program determines the optimum alternative among various courses of action available under uncertainty. It utilizes various decision criteria such as Laplace, maximin, maximax, Hurwicz, and minimax. The output will indicate either the maximum expected value or minimum expected loss by analyzing the alternatives under various states of nature.

12. Bayes' Decision Rule

This program computes the marginal probabilities and posterior probabilities, given that an event has taken place. It can deal with up to 20 states of nature and 20 different predictors associated with these states of nature.

13. Shortest Route

This program determines the shortest route from an origin to a destination through a connected network, given the distance associated with each branch of the network. Output shows the complete route from the starting node to the ending node. This program handles a problem with up to 40 nodes and 40 links.

14. Maximum Flow

This program determines a route that maximizes the total flow from a specified source to a specified destination in a network. This program handles a problem with up to 40 nodes and 40 branches.

15. Minimum Spanning Tree

This program determines the best way to connect all the network nodes such that the total branch lengths required would be minimum (distance, time, or cost). The program output indicates the total length of the minimum spanning tree and the branches that connect all of the nodes in the network. This program can solve a network of up to 40 nodes and 40 branches.

16. Pert/CPM

This program determines the minimum time required to complete a project. The minimum time required for project completion is equal to the longest time path (the critical path) of a sequence of connected activities. The program output includes the variance of the expected project-completion time, slack, critical path, the earliest start and latest finish times for each activity, and the probability of completing a project within a certain time period. This program can handle a project problem that has up to 40 activities.

17. Inventory Models

This program determines the economic-order quantity (EOQ) (either with or without shortage) and the optimum lot size. The output will present the order quantity (either with or without a discount situation), order frequency, reorder point, inventory cycle, total inventory cost, and/or the maximum required inventory level. For the inventory problem with uncertain demand rates and lead times, a simulation program is presented in "simulation" (program number 21).

18. Dynamic Programming

This program determines the optimum route, time, cost, or return for complex problems through a sequential decision-making approach. The output will include a description of the complete route from the starting state to the ending state. This program can handle problems with up to ten stages and ten states.

19. Queuing Models

This program determines the mean value (time or number of people, and so forth) in a system and in the queue under various conditions. The output will include an economic analysis of the solution. Economic analysis involves computation of the operating costs, waiting cost, and total costs.

20. Markov Models

This program provides probabilistic information about a future decision situation. The program determines the future probabilities of certain conditions based on a transition probability matrix. It also provides the equilibrium-state probabilities. This program can handle up to a 5×5 matrix for an infinite number of periods.

21. Simulation

This program simulates the following three categories of problems by generating random numbers: (1) Monte Carlo simulation, (2) inventory simulation, and (3) queuing simulation.

Monte Carlo Simulation

This program is limited to the simulation of events that have a given probability distribution.

Inventory Simulation

This program is limited to finding the optimum order quantity and reorder point under uncertain demand rates and lead times.

Queuing Simulation

This program is limited to computation of the queue length, total cost (time), waiting time (cost), and so forth.

Summary

This chapter has presented a comprehensive overview of the *Micro Manager*. This software package represents the most complete collection of microcomputer-based management science programs. The 21 programs in the *Micro Manager* also include many subprograms that deal with various special cases.

The *Micro Manager* is also completely user-friendly. The instructions provided in this chapter would be sufficient to install and use any of the programs in the two menu diskettes. The two primary purposes of the *Micro Manager* are: (1) to provide the user with the basic understanding about when and how to use management science for decision making; and (2) to solve simple management science problems or to be used as a learning/teaching aid. Many user-friendly commands, examples, and information make it fun to use the *Micro Manager*.

C H A P T E R 3

Break-Even Analysis

Break-even analysis, also referred to as cost–volume–profit analysis, is one of the most fundamental optimization techniques. The basic purpose of this analysis is to investigate the relationship among cost, volume, and profit to determine the volume at which we break even in an operation. The volume represents the level of operation in terms of quantity of products, total dollar amount of transactions, or the percentage of productive capacity. Thus, break even can be defined as the required volume at which total revenue equals total cost.

Basics

A large proportion of management science is concerned with optimization, which attempts to maximize or minimize an objective function subject to a set of constraints. Since break-even analysis is one of the simplest optimization techniques, it is a good starting point for us.

In break-even analysis, we attempt to determine the point of break-even volume where total revenue equals total cost. Information about the break-even point is very valuable for any organization involved in undertaking a project. For example, suppose that an individual is considering the purchase of an automobile dealership. An important factor for the decision is to determine the number of automobiles that need to be sold to cover the fixed and variable costs of operation. Managing a dealership requires a large parking facility, service center, office staff, sales personnel, and so on. To compete successfully in town, the dealer must sell a certain number of automobiles at a reasonable price. The dealer must know the break-even point so that the level of operation (the number of automobiles sold) would be at least at break-even volume.

Model Components

The break-even analysis model typically has the following components:

Total revenue (TR). Total revenue represents the total sales, which is the product of the selling price multiplied by the quantity sold.

Total cost (TC). Total cost is simply the sum of all costs involved. Typically, there are fixed costs and variable costs.

Fixed costs (FC). Fixed costs are those that remain constant regardless of the level of production or sales volume. Some examples of fixed costs are property rents, interest payments, taxes and insurance payments, depreciation, office personnel salaries, and others.

Variable costs (VC). Variable costs are those that are directly related to the level of production or sales volume. Thus, total variable costs are the product of the unit variable cost multiplied by the units of production or sales. Some examples of variable costs are direct material, direct labor, packaging, handling and freight, sales commissions, and the like.

Quantity (Q). The quantity represents the level of operation, sales volume, or dollar amount. Total revenue and total variable costs are directly related to quantity.

Price (P). Price is the sales price of the product involved.

The Break-Even Model

Now we are ready to develop mathematical models that represent relationships among the components discussed above. If we denote profit as Z, then we can develop the following models:

$$\text{Profit} = \text{Total Revenue} - \text{Total Cost}$$
$$Z = TR - TC \quad (1)$$

$$\text{Total Revenue} = \text{Price} \times \text{Quantity}$$
$$TR = P \cdot Q \quad (2)$$

$$\text{Total Cost} = \text{Fixed Costs} + (\text{Variable Cost} \times \text{Quantity})$$
$$TC = FC + (VC \cdot Q) \quad (3)$$

Thus, we can determine profit as

$$Z = (P \cdot Q) - FC - (VC \cdot Q). \quad (4)$$

Figure 3.1 Break-Even Analysis

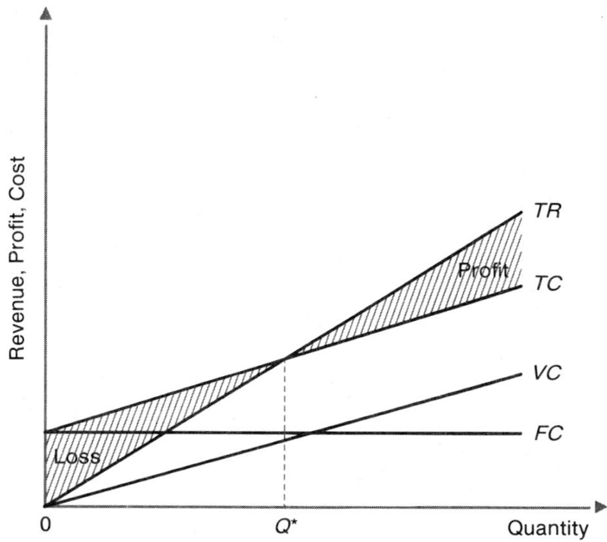

To determine the break-even point, we can solve for Q in Eq. (4) when total profit is zero. In other words, we can state

$$
\begin{aligned}
&Z = 0\\
&Z = (P \cdot Q) - FC - (VC \cdot Q)\\
&(P \cdot Q) - FC - (VC \cdot Q) = 0\\
&(P \cdot Q) - (VC \cdot Q) = FC\\
&Q\,(P - VC) = FC\\
&Q^* = \frac{FC}{P - VC},
\end{aligned}
\tag{5}
$$

where Q^* represents the break-even point quantity.

When the volume or quantity produced from the operation equals Q^*, total revenue will equal total cost. Thus, at the break-even point profit will be zero. In Eq. (5), $(P - VC)$ represents the unit contribution. The break-even quantity Q^* is determined by dividing fixed cost by unit contribution.

Figure 3.1 graphically illustrates the break-even model. As quantity is increased gradually from zero, the total revenue increases much faster than the increase of total cost. Thus, the break-even point is reached at Q^*, where profit Z equals zero. When quantity is increased beyond the break-even point Q^*, the total revenue exceeds total cost. Thus, a positive profit is achieved.

Modifications to the Basic Model

The basic break-even model can be modified in a number of different ways. For example, the volume could be expressed in a dollar amount rather than in quantity, a change in variable cost due to a quantity discount, a change in fixed cost due to a capacity expansion, nonlinear cost and revenue functions, and the like. We will discuss only four basic modifications.

a. *Break even with a dollar amount.* The decision maker may be interested in determining the break even in terms of the required sales volume. In such a case, the break-even dollar amount can be determined by multiplying both sides of the basic model by price P. Thus, we can determine

$$Q^* = \frac{FC}{P - VC}$$

$$(P \cdot Q)^* = P\left(\frac{FC}{P - VC}\right)$$

$$(P \cdot Q)^* = \frac{FC}{1 - (VC/P)} \qquad (6)$$

b. *Break even as a percentage of capacity.* It is also possible to determine the break-even point as a percentage of total productive capacity. If we denote Q_c as the total capacity quantity, we can divide both sides of the basic break-even model as follows to determine the break-even percentage of capacity:

$$Q^* = \frac{FC}{P - VC}$$

$$\left(\frac{Q}{Q_c}\right)^* = \frac{FC/(P - VC)}{Q_c}$$

$$\left(\frac{Q}{Q_c}\right)^* = \frac{FC}{(P - VC)Q_c} \qquad (7)$$

c. *Break in variable cost.* In real-world situations, the variable cost is not constant. As a matter of fact, the variable cost may decrease at several breakpoints because of the economies of scale in operations, quantity discounts on materials purchased, or the learning curve of the workers involved. If the breakpoint occurs at the left of Q^*, the break-even quantity will decrease. On the other hand, if the breakpoint is to the right of Q^*, the break-even quantity would not change, as shown in Fig. 3.2.

d. *Break in fixed cost.* The level of fixed cost cannot remain constant if an operation is expanded to increase limited productive capacity. In other words, the physical plant capacity has to be expanded at a certain point as the level of operation increases. If the breakpoint in fixed cost occurs, the fixed-cost function and, consequently, the total cost function will jump up stepwise. If the breakpoint occurs to the left of Q^*, it will increase the break-even quantity. If the breakpoint occurs to the right of Q^*, the break-even quantity will not change, even though the amount of profit will change. Figure 3.3 illustrates the case of a break in fixed cost.

Figure 3.2 Break-Even Model with a Break in Variable Cost

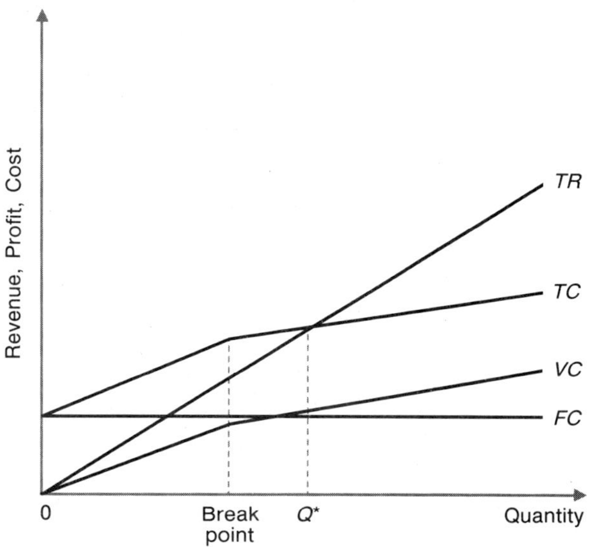

Figure 3.3 Break-Even Model with a Break in Fixed Cost

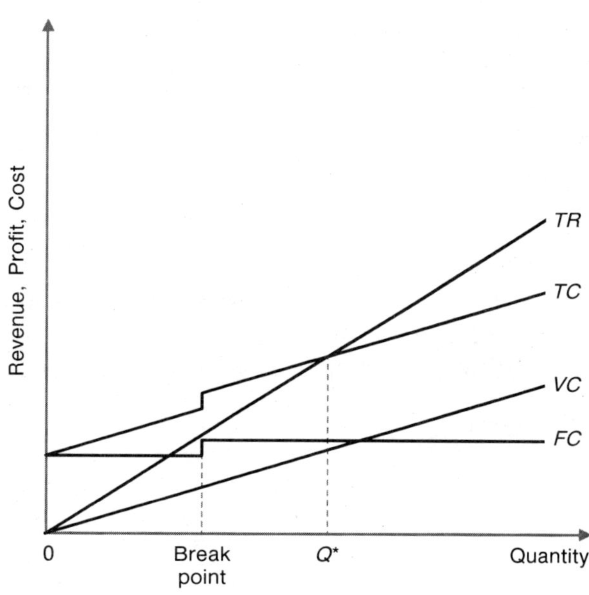

Illustrative Problems

Following are two problems that illustrate the use of break-even analysis. In the first example, break-even quantity is determined; in the second example, the profit from a given sales volume is determined.

Example 3.1 Mercury Corporation

Mercury Corporation is an electronics firm that produces several microcomputer-related products. The firm is considering an acquisition of Citron, Inc., a producer of keyboards. Based on the available financial data at Citron, the variable cost per keyboard is \$20 and the current wholesale price is \$45. The board of directors at Citron is requesting \$2.5 million for the plant. Mercury Corporation is trying to determine the quantity of keyboards it must sell to break even on this acquisition.

In this problem, we can easily determine the following:

$$P = \$45,\ VC = \$20,\ FC = \$2{,}500{,}000.$$

Thus,

$$\begin{aligned} Q^* &= \frac{FC}{P - VC} \\ &= \frac{2{,}500{,}000}{45 - 20} \\ Q^* &= 100{,}000 \text{ keyboards.} \end{aligned}$$

Example 3.2 Runza-U

Runza-U is an exclusive runza seller at the university football stadium. The company incurred a total of \$5,000 fixed costs, including the concession fee, a specially equipped truck, and stand rentals. Runza-U sells its runzas for eighty cents apiece to the Boy Scout sellers. The average cost of a runza is thirty cents apiece. The company's total revenue this season was \$26,000. Determine break-even sales and total profit in dollars.

Break-even sales are determined as follows:

$$\begin{aligned} (P \cdot Q)^* &= \frac{FC}{1 - (VC/P)} \\ &= \frac{5{,}000}{1 - (30/80)} \\ &= (5{,}000 \times 8/5) \\ &= \$8{,}000. \end{aligned}$$

The company's profit is

$$\begin{aligned} Q &= \$26{,}000/0.80 = 32{,}500 \\ Z &= 26{,}000 - (0.30 \times 32{,}500) - 5{,}000 \\ Z &= \$11{,}250. \end{aligned}$$

Application of the *Micro Manager*

In this section we present an application example of the *Micro Manager.* The program diskette provides the complete information about the purpose of the technique under study, the solution example of a sample problem, interactive input instructions, and the batch input procedure. Therefore, in this section we will present only the information (purpose of the technique and the batch input data format) and the solution of a sample problem using the interactive input format.

```
<< PURPOSE >>

BREAK-EVEN ANALYSIS determines the volume at which we break-even from an
operation by analyzing the relationship among costs, volume, and profit.  The
output will show you the level of operation in terms of the quantity of
products, total dollar amount of transactions, or the percentage of productive
capacity.  This program can handle almost any size break-even problem.

<<  BATCH INPUT DATA FORMAT  >>

Type in the values of the following input data requirements, after creating a
new file.  You may enter as many values as you want in a line, separating them
by commas for alphabetic characters and by commas or blank spaces for numeric
values.  However, the input data must be exactly in the following order:

1. Total fixed cost (TFC)
2. Unit variable cost (UVC)
3. Unit selling price (USP)
4. Expected sales units (ES) (0 if not available)

** Sample Batch Input Data Set (Example 3.1) **

2500000  ; total fixed cost
20       ; unit variable cost
45       ; unit selling price
0        ; no expected sales units

PROGRAM: Break-Even Analysis

Enter total fixed cost    : 2500000
Enter unit variable cost  : 20
Enter unit selling price  : 45
Enter expected sales units (if not available, enter 0): 0

PROGRAM: Break-Even Analysis

***** INPUT DATA ENTERED *****

  Total fixed cost    :     2500000.00
  Unit variable cost  :          20.00
  Unit selling price  :          45.00
  Expected sales units:           0

*****   PROGRAM OUTPUT   *****

                          Units          Dollars
-----------------+----------------+-----------------
Break-Even Point         100000         $ 4500000
```

Summary

Break-even analysis is perhaps the most fundamental optimization technique. This analysis has the basic purpose of investigating the relationships among cost, volume, and profit, in order to determine the break-even point of operation. The *Micro Manager* program can handle virtually any size problem. Also, the program can determine the break-even point in terms of the quantity of products, total amount of transactions, or the percentage of productive capacity.

References

Chase, R. B., and N. J. Aquilano. 1981. *Production and operations management.* Homewood, IL: Irwin.

Lee, S. M., and L. J. Moore. 1975. *Introduction to decision science.* New York: Petrocelli-Charter.

Problems

1. The Lambda Corporation has just acquired a new production plant at a cost of $1.2 million. The plant specializes in producing military antennae. The average variable cost per antenna is $175. The firm's contracted price with the Department of Defense is $300. How many antennae must the firm supply to the government to break even?

2. Given the following information, determine the break-even point in quantity and the break-even sales volume.

$$P = \$6.00 \qquad FC = \$10{,}000 \qquad VC = \$4.00$$

3. Romeo & Juliet is a new pizza shop in town. The owner of the shop invested $140,000 to acquire the store with all of the required equipment and furnishings. The average cost per pizza is $2.25. The average price per pizza is $6.25. What is the break-even quantity?

4. In Problem 3, determine the following:

   a. The break-even sales volume.
   b. If the owner sells 30,000 pizzas in the first year, what will be the profit or loss?
   c. If the owner is simply trying to break even in the first year, what price should he charge per pizza?

5. In Problem 3, the current capacity of the store is to produce and sell 50,000 pizzas per year. What is the break-even point in terms of percentage of its productive capacity?

6. Again in Problem 3, the owner is considering replacing the current pizza oven with a new gas oven. The cost of replacement is $2,000. The new oven is more energy efficient. Thus, the expected cost savings is twenty cents per pizza. Determine the new break-even quantity.

7. Western Pharmaceuticals, Inc., produces plastic disposable syringes. The company's production capacity is 20 million units per year. The estimated total annual fixed cost is $500,000. The syringes cost twenty-five cents each to produce and Western sells them for fifty cents apiece.

   a. What is the break-even quantity?
   b. At what percentage of capacity must the firm operate to break even?

8. Midwest Energy Corporation needs a fleet of 30 cars. The purchase price is $12,000 per car with an operating cost of eighteen cents per mile. The expected average usage per car is 50 miles per week. The cost of leasing per car is a flat $150 per week including the operating costs. Develop a decision rule that will help the company to decide whether to buy or lease automobiles. Midwest Energy has a policy to keep all purchased vehicles at least two years. The expected salvage value is negligible.

9. In Problem 8, if the company can get a discount of 10 percent from the purchase cost for purchasing more than 15 cars, what will be the change in the decision rule developed in Problem 8?

10. Again, in Problem 8, if the car-rental company provides 20 percent discount on leasing fees for more than 10 automobiles rented, what will be the change in the decision rule developed in Problem 8?

11. Given the following information, determine the break-even point in quantity and break-even sales volume.

    a. $P = \$100.00$, $FC = \$100{,}000$, $VC = \$50.00$
    b. $P = \$75.00$, $FC = \$50{,}000$, $VC = \$25.00$

12. Sweet Cake Company has just opened a new shop with an investment of $500,000. The average variable cost per cake is $7.00. The average price per cake is $15.00. What is the break-even quantity?

13. In Problem 12, determine the following:

a. The break-even sales volume.

b. If the company sells 70,000 cakes in the first year, what will be the profit or loss?

c. If the company just wants to break even in the first year, what price should it charge per cake?

14. In Problem 12, the current capacity of the shop is to produce and sell 80,000 cakes per year. What is the break-even point in terms of percentage of its productive capacity?

15. Lincoln Manufacturing Corporation has just built a new tennis racquet plant at a cost of $2 million. The average variable cost per racquet is $30.00. The average price of a racquet is $70.00. How many racquets must the firm produce to break even?

16. Century Electronics Company estimates its sales at $530,000 (1,000 units). The variable costs are expected to be 56 percent of sales and profit is expected to be $63,536.

a. Determine the break-even point in dollars.

b. Determine the sales if the company makes a profit of $21,500.

17. In Problem 16, if sales increased by 20 percent, what would be the profit of this company?

18. The normal production capacity of Good Calculator Company is 180,000 units and the unit sales price is $25.00. Costs are:

	Variable (per unit)	**Fixed**
Direct materials	$7.00	—
Direct labor	8.00	—
Factory overhead	1.50	$30,000
Nonmanufacturing cost	0.25	12,900

a. Determine the break-even point in dollars.

b. Determine the break-even point in units.

19. The following data of TXA Manufacturing Company are for July:

Plant capacity	20,000 units/month
Fixed cost	$40,000/month
Variable cost	$25.00/unit
Sales price	$50.00/unit

a. Determine the break-even point in dollars.

b. Determine the break-even point in units.

20. During the past year, ABC Company produced and sold 10,000 units. The unit sales price was $10.00. Actual costs per unit, based on a production of 10,000 units, were:

Variable cost	$2.50
Fixed cost	$5.00
Total	$7.50

a. Determine the profit of this company.

b. Determine the break-even point in dollars.

c. Determine the break-even point in units.

C H A P T E R 4

Linear Programming

Linear programming is one of the most widely applied techniques of management science. This technique is concerned with the allocation of limited resources to alternative uses to achieve organizational objectives to the greatest extent. In this chapter, we will discuss the basic linear-programming model and its solution by the *Micro Manager.*

Basics

Linear programming is a mathematical method of allocating scarce resources to achieve a *single* objective. The objective may be profit, cost, return on investment, sales, market share, space, time, and the like. Because of its effectiveness, linear programming has found wide applications in business, government, and nonprofit organizations. For example, management decision problems, such as production planning, capital budgeting, manpower scheduling, gasoline blending, personnel development, and the like, are concerned with the achievement of a single objective subject to resource and/or environmental constraints.

Many scholars pioneered linear programming, including J. von Neumann, L. Kantorovich, T. C. Koopmans, George B. Dantzig, A. Charnes, W. W. Cooper, and many others. However, George B. Dantzig has been recognized widely as the father of linear programming.

Application Areas of Linear Programming

Most organizations are concerned with the production or distribution of goods and services. Advanced Micro Devices, National Medical Enterprises, Mobil Oil, Chrysler, Burger King, IBM, the Department of Defense, state correctional departments, National Bank, and New York Life are all concerned about providing essential goods and services to their customers while achieving organizational goals. Many organizations use linear programming because it is an effective tool in determining the best mix of resources to derive the best outcome. Thus, when we study linear programming, it is rare to find a decision problem that has not been analyzed through the use of linear programming. The typical application examples of linear programming are shown in Table 4.1.

Table 4.1 Typical application examples of linear programming

Type of decision	Organizational problems
Resource allocation	Production scheduling
	Blending
	Inventory control
	Assembly-line balancing
	Sales effort allocation
	Advertising scheduling
	Capital budgeting
	Portfolio selection
	Manpower allocation
	Salary determination
	Operating room scheduling
	Office space allocation
Planning–scheduling	Corporate financial planning
	Manpower planning
	Production and inventory control
	Crop planning
	Urban and regional planning
	Police patrol planning
	Traveling salesperson scheduling
Diet problem	Menu determination
	C-ration determination
	Food relief programs
	Patient care
	School luncheon programs
Transportation problem	Merchandise transportation schedule
	Location–allocation problems
	Pipeline construction
	Emergency military airlift
Assignment problem	Police force assignment
	Snowplow assignment
	Manpower assignment
	Special staff allocation
	Computer-terminal assignment

Linear-Programming Model Formulation Steps

In any linear-programming application, the basic steps we take are as follows:

1. Define the Basic Variables

After we analyze the descriptive problem, we must identify the key variables whose values we attempt to determine. These are the decision variables. What quantity of product *A* must we produce? How much money should we invest in stock *X*? How many acres of corn should we plant? All of these questions are good examples of decision variables.

2. Determine the Objective Function

The second step is to decide what we are trying to do in the problem. For example, we may want to maximize total revenue, minimize total cost, maximize total return on investment, minimize total distance traveled, and the like. There must be only a single objective since multiple objectives cannot be solved by linear programming.

3. Formulate the Constraints

Once we have identified the decision variables and the objective function, the next step is to formulate a set of constraints. The constraints represent limited resources that will restrict the choice of permissible values of the decision variables. For example, the total production time is limited to 40 hours a week, the total investment budget must be less than $10 million, the total vitamin A intake required is at least 30 milligrams, and the like are some examples of constraints involving limited resources.

Assumptions Underlying a Linear-Programming Model

A typical linear-programming problem must satisfy a number of assumptions. We will discuss only the most basic assumptions underlying a linear-programming model.

1. Linearity

As the term "linear" implies, a linear-programming model must have all relationships among the decision variables in mathematically linear functions. Thus, the objective function and all constraints must be expressed in linear functions. A linear function must satisfy two basic requirements: proportionality and additivity. *Proportionality* requirement is necessary to assure a constant relationship between the output and input. For example, if we increase our input by 20 percent, we can expect the same 20 percent increase in output. *Additivity* means that the total value in either the objective function or a constraint is simply the sum of individual activities. For example, the total profit expected is the sum of profits from each of the products, or the total resources consumed is the sum of resources used for producing individual products.

2. Divisibility

In a linear-programming problem, the decision variable can take any nonnegative value. Thus, the value can be a whole number (i.e., an integer) or a continuous number (i.e., a value in decimal points). For example, the quantity of product A we produce may be 120 or it could be 119.2776 units. Also, the total amount of flour required may be 16 pounds or 16.333 pounds.

3. Deterministic

Another typical assumption underlying a linear-programming model is a set of deterministic parameters. We assume that all parameters (i.e., coefficients in the objective function and constraints) are assumed to be known and constant. For example, the unit profit we get from product A is \$10 and the amount of time required to process product B is 15 minutes are good examples of deterministic parameters.

4. Nonnegativity

Another typical assumption required in a linear-programming model is nonnegativity for the variables. For example, minus 10 units of production or a negative consumption of a nutrient is not conceivable in most problems. If we have a decision variable that is not restricted in sign (e.g., the change in interest rates), we must make a slight modification so that the nonnegativity constraint still applies in the model.

Illustrative Problems

In this section, three illustrative problems will be presented as means to show the model formulation process. Note the similarities as well as the model formulation steps that are being employed.

Example 4.1 Romeo's Pizza Shoppe

Romeo's Pizza Shoppe produces half-baked, frozen pizzas. Romeo Stefano, the owner, specializes in two very popular pizzas: Romeo's Special and Juliet's Pepperoni. Romeo uses two processes in pizza making: fixing (preparing the dough, putting on sauce, and adding various other ingredients) and baking. A Romeo's Special takes 2 minutes to fix and 6 minutes to bake. On the other hand, a Juliet's

Pepperoni requires 1.5 minutes to fix and 9 minutes to bake. Since Romeo is the only cook, the weekly production capacity is limited by Romeo's working hours and the oven capacity. Romeo has 40 hours of weekly fixing time available and 120 hours of oven time. The average unit profits for the two types of pizza are: Romeo's Special—$1.50; Juliet's Pepperoni—$1.00. Romeo Stefano is trying to determine the number of each type of pizza to produce to maximize total profit.

We can formulate a linear-programming model as follows:

Step 1 Decision Variables

x_1 = number of Romeo's Specials to produce per week

x_2 = number of Juliet's Pepperonis to produce per week

Step 2 The Objective Function

$$\text{Maximize } Z = 1.50x_1 + 1.00x_2$$

where Z = total profit

1.50 = unit profit for Romeo's Specials

1.00 = unit profit for Juliet's Pepperonis

Step 3 Constraints

$$\begin{aligned} 2x_1 + 1.5x_2 &\leq 2{,}400 && \text{fixing time} \\ 6x_1 + 9x_2 &\leq 7{,}200 && \text{oven time} \\ x_1, x_2 &\geq 0 && \text{nonnegativity} \end{aligned}$$

Now the complete model can be presented.

$$\begin{aligned} \text{Maximize } Z &= 1.50x_1 + 1.00x_2 \\ \text{subject to } 2x_1 + 1.5x_2 &\leq 2{,}400 \\ 6x_1 + 9x_2 &\leq 7{,}200 \\ x_1, x_2 &\geq 0 \end{aligned}$$

Example 4.2 Fashions Unlimited, Inc.

Fashions Unlimited, Inc., is a boutique that specializes in working-women's fashion clothing. To attract new customers, the company is thinking about launching a special advertising campaign. The company has selected four advertising vehicles: local television ads (30 seconds), local radio spot ads, local newspaper ads (one-quarter page), and direct mail. The current advertising costs for each of the vehicles are as follows:

TV ad—$1,000 per insertion

Radio ad—$150 per spot

Newspaper ad—$400 per 1/4 page

Direct mail—$5 per mailing

Fashions Unlimited attempts to maximize the weighted exposure (the exposure of the company to potential customers) through the advertising campaign. The weighted exposure points per insertion in each of the advertising vehicle are as follows:

TV ad—20,000 exposure points
Radio ad—4,000 exposure points
Newspaper ad—10,000 exposure points
Direct mail—200 exposure points

The company board of directors has set $30,000 as the advertising campaign budget. Also, the board has established the following policies about the advertising campaign: (1) the total advertising cost in direct mail should be at least 10 percent of the budgeted $30,000; (2) the amount of TV ads should be at least $5,000 because of a prior contract with the television station; (3) the total number of newspaper ads should be at least 10; and (4) the total amount of advertising costs in television and radio ads should be at least the total advertising costs in newspaper and direct-mail ads. Fashions Unlimited is trying to determine the number of insertions in each of the advertising vehicles to maximize the total weighted exposure points.

Decision Variables

x_1 = number of TV ads
x_2 = number of radio spot ads
x_3 = number of newspaper ads
x_4 = number of direct-mail ads

The Objective Function

$$\text{Maximize } Z = 20{,}000x_1 + 4{,}000x_2 + 10{,}000x_3 + 200x_4$$

Constraints

$$\begin{aligned}
1{,}000x_1 + 150x_2 + 400x_3 + 5x_4 &\leq 30{,}000 && \text{budget}\\
5x_4 &\geq 3{,}000 && \text{direct mail}\\
1{,}000x_1 &\geq 5{,}000 && \text{TV ads}\\
x_3 &\geq 10 && \text{newspaper}\\
1{,}000x_1 + 150x_2 - 400x_3 - 5x_4 &\geq 0 && \text{TV and radio ads}\\
x_1, x_2, x_3, x_4 &\geq 0 && \text{nonnegativity}
\end{aligned}$$

Example 4.3 Speedy Taco Hut

Speedy Taco Hut is a Mexican fast-food restaurant in a college town. One of the most frustrating problems of Mr. Sanchez, the owner, is the employees' working schedule. The restaurant has been successful mainly because of its low-labor cost. The company hires only college students as part-time employees.

Currently, the restaurant is open for 16 hours a day, from 10 A.M. to 2 A.M. The company hires students for a 4-hour working schedule each day either as cooks or order takers–food preparers. The cooks and order takers–food preparers are not interchangeable as they need specialized training. The workers can report to work only at 10 A.M., 12 M. (noon), 2 P.M., 4 P.M., 6 P.M., 8 P.M., or 10 P.M. Based on currently available data, the minimum number of workers required during each of the two-hour intervals and their hourly wages are as follows:

	Cooks	**Order takers–food preparers**	**Hourly wage**
10 A.M.–12 M. (noon)	4	2	\$3.60
12 M. (noon)–2 P.M.	6	4	3.60
2 P.M.–4 P.M.	3	1	3.80
4 P.M.–6 P.M.	5	4	3.80
6 P.M.–8 P.M.	3	3	3.80
8 P.M.–10 P.M.	2	2	4.00
10 P.M.–12 A.M. (midnight)	1	2	4.00
12 A.M.(midnight)–2 A.M.	1	1	4.20

In addition to the above manpower requirements, Mr. Sanchez feels that there should be at least as many cooks working during the entire day as the number of order takers–food preparers. Mr. Sanchez is trying to determine the number of student workers reporting to work at different time intervals for a 4-hour working schedule while minimizing the total payroll cost.

The problem is succinctly described in Fig. 4.1.

Decision Variables

x_i = number of cooks reporting at time interval i ($1 = 10$ A.M., $2 = 12$ M. (noon), . . . , $7 = 10$ P.M.)

y_i = number of order takers–food preparers reporting at time interval i ($1 = 10$ A.M., $2 = 12$ M. (noon), . . . , $7 = 10$ P.M.)

The Objective Function

$$\begin{aligned}\text{Minimize } Z = {} & 14.40x_1 + 14.80x_2 + 15.20x_3 + 15.20x_4 + \\ & 15.60x_5 + 16.00x_6 + 16.40x_7 + 14.40y_1 + \\ & 14.80y_2 + 15.20y_3 + 15.20y_4 + 15.60y_5 + \\ & 16.00y_6 + 16.40y_7\end{aligned}$$

Figure 4.1 The Speedy Taco Hut Problem

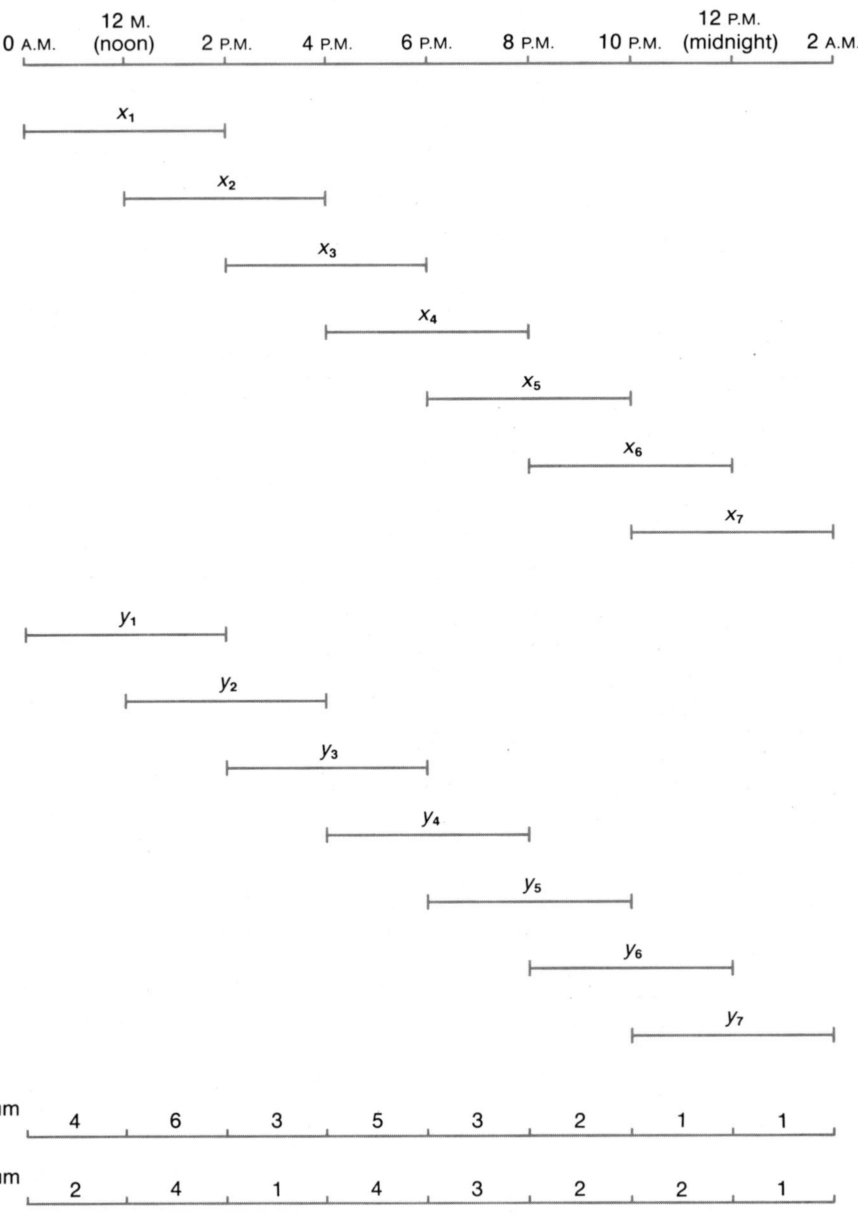

Constraints

$$
\begin{aligned}
x_1 &\geq 4 \\
x_1 + x_2 &\geq 6 \\
x_2 + x_3 &\geq 3 \\
x_3 + x_4 &\geq 5 \\
x_4 + x_5 &\geq 3 \\
x_5 + x_6 &\geq 2 \\
x_6 + x_7 &\geq 1 \\
x_7 &\geq 1 \\
y_1 &\geq 2 \\
y_1 + y_2 &\geq 4 \\
y_2 + y_3 &\geq 1 \\
y_3 + y_4 &\geq 4 \\
y_4 + y_5 &\geq 3 \\
y_5 + y_6 &\geq 2 \\
y_6 + y_7 &\geq 2 \\
y_7 &\geq 1 \\
\sum_{i=1}^{7} x_i - \sum_{i=1}^{7} y_i &\geq 0 \\
x_i, y_i &\geq 0
\end{aligned}
$$

Solution Methods of Linear Programming

In this section, we will restrict our discussion to two basic solution approaches of linear programming—the graphical method and the simplex method of linear programming.

A. The Graphical Method

The graphical method is useful in understanding the concept of the linear programming approach. However, we can effectively depict problems that involve only two dimensions. Thus, the graphical method is used only for those problems that have two decision variables. The basic solution procedure is as follows:

1. Plot all constraints on the graph.
2. Identify the feasible region or the area of feasible solutions.
3. Identify the optimum solution by plotting a series of the iso-profit function or the iso-cost function.
4. Determine the exact solution values of the decision variables and the objective function at the optimum solution.

Let us examine the following two simple problems.

A Maximization Problem

$$\begin{aligned} \text{Maximize } Z &= \$30x_1 + \$20x_2 \\ \text{subject to } x_1 + x_2 &\leq 50 \\ 2x_1 \quad\quad &\leq 80 \\ x_2 &\leq 30 \\ x_1, x_2 &\geq 0 \end{aligned}$$

Figure 4.2 presents the graphical illustration of the problem. The three constraints can be plotted graphically after each one is solved for the vertical axis x_2. For example, the first constraint can be solved as follows:

$$\begin{aligned} x_1 + x_2 &\leq 50 \\ x_2 &\leq 50 - x_1 \end{aligned}$$

Thus, the x_2 intercept is 50 and the slope of the line is -1. Since the feasible region is the overlapping area of the three constraints, the shaded area $0ABCD$ represents the feasible region.

Now we can plot a series of the iso-profit functions on the graph as well. When we solve the objective function for x_2, we obtain

$$\begin{aligned} Z &= 30x_1 + 20x_2 \\ 20x_2 &= Z - 30x_1 \\ x_2 &= Z/20 - 3/2\, x_1 \qquad \text{iso-profit function} \end{aligned}$$

Since the total profit Z is not known at this time, we cannot determine the x_2 intercept $Z/20$. However, we have the slope of the iso-profit function, $-3/2$. As we move out gradually from the origin with the slope, the total profit increases. Thus, the optimum solution is identified as point C.

The optimum solution is

$$x_1 = 40, x_2 = 10, Z = \$1{,}400.$$

A Minimization Problem

$$\begin{aligned} \text{Minimize } Z &= \$8x_1 + \$10x_2 \\ \text{subject to } 4x_1 + 3x_2 &\geq 60 \\ x_1 + 2x_2 &\geq 20 \\ x_2 &\leq 15 \\ x_1, x_2 &\geq 0 \end{aligned}$$

The three constraints are plotted on the graph as shown in Fig. 4.3. The constraints are all solved for the vertical axis variable x_2. The feasible region is the shaded area bordered by points A, B, and C. The objective function is also solved for x_2 to obtain the iso-cost function as shown below.

$$\begin{aligned} Z &= 8x_1 + 10x_2 \\ 10x_2 &= Z - 8x_1 \\ x_2 &= Z/10 - 4/5\, x_1 \qquad \text{iso-cost function} \end{aligned}$$

Figure 4.2 A Maximization Problem

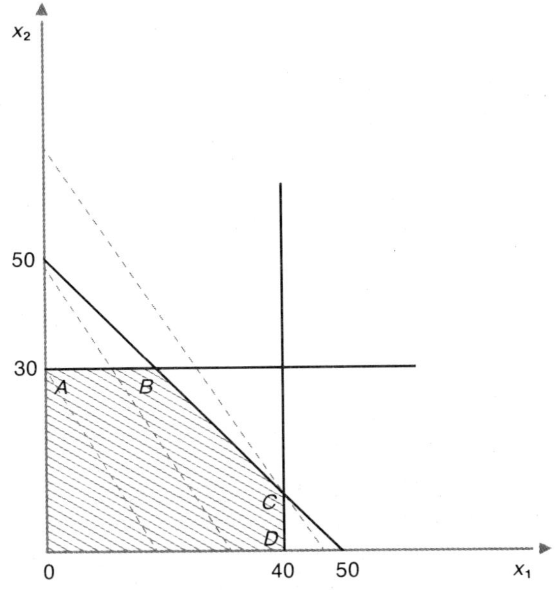

Figure 4.3 A Minimization Problem

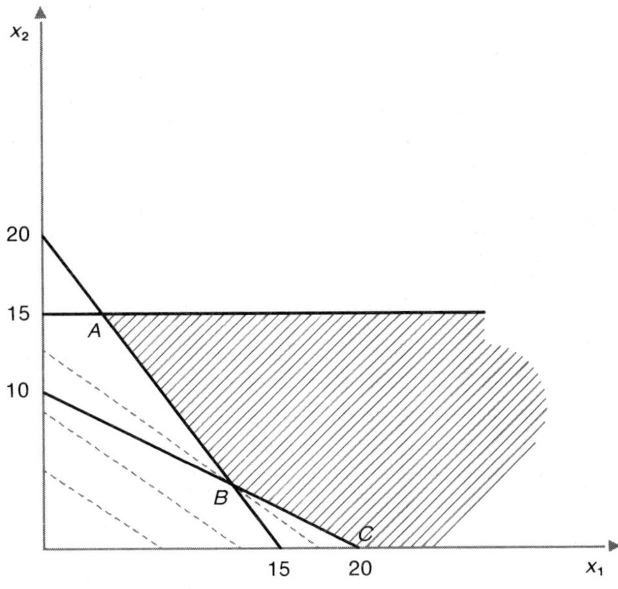

We can plot a series of the iso-cost function on the graph by moving out from the origin with a slope of $-4/5$. From Fig. 4.3 it is obvious that point B is the optimum point. Thus, we can determine the values of the basic variables at point B by solving the two intersecting equalities simultaneously.

$$\begin{aligned} 4x_1 + 3x_2 &= 60 && \text{constraint 1 equality} \\ x_2 &= 20 - 4/3\, x_1 \\ x_1 + 2x_2 &= 20 && \text{constraint 2 equality} \\ x_2 &= 10 - 1/2\, x_1 \\ 20 - 4/3\, x_1 &= 10 - 1/2\, x_1 \\ 5/6\, x_1 &= 10 \\ x_1 &= 12 \end{aligned}$$

Substituting $x_1 = 12$ into constraint 1, we obtain $x_2 = 4$. The optimum solution is $x_1 = 12$, $x_2 = 4$, $Z = \$136$.

B. The Simplex Method

The graphical solution method is useful for only those linear-programming problems that have two decision variables. However, virtually all real-world problems involve more than two decision variables. The simplex method, first developed by George B. Dantzig in 1947, is a systematic solution technique for solving complex linear-programming problems. The simplex technique employs an iterative process so that the optimum solution is achieved through progressive operations.

The simplex method presented here is just a prototype technique. The actual computer-based algorithm is often a modified version that takes advantage of special features of the model for computational efficiency. The simplex solution procedure will be summarized based on the maximization problem we presented earlier.

$$\begin{aligned} \text{Maximize } Z &= 30x_1 + 20x_2 \\ \text{subject to } \quad x_1 + x_2 &\leq 50 \\ 2x_1 \quad\quad &\leq 80 \\ x_2 &\leq 30 \\ x_1, x_2 &\geq 0 \end{aligned}$$

1. Develop the Initial Solution

The typical initial solution with which we start the solution process is at the origin. In other words, all decision variables have zero solution values, $x_j = 0 (j = 1, 2, \ldots, n)$. To determine the basic variables, those variables that have solution values, we must convert the constraints into simplex equalities as follows:

Constraint Type	**Adjustment Required**
Less than or equal to, $\leq$	Add a slack variable, s
Exactly equal to, $=$	Add an artificial variable, A
Greater than or equal to, $\geq$	Subtract a surplus variable and add an artificial variable, $-s + A$

Thus, the basic variable in the simplex tableau for each type of constraint can be determined as follows:

Constraint Type	**The Basic Variable**
Less than or equal to, $\leq$	The slack variable s
Exactly equal to, $=$	The artificial variable A
Greater than or equal to, $\geq$	The artificial variable A

The simplex equalities for the example problem are

$$\begin{aligned} x_1 + x_2 + s_1 &= 50 \\ 2x_1 \qquad + s_2 &= 80 \\ x_2 + s_3 &= 30 \end{aligned}$$

2. Set up the Initial Simplex Tableau

Since the simplex method is based on an iterative process, it is essential to use a simplified tableau for analysis and iteration. A number of different formats are suggested for the simplex method. In this text, we will use the tableau presented in Table 4.2. The initial simplex tableau is presented in Table 4.3. In Table 4.3, we note the following:

1. Since the initial solution is at the origin, the basic variables are s_1, s_2, and s_3.
2. The contribution rate, c_j, for each of the slack variables is zero.
3. z_j values are determined as follows:

$$\begin{aligned} z_j \text{ (basis column)} &= \Sigma\,(c_b \cdot \text{solution}) \\ &= (0 \times 50) + (0 \times 80) + (0 \times 30) \\ &= 0 \\ z_j \text{ (variable column)} &= \Sigma\,(c_b \cdot \text{coefficients}) \\ z_j\ (x_1 \text{ column}) &= (0 \times 1) + (0 \times 2) + (0 \times 0) \\ &= 0 \end{aligned}$$

4. Since the contribution rates of the basic variables are all zero ($c_b = 0$), z_j values are all zero.
5. Since z_j values are all zero, $c_j - z_j$ values are exactly the same as the c_j values.
6. The solution values are exactly the same as the right-hand side values of the constraints.
7. The coefficients in the variable columns are transcribed from the simplex equalities. These coefficients represent the marginal rates of substitution. For example, in the x_1 column, there is a coefficient of 1 in the s_1 row and a coefficient of 2 in the s_2 row. Thus, to produce one unit of x_1 we need one unit of s_1 and two units of s_2. Since there is a zero coefficient in the s_3 row, there is no substitution relationship between x_1 and s_3. When a coefficient is negative, an inverse rate of substitution exists.

Table 4.2 The simplex tableau

c_b \ c_j	Basis	Solution	c_1 x_1	c_2 x_2	. . . . . .	. . s_1	. . s_2	. . . .	. . A_1
	z_j $c_j - z_j$								

c_j = Unit contribution rate for each of the variables in the model (e.g., unit profit, unit cost, etc.). The variable columns start with the decision variables followed by the slack, surplus, and artificial variables.

c_b = Unit contribution rate for each of the basic variables.

Basis = Basis column where the basic variables for each of the constraints are listed.

Solution = Solution values of the basic variable.

z_j = Total value (contribution) of the objective function for the given solution in the basis column. In each of the variable columns, z_j value represents the total profit that needs to be sacrificed to produce one unit of each variable for a maximization problem.

$c_j - z_j$ = Net increase of profit associated with the production of one unit of each variable in a maximization problem.

Table 4.3 The initial simplex tableau for the example problem

c_b \ c_j	Basis	Solution	30 x_1	20 x_2	0 s_1	0 s_2	0 s_3	
0	s_1	50	1	1	1	0	0	
0	s_2	80	(2)	0	0	1	0	← Pivot row
0	s_3	30	0	1	0	0	1	
	z_j	0	0	0	0	0	0	
	$c_j - z_j$		30	20	0	0	0	
			↑ Pivot column					

3. Determine the Entering Variable

The initial solution is at the origin. Thus, the total profit is zero [z_j (solution) = 0]. To increase total profit, we must produce a product. The product that we should produce first is the one that has the maximum net contribution rate. Therefore, we are looking for the largest positive $c_j - z_j$ value in the initial simplex tableau shown in Table 4.3. The largest $c_j - z_j$ is 30 in the x_1 column.

This column x_1, with the largest $c_j - z_j$, is referred to as the "pivot column." The variable in this pivot column, x_1, is the incoming variable to the solution basis in the second tableau. The $c_j - z_j$ value of 30 indicates that every unit of x_1 that we produce will increase the total profit by 30.

The incoming variable is determined as x_1. However, since there should be only three basic variables (three constraints), one of the existing basic variables must be removed from the solution basis. This variable is often called the outgoing variable.

We have determined that x_1 is the incoming variable as it is in the pivot column. The maximum quantity of x_1 that can be produced is determined by dividing the solution values in the solution column by their respective coefficients in the pivot column (x_1 column). Thus, we can obtain the following:

	Solution		Coefficient	Quantity Possible
s_1 row:	50	÷	1	= 50
s_2 row:	80	÷	2	= 40 ← pivot row
s_3 row:	30	÷	0	= undefined

Production of one unit of x_1 requires one unit of s_1 and two units of s_2. Thus, in the first constraint we can process up to 50 units of x_1. In the second constraint we can process only up to 40 units of x_1. The third constraint is immaterial since its coefficient is zero. We must satisfy both constraints one and two simultaneously. Thus, the minimum nonnegative quantity possible is the maximum quantity of x_1 that can be produced. Thus, 40 is the maximum quantity as determined in the second constraint.

When we produce 40 units of x_1, s_2 will be all used up. The solution value for s_2 becomes zero. Consequently, s_2 is the outgoing variable from the solution basis. Therefore, the "pivot row" is the s_2 row. The pivot row is determined by identifying the row that has the minimum nonnegative quotient when we divide solution values by the *positive* coefficients in the pivot column.

4. Determine the Optimum Solution

Now we are ready to go through the iterative process and determine the optimum solution. The iterative process can be summarized as follows:

1. Develop a new simplex tableau with the new incoming variable in the solution basis. Table 4.4 presents the second simplex tableau. x_1 has replaced s_2.
2. Determine new solution values and coefficients as follows:

Pivot row: New value = Old value ÷ Pivot element

Other rows: New value = Old value − (Row element × New value in the pivot row).

The pivot element is the element that is located at the intersection of the pivot column and the pivot row. The row element for each row is the element at the intersection of each row other than the pivot row and the pivot column.

Table 4.4 The second simplex tableau

c_b \ c_j	Basis	Solution	30 x_1	20 x_2	0 s_1	0 s_2	0 s_3
0	s_1	10	0	(1)	1	−1/2	0
30	x_1	40	1	0	0	1/2	0
0	s_3	30	0	1	0	0	1
	z_j	1,200	30	0	0	15	0
	$c_j - z_j$		0	20	0	−15	0

← Pivot row (the s_1 row)

↑ Pivot column (the x_2 column)

Now we can determine new solution values as follows:

x_1 row:

Old value	÷	Pivot element	=	New value
80	÷	2	=	40
2	÷	2	=	1
0	÷	2	=	0
0	÷	2	=	0
1	÷	2	=	1/2
0	÷	2	=	0

	Old value	−	(Row element × New value in pivot row)	=	New value
s_1 row:	50	−	(1 × 40)	=	10
	1	−	(1 × 1)	=	0
	1	−	(1 × 0)	=	1
	1	−	(1 × 0)	=	1
	0	−	(1 × 1/2)	=	−1/2
	0	−	(1 × 0)	=	0
s_3 row:	30	−	(0 × 40)	=	30
	0	−	(0 × 1)	=	0
	1	−	(0 × 0)	=	1
	0	−	(0 × 0)	=	0
	0	−	(0 × 1/2)	=	0
	1	−	(0 × 0)	=	1

We can also compute new z_j and $c_j - z_j$ values as shown in Table 4.4. In the second solution, we produce 40 units of x_1 and, thus, the total profit is $1,200. The pivot column is x_2 since the largest $c_j - z_j$ of 20 is found in this column. The pivot row is s_1 because the minimum nonnegative quotient of 10 is found in this row when the solution values are divided by the positive coefficients in the pivot column.

Table 4.5 The optimum solution

c_b \ c_j	Basis	Solution	30 x_1	20 x_2	0 s_1	0 s_2	0 s_3
20	x_2	10	0	1	1	−1/2	0
30	x_1	40	1	0	0	1/2	0
0	s_3	20	0	0	−1	1/2	1
	z_j	1,400	30	20	20	5	0
	$c_j - z_j$		0	0	−20	−5	0

Now we can proceed and go through the second iteration. The third simplex tableau is presented in Table 4.5. This solution is the optimum solution since all $c_j - z_j$ values are zero or negative. The optimum solution is $x_1 = 40$, $x_2 = 10$, $s_3 = 20$, $z_j = 1{,}400$. This solution corresponds with the optimum solution derived through the graphical method as shown in Fig. 4.2.

C. Mixed Constraint Problems and Minimization Problems

Mixed Constraint Problems

The simplex solution procedure for the mixed constraint problem is identical to the maximization problem we discussed earlier except for one important adjustment. For an exactly equal to or a greater than or equal to type constraint, we must add an artificial variable. In the initial solution, which is at the origin ($x_j = 0$), the artificial variable always takes the right-hand side value. The artificial variable is used only to facilitate solutions that are outside of the feasible region for the given constraint. Thus, as long as at least one artificial variable exists in the solution basis, the solution is infeasible.

To remove an artificial variable from the basis as quickly as possible, we assign a very large negative profit to it as c_j. The typical value assigned is $-M$, where M is a sufficiently large number. One more thing we should remember is that an artificial variable can only get out of the basis, but never reenter it. Also, when we remove an artificial variable from the solution basis, we can eliminate this column from further consideration.

In a greater than or equal to type constraint, we subtract a surplus variable and add an artificial variable. The surplus variable is treated much like a slack variable in that we assign a zero c_j value to it.

The Minimization Problem

The simplex solution procedure for the minimization problem is exactly the same as the maximization problem with the following two exceptions:

1. Since the purpose of the model is to minimize the total cost, a very large positive cost M is assigned to an artificial variable.
2. In selecting the pivot column, we look for the largest positive $z_j - c_j$ value (or the largest negative $c_j - z_j$ number). The $z_j - c_j$ value represents the cost reduction associated with one unit of each variable.

D. Some Complications

In many real-world problems, we face various complications. Some of the complications are discussed here.

A Negative Right-Hand Side Value

In a typical linear-programming model, we must satisfy the nonnegativity constraint. Thus, a negative right-hand side value is not acceptable. Whenever we encounter a negative right-hand side value, we should make it a positive value by multiplying both sides of the constraint by -1. Let us consider the following example.

$$2x_1 - 6x_2 - x_3 \leq -5$$
$$-2x_1 + 6x_2 + x_3 \geq 5 \qquad \text{(multiply } -1 \text{ to both sides)}$$
$$-2x_1 + 6x_2 + x_3 - s_1 + A_1 = 5 \qquad \text{(simplex equality)}$$

A Tie in Selecting the Pivot Column

The pivot column is selected by finding the column with the largest $c_j - z_j$ for a maximization problem or the largest $z_j - c_j$ for a minimization problem. If we find two columns with the identical largest $c_j - z_j$ or $z_j - c_j$ values, a choice can be made on an arbitrary basis. If a tie is between a decision variable and a slack (or surplus) variable, we can select the decision variable as the entering variable.

A Tie in Selecting the Pivot Row (Degeneracy)

To determine the pivot row, we find the minimum nonnegative quotient when the solution values are divided by the positive coefficients in the pivot column. If there are two or more rows with the identical minimum nonnegative quotient, a case of degeneracy occurs. This situation arises when three or more constraints intersect at the same corner point. In most real-world problems, degeneracy presents no real difficulty for us. We select a row as the pivot row on an arbitrary basis and carry on with the simplex procedure.

Multiple-Optimum Solutions

As we can observe in Table 4.5, in the optimum solution simplex tableau, the $c_j - z_j$ values are zero for the basic variable columns and they are negative for the nonbasic variable columns. If one or more of the nonbasic variable columns has a zero $c_j - z_j$ value in the final simplex tableau, we have an alternate optimum solution. We can choose this nonbasic variable column as the pivot column and have an entirely different solution. Yet, the total profit will be exactly the same as the previous optimum solution.

An Infeasible Problem

If there are conflicting (mutually exclusive) constraints, the problem is infeasible and there is no feasible region. When we solve such a problem by the simplex method, the final solution will contain at least one artificial variable with a positive solution value. Then we know that the solution derived is infeasible.

An Unbounded Problem

An unbounded problem occurs only when one or more important contraints are left out in the model by mistake. In such a problem, the total profit can keep on increasing without any bounds. When we apply the simplex method to solve such a problem, the process initially continues as usual. However, during iterations when the pivot column is identified and the corresponding pivot row is to be identified, we would face an unusual situation. There is no positive coefficient in the pivot column with which to divide the solution values. When this situation occurs, we know that the problem is unbounded.

Application of the *Micro Manager*

In this section we will examine an application example of the *Micro Manager.* The software diskette provides the complete information about the purpose of linear programming, the solution of a sample problem, interactive input instructions, and the batch input procedure. Here we will present only the information (purpose and batch input data format) and the solution of a sample problem using the interactive input format by Linear Programming I. The program also provides a sensitivity analysis, which is discussed in Chapter 5.

```
<< PURPOSE >>

LINEAR PROGRAMMING I determines the optimum allocation of scarce resources to
achieve the minimum or maximum of a single objective criterion.  This program
can handle LP problems with up to 50 decision variables and 40 constraints.
This program also performs sensitivity analysis.
```

<< BATCH INPUT DATA FORMAT >>

Type in the values of the following input data requirements, after creating a new file. You may enter as many values as you want in a line, separating them by commas for alphabetic characters and by commas or blank spaces for numeric values. However, the input data must be exactly in the following order:

```
 1. Problem type:
      1    : maximization
      2    : minimization
 2. Number of decision variables (maximum 40)
 3. Number of constraints (maximum 50)
 4. Number of ' <= ' type constraints
 5. Number of '  = ' type constraints
 6. Number of ' >= ' type constraints
 7. Type of each constraint:
       L    : less than or equal to    ( <= )
       E    : equal to                 (  = )
       G    : greater than or equal to ( >= )
 8. Coefficient of each decision variable in the objective function
 9. Coefficient of each decision variable for each constraint
10. Right-hand side value of each constraint
```

** Sample Batch Input Data Set (Example 4.1) **

```
1           ; maximization problem
2           ; two decision variables
2           ; two constraints
2           ; two 'less than or equal to' constraints
0           ; no  'equal to' constraints
0           ; no  'greater than or equal to' constraints
L,L         ; type of constraint 1 and 2
1.5,1       ; coefficients in the objective function
2,1.5       ; coefficients of constraint 1
6,9         ; coefficients of constraint 2
40,120      ; right-hand side values
```

PROGRAM: Linear Programming I

```
Enter 1 for maximization or 2 for minimization: 1

Enter number of decision variables: 2
Enter number of constraints: 2
Enter number of 'LESS THAN OR EQUAL TO    (<=)' constraints: 2
Enter number of 'EQUAL TO                 ( =)' constraints: 0
Enter number of 'GREATER THAN OR EQUAL TO (>=)' constraints: 0

Type of Constraint: L for <=, E for =, and G for >=

Enter type of constraint  1 : L
Enter type of constraint  2 : L

Enter coefficient of decision variable  1  in the objective function:  1.5
Enter coefficient of decision variable  2  in the objective function:  1

Enter coefficient of decision variable  1  in constraint  1 :  2
Enter coefficient of decision variable  2  in constraint  1 :  1.5
```

Enter coefficient of decision variable 1 in constraint 2 : 6
Enter coefficient of decision variable 2 in constraint 2 : 9

Enter right-hand side value (RHS) of constraint 1 : 40
Enter right-hand side value (RHS) of constraint 2 : 120

PROGRAM: Linear Programming I

***** INPUT DATA ENTERED *****

Max Z = 1.5 x 1 + 1 x 2

Subject to:

C 1 2 x 1 + 1.5 x 2 <= 40
C 2 6 x 1 + 9 x 2 <= 120

***** PROGRAM OUTPUT *****

Simplex tableau: Iteration 0

\Cj			1.50	1.00	0.00	0.00
Cb	Basis	Bi	x 1	x 2	s 1	s 2
0.00	s 1	40.00	2.00	1.50	1.00	0.00
0.00	s 2	120.00	6.00	9.00	0.00	1.00
	Zj	0.00	0.00	0.00	0.00	0.00
	Cj-Zj		1.50	1.00	0.00	0.00

Simplex tableau: Iteration 1

\Cj			1.50	1.00	0.00	0.00
Cb	Basis	Bi	x 1	x 2	s 1	s 2
1.50	x 1	20.00	1.00	0.75	0.50	0.00
0.00	s 2	0.00	0.00	4.50	-3.00	1.00
	Zj	30.00	1.50	1.13	0.75	0.00
	Cj-Zj		0.00	-0.13	-0.75	0.00

Degenerate final optimal solution

Variable	Value
x 1	20.00
s 2	0.00
Z	30.00

Sensitivity Analysis

	Right-hand side Ranging		
Constraint Number	Lower Limit	Current Value	Upper Limit
1	0.00	40.00	40.00
2	120.00	120.00	No Limit

```
----------------------------------------------------------
                     Contribution Rate Ranging
              --------------------------------------------
                  Lower          Current          Upper
Variable          Limit          Rate             Limit
----------------------------------------------------------
    x 1*           1.33            1.50        No Limit
    x 2        No Limit            1.00            1.13

* indicates basic variable
```

Summary

Linear programming is undoubtedly one of the most popular and widely applied techniques of management science. It is primarily concerned with the optimum allocation of scarce resources to achieve a single objective. In this chapter, we have studied the basic application areas, model requirements, model formulation, graphical solution method, and the simplex method of linear programming. Also, the application of the *Micro Manager* via the interactive approach was examined. The *Micro Manager* demonstrated its effectiveness in solving simple linear-programming problems.

References

Charnes, A., and W. W. Cooper. 1961. *Management models and industrial applications of linear programming.* New York: John Wiley & Sons.

Dantzig, G. B. 1963. *Linear programming and extensions.* Princeton, NJ: Princeton University Press.

Hillier, F. S., and G. J. Lieberman. 1980. *Introduction to operations research.* 3d ed. San Francisco: Holden-Day.

Lee, S. M., L. J. Moore, and B. W. Taylor. 1985. *Management science.* 2d ed. Dubuque, IA: Wm. C. Brown Co. Publishers.

Problems

1. A plant produces two products—product *A* and product *B*. The resource requirements and selling prices are as follows:

	Materials (units)	**Labor (hr)**	**Selling price ($)**
Product *A*	2	3	12
Product *B*	6	3	20

Eighty units of materials and 60 hours of labor are available. Formulate a linear-programming model to determine the production schedule that will maximize sales and solve it by using the *Micro Manager.*

2. A farmer can use two brands of feed to raise his herd. Brand 1 costs 40 cents/lb and brand 2 costs 30 cents/lb. The contents of a pound of each of these brands and the daily requirement of nutritional elements *A* and *B* are given in the following table.

	Brand 1	**Brand 2**	**Total requirement**
Element *A*	2	5	40
Element *B*	6	3	60

Formulate a linear-programming model to determine the optimal feed mix that will minimize cost and solve it by using the *Micro Manager.*

3. A shoe manufacturer produces hiking boots and ski boots. Its manufacturing process consists of sewing and stretching. Thirteen hours per day for the sewing process and 16 hours per day for the stretching process are available. The firm realizes profits of \$15 per pair on hiking boots and \$10 per pair on ski boots. It requires 2 hours of sewing and 5 hours of stretching to produce one pair of hiking boots, and 3 hours of sewing and 2 hours of stretching to produce one pair of ski boots. How many pairs of each type of boots should be produced to maximize profits? Formulate a linear-programming model and solve it by using the *Micro Manager.*

4. Granite County in Montana has recently decided to spray insecticides into forest areas by using an airplane. It is estimated that one ton of insecticide *A* can eradicate 2,000 caterpillars and 6,000 moths, and one ton of insecticide *B* can eradicate 5,000 caterpillars and 2,000 moths. The county office estimates that approximately 20,000 caterpillars and 11,000 moths are in the forest and wishes to eradicate all of these noxious insects. The prices of insecticides *A* and *B* are \$100 and \$70 per ton, respectively. Formulate a linear-programming model to minimize the cost and solve it by using the *Micro Manager.*

5. A sorority plans to market three special fruit baskets for the upcoming festival season. Fruit basket *A* contains 3 apples, 4 oranges, and 1 honeydew melon. Fruit basket *B* contains 6 apples, 2 oranges, and 1 honeydew melon. Fruit basket *C* contains 4 apples, 3 oranges, and 2 honeydew melons. Fruit baskets *A, B,* and *C* sell for \$8, \$10, and \$12, respectively. The amounts available and costs of apples, oranges, and honeydews appear in the following table.

	Quantity available	Cost per piece
Apple	160 pieces	$0.30
Orange	300 pieces	$0.20
Honeydew	60 pieces	$1.20

It is assumed that the sorority can sell all the baskets that it makes up. Formulate a linear-programming model to maximize the profit and solve it by using the *Micro Manager.*

6. The Super-Duper Chemical Company produces "Super-Duper" bond. To produce the bond, it uses two kinds of raw materials. One ton of raw material *A* generates 0.6 ton of the bond, and 20 ppm of S (sulfur) and 30 ppm of P (phosphorus) in its exhaust gas. One ton of raw material *B* generates 0.8 ton of the bond, and 40 ppm of S and 30 ppm of P in its exhaust gas. Because of air-pollution regulations, the government permits a maximum exhaust of 200 ppm of S and 300 ppm of P per day. Formulate a linear-programming model to determine the optimum amount of each raw material that can be used to maximize production—by using the limitation of the government air-pollution regulation—and solve it by using the *Micro Manager.*

7. A fertilizer company plans to produce two types of fertilizers from components 1 and 2. Each component contains nitrogen and phosphorus in different amounts. The composition of each component and cost per pound are as follows:

Component	Cost ($)	Nitrogen(%)	Phosphorus (%)
1	0.60	50	20
2	0.50	20	40

Fertilizer *A* must contain more than 30% nitrogen and 20% phosphorus. Fertilizer *B* must contain more than 40% nitrogen and 10% phosphorus. The estimated demands for this season are 5,000 lb for fertilizer *A* and 3,000 lb for fertilizer *B.*

a. Formulate a linear-programming model to determine how many pounds of each component should be used to minimize costs and still satisfy the demands.
b. Solve the problem by using the *Micro Manager.*

8. ABC Steel has two processes to produce steel. An hour's operation of process 1 can produce 350 kg of steel and 120 kg of by-products, which requires 4 hours of labor, 200 kg of ore, and 100 kg of coal. An hour's

operation of process 2 can produce 375 kg of steel and 40 kg of by-products, which requires 6 hours of labor, 140 kg of ore, and 60 kg of coal. Up to 240 hours of labor, 6 tons of ore, and 5 tons of coal are available in a week. The cost of labor is $6 per hour. The prices of ore and coal are $100/ton and $50/ton, respectively. Steel sells at $200/ton. The by-products can be sold at $25/ton. This plant operates 40 hours per week. Formulate a linear-programming model that will maximize profits and solve it by using the *Micro Manager.*

9. The owner of a recently opened restaurant in a middle-sized city wishes to spend $5,000 on advertising using radio, television, and/or the newspaper. One unit of TV advertising costs $1,000 and reaches approximately 8,000 people. One unit of radio advertising costs $200 and can reach 2,000 people. One unit of newspaper advertising costs $300 and reaches 5,000 people. The owner wants to reach as many people as she can within the budget limitation. Because of the different effects of three mass media, the owner wants at least 1 unit of TV advertising, 3 units of radio advertising, and 2 units of newspaper advertising. Formulate a linear-programming model to determine the most efficient advertising planning and solve it by using the *Micro Manager.*

10. Lester Electrical manufactures generators for the commercial market. A salesperson who is paid $500/week can sell 10 generators per week. A sales trainee can be hired at $200 per week. The training cost is $100 per trainee. After training, the sales trainee can sell 7 generators per week. The company has budgeted $3,000 for the weekly payroll and $600 for the training program per week. To sell the generators, a salesperson spends about $100 per week and a trainee spends $200 per week for sales expenses. The budget for sales expenses is $1,400 per week. Formulate a linear-programming model to determine the optimum number of salespeople and trainees to have on payroll to maximize total sales. Solve it by using the *Micro Manager.*

11. A bakery company supplies fresh bread to five Mini-Marts from its two plants. Transportation costs, demands, and supplies are shown in the following table.

	Mini-Marts					
	1	**2**	**3**	**4**	**5**	**Supply (boxes)**
Plant 1	$1	2	4	3	1	60
Plant 2	2	3	1	2	3	50
Demand (boxes)	10	20	15	30	20	

Formulate a linear-programming model to meet all demands at minimum transportation cost and solve it by using the *Micro Manager.*

12. The ABC Company manufactures three products—*X*, *Y*, and *Z*. The company has three departments, all of which can produce any of the products. The firm must determine the optimum allocation of its resources to these three departments. Following are the required labor-hours for each product in each department and the maximum labor-hours available per day.

	X	Y	Z	Labor-hours/day
Dept. 1	2	6	2	80
Dept. 2	3	4	4	120
Dept. 3	4	5	5	60

The company should produce at least 30 units of product *X*, 40 units of product *Y*, and 50 units of product *Z* per day to meet the market demands. The average wage rate in department 1, 2, and 3 is $7.5, $8, and $7, respectively. The raw materials cost $8 for product *X*, $12 for product *Y*, and $10 for product *Z*. Formulate a linear-programming model to determine the production schedule that will minimize cost and solve it by using the *Micro Manager*.

13. Solve the following linear-programming problem by the graphical method.

$$\begin{aligned} \text{Minimize } Z &= 3x_1 + 4x_2 \\ \text{subject to } 2x_1 + 4x_2 &\geq 12 \\ 8x_1 + 2x_2 &\geq 20 \\ x_1 \qquad &\leq 3 \\ x_1, x_2 &\geq 0 \end{aligned}$$

14. Solve the following linear-programming problem by the graphical method.

$$\begin{aligned} \text{Maximize } Z &= 2x_1 + 4x_2 \\ \text{subject to } x_1 + 3x_2 &\leq 15 \\ 3x_1 + 4x_2 &\leq 24 \\ 5x_1 + 3x_2 &\leq 30 \\ x_1, x_2 &\geq 0 \end{aligned}$$

15. Solve the following linear-programming problem by the graphical method.

$$\begin{aligned} \text{Maximize } Z &= x_1 + x_2 \\ \text{subject to } 4x_1 + 2x_2 &\leq 16 \\ 2x_1 + 3x_2 &\geq 12 \\ x_2 &\leq 6 \\ x_1, x_2 &\geq 0 \end{aligned}$$

16. The Midland Oil Company produces two kinds of motor oil—10W/30 and 10W/40 by blending three components. The viscosity, the cost per barrel, and the maximum quantity available of each component are as follows:

Component	Viscosity	Cost/barrel	Available barrels/week
1	20	$6	8,000
2	35	$7.5	6,000
3	50	$9	4,000

The viscosity of each motor oil is proportional to the viscosities of its components. The selling prices and required viscosities of the two motor oils are as follows:

Motor oil	Minimum viscosity required	Selling price/barrel
10W/30	30	10
10W/40	40	12

a. Formulate a linear-programming model to determine how many barrels of each motor oil the company should produce each week to maximize profit.
b. Solve the problem by using the *Micro Manager.*

17. A firm wishes to advertise its new products through three mass media: radio, television, and the newspaper. The total budget available for advertising is $20,000. The following information has been obtained from an advertising agency.

	Radio	TV	Newspaper
Cost per advertising unit	$300	$3,000	$200
Number of individuals reached per unit	1,600	6,000	1,000
Number of men per unit	500	1,000	500
Number of women per unit	600	3,000	400
Number of children per unit	500	2,000	100

The company wishes to contact at least 40,000 people. At least 20 percent of those people should be men. The company wishes to reach at least 10,000 women and 5,000 children. Determine how much of each type of advertising the company should use to minimize advertising expenses. Formulate a linear-programming model and solve it by using the *Micro Manager.*

18. World Motors Company has plants in India, Singapore, and Taiwan. Each plant has the following capacity per month to export to foreign markets after covering its local demands.

Plant	Capacity to export
India	2,000
Singapore	1,000
Taiwan	2,000
	5,000 cars

The cost of sea transportation per car and the demands from three Asian countries—Korea, the Philippines, and Indonesia, are as follows:

From \ To	Korea	Philippines	Indonesia
India	$120	$130	$150
Singapore	$180	$80	$200
Taiwan	$90	$100	$110
Demand	2,500	1,000	1,000 cars

a. Develop the production and shipping schedule that minimizes transportation costs. Formulate a linear-programming model.

b. Solve the problem by using the *Micro Manager.*

19. A winner in a beauty contest has received the $200,000 award. She wishes to invest this money in common stocks, AAA bonds, A bonds, and saving certificates. The winner has obtained the following information from an investment counselor.

Alternative	Expected annual yield rate	Risk factor
Common stock	12.00%	0.25
AAA bonds	8.00	0.10
A bonds	9.50	0.15
Saving certificates	7.00	0.05

She wishes to determine the mix of investments that will maximize her return and has the following rules as a guideline for investments.

a. The probability of failing to obtain the expected earnings from the entire investment plan should be less than 18 percent.

b. Not more than 40 percent of the total money should be invested in AAA and A bonds.

c. The money invested in common stocks should be less than one half of the money invested in saving certificates.

Formulate a linear-programming model for this investment problem and solve it by using the *Micro Manager.*

20. Ohio Equipment Company has a government contract to produce 120 units of special tractors over the next four months. The delivery schedule and the required material and labor costs are as follows:

Months	Number of units	Material costs per units ($)	Labor cost per unit	
			Regular	*Overtime*
1	16	200	200	300
2	36	220	220	330
3	28	240	200	300
4	40	220	240	360

The normal capacity of this company is 24 units per month. An additional 10 units can be produced per month on an overtime basis. Inventory carrying costs per unit are $50 per month. Because these are custom orders, more than 120 special tractors are valueless.

a. Formulate a linear-programming model to determine the optimum production units each month that will minimize total cost.
b. Solve the problem by using the *Micro Manager.*

21. Tele-Bell Corporation has a scheduling problem. The operators required and their wages are shown in the following table.

Time period	Operators required	Wage ($/hour)
Midnight to 4 A.M.	2	16
4 A.M. to 8 A.M.	4	16
8 A.M. to noon	20	8
Noon to 4 P.M.	16	8
4 P.M. to 8 P.M.	12	12
8 P.M. to midnight	6	16

Operators work 8-hour shifts and can begin work at midnight, 4 A.M., 8 A.M., noon, 4 P.M., or 8 P.M. Formulate a linear-programming model to minimize the total labor cost and solve it by using the *Micro Manager.*

CHAPTER 5

Linear Programming—Sensitivity Analysis and Integer Problems

A model is an approximate representation of reality. Thus, the optimum solution to a given linear-programming model is a solution to the problem under many restrictive assumptions and generalizations. Obtaining the optimum solution to a model is important, of course, because it identifies the best decision alternative. However, this is not the sole objective of linear programming. In fact, analysis of the sensitivity of the optimum solution to changes in certain parameters under dynamic conditions is of vital importance to the decision maker. In this chapter, we will discuss the sensitivity of the optimum solution to the following changes in the model: (1) the unit contribution rate (c_j); (2) the amount of resources (b_i); (3) technological coefficients (a_{ij}); (4) addition of a new constraint; and (5) addition of a new variable.

In many real-world problems, decision variables must be integer-valued to have any significance. Such problems are referred to as integer-programming problems. Capital budgeting, assignment, project management, and construction of dams are good examples of integer problems. In this chapter, we will also examine the branch and bound and zero–one programming methods.

Basics

It is extremely important that the decision maker have information about the sensitivity of the optimum solution to changes in the decision environment. If the optimum solution is very sensitive to change in a model parameter, we must monitor that parameter very carefully. On the other hand, if the solution is not sensitive to change in that particular parameter, it will be a waste of time and effort to monitor the parameter very carefully. Such a procedural analysis is usually referred to as *sensitivity analysis, optimality analysis,* or *parametric programming.* The term sensitivity analysis is usually used for an analysis of the effects of discrete changes in model parameters, while parametric programming is used for the analysis of the effects of continuous changes in model parameters. In this chapter, we will discuss sensitivity analysis.

Changes in the Unit Contribution Rates (c_j)

In real-world situations, unit contribution rates (e.g., unit profits or unit costs) are seldom constant. Sometimes, contribution rates fluctuate in certain patterns within a range, and sometimes their fluctuations are totally unpredictable. Thus, the decision maker is vitally interested in the sensitivity of the optimum solution to changes in unit contribution rates.

A change in a unit contribution rate results in a change in the objective function and consequently a change in the iso-profit (cost) function. However, the feasible region will not be affected by such a change in a unit contribution rate. Consequently, the only area that we have to analyze is the optimality, not the feasibility, of the solution. In other words, we must check whether all nonbasic variables have nonpositive $c_j - z_j$ values after the change if a c_j is implemented in the solution. If all $c_j - z_j$ values are nonpositive, the previous optimum solution is still optimum. Otherwise, we will have to find a new optimum solution.

Change in c_j When x_j Is a Nonbasic Variable

Whether or not a decision variable becomes a basic variable is based on the variable's relative unit contribution rate and resource requirement as compared to other variables. If a decision variable is a nonbasic variable, it is clear that the unit contribution rate of this decision variable is not attractive enough to have a solution value for the variable. Thus, if the unit contribution rate decreases for a nonbasic decision variable in a maximization problem (the opposite will be true for a minimization problem), the variable will remain a nonbasic variable. Consequently, the previous optimum solution remains optimum.

Change in c_j When x_j Is a Basic Variable

When x_j is a basic variable, a change in its contribution rate will change c_j for the variable. Thus, the only changes in the final simplex tableau will be z_j values, and consequently $c_j - z_j$ values, in those nonbasic variable columns where nonzero coefficients are in the x_j row. As soon as the $c_j - z_j$ values of one of the nonbasic variable columns become positive, a new optimum solution will emerge.

Changes in the Resources (b_i)

In real-world situations, the amount of available resources changes frequently. In a maximization problem, if the right-hand side value of a constraint decreases, the solution values of the basic variables may decrease to the point where some of them may actually become negative. In other words, the previous optimum solution may become infeasible.

On the other hand, if the right-hand side value of a constraint increases, a new optimum solution with different solution values may result. Since a change in b_i does not affect $c_j - z_j$, we will not be concerned with optimality but only with a feasibility test.

The $c_j - z_j$ value in a slack variable column in the final simplex tableau represents the amount of profit that will be reduced if the resource of the constraint where the slack variable appears is decreased by one unit. Conversely, if the resource is increased by one unit in that constraint the total profit will be increased by the same amount of $c_j - z_j$. Thus, this $c_j - z_j$ value in the slack variable column is referred to as the *shadow price* for the constraint. The shadow price for a given constraint is valid within the feasibility range of b_i.

Changes in Technological Coefficients (a_{ij})

The technological coefficients represent the rates of resource usage in producing certain products in a typical maximization problem. In real-world situations, technological coefficients change almost constantly because of the changing efficiency of human resources or because of improvements in technologies used on the job.

Change in a_{ij} When x_j is a Nonbasic Variable

When a decision variable is nonbasic, it uses relatively more resources than other variables. Thus, if the technological coefficient of a nonbasic variable increases in a maximization problem, this variable will remain as a nonbasic variable. On the other hand, if the technological coefficient of this variable decreases, its $c_j - z_j$ values may increase sufficiently to become positive. Then, a new optimum solution will result.

Change in a_{ij} When x_j is a Basic Variable

When the technological coefficient of a basic variable is changed, we must check the feasibility as well as optimality of the previous solution. The procedure for doing this is somewhat complex. However, the basic approach is quite similar to the case of a change in a_{ij} when x_j is a nonbasic variable.

Addition of a New Constraint

There are many occasions when an additional constraint must be introduced to the problem under consideration. An additional constraint will be needed when the organization introduces a new policy, a government agency develops a new regulation, the production process requires a new fabrication center, and others.

The new constraint introduced to the model will not alter the objective function. Thus, the only area that we have to check is feasibility. If the previous optimum solution satisfies the new constraint just added to the model, the solution is still optimum. However, if the solution does not satisfy the new constraint, the previous optimum solution is now infeasible. Thus, we should derive a new solution by using the *Micro Manager*.

Addition of a New Variable

After finding the optimum solution, the decision maker may find that an important decision variable has been deleted from the model. An additional variable will completely change the nature of the problem. First of all, the decision space will be increased by another dimension. Also, the objective function will be changed.

We can check whether the new variable would be attractive enough to be brought into the solution basis. This can be done simply by analyzing the resource requirements for the new variable. Based on the shadow prices of the nonbasic variable columns, we can easily compute the total cost associated with introducing one unit of the new variable. If the total cost is more than the unit contribution of the variable, this new product will not be produced. Thus, the previous optimum solution is still optimum. On the other hand, if the total cost is less than the unit contribution rate of the variable, a profit can be made by producing the new product. Thus, we should obtain a new solution by using the *Micro Manager.*

Example 5.1 Commonwealth Chemical, Inc.

Commonwealth Chemical, Inc., specializes in producing three types of catalyzers. A unit of catalyzer *A* requires 20 liters of liquid 1, 5 liters of liquid 2, and 10 hours of laboratory time. A unit of catalyzer *B* requires none of liquid 1, 20 liters of liquid 2, and 10 hours of laboratory time. A unit of catalyzer *C* requires 20 liters of liquid 1, 10 liters of liquid 2, and 20 hours of laboratory time.

Commonwealth Chemical has secured 80 liters of liquid 1, 30 liters of liquid 2, and 60 hours of laboratory time for the production of these catalyzers. The unit contribution rate for each type of catalyzer is: *A*—$75 per unit; *B*—$150 per unit; and *C*—$100 per unit.

Commonwealth Chemical is attempting to determine the quantity of the three types of catalyzers to maximize total profit. The model can be developed as follows:

$$\begin{aligned} \text{Maximize } Z &= 75x_1 + 150x_2 + 100x_3 \\ \text{subject to } 20x_1 \qquad\qquad &+ 20x_3 \leq 80 \\ 5x_1 + 20x_2 &+ 10x_3 \leq 30 \\ 10x_1 + 10x_2 &+ 20x_3 \leq 60 \\ x_1, x_2, x_3 &\geq 0, \end{aligned}$$

where x_1 = quantity of catalyzer *A* to be produced
x_2 = quantity of catalyzer *B* to be produced
x_3 = quantity of catalyzer *C* to be produced

The optimum solution to the problem is derived by the *Micro Manager.* The optimum simplex solution tableau is presented in Table 5.1.

Table 5.1 The simplex tableau of the optimum solution

c_b \ c_j	Basis	Solution	75 x_1	150 x_2	100 x_3	0 s_1	0 s_2	0 s_3
75	x_1	4	1	0	1	0.0500	0	0
150	x_2	0.5	0	1	0.25	−0.0125	0.05	0
0	s_3	15	0	0	7.5	−0.3750	−0.5	1
	z_j	375	75	150	112.5	1.8750	7.5	0
	$c_j - z_j$		0	0	−12.5	−1.8750	−7.5	0

Change in the Unit Contribution Rate

As we discussed earlier, the unit contribution rate of a decision variable changes quite frequently. The process of sensitivity analysis differs depending on whether the decision variable, whose unit contribution rate has been changed, is a basic or a nonbasic variable.

Change in c_3 As shown in Table 5.1, x_3 is the only nonbasic decision variable. The $c_j - z_j$ value in the x_3 column indicates that the reason why x_3 is not in the solution is that the production of a unit of x_3 would decrease the total profit by \$12.50. The total cost associated with the production of a unit of x_3 is \$112.50 (z_j value in the x_3 column). Thus, unless c_3 (the unit contribution rate of x_3) is increased beyond \$112.50, x_3 will remain a nonbasic variable. Consequently, there is no lower limit in the change of c_3 and the upper limit is \$112.50.

Change in c_j For x_1 or x_2 When the unit contribution rate of a basic variable changes, the analysis process becomes somewhat complex. In Table 5.1, we can easily see that a change in the contribution rate of either x_1 or x_2 will only affect the z_j values of the nonbasic variable columns.

For example, if c_2 (contribution rate of x_2) is changed, z_j values of the nonbasic variable columns, x_3, s_1, and s_2, will be changed. If c_2 is increased, the z_j values of the nonbasic variable columns with positive coefficients in the x_2 row will increase and thus these variables will remain nonbasic. On the other hand, when c_2 is increased, those nonbasic variable columns with negative coefficients in the x_2 row will have increased $c_j - z_j$ values. As soon as their $c_j - z_j$ values become positive, a new optimum solution will result.

When c_2 decreases, those nonbasic variable columns with positive coefficients in the x_2 row will become more attractive. As soon as the $z_j - c_j$ value of one of these nonbasic variable columns becomes positive, a new optimum solution will result.

The upper (increase) and lower (decrease) limits of the change in c_2, within which the previous optimum solution remains optimum, can be determined as follows:

$$\begin{aligned}
\text{Upper limit} &= \min\left(c_k + \frac{c_j - z_j}{a_{kj}}\right), \text{ where } a_{kj} \text{ is negative} \\
&= \left(c_2 + \frac{c_{s_1} - z_{s_1}}{a_{x_2, s_1}}\right) \\
&= \left(150 + \frac{-1.8750}{-0.0125}\right) = \$300.
\end{aligned}$$

$$\begin{aligned}
\text{Lower limit} &= \max\left(c_k + \frac{c_j - z_j}{a_{kj}}\right), \text{ where } a_{kj} \text{ is positive} \\
&= \max\left(c_2 + \frac{c_{x_3} - z_{x_3}}{a_{x_2, x_3}} ; c_2 + \frac{c_{s_2} - z_{s_2}}{a_{x_2, x_3}}\right) \\
&= \max\left(150 + \frac{-12.5}{0.25} ; 150 + \frac{-7.5}{0.05}\right) \\
&= \max\,(150 - 50 ; 150 - 150) \\
&= \$100,
\end{aligned}$$

where c_k = the unit contribution rate of the kth basic variable
$c_j - z_j$ = $c_j - z_j$ value of the jth nonbasic variable column
a_{kj} = coefficient at the kth row and jth nonbasic variable column

We can use the same approach to analyze a change in c_1. Since there is no negative coefficient in the x_1 row, there is no upper limit. In other words, regardless of the amount of increase in c_1, x_1 will remain as a basic variable. The lower limit can be found as follows:

$$\begin{aligned}
\text{Lower limit} &= \max\left(c_1 + \frac{c_{x_3} - z_{x_3}}{a_{x_1, x_3}} ; c_1 + \frac{c_{s_1} - z_{s_1}}{a_{x_1, s_1}}\right) \\
&= \max\left(75 + \frac{-12.5}{1} ; 75 + \frac{-1.875}{0.05}\right) \\
&= \max\,(150 - 50 ; 150 - 150) \\
&= \$100,
\end{aligned}$$

The *Micro Manager* performs sensitivity analysis of c_j for the decision variables exactly the same way shown above.

Change in b_i

Changes in the right-hand side value may affect feasibility of the previous optimum solution. In the simplex equality of a constraint, the slack (or surplus) variable for the particular constraint appears only in the given equality. Thus, we can easily determine what multiples of b_i have been added to the solution values of the basic variables for other constraints by examining the coefficients in the s_i column.

Suppose we change the first constraint from $20x_1 + 20x_3 + s_1 = 80$ to $20x_1 + 20x_3 + s_1 = 100$. We denote a^*_{ki} as the coefficient in the s_i column and the kth row in the final simplex tableau, b_i as the original right-hand side value, and b^*_i as the new right-hand side value. Then $a^*_{ki}\ (b^*_i - b_i)$ should be added to the solution value of the basic variables to obtain the new solution. The coefficients in the s_1 column are: 0.05 in the x_1 row, -0.012 in the x_2 row, and -0.375 in the s_3 row. Thus, we can find the new solution values as follows:

x_1 row: $4 + 0.05\ (100 - 80) = 4 + 1 = 5$

x_2 row: $0.5 - 0.012\ (100 - 80) = 0.5 - 0.24 = 0.26$

s_3 row: $15 - 0.375\ (100 - 80) = 15 - 7.5 = 7.5$

We can easily see that this new solution is feasible. Thus, it is the new optimum solution. We can easily determine the range of b_i within which the previous optimum solution mix of the basic variables does not change. Also, within the range of b_i, the shadow price of a unit of resources in the given constraint remains valid. The range for the first constraint resource level (b_1) can be found as follows:

$$\begin{aligned}\text{Upper limit} &= \min\left(b_i - \frac{B_k}{a^*_{ki}}\right), \text{ where } a^*_{ki} \text{ is negative} \\ &= \min\left(80 - \frac{0.5}{-0.012}\,;\ 80 - \frac{15}{-0.375}\right) \\ &= \min\ (80 + 41.67\ ;\ 80 + 40) \\ &= 120.\end{aligned}$$

$$\begin{aligned}\text{Lower limit} &= \max\left(b_i - \frac{B_k}{a^*_{ki}}\right), \text{ where } a^*_{ki} \text{ is positive} \\ &= \max\left(80 - \frac{4}{0.05}\right) \\ &= \max\ (80 - 80) \\ &= 0,\end{aligned}$$

where b_i = the original right-hand side value of the ith constraint

B_k = the solution value of the kth basic variable

a^*_{ki} = coefficient at the kth row and the ith slack variable column

The previous optimum solution mix remains the same as long as change in b_i is within the range of 0 to 120. Also, the shadow price of 1.875 that we see in the s_1 column is valid within this range of b_1. The *Micro Manager* uses the same procedure outlined in this section to derive the right-hand side ranging.

Change in Technological Coefficients (a_{ij})

The technological coefficients associated with the decision variables represent the rates of resource usage in producing certain products in a typical maximization problem. The analysis process of a change in a_{ij} differs when the associated x_j is a basic or a nonbasic variable.

When x_j Is a Nonbasic Variable When a_{ij} of a nonbasic decision variable is changed, the only possible effect will be changed coefficients in that nonbasic variable column. Let us denote s_i as the slack variable in the constraint where a_{ij} has been changed to a_{ij}^*. Then a_{ki}^* can be denoted as the coefficient at the kth row and the s_i column in the final simplex tableau. Then, a_{ki}^* $(a_{ij}^* - a_{ij})$ should be added to the current coefficients in the x_j nonbasic variable column.

For example, suppose the second constraint is changed from $5x_1 + 20x_2 + 10x_3 + s_2 = 30$ to $5x_1 + 20x_2 + 8x_3 + s_2 = 30$. In other words, a_{23} has been changed from 10 to 8. The coefficients in the x_3 column will be changed as follows:

Row	Old coefficient in x_3 column	New coefficient in x_3 column
x_1	1	$1 + [0\ (8 - 10)] = 1$
x_2	0.25	$0.25 + [0.05\ (8 - 10)] = 0.15$
s_3	7.5	$7.5 + [-0.5\ (8 - 10)] = 8.5$

When we substitute these new coefficients in the x_3 column, the new $c_j - z_j$ becomes $100 - 91.5 = 8.5$. Thus, the previous optimum solution is no longer optimum and a new solution will be derived with x_3 as a basic variable. The *Micro Manager* analyzes the problem by the same basic approach.

When x_j Is a Basic Variable If a_{ij} changes for a basic decision variable, we use the same approach to compute a new set of coefficients in the x_j column. For example, suppose the first constraint is changed from $20x_1 + 20x_3 + s_1 = 80$ to $30x_1 + 20x_3 + s_1 = 80$. In other words, a_{11} is changed from 20 to 30. The new set of coefficients for the x_1 column can be computed as follows:

Row	Old coefficients in x_1 column	New coefficients in x_1 column
x_1	1	$1 + [0.05\ (30 - 20)] = 1.5$
x_2	0	$0 + [-0.012\ (30 - 20)] = -0.12$
s_3	0	$0 + [-0.375\ (30 - 20)] = -3.75$

Table 5.2 The new optimum solution with the changed a_{11}

c_b \ c_j	Basis	Solution	75 x_1	150 x_2	100 x_3	0 s_1	0 s_2	0 s_3
0	s_1	20	20	0	0	1	0.667	1.333
150	x_2	1.037	0.26	1	0	0	0.068	0.037
100	x_3	3	0.5	0	1	0	0.033	0.133
	z_j	455.55	89	150	100	0	13.533	18.883
	$c_j - z_j$		−14	0	0	0	−13.533	−18.883

Since x_1 is a basic variable, there should be only one nonzero coefficient in the x_1 column (1 at the intersection of the x_1 row and the x_1 column, as shown in Table 5.1). This basic variable condition is broken when the net set of coefficients are introduced in the x_1 column. To restore the basic variable condition, we select the x_1 column as the pivot column and the x_1 row as the pivot row. Table 5.2 presents a new solution. The *Micro Manager* solves for the new optimum solution in the same basic manner.

Addition of a New Constraint

When we must introduce an additional constraint to the model, we should first check to see whether the current optimum solution satisfies the new constraint. For example, suppose we need to add a new constraint $2x_1 + x_2 + x_3 \leq 10$. If we substitute the solution values ($x_1 = 4$, $x_2 = 0.5$, and $x_3 = 0$) into the new constraint, we obtain $2(4) + 0.5 = 8.5 < 10$. Thus, the previous optimum solution remains optimum.

If the previous optimum solution does not satisfy the new constraint, we need to solve the problem again with the new constraint added to the model. The *Micro Manager* has an interactive linear programming (LP) program that can quickly solve the new problem.

Addition of a New Variable

If we need to add a new decision variable to the model, we can easily check whether the new variable would be profitable to produce. For example, let us suppose that x_4 is being considered for possible production. One unit of x_4 requires 10 units of resource in constraint 1, 2 units in constraint 2, and 5 units in constraint 3. The unit contribution rate of this new variable is \$120. By examining the shadow prices ($c_j - z_j$ values of the nonbasic-variable columns) in the s_1, s_2, and s_3 columns, we can compute the total cost associated with the production of a unit of x_4 as follows:

$$10(1.875) + 2(7.5) + 5(0) = \$33.75.$$

Since we can produce net profit of \$86.25 from a unit of x_4, we should produce the new variable. The *Micro Manager* can easily derive a new solution. If the total production cost exceeds the unit contribution rate, the previous optimum solution remains optimum.

Integer Programming

One of the requirements of linear programming is divisibility of the variables. In a linear-programming model, each decision variable can take on any nonnegative continuous solution value. The divisibility requirement does not present any real problem in many decision problems. For example, we can easily accept such solution values as 1.27 tons of concrete, 0.667 hours, or 3.497 ounces of alcohol.

However, in many real-world problems, the divisibility assumption is totally unacceptable. For example, we cannot accept such solution values as 1.39 dams on a river system, 3.697 units of nuclear power plants, or 0.417 individuals assigned to a foreign mission. These variables require integer solution values. Also, some special cases of integer problems require solution values of either zero or one. For example, assignment and capital budgeting are good examples of zero–one integer-programming problems. These problems require a solution that either accepts or rejects each person or project.

A simple method of obtaining an integer solution is by rounding off the fractional values of the optimum continuous solution. A major pitfall of this approach is that an integer solution based on rounding may be either infeasible (violating one or more constraints) or suboptimum (inferior to other integer solutions).

The integer-programming model requires the same model characteristics (e.g., linear objective function and constraints, nonnegativity constraints, and so forth) as a regular linear-programming model and an integer value constraint for certain variables. When the model requires all integer values for the basic variables, it is referred to as an all-integer or pure-integer problem. On the other hand, if the model requires only certain variables to be integers, it is referred to as a mixed-integer problem. If a problem requires only zero or one solution values for the variable, it is called a zero–one integer problem.

If an integer-programming problem involves only two decision variables, we can easily identify the optimum integer solution by either a search technique or the iso-profit or iso-cost function approach. However, if the problem involves more than two decision variables, the most widely applied techniques are the branch and bound and implicit enumeration (for the zero–one problem) methods. In this section, we will discuss these two methods.

Branch and Bound Method

Many integer-programming problems have upper and/or lower bounds for the decision variables. The bounded integer-programming problem has a finite number of feasible integer solutions. Thus, we can search for the optimum solution by an enumeration procedure. The basic steps of the branch and bound method for a maximization problem are as follows:

Step 1. Solve the integer-programming problem by the regular simplex method of linear programming without the integer restrictions.

Step 2. If the solution derived in Step 1 satisfies integer requirements, the optimum integer solution is obtained. Stop. If the solution does not satisfy integer requirements, go to Step 3.

Step 3. The set of feasible noninteger solutions is branched into two subsets (subproblems) by introducing mutually exclusive constraints that are necessary to satisfy the integer requirement of one basic variable whose integer requirement has not been satisfied.

Step 4. For each subset, the objective function value of the optimum noninteger solution is determined as the upper bound. The objective function value of the best integer solution becomes the lower bound. Those subsets having upper bounds that are less than the current lower bound are excluded from further considerations. A feasible integer solution that is as good or better than the upper bound for any subset is sought. If such a solution is found, it is optimum. If such a solution does not exist, a subset with the best upper bound is selected for further branching. Return to Step 3.

Example 5.2 Colonial Furniture, Inc.

Colonial Furniture, Inc., specializes in producing Early American style furniture. The company has decided to produce EZ rockers and coffee tables. The production process requires three departments: cutting and assembly, finishing, and varnishing. An EZ rocker requires two hours of cutting and assembly, three hours of finishing, and one hour of varnishing work. A coffee table takes two hours of cutting and assembly, one hour of finishing, and two hours of varnishing work. The company has secured the following productive resources: 59 hours of cutting and assembly time; 75 hours of finishing time; and 50 hours of varnishing time.

The expected unit profit for each product is: EZ rocker—$40 and coffee table—$30. Since the company must retool the production facility after this production run, the solution values of EZ rockers and coffee tables must be integer-valued. Thus, this problem is an integer-programming problem.

This problem can be easily formulated as an integer-programming problem as follows:

$$\begin{aligned} \text{Maximize } Z &= 40x_1 + 30x_2 \\ \text{subject to } 2x_1 + 2x_2 &\leq 59 \\ 3x_1 + x_2 &\leq 75 \\ x_1 + 2x_2 &\leq 50 \\ x_1, x_2 &= 0 \text{ or nonnegative integers} \end{aligned}$$

Figure 5.1 Optimum solution: point A. $x_1 = 22.75$, $x_2 = 6.75$, and $Z =$ 1,112.50.

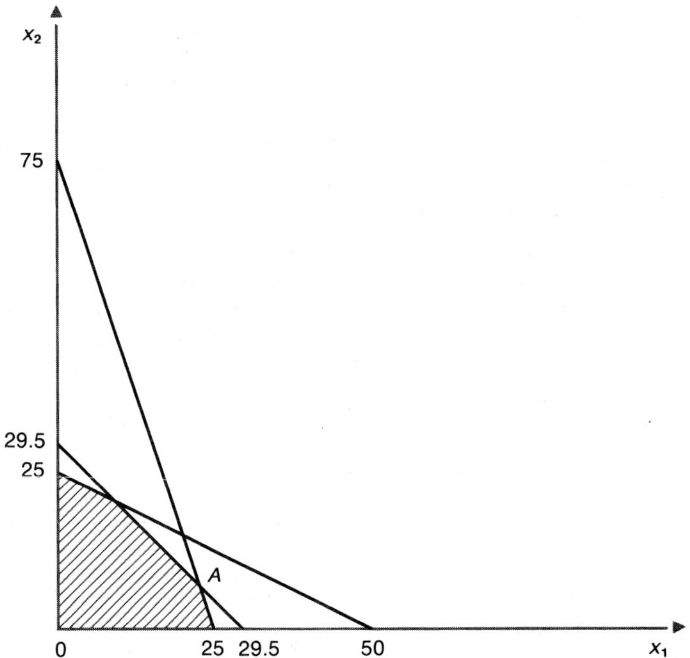

The optimum relaxed solution to this problem is $x_1 = 22.75$, $x_2 = 6.75$, and $Z = 1{,}112.50$, as shown in Fig. 5.1. This regular linear-programming solution represents the initial upper bound. The lower bound is the rounded-down solution of $x_1 = 22$, $x_2 = 6$, and $Z = 1{,}060.00$. The first step of the branch and bound method is to divide the problem into two subproblems to search for the possible integer solution values of x_1 and x_2. To accomplish this, the variable with the noninteger solution value that has the greatest fractional part is selected. In the above-determined linear-programming solution, we have a tie between x_1 and x_2 in their fractional values. Thus, we can select a variable arbitrarily for the branching operation.

Suppose we select x_1 for branching. To eliminate the fractional part of 22.75, two mutually exclusive constraints are created. In this case, the two integer values closest to 22.75 are 23 and 22. Thus, we formulate two subproblems by introducing two mutually exclusive constraints: $x_1 \leq 22$ and $x_1 \geq 23$.

Subproblem A

$$\begin{aligned} \text{Maximize } Z &= 40x_1 + 30x_2 \\ \text{subject to } 2x_1 + 2x_2 &\le 59 \\ 3x_1 + x_2 &\le 75 \\ x_1 + 2x_2 &\le 50 \\ x_1 &\le 22 \\ x_1, x_2 &\ge 0 \end{aligned}$$

Subproblem B

$$\begin{aligned} \text{Maximize } Z &= 40x_1 + 30x_2 \\ \text{subject to } 2x_1 + 2x_2 &\le 59 \\ 3x_1 + x_2 &\le 75 \\ x_1 + 2x_2 &\le 50 \\ x_1 &\ge 23 \\ x_1, x_2 &\ge 0 \end{aligned}$$

The above two subproblems are solved with integer restrictions relaxed by the simplex solution. Since this problem involves only two decision variables, graphical solutions are provided here in Fig. 5.2. Linear-programming solutions are

Subproblem *A:* $x_1 = 22$, $x_2 = 7.5$, $Z = 1{,}105.00$

Subproblem *B:* $x_1 = 23$, $x_2 = 6$, $Z = 1{,}100.00$

Figure 5.2(a) Optimum solution: point A. $x_1 = 22$, $x_2 = 7.5$, and $Z = 1{,}105.00$.

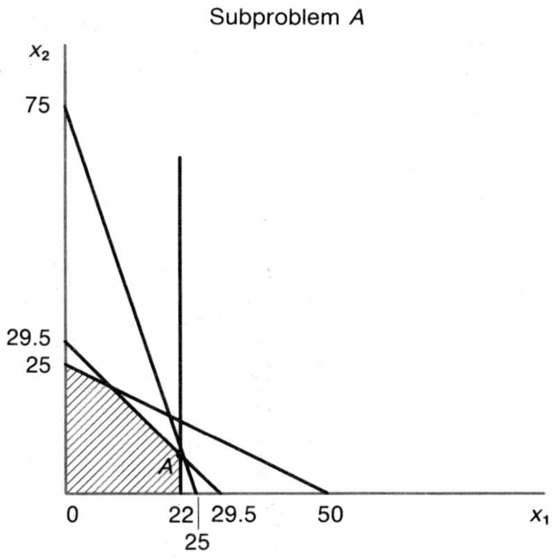

Figure 5.2(b) Optimum solution: point B. $x_1 = 23$, $x_2 = 6$, and $Z =$ 1,100.00.

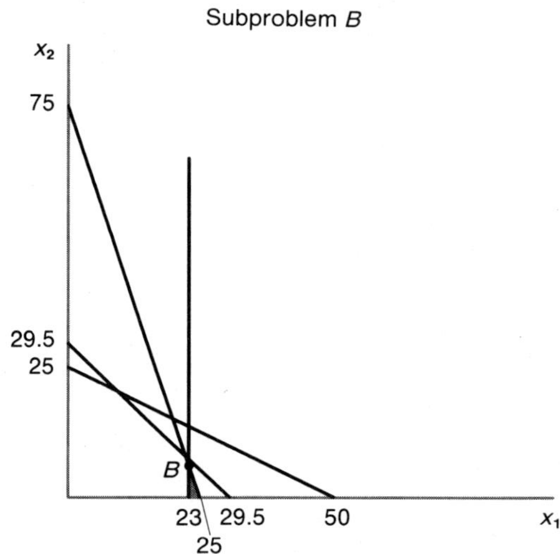

Subproblem B yields an all-integer solution. Thus, the lower bound is now $Z = 1{,}100.00$. Subproblem A's solution warrants a further search because its solution has a total profit that is greater than the lower bound. A further search of Subproblem A may yield an all-integer solution with total profit exceeding \$1,100.00.

We branch Subproblem A further into Subproblem $A1$ and Subproblem $A2$, the first with the constraint $x_1 \leq 7$ and the other with $x_1 \geq 8$. The two subproblems are

Subproblem *A*1

$$\begin{aligned}
\text{Maximize } Z &= 40x_1 + 30x_2 \\
\text{subject to } 2x_1 + 2x_2 &\leq 59 \\
3x_1 + x_2 &\leq 75 \\
x_1 + 2x_2 &\leq 50 \\
x_1 &\leq 22 \\
x_2 &\leq 7 \\
x_1, x_2 &\geq 0
\end{aligned}$$

Subproblem *A*2

$$\begin{aligned}
\text{Maximize } Z &= 40x_1 + 30x_2 \\
\text{subject to } 2x_1 + 2x_2 &\leq 59 \\
3x_1 + x_2 &\leq 75 \\
x_1 + 2x_2 &\leq 50 \\
x_1 &\leq 22 \\
x_2 &\geq 8 \\
x_1, x_2 &\geq 0
\end{aligned}$$

Figure 5.3A1 Optimum solution: point A. $x_1 = 22$, $x_2 = 7$, and $Z = 1{,}090$.

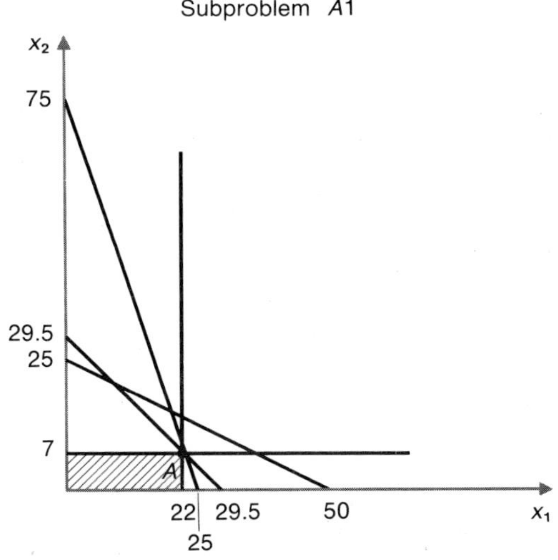

Figure 5.3A2 Optimum solution: point B. $x_1 = 21.5$, $x_2 = 8$, and $Z = 1{,}100$.

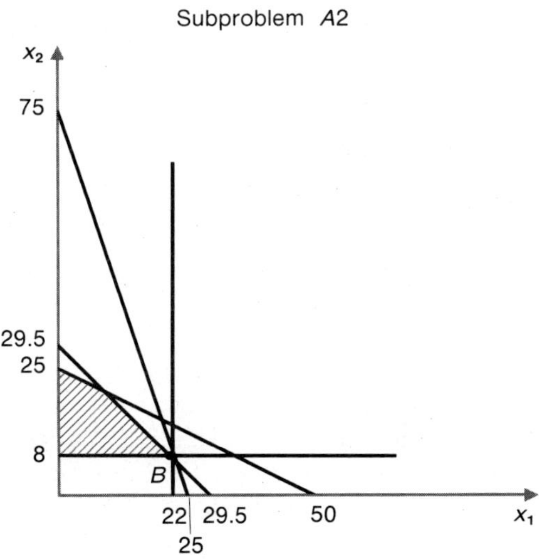

The graphical solutions for the above two subproblems are shown in Fig. 5.3. The simplex solutions are:

Subproblem $A1$: $x_1 = 22$, $x_2 = 7$, $Z = 1{,}090$
Subproblem $A2$: $x_1 = 21.5$, $x_2 = 8$, $Z = 1{,}100$

Figure 5.4(a) Complete Branch and Bound Solution

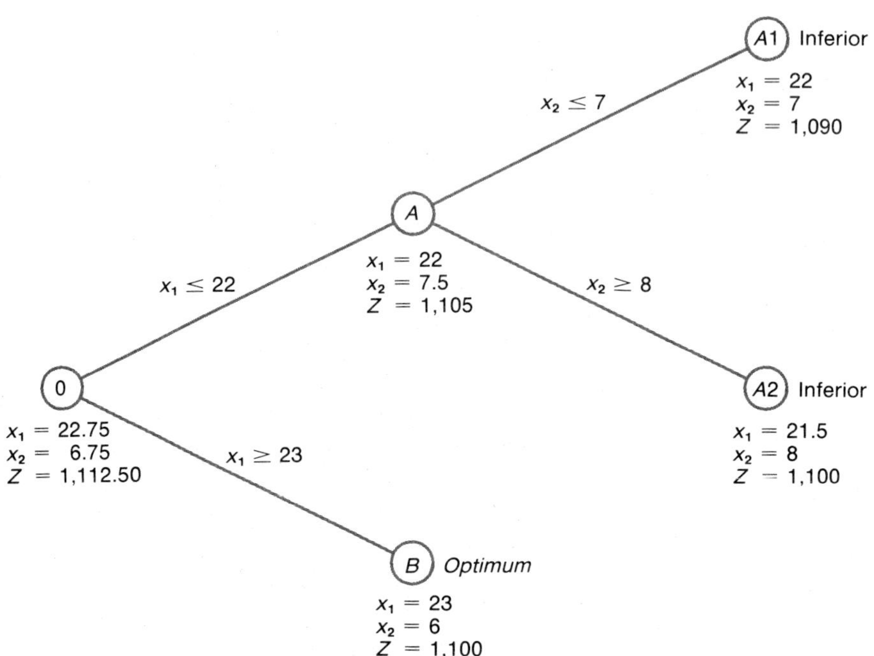

Subproblem $A1$ yields an all-integer solution. However, its $Z = 1{,}090$ is less than the previous lower bound $Z = 1{,}100$ found in Subproblem B. Thus, the previous lower bound remains to be the lower bound. Subproblem $A2$ still has a noninteger solution. Its $Z = 1{,}100$ is exactly equal to the current lower bound. Therefore, a further branching from Subproblem $A2$ will not yield an all-integer solution that is better than the current lower bound. In fact, the lower bound is equal to the new upper bound. The optimum integer solution is $x_1 = 23$, $x_2 = 6$, and $Z = 1{,}100.00$, which Subproblem B yields.

In the branching operation, further analysis is stopped when (a) a subproblem results in an inferior solution as compared with the feasible lower bound already identified, and (b) further branching yields infeasible solutions. The entire branch and bound procedure for this problem is shown in Fig. 5.4.

Figure 5.4(b) Another Solution from Computer Program

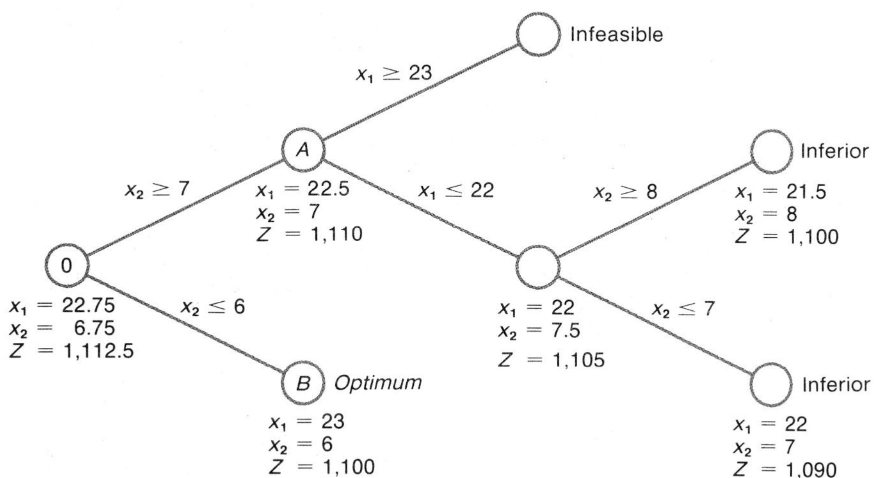

Zero–One Programming

Many decision problems require solutions with decision variables of only zero or one. Some examples are capital budgeting, project scheduling, fixed-cost, location–allocation, traveling salespeople, and assignment problems. A widely known zero–one programming technique is the implicit enumeration method that Egon Balas developed. The implicit enumeration method is based on Balas's additive algorithm and Fred Glover's backtracking method.

The solution process starts with an infeasible solution that is even better than the optimum solution. The procedure then forces the solution toward feasibility while maintaining the optimality condition. The solution procedure is somewhat involved and its discussion is beyond the scope of this book. Those interested in the solution procedure and illustrative examples should consult Lee, Moore, and Taylor (1985).

Application of the *Micro Manager*

In this section we present an application example of the *Micro Manager.* Since the program diskette contains the complete information about sensitivity analysis and integer programming, this section presents only the information (purpose of the technique and the batch input data format) and solutions of the sample problems using the interactive input format. We will apply Linear Programming I, Linear Programming II, All Integer Programming, and Zero-One Programming.

<< PURPOSE >>

The function of LINEAR PROGRAMMING II is the same as LP I except for the computation procedure. LP II utilizes the revised simplex method whereas LP I uses the standard simplex method. LP II presents just the final result without giving intermediate solution tableaus. This second version of LP is intended for LP problems with up to 50 decision variables and 40 constraints.

<< BATCH INPUT DATA FORMAT >>

Type in the values of the following input data requirements, after creating a new file. You may enter as many values as you want in a line, separating them by commas for alphabetic characters and by commas or blank spaces for numeric values. However, the input data must be exactly in the following order:

```
 1. Problem type:
      1    : maximization
      2    : minimization
 2. Number of decision variables (maximum 50)
 3. Number of constraints (maximum 40)
 4. Number of ' <= ' type constraints
 5. Number of '  = ' type constraints
 6. Number of ' >= ' type constraints
 7. Type of each constraint:
      L    : less than or equal to    ( <= )
      E    : equal to                 (  = )
      G    : greater than or equal to ( >= )
 8. Coefficient of each decision variable in the objective function
 9. Coefficient of each decision variable for each constraint
10. Right-hand side value of each constraint
```

** Sample Batch Input Data Set (Example 5.1) **

```
1           ; maximization problem
3           ; number of decision variables
3           ; number of constraints
3           ; three 'less than or equal to' constraints
0           ; no  'equal to' constraints
0           ; no  'greater than or equal to' constraints
L,L,L       ; type of constraint 1, 2, and 3
75,150,100  ; coefficients in the objective function
20,0,20     ; coefficients of constraint 1
5,20,10     ; coefficients of constraint 2
10,10,20    ; coefficients of constraint 3
80,30,60    ; right-hand side values
```

```
PROGRAM: Linear Programming II

Enter 1 for maximization or 2 for minimization: 1

Enter number of decision variables: 2
Enter number of constraints: 2
Enter number of 'LESS THAN OR EQUAL TO    (<=)' constraints: 2
Enter number of 'EQUAL TO                 ( =)' constraints: 0
Enter number of 'GREATER THAN OR EQUAL TO (>=)' constraints: 0

Type of Constraint: L for <=, E for =, and G for >=
```

```
Enter type of constraint  1 : L
Enter type of constraint  2 : L

Enter coefficient of decision variable  1  in the objective function:  1.5
Enter coefficient of decision variable  2  in the objective function:  1

Enter coefficient of decision variable  1  in constraint  1 :  2
Enter coefficient of decision variable  2  in constraint  1 :  1.5

Enter coefficient of decision variable  1  in constraint  2 :  6
Enter coefficient of decision variable  2  in constraint  2 :  9

Enter right-hand side value (RHS) of constraint  1 :  40
Enter right-hand side value (RHS) of constraint  2 :  120

PROGRAM: Linear Programming II

***** INPUT DATA ENTERED *****

Max  Z =  1.5 x 1 + 1 x 2

Subject to:

C 1   2 x 1 + 1.5 x 2 <=  40
C 2   6 x 1 + 9 x 2 <=  120

*****   PROGRAM OUTPUT   *****

Optimal solution is obtained in  1  iterations

  Optimal Z =        30.00000

Optimal solution in row order

Number      Basis        Solution

    1.      X 1           20.00000
    2.      S 2            0.


Variable summary

Variable      Value            Reduced Cost

  X  1        20.00000             0.
  X  2         0.                 -0.12500

Slack/Surplus summary

  Row Number    Slack/Surplus         Shadow Price

    S  1             0.                 -0.75000
    S  2             0.                  0.
```

<< PURPOSE >>

ALL INTEGER PROGRAMMING determines the optimum solution to meet integer requirements of a linear programming problem using the branch and bound method. This program is very restricted and time consuming. Although it can handle problems with up to 10 decision variables and 20 constraints, it is recommended that this program be used to solve problems with less than 5 variables and 5 constraints. During the execution, the program displays the search process starting from level 0 and node 0. The major purpose of this program is to provide you with an idea about how the technique works and how it can be applied to real-world problems.

<< BATCH INPUT DATA FORMAT >>

Type in the values of the following input data requirements, after creating a new file. You may enter as many values as you want in a line, separating them by commas for alphabetic characters and by commas or blank spaces for numeric values. However, the input data must be exactly in the following order:

1. Problem type:
   - 1 : maximization
   - 2 : minimization
2. Number of decision variables (maximum 10)
3. Number of constraints (maximum 20)
4. Number of ' <= ' type constraints
5. Number of ' = ' type constraints
6. Number of ' >= ' type constraints
7. Type of each constraint:
   - L : less than or equal to (<=)
   - E : equal to (=)
   - G : greater than or equal to (>=)
8. Coefficient of each decision variable in the objective function
9. Coefficient of each decision variable for each constraint
10. Right-hand side value of each constraint

** Sample Batch Input Data Set (Example 5.2) **

```
1           ; maximization problem
2           ; two decision variables
3           ; three constraints
3,0,0       ; three '<=', no '=', and no '>=' type constraints
L,L,L       ; type of each constraint
40,30       ; coefficients of variables in the objective function
2,2         ; coefficients of variables in constraint 1
3,1         ; coefficients of variables in constraint 2
1,2         ; coefficients of variables in constraint 3
59,75,50    ; right-hand side values of constraints
```

```
PROGRAM: All Integer Programming

Enter 1 for maximization or 2 for minimization: 1

Enter number of decision variables: 2
Enter number of constraints: 3
Enter number of 'LESS THAN OR EQUAL TO    (<=)' constraints: 3
Enter number of 'EQUAL TO                 ( =)' constraints: 0
Enter number of 'GREATER THAN OR EQUAL TO (>=)' constraints: 0
```

```
Type of Constraint: L for <=, E for =, and G for >=

Enter type of constraint  1 : L
Enter type of constraint  2 : L
Enter type of constraint  3 : L

Enter coefficient of decision variable  1  in the objective function:  40
Enter coefficient of decision variable  2  in the objective function:  30

Enter coefficient of decision variable  1  in constraint  1 :  2
Enter coefficient of decision variable  2  in constraint  1 :  2

Enter coefficient of decision variable  1  in constraint  2 :  3
Enter coefficient of decision variable  2  in constraint  2 :  1

Enter coefficient of decision variable  1  in constraint  3 :  1
Enter coefficient of decision variable  2  in constraint  3 :  2

Enter right-hand side value (RHS) of constraint  1 :  59
Enter right-hand side value (RHS) of constraint  2 :  75
Enter right-hand side value (RHS) of constraint  3 :  50

PROGRAM: All Integer Programming

***** INPUT DATA ENTERED *****

Max  Z =  40 x 1 + 30 x 2

Subject to:

C 1   2 x 1 + 2 x 2 <=  59
C 2   3 x 1 + 1 x 2 <=  75
C 3   1 x 1 + 2 x 2 <=  50

*****   PROGRAM OUTPUT   *****

Level 0  node  0 :   Optimal solution =    1112.50000

                              x 1 = 22.75
                              x 2 = 6.75

Level 1  node  1 :   Optimal solution =    1100.00000

                              x 1 = 23
                              x 2 = 6

Level 1  node  2 :   Optimal solution =    1110.00000

                              x 1 = 22.5
                              x 2 = 7

Level 2  node  3 :   Optimal solution =    1105.00000

                              x 1 = 22
                              x 2 = 7.5
```

```
Level 3  node  4 :   Optimal solution =    1090.00000

                          x 1 = 22
                          x 2 = 7

Level 3  node  5 :   Optimal solution =    1100.00000

                          x 1 = 21.5
                          x 2 = 8

Level 2  node  6 :   Infeasible solution

Final optimal solution =    1100.00000

    X 1 = 23
    X 2 = 6
```

<< PURPOSE >>

ZERO ONE PROGRAMMING determines the optimum solution to the zero or one type of linear programming problems. This program utilizes the implicit enumeration algorithm, which is computationally inefficient. Therefore, this program's capacity is quite limited. It can handle problems with up to 10 decision variables and 10 constraints. The major purpose of this program is to demonstrate how the technique works on the microcomputer.

<< BATCH INPUT DATA FORMAT >>

Type in the values of the following input data requirements, after creating a new file. You may enter as many values as you want in a line, separating them by commas for alphabetic characters and by commas or blank spaces for numeric values. However, the input data must be exactly in the following order:

1. Problem type:
   - 1 : maximization
   - 2 : minimization
2. Number of decision variables (maximum 10)
3. Number of constraints (maximum 10)
4. Number of ' <= ' type constraints
5. Number of ' = ' type constraints
6. Number of ' >= ' type constraints
7. Type of each constraint:
   - L : less than or equal to (<=)
   - E : equal to (=)
   - G : greater than or equal to (>=)
8. Coefficient of each decision variable in the objective function
9. Coefficient of each decision variable for each constraint
10. Right-hand side value of each constraint

```
** Sample Batch Input Data Set (Problem 5.24) **

2            ; minimization problem
5            ; five decision variables
3            ; three constraints
1,0,2        ; one '<=', no '=', and two '>=' type constraints
G,G,L        ; type of each constraint
2,1,3,2,4    ; coefficients of variables in the objective function
1,2,1,1,2    ; coefficients of variables in constraint 1
7,1,0,-3,3   ; coefficients of variables in constraint 2
9,-9,-6,0,3  ; coefficients of variables in constraint 3
4,6,3        ; right-hand side values

PROGRAM: Zero One Programming

Enter 1 for maximization or 2 for minimization: 2

Enter number of decision variables: 5
Enter number of constraints: 3
Enter number of 'LESS THAN OR EQUAL TO    (<=)' constraints: 1
Enter number of 'EQUAL TO                 ( =)' constraints: 0
Enter number of 'GREATER THAN OR EQUAL TO (>=)' constraints: 2

Type of Constraint: L for <=, E for =, and G for >=

Enter type of constraint  1 : G
Enter type of constraint  2 : G
Enter type of constraint  3 : L

Enter coefficient of decision variable  1  in the objective function:  2
Enter coefficient of decision variable  2  in the objective function:  1
Enter coefficient of decision variable  3  in the objective function:  3
Enter coefficient of decision variable  4  in the objective function:  2
Enter coefficient of decision variable  5  in the objective function:  4

Enter coefficient of decision variable  1  in constraint  1 :  1
Enter coefficient of decision variable  2  in constraint  1 :  2
Enter coefficient of decision variable  3  in constraint  1 :  1
Enter coefficient of decision variable  4  in constraint  1 :  1
Enter coefficient of decision variable  5  in constraint  1 :  2

Enter coefficient of decision variable  1  in constraint  2 :  7
Enter coefficient of decision variable  2  in constraint  2 :  1
Enter coefficient of decision variable  3  in constraint  2 :  0
Enter coefficient of decision variable  4  in constraint  2 :  -3
Enter coefficient of decision variable  5  in constraint  2 :  3

Enter coefficient of decision variable  1  in constraint  3 :  9
Enter coefficient of decision variable  2  in constraint  3 :  -9
Enter coefficient of decision variable  3  in constraint  3 :  -6
Enter coefficient of decision variable  4  in constraint  3 :  0
Enter coefficient of decision variable  5  in constraint  3 :  3

Enter right-hand side value (RHS) of constraint  1 :  4
Enter right-hand side value (RHS) of constraint  2 :  6
Enter right-hand side value (RHS) of constraint  3 :  3
```

```
PROGRAM: Zero One Programming

***** INPUT DATA ENTERED *****

Min  Z =  2 x 1 + 1 x 2 + 3 x 3 + 2 x 4 + 4 x 5

Subject to:

C 1   1 x 1 + 2 x 2 + 1 x 3 + 1 x 4 + 2 x 5 >=  4
C 2   7 x 1 + 1 x 2 - 3 x 4 + 3 x 5 >=  6
C 3   9 x 1 - 9 x 2 - 6 x 3 + 3 x 5 <=  3

*****   PROGRAM OUTPUT   *****

Iteration :  0
Assigned Variables:  0  0  0  0  0
Free     Variables:  1  1  1  1  1
This combination is infeasible.

Iteration :  1
Assigned Variables:  1  0  0  0  0
Free     Variables:  0  1  1  1  1
This combination is infeasible.

Iteration :  2
Assigned Variables:  1  1  0  0  0
Free     Variables:  0  0  1  1  1
This combination is infeasible.

Iteration :  3
Assigned Variables:  1  1  1  0  0
Free     Variables:  0  0  0  1  1
The value of this combination is  6

Iteration :  4
Assigned Variables:  1  1 -1  1  0
Free     Variables:  0  0  0  0  1
This combination is infeasible.

Iteration :  5
Assigned Variables:  1  1 -1  1  1
Free     Variables:  0  0  0  0  0
The value of this combination is  9

Iteration :  6
Assigned Variables:  1  1 -1 -1  1
Free     Variables:  0  0  0  0  0
The value of this combination is  7

Iteration :  7
Assigned Variables:  1 -1  1  0  0
Free     Variables:  0  0  0  1  1
This combination is infeasible.

Iteration :  8
Assigned Variables:  1 -1  1  1  0
Free     Variables:  0  0  0  0  1
This combination is infeasible.
```

```
Iteration :  9
Assigned Variables:  1 -1  1  1  1
Free     Variables:  0  0  0  0  0
This combination is infeasible.

Iteration :  10
Assigned Variables:  1 -1  1 -1  1
Free     Variables:  0  0  0  0  0
This combination is infeasible.

Iteration :  11
Assigned Variables:  1 -1 -1  1  0
Free     Variables:  0  0  0  0  1
This combination is infeasible.

Iteration :  12
Assigned Variables:  1 -1 -1  1  1
Free     Variables:  0  0  0  0  0
This combination is infeasible.

Iteration :  13
Assigned Variables:  1 -1 -1 -1  1
Free     Variables:  0  0  0  0  0
This combination is infeasible.

Iteration :  14
Assigned Variables: -1  1  0  0  0
Free     Variables:  0  0  1  1  1
This combination is infeasible.

Iteration :  15
Assigned Variables: -1  1  1  0  0
Free     Variables:  0  0  0  1  1
This combination is infeasible.

Iteration :  16
Assigned Variables: -1  1  1  1  0
Free     Variables:  0  0  0  0  1
This combination is infeasible.

Iteration :  17
Assigned Variables: -1  1  1  1  1
Free     Variables:  0  0  0  0  0
This combination is infeasible.

Iteration :  18
Assigned Variables: -1  1  1 -1  1
Free     Variables:  0  0  0  0  0
This combination is infeasible.

Iteration :  19
Assigned Variables: -1  1 -1  1  0
Free     Variables:  0  0  0  0  1
This combination is infeasible.

Iteration :  20
Assigned Variables: -1  1 -1  1  1
Free     Variables:  0  0  0  0  0
This combination is infeasible.
```

```
Iteration :  21
Assigned Variables: -1  1 -1 -1  1
Free     Variables:  0  0  0  0  0
This combination is infeasible.

Iteration :  22
Assigned Variables: -1 -1  1  0  0
Free     Variables:  0  0  0  1  1
This combination is infeasible.

Iteration :  23
Assigned Variables: -1 -1  1  1  0
Free     Variables:  0  0  0  0  1
This combination is infeasible.

Iteration :  24
Assigned Variables: -1 -1  1  1  1
Free     Variables:  0  0  0  0  0
This combination is infeasible.

Iteration :  25
Assigned Variables: -1 -1  1 -1  1
Free     Variables:  0  0  0  0  0
This combination is infeasible.

Iteration :  26
Assigned Variables: -1 -1 -1  1  0
Free     Variables:  0  0  0  0  1
This combination is infeasible.

Iteration :  27
Assigned Variables: -1 -1 -1  1  1
Free     Variables:  0  0  0  0  0
This combination is infeasible.

Iteration :  28
Assigned Variables: -1 -1 -1 -1  1
Free     Variables:  0  0  0  0  0
This combination is infeasible.

The optimal solution is 6

The solution values of decision variables are as follows:

 1   1   1   0   0
```

Summary

Sensitivity analysis is an important topic of linear programming. This analysis provides useful economic information about the sensitivity of an optimum solution to changes in model parameters. If a solution is very sensitive to changes in a parameter, one should direct a great deal of effort in estimating that parameter. On the other hand, if the solution is not very sensitive to that parameter, extra efforts are not warranted in estimating the parameter.

Many real-world problems often require solutions that are integer-valued. Some integer-programming problems require all-integer solutions while others may require zero–one solutions. In this chapter, we have examined the application of Linear Programming I and Linear Programming II for sensitivity analysis of linear programming. Also, we applied the programs of All-Integer Programming and Zero–One Programming for integer-programming problems.

References

Ackoff, R. L., and M. F. Sasiani. 1968. *Fundamentals of operations research.* New York: John Wiley & Sons.

Baumol, W. J. 1965. *Economic theory and operational analysis.* 2d ed. Englewood Cliffs, NJ: Prentice-Hall.

Dantzig, G. B. 1963. *Linear programming and extensions.* Princeton, NJ: Princeton University Press.

Hillier, F. S., and G. J. Lieberman. 1980. *Introduction to operations research.* 3d ed. San Francisco: Holden-Day.

Lee, S. M. 1976. *Linear optimization for management.* New York: Petrocelli-Charter.

———. 1983. *Introduction to management science.* Chicago: Dryden.

Lee, S. M., L. J. Moore, and B. J. Taylor. 1985. *Management science.* 2d ed. Dubuque, IA: Wm. C. Brown Co. Publishers.

Taha, H. A. 1982. *Operations research: An introduction.* 3d ed. New York: Macmillan.

Problems

1. Consider the following linear-programming problem.

$$\begin{aligned} \text{Maximize } Z &= 10x_1 + 15x_2 \\ \text{subject to } 2x_1 + 4x_2 &\leq 16 \\ 6x_1 + 4x_2 &\leq 24 \\ x_1, x_2 &\geq 0 \end{aligned}$$

a. Find the optimum solution.

b. Interpret the shadow prices for this problem.

2. Consider the following linear-programming problem.

$$\begin{aligned} \text{Maximize } Z &= 6x_1 + 8x_2 \\ \text{subject to } 6x_1 + 10x_2 &\le 30 \\ 4x_1 + 2x_2 &\le 16 \\ 2x_2 &\le 4 \\ x_1, x_2 &\ge 0 \end{aligned}$$

a. Find the optimum solution.

b. Interpret the sensitivity of contribution rates for this problem.

3. Consider the following linear-programming problem.

$$\begin{aligned} \text{Minimize } Z &= 60x_1 + 50x_2 \\ \text{subject to } 40x_1 + 80x_2 &\ge 800 \\ 60x_1 + 40x_2 &\ge 1000 \\ 50x_1 + 50x_2 &\ge 950 \\ 60x_1 + 30x_2 &\ge 1100 \\ x_1, x_2 &\ge 0 \end{aligned}$$

a. Find the optimum solution.

b. Interpret the right-hand-side ranges for this problem.

4. Consider the following linear-programming problem.

$$\begin{aligned} \text{Minimize } Z &= 8x_1 + 4x_2 + 6x_3 \\ \text{subject to } 2x_1 + 6x_2 &\ge 30 \\ 2x_1 + 4x_3 &\ge 20 \\ 4x_1 + 2x_2 &\ge 40 \\ x_1, x_2, x_3 &\ge 0 \end{aligned}$$

a. Find the optimum solution.

b. Find the sensitivity analysis.

5. Consider the following linear-programming problem.

$$\begin{aligned} \text{Maximize } Z &= 150x_1 + 300x_2 + 200x_3 \\ \text{subject to } 10x_1 + 10x_3 &\le 40 \\ 5x_1 + 20x_2 + 10x_3 &\le 30 \\ 10x_1 + 10x_2 + 20x_3 &\le 60 \\ x_1, x_2, x_3 &\ge 0 \end{aligned}$$

a. Find the optimum solution.

b. Interpret the shadow prices for this problem.

6. Consider the following linear-programming problem.

$$\begin{aligned} \text{Maximize } Z &= 700x_1 + 300x_2 \\ \text{subject to } 20x_1 + 10x_2 &\le 10 \\ 10x_1 + 80x_2 &\le 40 \\ x_1, x_2 &\ge 0 \end{aligned}$$

a. Find the optimum solution.

b. Find the range of optimality for each of the c_j values.

7. Consider the following linear-programming problem.

$$\begin{aligned} \text{Minimize } Z &= 10x_1 + 8x_2 \\ \text{subject to } 1.5x_1 + 0.5x_2 &\geq 3 \\ 0.5x_1 + 0.5x_2 &\geq 2 \\ x_1 + 3x_2 &\geq 6 \\ x_1, x_2 &\geq 0 \end{aligned}$$

a. Find the optimum solution.

b. Interpret the right-hand-side ranges for this problem.

c. What is the range of optimality for each of the c_j values?

8. Consider the following linear-programming problem.

$$\begin{aligned} \text{Minimize } Z &= 60x_1 + 20x_2 \\ \text{subject to } 30x_1 + 40x_2 &\geq 500 \\ 10x_1 + 20x_2 &= 200 \\ 20x_1 + 30x_2 &\leq 450 \\ x_1, x_2 &\geq 0 \end{aligned}$$

a. Find the optimum solution.

b. Interpret the shadow prices for this problem.

c. Find the range of optimality for each of the c_j values.

9. Consider the following linear-programming problem.

$$\begin{aligned} \text{Minimize } Z &= 10x_1 + 10x_2 \\ \text{subject to } 10x_1 &\geq 300 \\ 10x_2 &\geq 200 \\ 10x_1 + 20x_2 &\geq 800 \\ x_1, x_2 &\geq 0 \end{aligned}$$

a. Find the optimum solution.

b. Find the range of feasibility for each of the b_i values.

10. An electronics company daily produces two types of color TV sets. This company has resource constraints for production time, transistors, and integrated circuits. The problem has been formulated as:

$$\begin{aligned} \text{Maximize } Z &= 100x_1 + 180x_2 \\ \text{subject to } 20x_1 + 20x_2 &\leq 210 \quad \text{(production, hr)} \\ 10x_1 + 20x_2 &\leq 150 \quad \text{(transistor, ea.)} \\ 5x_1 + 8x_2 &\leq 70 \quad \text{(integrated circuits, ea.)} \\ x_1, x_2 &\geq 0 \end{aligned}$$

a. Find the optimum solution.

b. Interpret the shadow prices for this problem.

c. Find the range of feasibility for each of the b_i values.

11. A manufacturing company produces three types of skis: regular, professional, and children's. Each type of ski must go through three processes. The linear-programming model has been formulated as:

$$\begin{aligned} \text{Maximize } Z &= 40x_1 + 30x_2 + 20x_3 && \text{(profit, \$)} \\ \text{subject to } 2x_1 + 5x_2 + 10x_3 &\leq 900 && \text{(process 1, hr)} \\ 2x_1 + 5x_2 + 3x_3 &\leq 400 && \text{(process 2, hr)} \\ 4x_1 + 2x_2 + 2x_3 &\leq 600 && \text{(process 3, hr)} \\ x_1, x_2, x_3 &\geq 0 \end{aligned}$$

a. Find the optimum solution.

b. Find the range of optimality for each of the c_j's.

c. Find the range of feasibility for each of the b_i's.

12. A brewing company produces three kinds of whiskey: Olden Day, Today, and Tomorrow. This company has resource constraints for raw materials and labor-hours. The linear-programming model has been formulated as:

$$\begin{aligned} \text{Maximize } Z &= x_1 + 1.2x_2 + 2x_3 && \text{(profit/gallon, \$)} \\ \text{subject to } x_1 + 2x_2 &\leq 150 && \text{(material } A\text{, bushels)} \\ x_1 + 2x_3 &\leq 150 && \text{(material } B\text{, bushels)} \\ 2x_1 + x_2 &\leq 80 && \text{(material } C\text{, pounds)} \\ 2x_1 + 3x_2 + x_3 &\leq 225 && \text{(labor, hr)} \\ x_1, x_2, x_3 &\geq 0 \end{aligned}$$

a. Find the optimum solution.

b. Find the range of optimality for each of the c_j values.

c. Find the range of feasibility for each of the b_i values.

13. A pharmaceutical company produces cans of insect spray from compounds x_1 and x_2. Each compound contains four ingredients, and each can must contain a certain amount of these ingredients. Each pound of x_1 costs \$6, while each pound of x_2 costs \$5. The linear-programming model has been formulated as:

$$\begin{aligned} \text{Minimize } Z &= 6x_1 + 5x_2 && \text{(cost/lb, \$)} \\ \text{subject to } 4x_1 + 8x_2 &\geq 80 && \text{(ingredient } A\text{, lb)} \\ 6x_1 + 4x_2 &\geq 100 && \text{(ingredient } B\text{, lb)} \\ 5x_1 + 5x_2 &\geq 95 && \text{(ingredient } C\text{, lb)} \\ 6x_1 + 3x_2 &\geq 110 && \text{(ingredient } D\text{, lb)} \\ x_1, x_2 &\geq 0 \end{aligned}$$

a. Find the optimum solution.

b. Interpret the shadow prices for this problem.

c. Find the range of optimality for each of the c_j values.

14. Alma Johnson is attempting to decide on her birthday party menu that will provide an adequate diet at a minimal cost. The main courses of the menu are shrimp (x_1), rice (x_2), and potatoes (x_3). The linear-programming model has been formulated as:

$$\begin{aligned} \text{Minimize } Z &= 4x_1 + 2x_2 + 3x_3 && \text{(cost/lb, \$)} \\ \text{subject to } 4x_1 + 3x_2 + 2x_3 &\geq 55 && \text{(protein, mg)} \\ 3x_1 + 2x_2 + x_3 &\geq 40 && \text{(iron, mg)} \\ 3x_1 + 3x_2 + 2x_3 &\geq 45 && \text{(vitamin E, mg)} \\ x_1, x_2, x_3 &\geq 0 \end{aligned}$$

a. Find the optimum solution.
b. What is the range of each c_j value within which the current optimal solution can remain optimum?
c. What is the range of each b_i value within which the optimum solution can remain feasible?

15. Consider the following linear-programming problem.

$$\begin{aligned} \text{Maximize } Z &= 7x_1 + 3x_2 \\ \text{subject to } 0.2x_1 + 0.1x_2 &\leq 0.1 \\ 0.1x_1 + 0.8x_2 &\leq 0.4 \\ x_1, x_2 &\geq 0 \end{aligned}$$

The optimal simplex tableau for this problem is below.

c_b \ c_j	Basis	b_i^*	7 x_1	3 x_2	0 s_1	0 s_2
7	x_1	0.5	1	0.5	5	0
0	s_2	0.35	0	0.75	−0.5	1
	z_j	3.5	7	3.5	35	0
	$c_j - z_j$		0	−0.5	−35	0

a. Find the range of feasibility for each of the b_i values.
b. Find the range of optimality for each of the c_j values.
c. What will be the impact of the following additional constraint on the solution?

$$10x_1 + 3x_2 \leq 5$$

16. Consider the following linear-programming problem.

$$\begin{aligned} \text{Maximize } Z &= 5x_1 + 10x_2 + 2x_3 + 2x_4 \\ \text{subject to } \quad & 2x_1 + 2.8x_2 + 0.4x_3 + 1.6x_4 \leq 3{,}200 \\ & 4x_1 + 4x_2 + 3.2x_3 + 2x_4 \leq 2{,}600 \\ & 2.4x_1 + 2x_2 + 2x_3 + 2.4x_4 \leq 1{,}920 \\ & x_1, x_2, x_3, x_4 \geq 0 \end{aligned}$$

The optimum simplex solution tableau for this problem is below.

c_b \ c_j	Basis	b_i^*	5 x_1	10 x_2	2 x_3	2 x_4	0 s_1	0 s_2	0 s_3
0	s_1	1380	−0.8	0	−1.84	0.2	1	−0.7	0
10	x_2	650	1	1	0.8	0.5	0	0.25	0
0	s_3	620	0.4	0	0.4	1.4	0	−0.5	1
	z_j	6500	10	10	8	5	0	2.5	0
	$c_j - z_j$		−5	0	−6	−3	0	−2.5	0

a. Find the range of feasibility for each of the b_i values.

b. Find the range of optimality for each of the c_j values.

c. What will be the impact of the following additional constraint on the solution?

$$2x_1 + 2x_2 + 3x_3 + 2.5x_4 \leq 1{,}300$$

17. Consider the following linear-programming problem.

$$\begin{aligned} \text{Maximize } Z &= 15x_1 + 30x_2 + 20x_3 \\ \text{subject to } \quad & 4x_1 + 4x_3 \leq 16 \\ & x_1 + 4x_2 + 2x_3 \leq 6 \\ & 2x_1 + 2x_2 + 4x_3 \leq 12 \\ & x_1, x_2, x_3 \geq 0 \end{aligned}$$

The optimum simplex solution tableau for this problem is below.

c_b \ c_j	Basis	b_i^*	15 x_1	30 x_2	20 x_3	0 s_1	0 s_2	0 s_3
15	x_1	4	1	0	1	0.25	0	0
30	x_2	0.5	0	1	0.25	−0.063	0.25	0
0	s_3	3	0	0	1.5	−0.375	−0.5	1
	z_j	75	15	30	22.5	1.875	7.5	0
	$c_j - z_j$		0	0	−2.5	−1.875	−7.5	0

a. Find the range of feasibility for each of the b_i values.
b. Find the range of optimality for each of the c_j values.
c. What will be the impact of the following additional constraint on the solution?

$$3x_1 + 2x_2 + 2x_3 \leq 13$$

d. In the original problem, what will be the impact of the following additional constraint on the solution?

$$2x_1 + 3x_2 + x_3 \leq 9$$

18. Consider the following linear-programming problem.

$$\begin{aligned} \text{Minimize } Z &= 40x_1 + 30x_2 + 60x_3 \\ \text{subject to } 10x_1 + 5x_2 + 10x_3 &\geq 150 \\ 20x_2 + 10x_3 &\geq 300 \\ 10x_1 + 10x_2 + 20x_3 &\geq 200 \\ x_1, x_2, x_3 &\geq 0 \end{aligned}$$

The optimum simplex solution tableau for this problem is below.

c_b \ c_j	Basis	b_i^*	40 x_1	30 x_2	60 x_3	0 s_1	0 s_2	0 s_3
0	s_3	25	0	0	−7.5	−1	−0.25	1
30	x_2	15	0	1	0.5	0	−0.05	0
40	x_1	7.5	1	0	0.75	−0.1	0.025	0
	z_j	750	40	30	45	−4	−0.5	0
	$z_j - c_j$		0	0	−15	−4	−0.5	0

a. Find the range of feasibility for each of the b_i values.
b. Find the range of optimality for each of the c_j values.
c. What will be the impact of the following additional constraint on the solution?

$$10x_1 + 10x_2 + 10x_3 \geq 200$$

d. In the original problem, what will be the impact of the following additional constraint on the solution?

$$10x_1 + 4x_2 + 5x_3 \geq 150$$

19. The NICE Coat Company produces three kinds of fur coats. This company's production is restricted by the available quantities of fur 1, fur 2, and labor constraints. The resource requirements for each coat are shown in the following linear-programming formulation.

$$
\begin{array}{llr}
\text{Maximize } Z = 150x_1 + 300x_2 + 200x_3 & & \text{(profit/coat, \$)} \\
\text{subject to} \quad 40x_1 \qquad\qquad + 40x_3 \leq 160 & & \text{(fur 1, oz)} \\
\qquad 10x_1 + 40x_2 + 20x_3 \leq 60 & & \text{(fur 2, oz)} \\
\qquad 20x_1 + 20x_2 + 40x_3 \leq 120 & & \text{(labor, hr)} \\
\qquad x_1, x_2, x_3 \geq 0 & &
\end{array}
$$

The final simplex tableau for this problem is below.

c_b \ c_j	Basis	b_i^*	150 x_1	300 x_2	200 x_3	0 s_1	0 s_2	0 s_3
150	x_1	4	1	0	1	0.025	0	0
300	x_2	0.5	0	1	0.25	−0.006	0.025	0
0	s_3	30	0	0	15	−0.375	−0.5	1
	z_j	750	150	300	225	1.875	7.5	0
	$c_j - z_j$		0	0	−25	−1.875	−7.5	0

a. What is the maximum price the company would be willing to pay for an additional ounce of fur 2?

b. How much of fur 2 would be purchased at that price?

c. What is the marginal value of fur 1?

d. What is the range of feasibility for fur 1?

e. If the company can increase the availability of fur 1 from 160 to 200 ounces, will this affect the optimal solution?

f. The company is considering adding a third fur to improve the quality of the coats it produces. The requirement for fur 3 is given as

$$10x_1 + 20x_2 + 25x_3 \leq 50.$$

What effect will this additional constraint have on the solution?

g. Calculate the range of optimality for each of the c_j values.

h. Calculate the range of optimality for a_{23}.

i. Through improving labor and productivity, the company can increase the unit profit of x_3 from \$200 to \$250. What is the impact of this change?

20. A brewing company produces three kinds of wines: snow (x_1), rain (x_2), and wind (x_3). The company is restricted by material 1, material 2, and labor-hour constraints. The linear-programming model is formulated as:

$$
\begin{array}{lrl}
\text{Maximize } Z = 10x_1 + 9x_2 + 2x_3 & & \text{(Profit/bottle, \$)} \\
\text{subject to } 30x_1 + 31.6x_2 & \leq 300 & \text{(material 1, lb)} \\
5.6x_2 + 23.2x_3 & \leq 72 & \text{(material 2, lb)} \\
10x_1 + 12.8x_2 + 30x_3 & \leq 154 & \text{(labor, hr)} \\
x_1, x_2, x_3 & \geq 0 &
\end{array}
$$

The final simplex tableau for this problem is below.

c_b \ c_j	Basis	b_i^*	10 x_1	9 x_2	2 x_3	0 s_1	0 s_2	0 s_3
10	x_1	10	1	1.053	0	0.033	0	0
0	s_3	30.24	0	3.847	0	−0.258	−0.773	1
2	x_3	1.8	0	0.076	1	−0.011	0.033	0
	z_j	103.6	10	10.684	2	0.311	0.067	0
	$c_j - z_j$		0	−1.684	0	−0.311	−0.067	0

a. What is the maximum price the company would be willing to pay for an additional pound of material 1?

b. How much of material 1 would be purchased at that price?

c. What is the marginal value of material 2?

d. What is the range of feasibility for material 2?

e. If the company can increase the available labor-hours from 154 to 180, will this affect the optimal solution?

f. The company is considering an addition of material 3 to improve the taste of the wines. The requirement for material 3 is given as

$$2x_1 + 3x_2 + 10x_3 \leq 40$$

What effect will this have on the solution?

g. Calculate the range of optimality for a_{12}.

h. This company can purchase an additional 100 pounds of material 2 from a new supplier. What is the impact of this change on the current optimum solution?

21. Solve the following integer-programming problem by the branch and bound technique.

$$
\begin{array}{lrl}
\text{Maximize } Z = & 10x_1 + 20x_2 & \\
\text{subject to} & 5x_1 + 7x_2 & \leq 21 \\
& -4x_1 + 12x_2 & \leq 32 \\
& x_1, x_2 & = 0 \text{ or nonnegative integers}
\end{array}
$$

22. Solve the following integer-programming problem by the branch and bound technique.

$$\begin{aligned}
\text{Maximize } Z &= 12x_1 + 16x_2 \\
\text{subject to } 2x_1 + 2x_2 &\leq 1{,}000 \\
x_1 + x_2 &\geq 400 \\
4x_1 - 8x_2 &= 0 \\
3x_1 - 2x_2 &\geq 0 \\
x_1, x_2 &= 0 \text{ or nonnegative integers}
\end{aligned}$$

23. Solve the following integer-programming problem by the branch and bound technique.

$$\begin{aligned}
\text{Minimize } Z &= 6x_1 + 6x_2 \\
\text{subject to } 3x_1 + 2x_2 &\geq 12 \\
3x_1 + 8x_2 &\geq 24 \\
x_1 &\geq 2 \\
x_1, x_2 &= 0 \text{ or nonnegative integers}
\end{aligned}$$

24. Solve the following zero–one problem.

$$\begin{aligned}
\text{Minimize } Z &= 2x_1 + x_2 + 3x_3 + 2x_4 + 4x_5 \\
\text{subject to } \quad x_1 + 2x_2 + x_3 + x_4 + 2x_5 &\geq 4 \\
7x \qquad & \\
x_2 \qquad - 3x_4 + 3x_5 &\geq 6 \\
-9x_1 + 9x_2 + 6x_3 \qquad - 3x_5 &\geq -3 \\
x_j &= 0 \text{ or } 1
\end{aligned}$$

25. Solve the following zero–one problem.

$$\begin{aligned}
\text{Minimize } Z &= 10x_1 + 5x_2 + 15x_3 + 10x_4 + 20x_5 \\
\text{subject to } \quad 2x_1 + 4x_2 + 2x_3 + 2x_4 + 4x_5 &\geq 8 \\
7x_1 + x_2 \qquad - 3x_4 + 3x_5 &\geq 2 \\
-6x_1 + 6x_2 + 4x_3 \qquad - 2x_5 &\geq -2 \\
x_j &= 0 \text{ or } 1
\end{aligned}$$

C H A P T E R 6

The Transportation Problem

Transporting goods from a number of sources to numerous destinations while minimizing distribution costs is a prevalent management decision problem. Many retail, wholesale, public utility, and military organizations face such transportation problems on a regular basis. The transportation problem is a special type of linear-programming problem. Even though the transportation problem can be solved by linear programming, it can be analyzed more efficiently by using special techniques. In this chapter, we will study several solution techniques for the transportation problem.

Basics

Many organizations frequently face transportation-related problems. For example, a department store chain may have 10 warehouses (sources) and 40 stores (destinations) in various geographical locations. For a given point in time, each warehouse may have a specific capacity of supply and each store may have a specific demand for certain merchandise. If we know the unit transportation cost from each warehouse to each store, we may be able to determine the quantity of merchandise to be distributed from warehouses to stores in such a manner as to minimize the total transportation cost.

Some of the typical problems that could be analyzed by the transportation-related techniques are as follows:

Retail and wholesale industry

Merchandise distribution

Truck routing

Sales effort allocation

Manufacturing industry

Production quota determination

Warehouse location

Product distribution systems

Service industry

Advertising media scheduling

Portfolio analysis

Nonprofit organizations

Military logistics planning (rapid deployment)

Government inspectors allocation

Blood-collection and rotation schedules

Ambulance service location

Fire-station location

In a typical transportation problem, the total supply quantity rarely equals that of total demand. Such a problem is referred to as an *unbalanced* transportation problem. Although a *balanced* transportation problem is a rarity in real-world situations, we analyze transportation problems as balanced cases because of simplicity. We can easily transform any unbalanced case into a balanced problem by introducing a dummy source (row) or a dummy destination (column).

Solution Methods for the Transportation Problem

To solve a transportation problem, we must first determine the initial solution. Once we derive an initial solution, then we can implement the solution procedure. To illustrate the transportation solution process, let us consider the following simple example.

Example 6.1 Blacksburg Concrete Company

The Blacksburg Concrete Company has a contract to supply concrete for three construction projects, located in the towns of Pulaski, Christiansburg, and Radford. The amount of concrete required per day at each of the three construction sites is as follows:

Site	Location	Daily demand (truckloads)
1	Pulaski	150
2	Christiansburg	70
3	Radford	60
Total		280

Table 6.1 Tableau form of the Blacksburg Concrete Company problem

Sources \ Destinations	Site 1	Site 2	Site 3	Supply
Plant 1	$ 8	$ 5	$ 6	120
Plant 2	15	10	12	80
Plant 3	3	9	10	80
Demand	150	70	60	280

The Blacksburg Concrete Company has three concrete mixing plants, located in the towns of Blacksburg, Roanoke, and Hillsville. The maximum production capacities per day of these three plants are as follows:

Plant	**Location**	**Daily production (truckloads)**
1	Blacksburg	120
2	Roanoke	80
3	Hillsville	80
Total		280

Each of the above three plants can supply the required concrete to each of the three construction projects. This transportation problem is a balanced one, since the total supply of the three plants is exactly equal to the total demand of the three construction projects. Certainly, it is rare in reality to observe a balanced transportation problem. However, an analysis of the balanced problem is a good starting point for studying the transportation method. Once we learn to analyze the balanced problem, it will be an easy task to attack the unbalanced problem by making minor adjustments.

The cost-accounting department of Blacksburg Concrete has estimated the transportation cost per truckload of concrete from the plants to the construction sites as shown in Table 6.1. Given the production capacity of the plants, the amount of concrete that the construction projects demand, and the unit transportation costs, the company seeks to determine the optimum transportation scheme that will minimize the total transportation cost. We have all the information we need to analyze the transportation problem of the Blacksburg Concrete Company. The transportation method involves the following steps.

1. Define the problem and set up the transportation tableau.
2. Develop an initial solution.
3. Determine the optimum solution.
4. Evaluate the optimum solution.

Now, we will follow the preceding steps to solve the Blacksburg Concrete Company case.

Table 6.2 Transportation tableau for the Blacksburg Concrete Company problem

From \ To	1	2	3	Supply
1	[8] x_{11}	[5] x_{12}	[6] x_{13}	120
2	[15] x_{21}	[10] x_{22}	[12] x_{23}	80
3	[3] x_{31}	[9] x_{32}	[10] x_{33}	80
Demand	150	70	60	280

1. Define the Problem and Set up the Transportation Tableau

First, let us set up the complete transportation tableau for the problem, as shown in Table 6.2. We list the concrete plants (sources) as rows and the construction sites (destinations) as columns. Since we have three plants and three construction sites, the tableau has $3 \times 3 = 9$ cells. In each cell, the unit transportation cost is recorded in the small box at the upper left-hand corner. In the bottom row, the total demand of each construction site is recorded. In the last column, the total supply (production capacity) of each plant is listed. Therefore, in the cell at the lower right-hand corner we can find the total supply and total demand (280) of the problem.

The management problem of Blacksburg Concrete is to determine the quantity of concrete to be transported, in the most economical manner, from each plant to each construction site. If we denote the quantity to be transported from each plant to each construction site as x_{ij} (from the ith plant to the jth construction site), as shown in Table 6.2, the quantity to be transported can be interpreted as follows:

x_{11} = quantity to be transported from plant 1 to construction site 1.
x_{12} = quantity to be transported from plant 1 to construction site 2.
⋮ ⋮
x_{33} = quantity to be transported from plant 3 to construction site 3.

Then the objective function of the problem (minimization of total transportation cost) can be described as

$$\text{Minimize } Z = 8x_{11} + 5x_{12} + 6x_{13} + 15x_{21} + 10x_{22} + 12x_{23} + 3x_{31} + 9x_{32} + 10x_{33}.$$

The above objective function is to be minimized subject to the supply and demand constraints. Since this problem is a balanced case, where total supply is exactly equal to total demand, we will have "exactly equal-to" type constraints. Plant 1 has a total production capacity (supply) of 120 truckloads of concrete. The total amount of concrete we can transport from plant 1 to construction sites 1, 2, and 3 will be $x_{11} + x_{12} + x_{13}$. Therefore, the supply constraint of plant 1 becomes $x_{11} + x_{12} + x_{13} = 120$. By employing the same approach, we can easily determine the supply constraints of plant 2 and plant 3, as follows:

$$x_{21} + x_{22} + x_{23} = 80$$
$$x_{31} + x_{32} + x_{33} = 80$$

The total amount of concrete that construction site 1 receives will be the sum of x_{11}, x_{21}, and x_{31}. Hence, the demand constraint for construction site 1 becomes

$$x_{11} + x_{21} + x_{31} = 150.$$

For construction sites 2 and 3, the demand constraints will be

$$x_{12} + x_{22} + x_{32} = 70$$

and

$$x_{13} + x_{23} + x_{33} = 60.$$

Now, we can formulate the complete linear-programming model for the transportation problem of the Blacksburg Concrete Company.

$$\begin{aligned}
\text{Minimize } Z = {} & 8x_{11} + 5x_{12} + 6x_{13} + 15x_{21} + 10x_{22} + 12x_{23} + 3x_{31} + 9x_{32} + 10x_{33} \\
\text{subject to } & \left.\begin{aligned} x_{11} + x_{12} + x_{13} &= 120 \\ x_{21} + x_{22} + x_{23} &= 80 \\ x_{31} + x_{32} + x_{33} &= 80 \end{aligned}\right\} \text{Supply} \\
& \left.\begin{aligned} x_{11} + x_{21} + x_{31} &= 150 \\ x_{12} + x_{22} + x_{32} &= 70 \\ x_{13} + x_{23} + x_{33} &= 60 \end{aligned}\right\} \text{Demand} \\
& x_{ij} \geq 0 \quad i,j = 1,2,3
\end{aligned}$$

In the above linear-programming problem, we have nine decision variables and six constraints. If we decide to solve the above problem by the simplex method, it may take a considerable amount of time. Therefore, we will use the transportation method instead.

2. Develop an Initial Solution

In the transportation method, as in the linear- and goal-programming methods, we must develop the initial solution as the starting point for the iterative algorithm. There are several methods available to develop an initial solution. It is obvious, however, that the better the initial solution (in terms of total transportation cost), the fewer the number of iterations required to reach the optimum solution. In this discussion, we will examine three different methods to develop the initial solution: the northwest-corner method, the minimum cell-cost method, and the Vogel's approximation method.

The Northwest-Corner Method The simplest way to set up the initial solution is the northwest-corner method that George Dantzig first suggested. This is a systematic, but not very scientific, method. However, this method is extremely useful if a computer program is readily available for the transportation problem. The northwest-corner method can be summarized as follows:

1. Starting from the northwest corner (upper left-hand corner) of the tableau, allocate as many units as possible into each cell as we move toward the southeast corner of the tableau.
2. Check whether supply and demand are met.

For the Blacksburg Concrete problem, the initial solution by the northwest-corner method is shown in Table 6.3. The initial solution via the northwest-corner method is achieved by following these steps:

Step 1: Cell (1,1). Transport as much as possible from plant 1 to site 1. Cell (1,1) is the northwest-corner cell in the tableau. The supply capacity of plant 1 is 120 and demand of site 1 is 150. Therefore, the maximum capacity we can transport to cell (1,1) will be 120. By transporting 120 to cell (1,1), we have exhausted the supply capacity of plant 1. However, the demand of site 1 has not been completely met as yet, since we are short 30 truckloads.

Step 2: (Cell 2,1). The unsatisfied demand of 30 truckloads of site 1 should be supplied by plant 2 as we follow the northwest-corner procedure. The total quantity being transported to site 1 from plants 1 (120) and 2 (30) satisfies the total demand.

Step 3: (Cell 2,2). Since we have satisfied the demand of construction site 1, we move on to the next column, construction site 2. The total demand of site 2 is 70 truckloads. After transporting 30 truckloads to site 1, plant 2 can ship only the remaining supply capacity of 50 truckloads to site 2.

Step 4: (Cell 3,2). Construction site 2 still requires 20 additional truckloads to meet the total demand of 70. Since plants 1 and 2 have already exhausted their supply capacities, this amount has to be shipped from plant 3.

Step 5: (Cell 3,3). Because this problem is a balanced case where total demand is exactly equal to total supply, the demand of construction site 3 (60 truckloads) must be exactly equal to the remaining supply capacity of plant 3 (60 truckloads).

Table 6.3 The initial solution by the northwest-corner method

From \ To	1	2	3	Supply
1	[8] 120	[5]	[6]	120
2	[15] 30	[10] 50	[12]	80
3	[3]	[9] 20	[10] 60	80
Demand	150	70	60	280

Now we can check each column and row to see whether demand and supply requirements are completely satisfied. The initial solution shown in Table 6.3 clearly indicates that we have indeed met all the demand and supply requirements. In this problem we have nine cells altogether and we have transported to (filled in) five cells. Consequently, there are four empty cells where we did not transport any quantity.

Let us now calculate the total transportation cost of the initial solution derived by the northwest-corner method, multiplying the quantity transported by the unit cost as follows:

Cell	**Σ (Quantity transported**	**×**	**Unit cost)**	**=**	**Total cost**
(1,1)	120	×	$ 8	=	$960
(2,1)	30	×	15	=	450
(2,2)	50	×	10	=	500
(3,2)	20	×	9	=	180
(3,3)	60	×	10	=	600
			Total transportation cost	=	$2,690

The total transportation cost of this initial solution is $2,690. One distinctive feature of the northwest-corner solution is that the occupied cells generally form a stair-step effect from the upper left-hand corner of the tableau.

The Minimum Cell-Cost Method As we have observed, the northwest-corner method is a simple procedure, but it is not a scientific way to set up an initial solution. Consequently, it may require a large number of iterations to find the optimal solution when we start the solution with the northwest-corner method.

One way to reduce the number of iterations is to use good common sense in formulating the initial solution. For example, we should try to transport as much as possible to those cells with the minimum unit costs. This approach is called the minimum cell-cost method and can be summarized as follows:

1. Select the cell with the minimum cell cost and allocate as much to this cell as possible.
2. Select the cell with the next minimum cell cost and allocate as much as possible.
3. Repeat the procedure until all of the supply and demand requirements are satisfied. In case of a tie, it is recommended that you select the cell that can accommodate the greater quantity.

Now, let us go back to the Blacksburg Concrete case. The cell with the minimum unit transportation cost is \$3 in cell (3,1). The maximum quantity we can allocate to this cell is 80, as the maximum supply capacity of plant 3 is 80, even though site 1 requires 150. First, we allocate 80 to cell (3,1). The requirement of site 1 is now reduced to 70. The cell with the next minimum cell cost is cell (1,2) with \$5. The maximum we can allocate to cell (1,2) is 70, since the requirement of site 2 is only 70, even though plant 1 has a supply capacity of 120. Next, we allocate to cell (1,3). By allocating 50 to cell (1,3), we will exhaust the capacity of plant 1. Because we exhausted the capacity of plants 1 and 3, the only plant that still has some supply capacity left is 2. Plant 2 has 80 available. On the other hand, sites 1 and 3 require 70 and 10, respectively. This implies that we have no further choice but to allocate 70 to cell (2,1) and 10 to cell (2,3). Table 6.4 presents the complete initial solution by the minimum cell-cost method. The total transportation cost of the initial solution by the minimum cell-cost method shown in Table 6.4 (p. 117) is \$2,060, calculated as follows:

Cell	Σ (Quantity transported	×	Unit cost)	=	Total cost
(1,2)	70	×	\$ 5	=	\$ 350
(1,3)	50	×	6	=	300
(2,1)	70	×	15	=	1,050
(2,3)	10	×	12	=	120
(3,1)	80	×	3	=	240
			Total transportation cost	=	\$2,060

As we compare the total transportation costs derived by the northwest-corner and the minimum cell-cost methods, it should be apparent that the use of common sense has reduced the total cost by \$630. This implies that the optimal solution can be reached faster by using the minimum cell-cost method rather than the northwest-corner method.

Table 6.4 Initial solution by the minimum cell-cost method

From \ To	1	2	3	Supply
1	[8]	[5] 70	[6] 50	120
2	[15] 70	[10]	[12] 10	80
3	[3] 80	[9]	[10]	80
Demand	150	70	60	280

The Vogel's Approximation Method Another technique one can use to develop an initial solution is Vogel's approximation method (VAM). This method makes allocations based on a rational approach—minimization of the penalty (or opportunity) cost. The penalty cost can be defined as the amount we lose because of our failure to select the best alternative.

The steps of VAM, which are also referred to as the penalty or regret method, can be summarized as follows:

1. Set up the transportation tableau with all the cells empty.
2. Calculate the penalty cost for each row and each column.
3. Select the row or column with the largest penalty cost (a tie can be broken by selecting the cell that can accommodate the greatest quantity).
4. Allocate as much as possible to the cell with the minimum cost in the chosen row or column.
5. Adjust the demand and supply requirements after the allocation.
6. Eliminate rows and columns that have met fully either demand or supply.
7. Recalculate the penalty cost for each row and each column.
8. Stop if no rows or columns remain to be evaluated; otherwise, go to Step 3.

Now, let us use the penalty method to set up the initial solution of the Blacksburg Concrete problem. In Table 6.5, we have calculated the penalty costs for the rows and columns. For example, in the first row (plant 1), the minimum cell cost is \$5 in cell (1,2) and the next smallest cost is \$6 in cell (1,3). Therefore, the penalty cost will be \$6 − \$5 = \$1. This penalty cost of \$1 is the amount we have to pay per unit if we fail to allocate to cell (1,2) and subsequently choose cell (1,3). The same procedure is used for calculating penalty costs for all the rows and columns.

Table 6.5 Initial solution by VAM

From \ To	1	2	3	Supply	
1	[8] ~~70~~	[5]	[6] ~~50~~	~~120~~	~~1~~
2	[15]	[10] 70	[12] 10	80	2
3	[3] ~~80~~	[9]	[10]	~~80~~	~~6~~
Demand	~~150~~	70	60	280	
	~~5~~	~~4~~	~~4~~		
	7	5	6		

The largest penalty cost in Table 6.5 is $6 in the third row (plant 3). This penalty indicates that if we fail to allocate to the cell (3,1) that has the minimum cost, we have to pay a $6 penalty per unit to allocate to the next best cell (3,2). To avoid paying this penalty, we should allocate to cell (3,1) as much as possible. The maximum quantity we can allocate to cell (3,1) is 80 units, since the capacity of plant 3 is only 80. After allocating 80 to cell (3,1), we can eliminate row 3 from further consideration, since we have exhausted the capacity of plant 3. Next, we adjust the demand of site 1 from 150 to 70 (150 − 80 = 70). The penalty cost of the columns must be recalculated, since we have eliminated the third row.

In Table 6.5, it should be clear that column 1 has the largest penalty cost. To avoid paying this penalty, we should allocate as much as possible to cell (1,1). The maximum quantity we can allocate to completely satisfy the demand of site 1 is 70.

After transporting 70 to cell (1,1), we can eliminate column 1. We repeat the procedure of adjusting the supply and/or demand figure and recalculating the penalty costs. The maximum penalty cost now appears in column 3. Therefore, we should allocate as much as possible to cell (1,3). The maximum quantity we can allocate to cell (1,3) is 50. Now, only two empty cells are left. Therefore, we do not have any further choice left but to allocate 70 to cell (2,2) and 10 to cell (2,3). Checking the entire tableau, we have completely satisfied the demand and supply requirements. The total transportation cost of this initial solution derived by VAM is $1,920, calculated as shown in the table that follows:

Cell	Σ (Quantity transported	×	Unit cost)	=	Total cost
(1,1)	70	×	$ 8	=	$560
(1,3)	50	×	6	=	300
(2,2)	70	×	10	=	700
(2,3)	10	×	12	=	120
(3,1)	80	×	3	=	240
			Total transportation cost	=	$1,920

Although the Vogel's approximation method takes the relative cost (opportunity cost) into account in analyzing the solution, this method is more logical than the minimum cell-cost method, which is based on good common sense. In general, VAM greatly reduces the subsequent number of iterations required to reach the optimal solution. As a matter of fact, Vogel's method often yields the optimal solution itself for simple transportation problems.

3. Determine the Optimum Solution

Once we obtain the initial solution to the given transportation problem, the next step is to evaluate whether the solution can be further improved in terms of reduced total cost. The evaluation process involves an analysis of the empty cells (cells where no allocations have been made) to determine whether it is desirable to make a transfer to one of these empty cells. To evaluate all the empty cells in the tableau, we must meet one requirement. The number of occupied cells (cells where allocations are already made) must be exactly equal to the sum of the number of rows and columns minus one, i.e., the number of occupied cells = (number of rows + number of columns) − 1. If a solution does not meet the above requirement, the solution is called degenerate. The problem of the degeneracy will be discussed later. We will now discuss two alternative methods to evaluate the solution for improvement: the stepping-stone method and the modified-distribution (MODI) method.

The Stepping-Stone Method Let us evaluate the initial solution we derived by the northwest-corner method, as shown in Table 6.6. We select cell (1,2) as the first empty cell to evaluate whether we can improve the solution by transferring some units from cell (1,1) to cell (1,2). We must always remember that we can transport some concrete only from plants to construction sites but never from a site to itself; in other words, a transfer must be initiated within the given row.

Suppose that we transfer one truckload of concrete from cell (1,1) to cell (1,2) (that is, we ship only 119 from plant 1 to site 1 and ship one from plant 1 to site 2). To allow this transfer of one unit from cell (1,1) to cell (1,2) while satisfying the supply and demand requirements, we have to also transfer one unit from column 2 to column 1. The question is from which cell in column 2 to which cell in column 1 should the transfer of one unit be made? Remembering that we

Table 6.6 Stepping-stone for cell (1,2)

From \ To	1	2	3	Supply
1	[8] 120 −	[5] +	[6]	120
2	[15] 30 +	[10] − 50	[12]	80
3	[3]	[9] 20	[10] 60	80
Demand	150	70	60	280

Cell (1,2) = +(1,2) − (1,1) + (2,1) − (2,2)
CII (1,2) = +5 − 8 + 15 − 10 = +2

can step only on the stepping-stones (occupied cells), the transfer has to be made from cell (2,2) to cell (2,1). Since cell (3,1) is an empty cell, the transfer cannot be made from cell (3,2) to cell (3,1). When we make this transfer, we can still satisfy the demand and supply requirements, as follows:

	Site 1	**Site 2**	**Supply**
1	119	1	120
2	31	49	80
3	0	20	
Demand	150	70	

Now, referring back to Table 6.6, we indicated the flow of the transfer by arrow lines. The change of quantity transported to each cell is indicated by a plus (increase) or a minus (decrease) sign. The path we follow (the arrow lines) in order to evaluate the empty cell is called the "stepping-stone path." The stepping-stone path involves vertical and horizontal movements but never diagonal short-cuts. Thus, the closed path for cell (1,2) will be

$$\text{Cell } (1,2) = +(1,2) - (1,1) + (2,1) - (2,2).$$

The reason we trace the stepping-stone path is to determine whether the transfer of one unit will decrease or increase the total transportation cost. From the stepping-stone path we identified above, we can determine the net effect in terms of the change in transportation cost. By shipping one unit from plant 1 to site 2, we have to incur a \$5 cost. But by shipping one unit less (only 119 units) from plant 1 to site 1, we can save \$8. Likewise, by transferring one unit from cell (2,2) to cell (2,1) the cost at cell (2,1) is increased by \$15 and it is decreased by \$10 at cell (2,2). By following the closed path and analyzing the unit transportation cost in each cell, we can derive the cost-improvement index (CII) as

$$\begin{aligned} \text{Cell } (1,2) &= +(1,2) - (1,1) + (2,1) - (2,2) \\ \text{CII } (1,2) &= +\$5 - \$8 + \$15 - \$10 = \$2 \end{aligned}$$

The amount \$2 indicates that if we make a transfer of one unit from cell (1,1) to cell (1,2), it will increase the total transportation cost by \$2. Certainly, we are not willing to make that kind of a transfer. Therefore, we should evaluate all the empty cells first and select a cell with the largest negative CII. If there is no negative CII, the existing solution is the optimum solution.

We now continue to evaluate other empty cells. Let us select cell (3,1) because it is an easy cell to evaluate since it is surrounded by three occupied cells. The CII for cell (3,1) can be found by tracing the stepping-stone path as follows:

$$\begin{aligned} \text{Cell } (3,1) &= +(3,1) - (3,2) + (2,2) - (2,1) \\ \text{CII } (3,1) &= +\$3 - \$9 + \$10 - \$15 = -\$11 \end{aligned}$$

The CII for cell (3,1) indicates that if we transfer some units from cell (3,2) to cell (3,1), we can reduce the total transportation cost by \$11 per unit.

We can evaluate cell (2,3) in a similar manner since it is also surrounded by three occupied cells.

$$\begin{aligned} \text{Cell } (2,3) &= +(2,3) - (2,2) + (3,2) - (3,3) \\ \text{CII } (2,3) &= +\$12 - \$10 + \$9 - \$10 = +\$1 \end{aligned}$$

The analysis of cell (1,3), which we have postponed long enough, is a rather difficult task because its stepping-stone path is relatively hard to trace. Observing row 1, it is clear that the only occupied cell from which we can transfer one unit to cell (1,3) is cell (1,1). Now, we have to increase one unit in column 1. The only occupied cell other than cell (1,1) that can accept an additional unit is cell (2,1). Analyzing row 2, the only occupied cell that can transfer one unit to cell (2,1) is cell (2,2). If we transfer a unit from cell (2,2) to cell (2,1), we need one additional unit in column 2. The only cell where we can accept a transfer of one unit other than cell (2,2) in column 2 is cell (3,2). Investigating row 3, this unit must come from cell (3,3). The stepping-stone path and CII for cell (1,3) can be determined as follows:

$$\begin{aligned} \text{Cell } (1,3) &= +(1,3) - (1,1) + (2,1) - (2,2) + (3,2) - (3,3) \\ \text{CII } (1,3) &= +\$6 - \$8 + \$15 - \$10 + \$9 - \$10 = +\$2 \end{aligned}$$

It should be apparent from the above discussion that we can jump over empty cells to step on the occupied cells when we trace the stepping-stone path.

Now that we have evaluated all the empty cells, we can list their improvement indices in the tableau, shown in Table 6.7. Clearly, the best empty cell to which we can make some transfer is cell (3,1). This cell indicates that the total transportation cost could be reduced by \$11 per truckload of concrete that we transfer from other cells. The next question we have to answer is how much can

Table 6.7 Initial solution showing CIIs for empty cells

From \ To	1	2	3	Supply
1	[8] 120	[5] +2	[6] +2	120
2	[15] 30	[10] 50	[12] +1	80
3	[3] −11	[9] 20	[10] 60	80
Demand	150	70	60	280

Table 6.8 Determining maximum quantity transferable to cell (1,3)

(a)

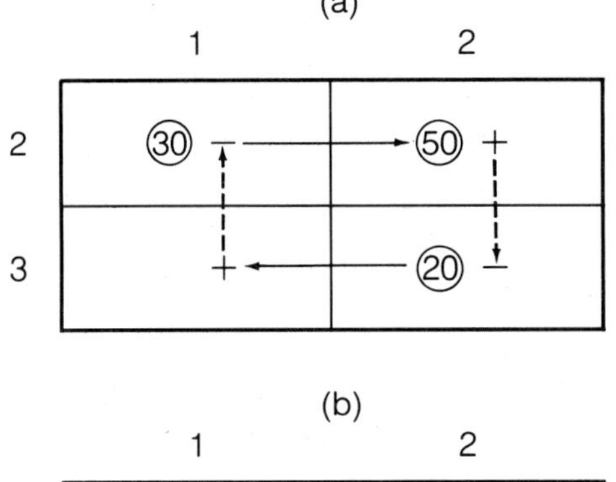

(b)

	1	2
2	30 − 20 = 10	50 + 20 = 70
3	0 + 20 = 20	20 − 20 = 0

we transfer to cell (3,1). The stepping-stone path for cell (3,1) has positive stones (cells with a plus sign) at cells (2,2) and (3,1) and negative stones (cells with a minus sign) at cells (2,1) and (3,2) as shown in Table 6.8(a). The maximum quantity we can transfer to cell (3,1) is exactly the minimum quantity we find in the negative stones of the stepping-stone path. Cell (2,1) has 30 and cell (3,2) has 20. Therefore, the minimum quantity we find is 20, and 20 is the maximum

Table 6.9 The second solution by the stepping-stone method

From \ To	1	2	3	Supply
1	[8] 120	[5]	[6]	120
2	[15] 10	[10] 70	[12]	80
3	[3] 20	[9]	[10] 60	80
Demand	150	70	60	280

Total transportation cost

120 × 8 =	$ 960
10 × 15 =	150
70 × 10 =	700
20 × 3 =	60
60 × 10 =	600
	$2,470

quantity that we can transfer to cell (3,1). It should be obvious that if we transfer more than 20 units to cell (3,1), we have to assign some negative value to cell (3,2) to meet the demand and supply requirements. Since we cannot transport a negative quantity, the maximum quantity to be transferred to cell (3,1) has to be 20, as shown in Table 6.8(b). The new solution is shown in Table 6.9. We now have completed one iteration.

The transportation cost of the improved solution is $2,470, as shown in Table 6.9, a reduction of $220 from $2,690 of the initial solution. Since the CII of cell (3,1) was −$11 and the quantity we transferred to cell (3,1) was 20, total cost improvement has to be $220 ($11 × 20 = $220). Now, we will start the second iteration by evaluating all the empty cells. Before evaluating all the empty cells, we can easily determine the CII of cell (3,2), the cell that we just emptied in the first iteration. We emptied cell (3,2) because cell (3,1) had a CII of −$11. Therefore, if we evaluate cell (3,2) by using exactly the same stepping-stone path, its CII will be +$11. We can easily determine the CII's of all the remaining empty cells, as shown in Table 6.10. The cell with the best CII is cell (2,3) with −$10. We can reduce the total transportation cost by $10 per truckload if we transfer concrete from cell (2,1) to cell (2,3). The maximum quantity we can transfer is 10 because this is the minimum quantity in the negative stones of the stepping-stone path. Thus, the total transportation cost will be reduced by $100 ($10 × 10) and hence the total cost becomes $2,370. The result of the second iteration is shown in Table 6.11.

Table 6.10 The stepping-stone paths and CII's for empty cells

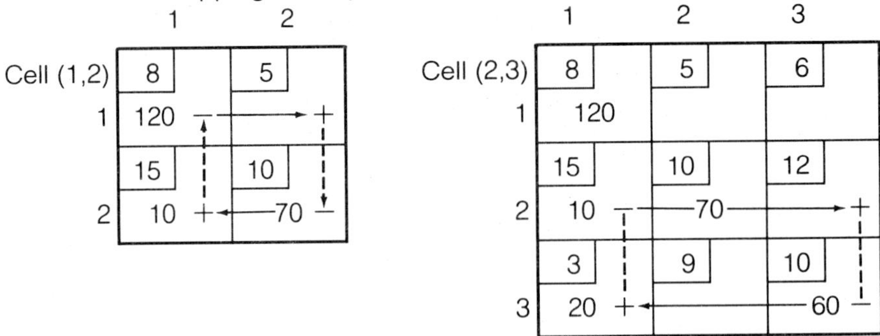

1 2
Cell (1,2)
8 5
1 120 − +
15 10
2 10 + 70 −
1 2 3
Cell (2,3)
8 5 6
1 120
15 10 12
2 10 − 70 +
3 9 10
3 20 + 60 −

Cell (1,2) = + (1,2) − (1,1) + (2,1) − (2,2)
CII (1,2) = + 5 − 8 + 15 − 10 = +2

Cell (2,3) = + (2,3) − (2,1) + (3,1) − (3,3)
CII (2,3) = + 12 − 15 + 3 − 10 = −10

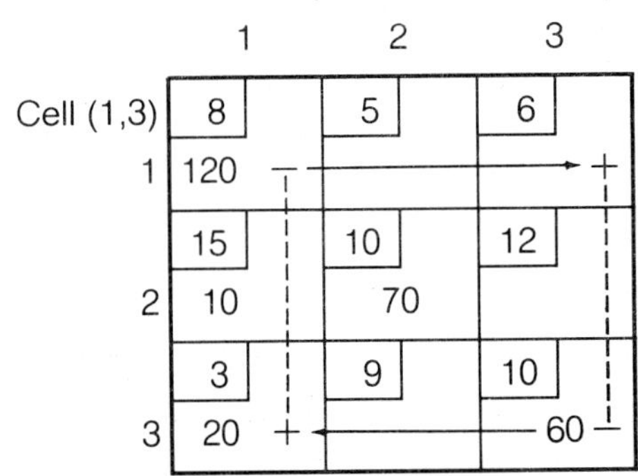

1 2 3
Cell (1,3)
8 5 6
1 120 − +
15 10 12
2 10 70
3 9 10
3 20 + 60 −

Cell (1,3) = + (1,3) − (1,1) + (3,1) − (3,3)
CII (1,3) = + 6 − 8 + 3 − 10 = −9

Table 6.11 The third solution by the stepping-stone method

From \ To	1	2	3	Supply
1	[8] 120	[5]	[6]	120
2	[15]	[10] 70	[12] 10	80
3	[3] 30	[9]	[10] 50	80
Demand	150	70	60	280

Total transportation cost

120 × $ 8	=	$ 960
70 × 10	=	700
10 × 12	=	120
30 × 3	=	90
50 × 10	=	500
		$2,370

Table 6.12 The optimum solution after three iterations

From \ To	1	2	3	Supply
1	[8] 70	[5]	[6] 50	120
2	[15]	[10] 70	[12] 10	80
3	[3] 80	[9]	[10]	80
Demand	150	70	60	280

Total transportation cost

70 × $ 8 = $ 560
50 × 6 = 300
70 × 10 = 700
10 × 12 = 120
80 × 3 = 240
$1,920

We shall now begin the third iteration. Without calculating, we already know that the CII of cell (2,1) is +$10, since we just emptied this cell. We can evaluate the remaining empty cells in the following manner:

Empty cell	Stepping-stone path	CII
(1,2)	+ (1,2) − (1,1) + (3,1) − (3,3) + (2,3) − (2,2)	+ 5 − 8 + 3 − 10 + 12 − 10 = −8
(1,3)	+ (1,3) − (1,1) + (3,1) − (3,3)	+ 6 − 8 + 3 − 10 = −9
(3,2)	+ (3,2) − (3,3) + (2,3) − (2,2)	+ 9 − 10 + 12 − 10 = +1

Clearly, cell (1,3) has the best CII with −$9. Now, the minimum quantity that can be transferred to cell (1,3) is 50 [50 units in cell (3,3)]. The solution we derive after the third iteration is shown in Table 6.12. The total transportation cost will be reduced by $450 ($9 × 50 = $450). Hence, the new total transportation cost is $1,920.

We repeat the procedure of evaluating the empty cells. Of course, we need not evaluate cell (3,3) because we already know that this cell has a \$9 CII. The remaining three empty cells are analyzed below.

Empty cell	Stepping-stone path	CII	
(1,2)	+ (1,2) − (1,3) + (2,3) − (2,2)	+ 5 − 6 + 12 − 10	= + 1
(2,1)	+ (2,1) − (2,3) + (1,3) − (1,1)	+ 15 − 12 + 6 − 8	= + 1
(3,2)	+ (3,2) − (3,1) + (2,3) − (2,2) + (1,1) − (1,3)	+ 9 − 3 + 12 − 10 + 8 − 6	= + 10

It is readily evident that no empty cell has a negative CII. In other words, there is no way we can improve the solution. Therefore, we have reached the optimum solution. We should note here that in a balanced transportation problem when all supplies and demands are integer values, the solution will also be in integer values.

The Modified-Distribution (MODI) Method The modified-distribution method (MODI) is an efficient procedure in evaluating the empty cells. In the MODI method, we evaluate all of the empty cells simultaneously. Thus, we do not have to trace all of the stepping-stone paths of the empty cells. We trace the stepping-stone path of only the one empty cell that has the best CII. In using this method, we eliminate the major portion of the cumbersome task of tracing the stepping-stone path. Thus, the *Micro Manager* utilizes MODI in solving transportation problems.

The MODI method is based on the dual formulation of the primal transportation problem. To demonstrate this method, let us go back to the initial solution obtained by the northwest-corner method for the Blacksburg Concrete problem, shown in Table 6.13. For the MODI operation, however, we must make a slight modification in the transportation tableau. We add the r_i column for row values and the k_j row for column values, as shown in Table 6.13.

For the *occupied cells* [cells where some quantities have been allocated, e.g., cells (1,1), (2,1), (2,2), (3,2), and (3,3)], the following relationships exist:

$$c_{ij} = r_i + k_j$$

where c_{ij} = unit transportation cost at the occupied cell ij
r_i = ith row value
k_j = jth column value

Table 6.13 Initial transportation tableau by the MODI method

r_i \ k_j		$k_1 = 8$	$k_2 = 3$	$k_3 = 4$	
	From \ To	1	2	3	Supply
$r_1 = 0$	1	[8] 120	[5]	[6]	120
$r_2 = 7$	2	[15] 30	[10] 50	[12]	80
$r_3 = 6$	3	[3] +	[9] 20	[10] 60	80
	Demand	150	70	60	280

Total transportation cost = \$2,690

The unit transportation cost for the five occupied cells can be described as follows:

$$
\begin{aligned}
c_{11} &= r_1 + k_1 = 8 && \text{cell (1,1)}\\
c_{21} &= r_2 + k_1 = 15 && \text{cell (2,1)}\\
c_{22} &= r_2 + k_2 = 10 && \text{cell (2,2)}\\
c_{32} &= r_3 + k_2 = 9 && \text{cell (3,2)}\\
c_{33} &= r_3 + k_3 = 10 && \text{cell (3,3)}
\end{aligned}
$$

In the above equations, to solve for the six unknown variables, we must select one of the variables and assign it an arbitrary value. We will select r_1 and assign a zero value to it. With $r_1 = 0$, it is simple to identify the values of the remaining variables as in the table below.

Occupied cell	$c_{ij} = r_i + k_j$	Row or column value
$r_1 + k_1 = 8$	$0 + k_1 = 8$	$k_1 = 8$
$r_2 + k_1 = 15$	$r_2 + 8 = 15$	$r_2 = 7$
$r_2 + k_2 = 10$	$7 + k_2 = 10$	$k_2 = 3$
$r_3 + k_2 = 9$	$r_3 + 3 = 9$	$r_3 = 6$
$r_3 + k_3 = 10$	$6 + k_3 = 10$	$k_3 = 4$

As we can see in the above calculations, the row and column values are not always positive. We list these values in the transportation tableau (as shown in Table 6.13). We can now evaluate all of the empty cells.

For the *empty cells,* the cost-improvement index (CII) can be determined as

$$\text{CII} = c_{ij} - r_i - k_j$$

If a cell has a negative CII, it indicates that an improvement is possible. If all of the CII values are zero or positive, an optimum solution is obtained. The CII for each of the empty cells can be computed as below.

Empty cell	$c_{ij} - r_i - k_j$	CII
(1,2)	5 − 0 − 3	+2
(1,3)	6 − 0 − 4	+2
(2,3)	12 − 7 − 4	+1
(3,1)	3 − 6 − 8	−11

These CII values correspond with those we calculated in the stepping-stone method. The empty cell with the negative CII is cell (3,1) with −\$11. The maximum quantity that can be transferred to cell (3,1) is the minimum quantity in the negative cells of the stepping-stone path. We must determine the stepping-stone path for cell (3,1), which has the best CII. From the stepping-stone method we know that the stepping-stone path for cell (3,1) is + (3,1) − (3,2) + (2,2) − (2,1), as shown in Table 6.13. The maximum quantity we can transfer to cell (3,1) is 20.

After this transfer, we obtain the second solution. The second solution is evaluated by recalculating the row and column values and the CII as follows:

Occupied cell	$c_{ij} = r_i + k_j$	Row or column value
(1,1)	$8 = 0 + k_1$	$k_1 = 8$
(2,1)	$15 = r_2 + 8$	$r_2 = 7$
(2,2)	$10 = 7 + k_2$	$k_2 = 3$
(3,1)	$3 = r_3 + 8$	$r_3 = -5$
(3,3)	$10 = -5 + k_3$	$k_3 = 15$

Empty cell	$c_{ij} - r_i - k_j$	CII
(1,2)	5 − 0 − 3	+2
(1,3)	6 − 0 − 15	−9
(2,3)	12 − 7 − 15	−10
(3,2)	9 − (−5) − 3	+11

Table 6.14 The second solution by the MODI method

	k_j	$k_1 = 8$	$k_2 = 3$	$k_3 = 15$	
r_i	From \ To	1	2	3	Supply
$r_1 = 0$	1	[8] 120	[5]	[6]	120
$r_2 = 7$	2	[15] 10 −	[10] 70	[12] +	80
$r_3 = -5$	3	[3] 20 +	[9]	[10] 60 −	80
	Demand	150	70	60	280

Total transportation cost = $2,470

Table 6.14 presents the second solution. The cell with the best CII is cell (2,3) with −$10. Therefore, we can easily determine the maximum quantity that we can transfer: 10, the quantity in cell (2,1) as shown in Table 6.14.

By repeating the process we can derive the third solution, as shown in Table 6.15 (p. 130). The new row and column values and the CIIs are determined as follows:

Occupied cell	$c_{ij} = r_i + k_j$	**Row or column value**
(1,1)	$8 = 0 + k_1$	$k_1 = 8$
(3,1)	$3 = r_3 + 8$	$r_3 = -5$
(3,3)	$10 = -5 + k_3$	$k_3 = 15$
(2,3)	$12 = r_2 + 15$	$r_2 = -3$
(2,2)	$10 = -3 + k_2$	$k_2 = 13$

Empty cell	$c_{ij} - r_i - k_j$	**CII**
(1,2)	$5 - 0 - 13$	−8
(1,3)	$6 - 0 - 15$	−9
(2,1)	$15 - (-3) - 8$	+10
(3,2)	$9 - (-5) - 13$	+1

Table 6.15 The third solution by the MODI method

	k_j	$k_1 = 8$	$k_2 = 13$	$k_3 = 15$	
r_i	From \ To	1	2	3	Supply
$r_1 = 0$	1	[8] 120 −	[5]	[6] +	120
$r_2 = -3$	2	[15]	[10] 70	[12] 10	80
$r_3 = -5$	3	[3] 30 +	[9]	[10] 50 −	80
	Demand	150	70	60	280

Total transportation cost = $2,370

In Table 6.15, the cell with the best CII is cell (1,3) with −$9. The maximum quantity we can transfer to cell (1,3) is 50. When we transfer 50 units to cell (1,3), we obtain the fourth solution, as shown in Table 6.16.

We can determine the row and column values and the CIIs for the empty cells as follows:

Occupied cell	$c_{ij} = r_i + k_j$	Row or column value
(1,1)	$8 = 0 + k_1$	$k_1 = 8$
(3,1)	$3 = r_3 + 8$	$r_3 = -5$
(1,3)	$6 = 0 + k_3$	$k_3 = 6$
(2,3)	$12 = r_2 + 6$	$r_2 = 6$
(2,2)	$10 = 6 + k_2$	$k_2 = 4$

Empty cell	$c_{ij} - r_i - k_j$	CII
(1,2)	$5 - 0 - 4$	+1
(2,1)	$15 - 6 - 8$	+1
(3,2)	$9 - (-5) - 4$	+10
(3,3)	$10 - (-5) - 6$	+9

The CII values determined are all positive. Thus, we have reached the optimum solution. This solution is identical to the one we derived through the stepping-stone method.

Table 6.16 The optimum solution obtained by the MODI method

r_i \ k_j	From \ To	1 ($k_1 = 8$)	2 ($k_2 = 4$)	3 ($k_3 = 6$)	Supply
$r_1 = 0$	1	[8] 70	[5]	[6] 50	120
$r_2 = 6$	2	[15]	[10] 70	[12] 10	80
$r_3 = -5$	3	[3] 80	[9]	[10]	80
	Demand	150	70	60	280

Total transportation cost = \$1,920

The Unbalanced Transportation Problem

In real-world situations, a balanced case is a rarity. In fact, virtually all transportation problems are unbalanced cases in which either supply exceeds demand or demand exceeds supply.

Demand Exceeds Supply

In the Blacksburg Concrete Company, let us suppose that a new apartment complex has been added to the project in construction site 3 and its requirement has been increased from 60 truckloads to 90 truckloads of concrete. The total demand is now 310 truckloads, while total supply remains at 280. The scheme we can use to balance the supply and demand requirements for this type of problem is to create an imaginary plant that can take up the excess demand. We introduce dummy plant 4 to supply the increased demand of 30 truckloads at site 3.

By creating a new row for plant 4 we can now balance supply and demand. Since 4 is only an imaginary plant, the unit transportation costs to the three sites are zero, as shown in Table 6.17.

The initial solution for the problem can be determined by the northwest-corner, minimum cell-cost, or VAM methods. When we use the northwest-corner method or VAM, the dummy row is treated as if it were one of the regular rows. If we use the minimum cell-cost method, we cannot make a unique first assignment among the three zero-cost cells in the dummy row. Thus, for the minimum cell-cost method, it is better that we leave out the dummy row (or dummy column) from consideration until the end.

Table 6.17 Initial solution by the minimum cell-cost method for the unbalanced problem

From \ To	1	2	3	Supply
1	[8]	[5] 70	[6] 50	120
2	[15] 40	[10]	[12] 40	80
3	[3] 80	[9]	[10]	80
4 Dummy	[0] 30	[0]	[0]	30
Demand	150	70	90	310

The problem can now be solved by using either the stepping-stone or the MODI method. In the optimum solution, if the dummy row is required to transport some quantity to one or more destinations, this implies that the destination(s) will receive less than the quantity required. For example, in Table 6.17 the dummy row is supplying 30 units to destination 1. In reality, destination 1 is receiving only 120 units rather than the 150 it demanded.

Supply Exceeds Demand

We can also analyze the opposite case, where supply exceeds demand, in a similar manner. In the original Blacksburg Concrete problem, let us suppose that the project in construction site 1 now requires only 100 truckloads instead of the original 150. The total demand amounts to only 230, while the total supply remains at 280.

To balance the supply and demand, we create a dummy construction site that can absorb the excess supply of 50 truckloads. Let us label this dummy construction site as site 4. We have added a new column to the tableau, as shown in Table 6.18. The unit transportation costs from various plants to site 4 should be zero. Table 6.18 presents the initial solution using the northwest-corner method. As usual, we can proceed to improve the solution by using either the stepping-stone or MODI methods.

If site 4 receives some quantity from a source (or sources), this implies that the source (or sources) is (are) not supplying up to its (their) production capacity. For example, if site 4 received 50 truckloads from plant 3, as shown in Table 6.18, plant 3 in reality is supplying only 30 truckloads to site 3, 50 truckloads below its supply capacity of 80 truckloads.

Table 6.18 Initial solution by the northwest-corner method for the second unbalanced problem

From \ To	1	2	3	4 Dummy	Supply
1	[8] 100	[5] 20	[6]	[0]	120
2	[15]	[10] 50	[12] 30	[0]	80
3	[3]	[9]	[10] 30	[0] 50	80
Demand	100	70	60	50	280

Some Complications

In real-world transportation problems, we often face several complicated situations that may cause some difficulty. Let us discuss several such complications.

Degeneracy

To evaluate all of the empty cells for solution improvement, there must be $m + n - 1$ number of occupied cells (m = number of rows and n = number of columns). When there is an insufficient number of occupied cells, we have a case of degeneracy. However, degeneracy does not necessarily present us with a difficulty. The only thing we have to do is designate one of the empty cells as an occupied cell by assigning zero quantity.

In a given transportation tableau, there may be several empty cells that could be candidates for the occupied cell designation. The key is that this cell must connect all the missing links in evaluating the empty cells whether we use the stepping-stone or the MODI method.

The case of degeneracy may occur at the initial solution or during solution iterations. In either case, the procedure we use to resolve the problem is the same.

Prohibited Routes

In some transportation problems, it is possible that distribution through a certain route may be prohibited or impossible due to local government ordinances, union agreements, road construction, or seasonal weather conditions. In such situations, the best way to handle an impossible or prohibited route is to assign an arbitrarily large transportation cost to the cell. Then, it becomes so prohibitively expensive to transport to the cell that this particular route will be avoided.

Multiple-Optimum Solutions

The solution technique, whether we use the stepping-stone or the MODI method, will terminate as soon as all CII values are zero or positive. If one or more of the empty cells has zero CII values, there are multiple-optimum solutions. We can transfer some units to the empty cell with a zero CII and find a different solution. However, since its CII is zero, the transfer of some quantity to this cell will have no effect on the total transportation cost.

The Transportation Problem with Multiple Objectives

Many real-world transportation problems involve multiple objectives. Minimization of total transportation cost is only one objective. For example, location–allocation, manpower scheduling, and school-busing problems involve many noneconomic objective criteria. For such transportation problems, we can effectively apply goal programming, which will be discussed in chapter 8.

Application of the *Micro Manager*

The program diskette provides the complete information about the transportation problem, including the purpose of the technique, the solution of a sample problem, interactive input instructions, and the batch input procedure. In this section we will examine an application example of the *Micro Manager.* We present the information (purpose of the technique and the batch input data format) and the solution of a sample problem using the interactive input format.

```
<< PURPOSE >>

TRANSPORTATION solves a special type of linear programming problem by finding
either the minimum total transportation cost or the maximum payoff from a
distribution problem where items are shipped from a set of sources to a set of
destinations.  This program can handle problems with up to a 40 by 40 size
matrix.

<<  BATCH INPUT DATA FORMAT  >>

Type in the values of the following input data requirements, after creating a
new file.  You may enter as many values as you want in a line, separating them
by commas for alphabetic characters and by commas or blank spaces for numeric
values.  However, the input data must be exactly in the following order:

1. Problem type:
      1    : maximization
      2    : minimization
2. Number of supply (source) points (maximum 40)
3. Number of demand (destination) points (maximum 40)
4. Capacity for each supply (source) points
5. Capacity for each demand (destination) points
6. Unit transportation cost for each cell
```

```
** Sample Batch Input Data Set (Example 6.1) **

2          ; minimization problem
3,3        ; three suply and three demand points
120,80,80  ; capacities of each supply points
150,70,60  ; capacities of each demand points
8,5,6      ; unit costs for row 1
15,10,12   ; unit costs for row 2
3,9,10     ; unit costs for row 3

PROGRAM: Transportation

Enter 1 for maximization or 2 for minimization: 2
Enter number of supply (source) points (greater than 1):  3
Enter number of demand (destination) points (greater than 1):  3

Enter available capacity for supply (source) point 1 :  120
Enter available capacity for supply (source) point 2 :  80
Enter available capacity for supply (source) point 3 :  80

Enter available capacity for demand (destination) point 1 :  150
Enter available capacity for demand (destination) point 2 :  70
Enter available capacity for demand (destination) point 3 :  60

Enter unit transportation cost for all routes.

From supply 1 to demand 1 :  8
From supply 1 to demand 2 :  5
From supply 1 to demand 3 :  6

From supply 2 to demand 1 :  15
From supply 2 to demand 2 :  10
From supply 2 to demand 3 :  12

From supply 3 to demand 1 :  3
From supply 3 to demand 2 :  9
From supply 3 to demand 3 :  10

PROGRAM: Transportation

***** INPUT DATA ENTERED *****

Minimization problem :

      :      1          2          3   :   Supply
--------------------------------------------------
 1    :     8.00       5.00       6.00:   120.00
 2    :    15.00      10.00      12.00:    80.00
 3    :     3.00       9.00      10.00:    80.00
--------------------------------------------------
Demand:   150.00      70.00      60.00:   280.00
```

```
*****  PROGRAM OUTPUT  *****

      :     1          2          3  :  Supply
-------------------------------------------------
1     :    70.00      0.00     50.00:   120.00
2     :     0.00     70.00     10.00:    80.00
3     :    80.00      0.00      0.00:    80.00
-------------------------------------------------
Demand:   150.00     70.00     60.00:   280.00

Optimal solution  :  1920
```

Summary

The transportation problem involves distribution of a product from a number of sources to numerous destinations while minimizing the total distribution cost. The transportation problem is a special type of linear-programming problem. It can be solved more simply by using special techniques. In this chapter, we have discussed the basic nature, solution methods, and application of the transportation model. We applied the *Micro Manager* to solve a transportation problem as a demonstration of its effectiveness as well as its user-friendliness.

References

Charnes, A., and W. W. Cooper. 1961. *Management models and industrial applications of linear programming.* New York: John Wiley & Sons.

Dantzig, G. B. 1963. *Linear programming and extensions.* Princeton, NJ: Princeton University Press.

Hillier, F. S., and G. L. Lieberman. 1980. *Introduction to operations research.* 3d ed. San Francisco: Holden-Day.

Lee, S. M., and L. J. Moore. 1973. Optimizing transportation problems with multiple objectives. *AIIE Transactions* 5:4, 333–38.

———. 1975. *Introduction to decision science.* New York: Petrocelli-Charter.

Lee, S. M., L. J. Moore, and B. W. Taylor. 1985. *Management science.* 2d ed. Dubuque, IA: W. C. Brown Co. Publishers.

Problems

1. Given the following linear-programming formulation of a transportation problem:

$$\begin{aligned}\text{Minimize } Z = {} & 4x_{11} + 10x_{12} + 6x_{13} + 8x_{21} + 16x_{22} + 6x_{23} + \\ & 14x_{31} + 18x_{32} + 10x_{33}\\ \text{subject to } & x_{11} + x_{12} + x_{13} = 100\\ & x_{21} + x_{22} + x_{23} = 300\\ & x_{31} + x_{32} + x_{33} = 300\\ & x_{11} + x_{21} + x_{31} = 200\\ & x_{12} + x_{22} + x_{32} = 300\\ & x_{13} + x_{23} + x_{33} = 200\\ & x_{ij} \geq 0\end{aligned}$$

a. Set up the transportation tableau for this problem.
b. Find the initial solution using the northwest-corner method.

2. Given the following linear-programming problem:

$$\begin{aligned}\text{Minimize } Z = {} & 20x_{11} + 16x_{12} + 24x_{13} + 10x_{21} + 10x_{22} + 8x_{23}\\ & + 12x_{31} + 18x_{32} + 10x_{33}\\ \text{subject to } & x_{11} + x_{12} + x_{13} = 300\\ & x_{21} + x_{22} + x_{23} = 500\\ & x_{31} + x_{32} + x_{33} = 100\\ & x_{11} + x_{21} + x_{31} = 200\\ & x_{12} + x_{22} + x_{32} = 400\\ & x_{13} + x_{23} + x_{33} = 300\\ & x_{ij} \geq 0\end{aligned}$$

a. Set up the transportation tableau for this problem.
b. Find the initial solution using the minimum cell-cost method.

3. Given the following transportation problem:

From \ To	1	2	3	Supply
A	$18	20	21	200
B	19	28	17	400
C	26	19	22	600
Demand	300	560	340	1,200

a. Find the initial solution by using the northwest-corner method.
b. Formulate this problem as a general linear-programming model.
c. Solve this problem by using the *Micro Manager*.

4. Given the following transportation problem:

From \ To	1	2	3	Supply
A	$20	18	16	100
B	22	16	17	200
C	24	22	23	600
Demand	200	300	400	900

a. Find the initial solution by using the minimum cell-cost method.
b. Formulate this problem as a general linear-programming model.
c. Solve this problem by using the *Micro Manager.*

5. Given the following transportation problem:

From \ To	1	2	3	Supply
A	$10	12	8	1,500
B	15	14	15	2,500
C	13	15	15	2,800
D	18	20	14	1,200
Demand	2,000	3,000	3,000	8,000

a. Find the initial solution by using the minimum cell-cost method.
b. Solve this problem by using the *Micro Manager.*

6. Given the following transportation problem:

From \ To	1	2	3	Supply
A	\$12	18	M	80
B	24	6	10	70
C	8	16	22	100
Demand	80	110	60	250

a. Find the initial solution by using the VAM method.
b. Solve this problem by using the *Micro Manager.*

7. Given the following linear-programming model:

$$\begin{aligned}\text{Minimize } Z = {} & x_{11} + 3x_{12} + 4x_{13} + 2x_{21} + 6x_{22} + 8x_{23} + 2x_{31} \\ & + 5x_{32} + 7x_{33}\end{aligned}$$

$$\begin{aligned}\text{subject to } x_{11} + x_{12} + x_{13} &\leq 200 \\ x_{21} + x_{22} + x_{23} &\leq 500 \\ x_{31} + x_{32} + x_{33} &\leq 300 \\ x_{11} + x_{21} + x_{31} &= 200 \\ x_{12} + x_{22} + x_{32} &= 100 \\ x_{13} + x_{23} + x_{33} &= 400 \\ x_{ij} &\geq 0\end{aligned}$$

a. Set up the transportation tableau for this problem.
b. Find the initial solution by using the VAM method.
c. Solve this problem by using the *Micro Manager.*

8. Given the following linear-programming problem:

$$\begin{aligned}\text{Minimize } Z = {} & 9x_{11} + 14x_{12} + 12x_{13} + 17x_{14} + 11x_{21} + 10x_{22} \\ & + 6x_{23} + 10x_{24} + 12x_{31} + 8x_{32} + 15x_{33} + 7x_{34}\end{aligned}$$

$$\begin{aligned}\text{subject to } x_{11} + x_{12} + x_{13} + x_{14} &\leq 400 \\ x_{21} + x_{22} + x_{23} + x_{24} &\leq 400 \\ x_{31} + x_{32} + x_{33} + x_{34} &\leq 400 \\ x_{11} + x_{21} + x_{31} &= 260 \\ x_{12} + x_{22} + x_{32} &= 340 \\ x_{13} + x_{23} + x_{33} &= 200 \\ x_{14} + x_{24} + x_{34} &= 300 \\ x_{ij} &\geq 0\end{aligned}$$

a. Set up the transportation tableau for this problem.
b. Find the initial solution by using the minimum cell-cost method.
c. Solve this problem by using the *Micro Manager.*

9. Given the following transportation problem:

From \ To	1	2	3	4	Supply
A	$24	18	32	36	300
B	22	16	14	32	420
C	32	24	20	44	640
Demand	260	140	360	480	

a. Find the initial solution by using the minimum cell-cost method.
b. Solve this problem by using the *Micro Manager.*
c. If there are alternative solutions, identify them.
d. Formulate this problem as a general linear-programming model.

10. Given the following transportation problem:

From \ To	1	2	3	Supply
A	$ 3	12	8	180
B	10	5	6	60
C	6	7	10	200
Demand	140	220	160	

a. Find the initial solution by using the VAM method.
b. Solve this problem by using the *Micro Manager.*
c. Formulate this problem as a general linear-programming model.

11. Given the following transportation problem:

From \ To	1	2	3	Supply
A	$ 5	6	4	750
B	7.50	7	7.50	1,100
C	6.50	7.50	7.50	1,400
D	9	10	7	500
Demand	1,000	1,500	1,500	

a. Find the initial solution by using the northwest-corner method.
b. Solve this problem by using the *Micro Manager*.

12. Given the following transportation problem:

From \ To	1	2	3	Supply
A	$10	12	9	150
B	13	14	12	150
C	11	10	12	100
Demand	200	50	120	

a. Find the initial solution by using the minimum cell-cost method.
b. Solve this problem by using the *Micro Manager*.
c. If there are alternative solutions, identify them.

13. Given the following transportation problem:

From \ To	1	2	3	4	Supply
A	$24	20	18	30	360
B	20	16	4	20	250
C	18	10	26	16	300
Demand	260	400	250	300	

a. Find the initial solution by using the VAM method.
b. Solve this problem by using the *Micro Manager.*

14. Given the following transportation problem:

From \ To	1	2	3	4	5	Supply
A	$42	24	56	34	18	500
B	30	26	40	100	24	600
C	36	34	44	20	16	400
D	M	4	20	10	2	700
E	66	58	70	54	46	300
Demand	400	300	500	600	500	

a. Find the initial solution by using the VAM method.
b. Formulate this problem as a general linear-programming model.
c. Solve this problem by using the *Micro Manager.*

15. The Foot Company produces shoes, then stores them in warehouses in three cities.

Warehouse	Capacity (boxes)
A. Lincoln	200
B. Nashville	400
C. Tucson	600

This company supplies shoes to markets in three cities, which have the following demands.

Market	Demand
1. St. Louis	300
2. Atlanta	400
3. Los Angeles	500

The shipping costs per box for each route are below.

From \ To	1	2	3
A	$5	2	3
B	8	4	3
C	9	7	5

a. Set up the transportation tableau for this problem.
b. Find the initial solution by using the VAM method.
c. Solve this problem by using the *Micro Manager.*

16. The Sweet Company produces candy in three cities: Omaha, Dallas, and Memphis. The production capacity of each plant per month is below.

Plant	Production
A. Omaha	300
B. Dallas	400
C. Memphis	250

These plants supply candy to markets in four cities, which have the following demands per month.

Market	Demand
1. Denver	150
2. San Francisco	300
3. Atlanta	300
4. Phoenix	200

The shipping costs for these routes are below.

From \ To	1	2	3	4
A	$7	6	10	3
B	8	10	4	9
C	5	6	5	11

a. Set up the transportation tableau for this problem.
b. Find the initial solution by using the minimum cell-cost method.
c. Solve this problem by using the *Micro Manager.*

17. The Big Wheel Company produces tires, then stores them in warehouses in four cities. The capacity of each warehouse is below.

Warehouse	Capacity
A. Denver	3,000
B. Detroit	4,000
C. Louisville	2,500
D. Jacksonville	3,500

These warehouses supply tires to markets in four cities, which have the following demands.

Market	Demand
1. Las Vegas	2,000
2. Chicago	3,500
3. Atlanta	2,500
4. New York	5,000

The shipping cost per pair for each route is below.

From \ To	1	2	3	4
A	$20	8	17	19
B	15	6	10	14
C	8	11	7	9
D	12	17	20	16

However, due to the truck company's policy, shipments are presently prohibited from Denver to Chicago, Detroit to Chicago, and Louisville to Atlanta.

a. Set up the transportation tableau for this problem.
b. Find the initial solution by using the VAM method.
c. Solve this problem by using the *Micro Manager.*

18. The Big Red Company grew, picked, and then stored corn in warehouses in Grand Island, Scotts Bluff, and Omaha. These warehouses supply corn to markets in Chicago, Houston, and Louisville. The following shipping costs per ton and supply and demand requirements exist.

From \ To	Chicago	Houston	Louisville	Supply
Grand Island	$ 12	16	16	200
Scotts Bluff	36	24	28	500
Omaha	16	24	20	300
Demand	200	100	400	

a. Set up the transportation tableau for this problem.
b. Find the initial solution by using the minimum cell-cost method.
c. Solve this problem by using the *Micro Manager.*
d. If there are alternate solutions, identify them.

19. The Unleaded Oil Company produces a catalyst in two cities, San Antonio and Dallas. The company is able to produce the catalyst as below.

Plant	Production
A. San Antonio	500
B. Dallas	300

The demand for this catalyst from four wholesalers is below.

Wholesalers	Demand
1. Houston	200
2. Chicago	500
3. Detroit	300
4. Atlanta	200

The following railroad shipping costs per ton have been determined.

From \ To	1	2	3	4
A	$16	17	16	20
B	17	15	14	19

a. Set up the transportation tableau for this problem.
b. Find the initial solution by using the VAM method.
c. Solve this problem by using the *Micro Manager*.

20. The West Company produces lawn-mower blades in three cities—Tucson, St. Louis, and Omaha. The production capacity of each plant is below.

Plant	Production
A. Tucson	400
B. St. Louis	300
C. Omaha	600

These plants supply lawn mowers to markets in five cities, which have the following demands.

Market	Demand
1. Iowa City	140
2. Denver	300
3. Tulsa	180
4. Dallas	225
5. San Diego	80

The following shipping cost for each route has been determined.

From \ To	1	2	3	4	5
A	$18	16	13	6	3
B	16	12	9	2	6
C	8	10	11	12	16

a. Set up the transportation tableau for this problem.
b. Find the initial solution by using the northwest-corner method.
c. Find the initial solution by using the minimum cell-cost method.
d. Find the initial solution by using the VAM method.
e. Solve this problem by using the *Micro Manager.*
f. If there are alternate solutions, identify them.

CHAPTER 7

The Assignment Problem

Assignment of people or other resources to various workstations or certain equipment to accomplish certain tasks while minimizing the total cost is a frequent management decision problem. For example, assigning employees to various tasks, teachers to different classes, crews to projects, ambulances to first-aid stations are good, real-world examples of assignment problems. The basic goal of the assignment problem is either to minimize the total cost of completing all of the required tasks or to maximize the total payoff (or benefits) from the assignments.

Basics

In chapter 6, we studied the transportation problem as a variation of the general linear-programming problem. Another special type of the linear-programming problem is the assignment problem. The assignment problem is closely related to the transportation problem. As a matter of fact, the assignment problem is a special case of the transportation problem where there are equal numbers of sources and destinations. Furthermore, the supply of each source and the demand of each destination are exactly one. Consequently, the quantity we assign to a given cell must be either 0 (no assignment) or 1 (assignment).

Because of its unique structure, the assignment problem can be solved more efficiently by a different solution method from linear programming or transportation techniques. Some of the typical assignment problems in real-world situations are as follows:

Production industry

Assignment of managers to plants

Assignment of production crews to product lines

Assignment of employees to tasks or equipment

Assignment of forklifts to workstations

Wholesale or retail industry

Assignment of salespeople to sales territories

Assignment of automobiles to salespeople

Transportation industry

Assignment of ships to docks

Assignment of trucks to unloading areas

Nonprofit organizations

Assignment of teachers to classes

Assignment of officers to command posts

Assignment of detective teams to criminal cases

Assignment of ambulances to first-aid stations

Assignment of snowplows to city areas

Solution Methods for the Assignment Problem

Several solution methods have been proposed for the assignment problem. Among the best known are the Hungarian method and the branch and bound integer-programming method. In this chapter, we will discuss only the Hungarian method, which the *Micro Manager* utilizes.

The Hungarian method, so named because the Hungarian mathematician, D. König, first proved the underlying theorem, is by far the best-known solution technique for the assignment problem. The Hungarian method is based on the concept of opportunity cost, which we discussed briefly in the Vogel's approximation method in chapter 6. The opportunity cost is the cost associated with failing to take the best course of action. Thus, the Hungarian method attempts to minimize the total opportunity cost.

Example 7.1 Kabuki Electronics, Inc.

Kabuki Electronics specializes in producing electronic scanners. The company received a special order from a large cash-register company for optical scanners. To produce important components required for the scanner, the company has selected four employees for assignment to four different machines to complete the necessary tasks. Because of different individual training and experience, the cost of successful completion of the given task on each machine is different for the four employees.

Table 7.1 Assignment problem tableau

Employee \ Machine	*A*	*B*	*C*	*D*	Supply
1	20	10	14	13	1
2	18	10	22	18	1
3	28	14	20	28	1
4	6	10	8	6	1
Demand	1	1	1	1	4

Only one employee can be assigned to each machine. Also, each task is completed independently by an employee on a machine. The assignment problem at Kabuki, along with the cost involved for each employee to complete each task on each machine, is presented in Table 7.1. Notice that there are the same number of rows (employees) and columns (machines). Also, the amount of supply and demand for each row and each column is exactly one.

In Table 7.1, we can easily see that it costs $20 for employee 1 to complete the task by using machine *A*, $10 using machine *B*, and so on. The cost required for each employee to complete each task may be determined by the amount of time required and the amount of other resources (i.e., materials) used to complete the task. The objective of the above assignment problem is to find the employees' optimum assignment schedule to each machine to minimize the total cost to complete the tasks. The problem can be solved by the regular transportation method studied earlier. However, it can be solved more efficiently by the Hungarian method.

The Hungarian Method of Assignment

The Hungarian method is based on the concept of opportunity cost, or penalty cost, which we discussed in Vogel's approximation method of transportation in chapter 6. The Hungarian method of assignment involves the following steps.

The Opportunity-Cost Table

The first step of the Hungarian method of assignment is to develop a table of opportunity costs. The concept of opportunity cost is important in any decision analysis. The amount of opportunity cost represents the implicit cost associated with the failure of taking the best course of action. For example, in our problem shown in Table 7.2, if employee 1 is assigned to machine *B*, it will cost the firm $10. Therefore, the best possible assignment for employee 1, while disregarding

Table 7.2 The assignment problem

Employee \ Machine	*A*	*B*	*C*	*D*
1	20	10	14	13
2	18	10	22	18
3	28	14	20	28
4	6	10	8	6

Table 7.3 The initial row-wise opportunity-cost table

Employee \ Machine	*A*	*B*	*C*	*D*
1	10	0	4	3
2	8	0	12	8
3	14	0	6	14
4	0	4	2	0

other employees for the time being, is clearly to machine *B*. The failure to assign employee 1 to machine *B*, assigning the person instead to *A*, for instance, will cost the firm \$10 (20 − 10 = 10). Since we are trying to minimize the total cost, our strategy should be to minimize the opportunity cost. We should note that opportunity costs also exist for each column. First, let us find the initial table of opportunity costs by analyzing each row. The procedure we follow in determining the row opportunity costs is to subtract the minimum value in each row from each of the other values in that row. Table 7.3 presents the opportunity cost for each of the rows.

From our discussion thus far, it should be clear that the opportunity cost also exists for columns. Any of the four employees can be assigned to machine *A*. Employee 4 has the minimum cost of \$6. If employee 2 is assigned to machine *A*, we must absorb the opportunity cost of \$12 (18 − 6 = 12) because we failed to assign employee 4 to that machine. The column opportunity cost must be computed from the row opportunity-cost table we derived in Table 7.3. The complete opportunity-cost table after the column reduction is shown in Table 7.4.

Table 7.4 The complete opportunity-cost table

Employee \ Machine	*A*	*B*	*C*	*D*
1	10	0	2	3
2	8	0	10	8
3	14	0	4	14
4	0	4	0	0

Table 7.5 The first test of optimum assignment feasibility

Employee \ Machine	*A*	*B*	*C*	*D*
1	10	0	(2)	3
2	8	0	10	8
3	14	0	4	14
4	0	4	0	0

Analysis of Optimum Assignment Feasibility

Once a complete opportunity-cost table is developed, the next step is to determine whether an optimum assignment is possible. An optimum assignment can be made if the final opportunity-cost table has as many *independent zeros* as the number of rows or columns. The "independent" zero permits the assignment of an employee to a cell with zero opportunity cost without excluding assignment to other cells having zero costs.

When an assignment is made to a cell with zero opportunity cost, the best possible assignment is possible for a given row and a given column. A convenient way to check optimality is to draw a *minimum* number of straight lines, horizontally or vertically but never diagonally, to cross out all of the zero elements in the opportunity-cost table. By minimizing the number of straight lines required to cover all of the zero elements, we identify the number of independent zeros in the opportunity-cost table. The minimum number of straight lines must equal the number of rows or columns to make an optimum assignment. If the number of straight lines is less than the number of rows or columns, we do not have a sufficient number of independent zeros to make an optimum assignment.

From Table 7.5, it is evident that we need only two lines to cross out all of the zeros. Thus, an optimum assignment is not possible at this point.

Table 7.6 The revised opportunity-cost table

Employee \ Machine	*A*	*B*	*C*	*D*
1	8	0	0	1
2	6	0	8	6
3	12	0	(2)	12
4	0	0	0	0

The Revised Opportunity-Cost Table

Since we need only two lines to cover all of the zeros in the opportunity-cost table, we have only two independent zero cells to use in making assignments. Thus, two other employees must be assigned to cells in which we have positive opportunity costs. To identify the least-expensive cells to which the third and fourth employees can be assigned, we must revise the opportunity-cost table. The procedure we use can be summarized as follows:

1. Identify the minimum opportunity cost that has not been crossed out by a straight line.
2. Subtract this value from all of the other opportunity costs that have not been crossed out by straight lines.
3. Add this same minimum value to those opportunity costs that are at the intersection of two straight lines.
4. All the remaining cells have the same opportunity costs as in the previous table.

This procedure of reviewing the opportunity cost is in effect until we find a sufficient number of independent zeros. Each new independent zero is determined on the basis of the opportunity costs among the cells not crossed out. In fact, we are creating an opportunity-cost table within an opportunity-cost table.

In Table 7.5, among the nine opportunity costs not crossed out, the minimum cost is 2 in cell (1,*C*). We subtract this value from all of the costs not lined out, and we also add this value to the one intersection value in cell (4,*B*). The cost elements that are crossed out by only one line are unchanged in the revised opportunity-cost table. The revised opportunity-cost tables are presented in Table 7.6 and Table 7.7.

Tables 7.6 and 7.7 both show that we need only three lines to cross out all of the zeros. Thus, we need further revision of the opportunity-cost table. Table 7.8 presents the complete opportunity-cost table. Finally, we need four straight lines to cover all of the zeros. Consequently, it is possible to make an optimum assignment for the problem.

Table 7.7 The second revised opportunity-cost table

Employee \ Machine	A	B	C	D
1	8	2	0	(1)
2	4	0	6	4
3	10	0	0	10
4	0	8	0	0

Table 7.8 Complete opportunity-cost table

Employee \ Machine	A	B	C	D
1	7	2	0	0
2	3	0	6	3
3	9	0	0	9
4	0	9	1	0

In the revised opportunity-cost table shown in Table 7.8, two zeros are in each row and each column except the first column and second row. The first assignment must be made in a row or column where there is only one zero because it represents a unique assignment. Since there is only one zero in the second row, we will assign employee 2 to machine *B*. We also assign employee 4 to machine *A* for the same reason. Next, employees 1 and 3 must be assigned to machine *D* and *C*, respectively, without any other alternative choice. The optimum assignment and total cost are as follows.

	Optimal Assignment	
Employee	**Machine**	**Cost**
1	*D*	$13
2	*B*	10
3	*C*	20
4	*A*	6
	Total cost =	$49

Some Complications

As in the transportation problem, we may face a number of unique situations in real-world assignment problems. We will discuss several such situations here.

A Maximization Problem

The Hungarian method is equally efficient in solving any maximization assignment problems. Since the objective is to maximize the total payoff or benefit from the assignment, we must make assignments to cells where the assignment payoff is the greatest, if possible. Thus, the only difference is that in determining the row-wise opportunity cost, we should find a difference between the *highest* row score and each of the row scores. On the other hand, the columnwise reduction procedure remains the same. Once the complete opportunity cost is derived, the other steps are exactly the same as the minimization problem.

Unequal Rows and Columns

An important requirement of the Hungarian method of assignment is the square matrix, i.e., the number of rows must be exactly the same as the number of columns. However, such a square-matrix assignment problem is very rare in real-world situations. In an uneven assignment problem, we introduce either a dummy row or a dummy column and balance the row–column requirements. The assignment costs for the dummy row or column will be zero.

Impossible or Prohibited Assignments

There are many instances where certain specific assignments cannot be made because of contracts or certain physical constraints. For example, a janitor cannot be assigned as a nurse, certain ships cannot be unloaded at certain docks, and the like. Just as in the transportation problem with prohibited routes, we can assign prohibitively large costs to the impossible assignment cells and solve the problem by the usual Hungarian method.

Multiple-Optimum Solutions

For a given assignment problem, there may be more than exactly the required number of independent zero elements. Thus, there will be multiple-optimum solutions with the same total cost (profit) of assignment. The decision maker has the option to exercise his or her judgment and select one particular optimum solution for the problem.

An Assignment Problem with Multiple Objectives

Most assignment problems involve a set of multiple conflicting objectives. For example, a new fire-station location, a new school-site decision, a warehouse location, and manpower allocation are such problems involving multiple objectives.

The zero–one goal programming approach has been applied to many assignment-related problems involving multiple objectives. Chapter 8 presents goal programming for multiple-objective decision making.

Application of the *Micro Manager*

In this section, we present an application example of the *Micro Manager.* The program diskette provides the complete information about the purpose of the assignment problem, the solution of a sample problem, interactive input instructions, and the batch input procedure. In this section, therefore, we will present only the information (purpose of the technique and the batch input data format) and the solution example of a sample problem using the interactive input format.

```
<< PURPOSE >>

ASSIGNMENT solves another special type of linear programming problems where the
objective is to find the maximum payoff or minimum cost that can be obtained by
assigning a set of objects to a set of stations.  This program can solve
problems with up to a 40 by 40 matrix.

<<  BATCH INPUT DATA FORMAT  >>

Type in the values of the following input data requirements, after creating a
new file.  You may enter as many values as you want in a line, separating them
by commas for alphabetic characters and by commas or blank spaces for numeric
values.  However, the input data must be exactly in the following order:

1. Problem type:
     1    : maximization
     2    : minimization
2. Number of rows (maximum 40)
3. Number of columns (maximum 40)
4. Unit cost (profit) for each cell

** Sample Batch Input Data Set (Example 7.1) **

2            ; minimization problem
4            ; four rows
4            ; four columns
20,10,14,13  ; unit costs of row 1
18,10,22,18  ; unit costs of row 2
24,14,20,28  ; unit costs of row 3
6,10,8,6     ; unit costs of row 4
```

```
PROGRAM: Assignment

Enter 1 for maximization or 2 for minimization: 2
Enter number of rows (greater than 1)    : 4
Enter number of columns (greater than 1): 4

Enter unit cost (profit) for row 1 column 1 : 20
Enter unit cost (profit) for row 1 column 2 : 10
Enter unit cost (profit) for row 1 column 3 : 14
Enter unit cost (profit) for row 1 column 4 : 13

Enter unit cost (profit) for row 2 column 1 : 18
Enter unit cost (profit) for row 2 column 2 : 10
Enter unit cost (profit) for row 2 column 3 : 22
Enter unit cost (profit) for row 2 column 4 : 18

Enter unit cost (profit) for row 3 column 1 : 24
Enter unit cost (profit) for row 3 column 2 : 134
Enter unit cost (profit) for row 3 column 3 : 20
Enter unit cost (profit) for row 3 column 4 : 28

Enter unit cost (profit) for row 4 column 1 : 6
Enter unit cost (profit) for row 4 column 2 : 10
Enter unit cost (profit) for row 4 column 3 : 8
Enter unit cost (profit) for row 4 column 4 : 6

PROGRAM: Assignment

***** INPUT DATA ENTERED *****

Minimization problem:

   ¦         1         2         3         4  ¦
-------------------------------------------------
 1 ¦     20.00     10.00     14.00     13.00  ¦
 2 ¦     18.00     10.00     22.00     18.00  ¦
 3 ¦     24.00    134.00     20.00     28.00  ¦
 4 ¦      6.00     10.00      8.00      6.00  ¦
-------------------------------------------------

*****   PROGRAM OUTPUT   *****

   ¦ 1  2  3  4 ¦
----------------
 1 ¦ 0  0  0  1 ¦
 2 ¦ 0  1  0  0 ¦
 3 ¦ 0  0  1  0 ¦
 4 ¦ 1  0  0  0 ¦
----------------

Optimal solution :  49
```

Summary

The assignment problem involves assigning a number of people or other resources to various workstations or projects to accomplish certain tasks while minimizing the total cost. The assignment problem is also a special type of linear programming. We can solve the assignment problem more efficiently by a different solution method that takes advantage of the unique structure of the problem. This chapter has presented the basic nature, solution methods, and application areas of the assignment model. The *Micro Manager* application example was presented to demonstrate its effectiveness in solving assignment problems.

References

Kwak, N. K. 1973. *Mathematical programming with business applications.* New York: McGraw-Hill.

Lee, S. M. 1976. *Linear optimization for management.* New York: Petrocelli-Charter.

Lee, S. M., L. J. Moore, and B. W. Taylor. 1985. *Management science.* 2d ed. Dubuque, IA: Wm. C. Brown Co. Publishers.

Problems

1. In a job shop operation, three jobs may be performed on any of three machines. The hours required for each job on each machine are presented in the following table.

	Machine		
Job	**1**	**2**	**3**
A	12	12	20
B	10	12	24
C	15	15	24

The foreman would like to assign the jobs so that the total time required to finish all three jobs would be minimized. Find the optimum solution by using the *Micro Manager.*

2. Sunny Electronics, Inc. has just hired three new sales managers who are going to be assigned to three new locations. The personnel director wishes to assign the managers so that moving expenses can be minimized. The estimated moving expenses are below.

Manager	New Location		
	Omaha	Kansas City	Jackson
Albert	$4,000	$5,000	$6,000
Marian	8,000	3,000	1,000
Chuck	5,000	7,000	2,000

Solve the assignment problem by using the *Micro Manager.*

3. A plant has four operators to be assigned to four machines. The cost required to complete required work on each machine by each operator is below.

Operator	Machine			
	1	2	3	4
A	$ 9	$10	$ 8	$ 6
B	14	8	11	12
C	8	10	9	10
D	11	7	8	14

Determine the optimum assignment by using the *Micro Manager.*

4. There are five empty offices in the research department. Five newly hired employees will be assigned to these offices. Since there are no priorities involved in assigning these offices, maximizing the aggregate preferences of these five individuals is desired. The preference of each employee is shown in the following table (p. 161).

Employee	Office				
	1	2	3	4	5
A	5	2	1	3	4
B	2	3	5	1	4
C	5	3	4	2	1
D	5	4	3	2	1
E	3	4	2	5	1

Determine the optimum assignment by using the *Micro Manager.*

5. The Blue Cab Company has a taxi waiting at each of four posts. Four customers have called and requested service. The distances, in miles, from the waiting taxis to the four customers are given below.

Post	Customer			
	1	2	3	4
A	8	14	12	16
B	16	8	6	14
C	12	18	14	12
D	10	12	8	10

Solve the problem by using the *Micro Manager.*

6. The Super Aerospace Company has just been awarded a rocket-engine development contract. The contract terms require that at least five other smaller companies be awarded subcontracts for a portion of the total work. So Super requested bids from five small companies to do subcontract work in five areas. The bids are as follows (in thousands of dollars).

Company	Work Area				
	1	2	3	4	5
A	$10	$ 6	$ 4	$8	$3
B	2	9	7	7	6
C	6	11	12	5	9
D	5	4	2	1	4
E	5	9	8	5	9

Because of the production capacity, each company can work only in one area. Which bids should Super accept to minimize the cost?

7. The town of Columbus is putting up bids for four used police vehicles. The town will allow individuals to make bids on all four vehicles, but will accept only one bid per individual. Four individuals have made the following bids:

Individual	Vehicle 1	2	3	4
A	$1,000	$ 700	$ 800	$ 600
B	900	1,000	1,100	900
C	1,200	700	1,400	1,400
D	800	600	400	700

How should the bids be awarded to maximize total sales revenue?

8. U-MOVE Company rents car trailers to individuals making one-way moves. Occasionally, the company has to redistribute the trailers to eliminate a surplus in some cities and a deficit in others. The company currently has a surplus of trailers in cities *A, B, C, D, E,* and *F* and a deficit of one trailer each in cities 1, 2, 3, 4, 5, and 6. The following table provides mileages between various cities with a surplus and cities with a deficit. How should U-MOVE redistribute the trailers so that total mileage traveled is minimized?

Surplus city	Deficit city 1	2	3	4	5	6
A	30	51	60	40	40	82
B	33	30	26	39	40	29
C	43	37	52	48	50	45
D	32	32	51	60	39	27
E	50	81	65	49	29	22
F	51	25	52	39	72	41

9. Peanut Computer, Inc. has five types of personal computers that can be assembled by five assembly lines. The cost per unit for each type of PC by each assembly line is below.

Assembly line	Computer type A	B	C	D	E
1	$1,010	$ 960	$590	$840	$ 730
2	800	1,040	940	970	790
3	680	880	830	900	590
4	580	880	860	640	700
5	1,120	770	700	950	1,020

Which assembly line should be assigned to assemble which computer to minimize the cost? Solve the problem by using the *Micro Manager.*

10. Jim Henderson is a sales manager facing a decision. He has four good salespeople and four important customers to be called and shown a new line of products. However, because of the four salespeople's different experiences and abilities, it will take some salespeople more calls to close the sale with some customers than with others. The table below gives the estimated number of visits each of the four salespeople will need to close each of the four accounts. Determine the assignment that will minimize the total number of visits for all the salespeople.

Salesperson	Account A	B	C	D
1	3	5	2	2
2	4	2	1	3
3	5	2	4	3
4	1	3	4	2

11. Trans-America Cargo Transportation Company has five types of trucks that need to be assigned to five different routes. Because of variations among the routes (distances, cargo characteristics, weather, and so on), the trucks are not all equally adaptable to each route. The cost for each truck over each route is as follows (p. 164).

Truck	Omaha–Chicago	San Jose–Denver	Detroit–Kansas City	New York–Reno	St. Louis–Tucson
1	$1,000	$1,500	$1,700	$4,000	$4,500
2	800	1,200	2,000	3,800	4,300
3	700	1,400	1,800	3,400	3,700
4	600	1,300	1,200	3,000	3,200
5	900	1,200	2,100	4,200	4,100

Solve this problem by using the *Micro Manager.*

12. A manufacturing company has five machines that need to be staffed by five operators. The time required to complete the given tasks by each operator with a given machine is shown below.

	Machine				
Operator	*A*	*B*	*C*	*D*	*E*
1	9	11	11	16	3
2	15	22	18	11	3
3	16	20	24	27	5
4	17	20	21	25	3
5	9	12	12	11	3

Determine the optimum assignment to minimize the total time.

13. The Anderson Corporation owns four television plants, which it must now assign to four rush orders of about equal size. The estimated costs (in thousands of dollars) at each plant for each order are below.

	Order			
Plant	1	2	3	4
A	$11	$12	$11	$15
B	15	9	13	18
C	17	13	18	19
D	19	18	20	20

How should the plants be assigned to minimize the total cost of the four rush orders? Solve the problem by using the *Micro Manager.*

14. A transportation company has five service stalls at its headquarters, each equipped to handle general maintenance. The company has four trucks scheduled for maintenance today. However, because of some special requirements, the time required to service the trucks will vary, depending on which truck is assigned to which stall. The estimated service time for each truck is as follows.

	Stall				
Truck	***A***	***B***	***C***	***D***	***E***
1	12	9	8	7	12
2	17	15	11	12	6
3	14	10	14	16	8
4	5	4	6	5	5

Find the optimum assignment.

15. A tobacco company has three plants located in three cities. The tobacco is purchased from four dealers in cities *A, B, C,* and *D.* The railroad-shipping costs per ton between each plant and each dealer have been estimated as follows.

	Plant		
Dealer	**1**	**2**	**3**
A	7	10	5
B	12	9	4
C	7	3	11
D	9	5	7

Find the optimum assignment.

16. The traffic manager of the Atlas Corporation has seven trucks, now located at various cities, available to pick up six loaded trailers, scattered over the territory. The estimated hours for each truck to load the trailers are below.

	Trailer					
Truck	**1**	**2**	**3**	**4**	**5**	**6**
A	12	30	20	18	22	20
B	8	7	13	18	10	12
C	15	23	18	27	30	18
D	10	30	8	10	40	20
E	10	20	32	13	23	33
F	42	15	15	35	20	25
G	24	42	19	32	30	43

Determine the optimum assignment to minimize the total time by using the *Micro Manager.*

17. An electronics firm produces electronic components that it supplies to various electrical manufacturers. Past quality-control records indicate that the number of defective items produced were different for each employee. The average number of defects produced by each employee per week for each of seven components is given in the following table.

	Components						
Employee	***A***	***B***	***C***	***D***	***E***	***F***	***G***
1	15	19	13	16	16	13	18
2	14	11	15	14	13	15	13
3	11	16	17	18	15	13	17
4	11	19	15	12	16	12	17
5	18	17	14	14	19	14	18
6	13	18	15	14	11	12	12
7	18	15	16	14	17	16	11

Determine the optimum assignment that will minimize the total average weekly defects.

18. A manufacturing firm has four employees and five machines. The hourly cost required to operate each machine by each employee is below.

Employee	Machine				
	A	*B*	*C*	*D*	*E*
1	$12	$11	$ 8	$14	$14
2	10	9	10	8	20
3	14	8	7	11	9
4	6	8	10	9	16

However, according to union rules, employee 3 cannot be assigned to machine *E*, and employee 4 cannot be assigned to machine *B*. Find the optimum assignment.

19. An insurance firm has five salespeople that the firm wants to assign to five sales regions. Because of previously acquired contracts, the salespeople are able to cover the regions in different amounts of time. The amount of time (in days) required by each salesperson to cover each region is below.

Salesperson	Region				
	A	*B*	*C*	*D*	*E*
1	15	12	14	16	18
2	14	10	15	10	14
3	16	13	10	19	16
4	18	17	12	17	14
5	12	16	10	14	13

Determine the optimum assignment to minimize the total time.

20. The public works department of Starkville has six snowplows. The director wants to assign these plows to six districts in the city to clean up the new snow in the shortest possible time. The amount of time (in minutes) required to clean up all major streets in each district by different snowplows is given in the following table.

Plow	District					
	A	*B*	*C*	*D*	*E*	*F*
1	70	64	56	66	70	62
2	62	68	54	70	60	53
3	58	56	65	54	52	62
4	54	62	58	63	61	70
5	65	58	54	56	56	68
6	72	54	50	54	58	60

Solve the assignment problem by using the *Micro Manager.*

C H A P T E R 8

Multiple-Objective Decision Making

Linear programming, as presented in chapters 4 and 5, is an effective technique for solving problems that involve a single objective. However, most decision problems involve multiple objectives, and often conflicting ones. Profit maximization or cost minimization is undoubtedly an important objective. Nevertheless, organizations frequently place higher priorities on noneconomic objectives such as social responsibility, public relations, employee relations, environmental protection, long-term growth of the organization, and others.

A number of techniques have been proposed for multiple-objective decision making. One of the most widely used management science techniques for multiple-objective decision making is goal programming. In this chapter we will discuss the concept, application areas, model formulations, and solution methods of goal programming.

Basics

Virtually all decision problems in organizations involve multiple objectives. Such problems are not simple to analyze by optimization techniques such as linear programming. Organizations attempt to achieve satisfactory levels of multiple objectives while satisfying system constraints. This general approach is often referred to as "satisficing." The *satisficing* approach, rather than optimizing, based on the concept of bounded rationality, as suggested by Nobel laureate Herbert A. Simon, has emerged as a pragmatic methodology of decision making. In this approach, a set of tangible, multiple-aspiration criteria is determined rather than developing a single global optimization criterion.

Multiple-criteria decision making (MCDM) or multiple-objective decision making (MODM) has been a popular topic of management science during the past decade. A number of different approaches of MCDM or MODM have been proposed, such as multiattribute utility theory, multiple-objective linear programming, goal programming, compromise programming, and various heuristics. Among these, goal programming has been the most widely accepted and applied technique. The primary reason for the wide popularity of goal programming appears to be its underlying philosophy of "satisficing." Goal programming captures a rich set of properties of a real decision environment by incorporating the decision-maker's judgment about organizational goals and their priorities. Goal programming is a powerful tool that draws upon the highly developed technique of linear programming while providing a simultaneous solution to a complex system of competing goals.

The concept of goal programming was originally developed as an extension of linear programming by A. Charnes and W. W. Cooper. In goal programming, we attempt to "satisfice" or come as close to satisfying the various goals as possible. The decision-maker's multiple aspiration goals are expressed in either ordinal (preemptive or lexicographic) or numerical terms so that multiple goals can be analyzed on the basis of their importance.

Since 1968, a large number of goal-programming related studies have been published. In the process, many important, new developments and refinements have been made in the areas of new solution algorithms, interactive approaches, sensitivity analysis, duality, integer methods, nonlinear models, large-scale models, stochastic approaches, and applications to many real-world problems. Thus, goal programming has been well established as a major solution approach for solving multiple-criteria decision problems.

Application Areas of Goal Programming

Goal programming has been widely applied to various decision problems in business firms, government agencies, and nonprofit institutions. Some of the best-known applications of goal programming include the following problem areas:

Academic planning and administration
Accounting analysis
Advertising media scheduling
Blood collection and distribution
Capital budgeting
Computer resource planning and allocation
Decision-support system design
Economic policy analysis
Educational system planning
Energy resources planning
Environmental protection
Facilities location and layout planning
Financial planning
Health-care delivery system design
Inventory management
Location and allocation decisions
Manpower planning
Marketing logistics
Military strategies and planning
Network scheduling
Organizational analysis
Personnel administration
Policy analysis
Portfolio determination
Production scheduling
Project scheduling
Quality control
Research and development
Transportation logistics
Urban planning
Water resources planning

Goal-Programming Model Formulation

To gain some hands-on experience in formulating goal-programming models, let us consider the following examples.

Example 8.1 Digital Devices, Inc.

Digital Devices is a firm that specializes in producing disk drives for various computer manufacturers. Currently, the company produces two types of disk drives—XT100 and DD11. The XT100 drive requires 8 minutes of processing time in assembly center one and 3 minutes in assembly center two. A DD11 drive requires 4 minutes of processing time in assembly center one and also 4 minutes in assembly center two. The normal operation time is 60 hours per week in assembly center one and 40 hours per week in assembly center two.

Digital Devices currently has a contract to deliver 400 XT100 drives. There is almost unlimited demand for DD11 drives. The current market prices provide the following unit profits: XT100—$100 and DD11—$60. The management of Digital Devices has set the following goals in the order of their importance:

1. Produce at least 400 XT100 drives.
2. Avoid any underutilization of normal operation hours in the two assembly centers.
3. Avoid any overtime operation in assembly center one.
4. Achieve the profit goal of $60,000.

Decision Variables

x_1 = number of XT100 disk drives produced

x_2 = number of DD11 disk drives produced

Goal Constraints

XT100 Disk Drives The first goal is to produce at least 400 XT100 disk drives.

$$x_1 + d_1^- - d_1^+ = 400,$$

where d_1^- = underachievement of sales goal for XT100 drives

d_1^+ = overachievement of sales goal for XT100 drives

The above two variables are referred to as *deviational variables*. If $x_1 < 400$, then $d_1^- > 0$ and $d_1^+ = 0$. On the other hand, if $x_1 > 400$, then $d_1^+ > 0$ and $d_1^- = 0$. If $x_1 = 400$, then $d_1^- = d_1^+ = 0$. One important requirement for a goal constraint is that at least one of the deviational variables must always be zero. Thus, $d_1^- \times d_1^+ = 0$. To achieve the sales goal of 400 XT100 drives, we must minimize d_1^- to zero. This is accomplished by

$$\text{Minimize } Z = P_1 d_1^-$$

Operation Hours of Assembly Centers The second goal is to avoid underutilization of normal operation hours in the two assembly centers.

$$8x_1 + 4x_2 + d_2^- - d_2^+ = 3{,}600 \qquad \text{assembly center one}$$
$$3x_1 + 4x_2 + d_3^- - d_3^+ = 2{,}400 \qquad \text{assembly center two}$$

where d_2^- = underutilization of normal operation time of 3,600 minutes in assembly center one
d_2^+ = overtime operation in assembly center one
d_3^- = underutilization of normal operation time of 2,400 minutes in assembly center two
d_3^+ = overtime operation in assembly center two

To achieve the second goal, we should minimize the negative deviations in the above goal constraints.

$$\text{Minimize } Z = P_1d_1^- + \boxed{P_2d_2^- + P_2d_3^-}$$

where $P_1 >\!\!>\!\!> P_2$.

The sign $>\!\!>\!\!>$ means the left-hand side is very much greater than the right-hand side.

Overtime Operation in Assembly Center One To achieve the second goal, we developed the normal operation hour constraint for assembly center one. Thus, we have already defined d_2^+ as overtime operation in assembly center one. Consequently, we do not need to develop a new goal constraint to achieve the third goal. The only thing we need to do is simply to minimize d_2^+.

$$\text{Minimize } Z = P_1d_1^- + P_2d_2^- + P_2d_3^- + \boxed{P_3d_2^+}$$

Profit Goal Management's final goal is to achieve the profit goal of \$60,000. This goal constraint can be formulated as

$$100x_1 + 60x_2 + d_4^- - d_4^+ = 60{,}000,$$

where d_4^- = underachievement of \$60,000 profit
d_4^+ = overachievement of \$60,000 profit

This goal can be achieved by minimizing d_4^- as follows:

$$\text{Minimize } Z = P_1d_1^- + P_2d_2^- + P_2d_3^- + P_3d_2^+ + \boxed{P_4d_4^-}$$

Now the complete model can be presented as follows:

$$\begin{aligned} \text{Minimize } Z &= P_1d_1^- + P_2d_2^- + P_2d_3^- + P_3d_2^+ + P_4d_4^- \\ \text{subject to } x_1 + \quad & d_1^- - d_1^+ = 400 \\ 8x_1 + 4x_2 + \; & d_2^- - d_2^+ = 3{,}600 \\ 3x_1 + 4x_2 + \; & d_3^- - d_3^+ = 2{,}400 \\ 100x_1 + 60x_2 + \; & d_4^- - d_4^+ = 60{,}000 \\ & x_i, d_i^-, d_i^+ \geq 0 \end{aligned}$$

Example 8.2 Uptown Life, Inc.

Uptown Life, Inc., just purchased an old school building in the middle of the downtown area. The firm specializes in converting old buildings into offices, condominiums, and specialty shops. The new building has a total floor space of 250,000 square feet. Uptown Life is thinking of creating a truly outstanding "uptown" life center with a number of nice stores, several restaurants, condominiums, and business or service office units.

Because of the attractive location of the building and the fine reputation of Uptown Life, it has received a large number of requests about space for specialty shops, restaurants, accounting and stock-brokerage offices, and medical and dental offices. The company is trying to decide the best mix of various types of units that will make the building a real showcase for Uptown Life.

Based on the firm's past experience and the demand of floor space for various purposes, the following represents the typical floor-space requirements for each of the possible units.

Unit type	**Floor-space requirement**
Condominium	750 square feet
Shop	1,000
Office	1,200
Restaurant	3,000
Lounge, management office, open space	30,000

After considerable deliberation and consultation with architectural consultants, management of the company has set the following goals arranged in order of their priorities:

1. Utilize the entire floor space of 250,000 square feet.
2. The building must have enough condominiums to satisfy the city council request that at least 40 percent of the floor space should be devoted to housing units.
3. To have an attractive total living complex, there should be at least 30,000 square feet dedicated to a spacious lounge, information desk, front-desk area, management office, and open space.
4. There should be at least two restaurants in the building.
5. At least 50 percent of the total rental space (excluding condos and open space) should be allocated to shops and offices.
6. Maximize the total income. The expected annual income from each of the units is as follows:

Unit type	**Annual income**
Condo	$ 6,000
Shop	12,000
Office	15,000
Restaurant	30,000

Variables

x_1 = number of condominium units to be housed in the building
x_2 = number of specialty shops to be housed in the building
x_3 = number of offices to be housed in the building
x_4 = number of restaurants to be housed in the building
x_5 = number of the open-space area

System Constraints

A system constraint represents a strict restriction that must be satisfied before any of the goal constraints are considered. In a system constraint, underachievement (d^-), overachievement (d^+), or both under- and overachievement ($d^- + d^+$) must be prohibited. In effect, system constraints accomplish the same thing as $\leq$, $=$, $\geq$ type constraints. Since the building has only 250,000 square feet of floor space, the total space utilized by different types of units cannot exceed 250,000. Thus, d_1^+ cannot exist in the following constraint.

$$750x_1 + 1{,}000x_2 + 1{,}200x_3 + 3{,}000x_4 + 30{,}000x_5 + d_1^- = 250{,}000$$

Another system constraint we need in this problem is that regardless of the mix of various types of units housed in the building, there should be the required open space with other necessary management and support offices.

$$x_5 = 1$$

Goal Constraint

The first goal of the management is to utilize the entire 250,000 square feet of floor space. Management can accomplish this by simply minimizing d_1^- in the first system constraint.

The second goal of the management is to allocate at least 40 percent of the available floor space to condominiums. Management can achieve this goal if it minimizes d_2^- in the following goal constraint.

$$750x_1 + d_2^- - d_2^+ = 100{,}000$$

The third goal is to allocate at least 30,000 square feet for a spacious lounge area, information desk, front-desk area, management office, and an open space. Management can achieve this goal by minimizing d_3^+ in the following constraint.

$$750x_1 + 1{,}000x_2 + 1{,}200x_3 + 3{,}000x_4 + d_3^- - d_3^+ = 220{,}000$$

The fourth goal is to have at least two restaurants in the building. This goal can be attained by minimizing d_4^- in the following goal constraint.

$$x_4 + d_4^- - d_4^+ = 2$$

The fifth goal is to allocate at least 50 percent of the total rental space to shops and offices. The rental space represents leftover space after floor space has been allocated to the open space and condos. Thus, management should minimize d_5^- in the following constraint.

$$\begin{aligned}&1{,}000x_2 + 1{,}200x_3 + d_5^- - d_5^+ \\ &= 0.5\,(250{,}000 - 750x_1 - 30{,}000x_5), \text{ or} \\ &375x_1 + 1{,}000x_2 + 1{,}200x_3 + 15{,}000x_5 + d_5^- - d_5^+ = 125{,}000\end{aligned}$$

The last goal of management is to maximize total income from the building. To maximize total profit, management must minimize d_6^- from the following constraint. Notice that the right-hand side value is an arbitrarily large number (M). Thus, d_6^+ is eliminated in the constraint.

$$6{,}000x_1 + 12{,}000x_2 + 15{,}000x_3 + 30{,}000x_4 + d_6^- = 100{,}000{,}000$$

Now the complete model can be formulated as follows:

$$\text{Minimize } Z = P_1d_1^- + P_2d_2^- + P_3d_3^+ + P_4d_4^- + P_5d_5^- + P_6d_6^-$$

subject to

$$\begin{array}{lr}750x_1 + 1{,}000x_2 + 1{,}200x_3 + 3{,}000x_4 + 30{,}000x_5 + d_1^- = & 250{,}000\\ x_5 = & 1\\ 750x_1 + d_2^- - d_2^+ = & 100{,}000\\ 750x_1 + 1{,}000x_2 + 1{,}200x_3 + 3{,}000x_4 + d_3^- - d_3^+ = & 220{,}000\\ x_4 + d_4^- - d_4^+ = & 2\\ 375x_1 + 1{,}000x_2 + 1{,}200x_3 + 15{,}000x_5 + d_5^- - d_5^+ = & 125{,}000\\ 6{,}000x_1 + 12{,}000x_2 + 15{,}000x_3 + 30{,}000x_4 + d_6^- = & 100{,}000{,}000\\ x_j,\ d_i^-,\ d_i^+ \geq & 0\end{array}$$

Example 8.3 *First Federal Bank & Trust Co.*

Robert Heins is executive vice president of First Federal Bank & Trust Company. He is in charge of the trust department. Currently, the trust department has $10 million to invest in several preselected investment alternatives. The selected investment alternatives are: stocks, bonds, treasury notes, mutual funds, real estate, and gold futures.

Based on the research department, the expected returns during the next year from the investment alternatives are as follows: stocks—6%; bonds—7%; treasury notes—8%; mutual funds—10%; real estate—15%; and gold futures—0%. Heins consulted with the investment committee and established the following goals in order of their importance.

P_1: The first goal is to invest at least 50 percent of the total amount of funds in stocks, bonds, and mutual funds in view of the expected bullish market in the coming year.

P_2: Invest at least $2 million in the development of a new shopping center in a suburban community.

P_3: The amount of money invested in speculative alternatives (stocks and gold futures) should not exceed 40 percent of total investment.

P_4: The amount invested in each alternative should be at least 5 percent of total investment.

P_5: Secure at least 7 percent return from the total funds during the coming year.

Variables

x_1 = amount invested in stocks
x_2 = amount invested in bonds
x_3 = amount invested in treasury notes
x_4 = amount invested in mutual funds
x_5 = amount invested in real estate
x_6 = amount invested in gold futures

System Constraint

There is only one system constraint in this problem. There is only $10 million to invest. Thus, the total amount invested in the available alternatives must not exceed $10 million.

$$x_1 + x_2 + x_3 + x_4 + x_5 + x_6 \leq 10{,}000{,}000$$

Goal Constraints

1. Invest at least 50 percent of the total amount of funds available in stocks, bonds, and mutual funds.

$$x_1 + x_2 + x_4 + d_1^- - d_1^+ = 5{,}000{,}000$$

2. Invest at least $2 million in real estate (shopping center).

$$x_5 + d_2^- - d_2^+ = 2{,}000{,}000$$

3. Investment in stocks and gold futures should be less than 40 percent of total investment.

$$x_1 + x_6 + d_3^- - d_3^+ = 0.4\,(x_1 + x_2 + x_3 + x_4 + x_5 + x_6), \text{ or}$$
$$0.6x_1 - 0.4x_2 - 0.4x_3 - 0.4x_4 - 0.4x_5 + 0.6x_6 + d_3^- - d_3^+ = 0$$

4. Invest at least 5 percent of total investment in each alternative.

$$x_1 + d_3^- - d_3^+ = 0.05\,(x_1 + x_2 + x_3 + x_4 + x_5 + x_6), \text{ or}$$
$$0.95x_1 - 0.05x_2 - 0.05x_3 - 0.05x_4 - 0.05x_5 - 0.05x_6$$
$$+ d_4^- - d_4^+ = 0$$
$$-0.05x_1 + 0.95x_2 - 0.05x_3 - 0.05x_4 - 0.05x_5 - 0.05x_6$$
$$+ d_5^- - d_5^+ = 0$$
$$-0.05x_1 - 0.05x_2 + 0.95x_3 - 0.05x_4 - 0.05x_5 - 0.05x_6$$
$$+ d_6^- - d_6^+ = 0$$

$$-0.05x_1 - 0.05x_2 - 0.05x_3 + 0.95x_4 - 0.05x_5 - 0.05x_6 + d_7^- - d_7^+ = 0$$
$$-0.05x_1 - 0.05x_2 - 0.05x_3 - 0.05x_4 + 0.95x_5 - 0.05x_6 + d_8^- - d_8^+ = 0$$
$$-0.05x_1 - 0.05x_2 - 0.05x_3 - 0.05x_4 - 0.05x_5 + 0.95x_6 + d_9^- - d_9^+ = 0$$

5. Secure at least 7 percent return on $10 million.

$$0.06x_1 + 0.07x_2 + 0.08x_3 + 0.10x_4 + 0.15x_5 + d_{10}^- - d_{10}^+ = 700{,}000$$

The Objective Function

$$\text{Minimize } Z = P_1d_1^- + P_2d_2^- + P_3d_3^+ + P_4 \sum_{i=4}^{9} d_i^- + P_5d_{10}^-$$

Solution Methods of Goal Programming

In this section, we will discuss two solution methods of goal programming: the graphical method and the modified simplex method. The *Micro Manager* applies the modified simplex method in solving goal-programming problems. The graphical method is useful for those goal-programming problems that involve only two decision variables. On the other hand, the modified simplex method is a more general solution technique for all types of goal-programming problems.

Before we discuss the solution methods, we should discuss a couple of important features of goal programming. First of all, goal programming is useful for three types of analyses: (1) to determine the input (resource) requirements to achieve a set of goals; (2) to determine the degree of attainment of defined goals with the given amount of resources; and (3) to obtain the most satisfactory solution under the varying inputs, aspiration levels, and priority structures.

In goal programming, we attempt to achieve multiple aspirations or goals to satisfactory levels rather than trying to optimize a single global objective function. The basic approach we take is to minimize deviations between our goals and what can be actually achieved under the given set of constraints and priorities of goals. To achieve various goals, we have the following three basic options open in the objective function:

Minimize	**Goal**	**If goal is achieved**
d_i^-	Minimize the underachievement	$d_i^- = 0, d_i^+ \geq 0$
d_i^+	Minimize the overachievement	$d_i^- \geq 0, d_i^+ = 0$
$d_i^- + d_i^+$	Minimize both under- and overachievement	$d_i^- = 0, d_i^+ = 0$

Figure 8.1 A Graphical Solution

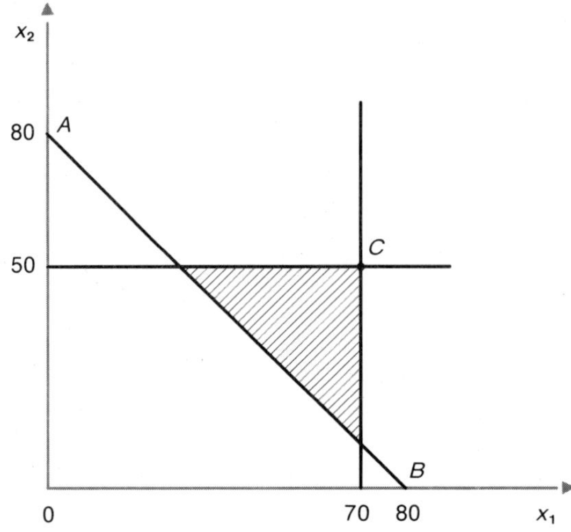

The Graphical Method

The graphical method is useful only for those problems with two decision variables. Let us consider the following example.

$$
\begin{aligned}
\text{Minimize } Z &= P_1d_1^- + P_2d_2^- + P_3d_3^- \\
\text{subject to } x_1 + x_2 + d_1^- - d_1^+ &= 80 \quad \text{Production goal constraint} \\
x_1 + \qquad d_2^- &= 70 \\
x_2 + d_3^- &= 50 \quad \text{(Sales goal constraint)} \\
x_j, d_i^-, d_i^+ &\geq 0
\end{aligned}
$$

In goal programming, we attempt to minimize the deviation from the goal with the highest priority to its fullest possible extent. Then the goal with the second highest priority factor is considered, and so on. The sequential "satisficing" procedure is used in the graphical method.

First, the production goal constraint is plotted on a graph as shown in Fig. 8.1. Since the first goal is to minimize d_1^-, the feasible region becomes on or above the straight line *AB*. Any solution in this feasible region will achieve the first goal because $d_1^- = 0$. The second goal is to minimize d_2^-. Since d_2^+ does not exist in the constraint, when we minimize d_2^- all the way to zero the solution must be exactly on the straight line $x_1 = 70$. The third goal is to minimize d_3^-. Again, there is no d_3^+ in the goal constraint. Thus, the solution must be exactly on the line $x_2 = 50$. The solution point that satisfies all three goals is at point *C*.

The optimum solution is point *C*, where $x_1 = 70$, $x_2 = 50$, $d_1^+ = 40$. At this solution point all three goals are completely attained because there is no conflict among the goals.

The Modified Simplex Method

The modified simplex method is an iterative algorithm just like the regular simplex method for linear programming. Because of the unique features of the goal-programming model, a number of modifications are necessary in the simplex operation. Let us consider the following slightly modified version of the problem we solved by the graphical method.

$$\begin{aligned}
\text{Minimize } Z &= P_1d_1^- + P_2d_4^+ + 2P_3d_2^- + 3P_3d_3^- \\
\text{subject to } x_1 + x_2 + d_1^- - d_1^+ &= 80 \\
x_1 + d_2^- &= 70 \\
x_2 + d_3^- &= 50 \\
x_1 + 2x_2 + d_4^- - d_4^+ &= 150 \\
x_j, d_i^-, d_i^+ &\geq 0
\end{aligned}$$

The modified simplex method of goal programming involves the following steps.

Developing the Initial Simplex Tableau

Similar to linear programming, the initial solution always starts at the origin where all the decision variables and positive deviational variables have a value of zero. This leaves all of the negative deviational variables, each with a solution value. Like linear programming, these variables represent the initial solution and are entered into the basis column. Their solution values are also entered into the solution column. It is a rule that negative deviational variables (d_i^-) in each of the constraints become the basic variables in the initial tableau. In our example, when zero is substituted into the decision variables, the system of constraints becomes

$$\begin{aligned}
d_1^- &= 80 \\
d_2^- &= 70 \\
d_3^- &= 50 \\
d_4^- &= 150
\end{aligned}$$

Then the variables and their solution values are entered into the initial simplex tableau as shown in Table 8.1.

As discussed earlier, c_j values are replaced by the preemptive priority factors or differential weights. Variables without preemptive priority factors are considered to have zero c_j value. The c_j values of the variables in our example are also shown in Table 8.1. (See p. 180.)

All coefficients are recorded in the tableau exactly the same way as in the simplex method of linear programming. The z_j-value row is completely eliminated in the modified simplex tableau for goal programming. This may result in more calculation. However, for simplicity and readability, it is well worth the inconvenience.

Table 8.1 The initial simplex tableau

c_b \ c_j	Basis	Solution	0	0	P_1	$2P_3$	$3P_3$	0	0	P_2	
			x_1	x_2	d_1^-	d_2^-	d_3^-	d_4^-	d_1^+	d_4^+	
P_1	d_1^-	80	1	1	1	0	0	0	−1	0	
$2P_3$	d_2^-	70	1	0	0	1	0	0	0	0	
$3P_3$	d_3^-	50	0	1	0	0	1	0	0	0	←Pivot row
0	d_4^-	150	1	2	0	0	0	1	0	−1	
$z_j - c_j$	P_3	290	2	3	0	0	0	0	0	0	
	P_2	0	0	0	0	0	0	0	0	−1	
	P_1	80	1	1	0	0	0	0	−1	0	

↑ Pivot column (x_2)

Since goal programming is always a minimization technique, $z_j - c_j$ values are used. All $z_j - c_j$ values are stored in a $k \times n$ matrix, where k is the number of preemptive priority levels and n is the total number of decision and deviational variables. Before obtaining the $z_j - c_j$ values, the z_j values must be computed. They are computed in exactly the same way as in the simplex method of linear programming. The calculation is shown as follows:

Column	**Σ (c_b × solution values)**	**= z_j (solution)**	**$z_j - c_j$**
Solution	$P_1 \times 80 + 2P_3 \times 70 + 3P_3 \times 50 + 0 \times 150$	$= 80P_1 + 0P_2 + 290P_3$	$80P_1 + 0P_2 + 290P_3$

Variable	**Σ (c_b × coefficients)**	**$=z_j$**	**c_j**	**$z_j - c_j$**
x_1	$P_1 \times 1 + 2P_3 \times 1 + 3P_3 \times 0 + 0 \times 1$	$= 1P_1 + 2P_3$	0	$1P_1 + 2P_3$
x_2	$P_1 \times 1 + 2P_3 \times 0 + 3P_3 \times 1 + 0 \times 2$	$= 1P_1 + 3P_3$	0	$1P_1 + 3P_3$
d_1^-	$P_1 \times 1 + 2P_3 \times 0 + 3P_3 \times 0 + 0 \times 0$	$= P_1$	P_1	0
d_2^-	$P_1 \times 0 + 2P_3 \times 1 + 3P_3 \times 0 + 0 \times 0$	$= 2P_3$	$2P_3$	0
d_3^-	$P_1 \times 0 + 2P_3 \times 0 + 3P_3 \times 1 + 0 \times 0$	$= 3P_3$	$3P_3$	0
d_4^-	$P_1 \times 0 + 2P_3 \times 0 + 3P_3 \times 0 + 0 \times 1$	$= 0$	0	0
d_1^+	$P_1 \times (-1) + 2P_3 \times 0 + 3P_3 \times 0 + 0 \times 0$	$= -1P_1$	0	$-1P_1$
d_4^+	$P_1 \times 0 + 2P_3 \times 0 + 3P_3 \times 0 + 0 \times (-1)$	$= 0$	P_2	$-1P_2$

Once the $z_j - c_j$ values of each column are calculated, they are filled into the $z_j - c_j$ matrix. Since preemptive priority factors P_j are not commensurable, each of their coefficients is entered separately into the appropriate row and column as shown in Table 8.1. In our example, the $z_j - c_j$ matrix has a dimension of 3 × 8 since there are three preemptive priority levels and eight variables (two decision and six deviational). Notice that the $z_j - c_j$ of the solution column has as its second row $P_2 = 0$. When a $z_j - c_j$ element has a zero value in the solution column, it merely means that the goal is completely achieved. In our case, $P_2 = 0$. Thus, the goal assigned with priority P_2 is fulfilled. However, we should understand the reason behind it. At the origin, everything is idle and there is no production. Obviously, there is no overtime involved for the labor force.

The finished initial simplex tableau of our goal-programming problem is shown in Table 8.1.

Selecting the Pivot Column

Similar to the simplex method of linear programming, the basic approach in selecting the pivot column is to choose the column with the largest nonnegative $z_j - c_j$ value. Recall the relationship of preemptive priority factors $P_1 >>> P_2 >>> P_3 >>> P_{k-1} >>> P_k$, where $>>>$ means "very much greater than." When this is applied, the values of each $z_j - c_j$ column can easily be compared and the one with the largest value is chosen as the pivot column. The largest $z_j - c_j$ values must be nonnegative values at the highest priority level where the goal is not completely attained.

The following procedure shows another approach for selecting the pivot column. Starting from the bottom row of the $z_j - c_j$ matrix, select the column with the largest $z_j - c_j$ value. If only one column is found, it is the pivot column. If there is no positive value in this row, move up one row and find the column with the largest positive $z_j - c_j$ value. If this column has no negative elements at higher-priority levels, it is the pivot column. This process is repeated. If no such column can be found, the solution is reached. If there exists a tie between columns, check the next row with a lower-priority level. The column with a larger positive value at the lower-priority level breaks the tie and will be selected as the pivot column. If the tie remains when it reaches the lowest $z_j - c_j$ row, select one on an arbitrary basis.

In our example, the initial simplex tableau is shown in Table 8.1. The second column (x_2) is chosen as the pivot column. There is a tie between the columns of x_1 and x_2 in the P_1 row. The tie remains when the next level of priority (P_2) is considered. However, when we move up to the third row (P_3), the column of x_2 has a larger positive value and thus it is chosen as the pivot column. Now x_2 is the entering variable.

Determining the Pivot Row

To select the pivot row, divide each solution value by the coefficient on the same row in the pivot column. The row that has the minimum nonnegative quotient is chosen as the pivot row. If a tie between rows exists, select the one with a higher-priority deviational variable. In our example, the outgoing variable is found to be d_3^- in row number 3.

Table 8.2 The second simplex tableau

c_b \ c_j	Basis	Solution	0 x_1	0 x_2	P_1 d_1^-	$2P_3$ d_2^-	$3P_3$ d_3^-	0 d_4^-	0 d_1^+	P_2 d_4^+	
P_1	d_1^-	30	(1)	0	1	0	−1	0	−1	0	←Pivot row
$2P_3$	d_2^-	70	1	0	0	1	0	0	0	0	
0	x_2	50	0	1	0	0	1	0	0	0	
0	d_4^-	50	1	0	0	0	−2	1	0	−1	
	P_3	140	2	0	0	0	−3	0	0	0	
$z_j - c_j$	P_2	0	0	0	0	0	0	0	0	−1	
	P_1	30	1	0	0	0	−1	0	−1	0	
			↑ Pivot column								

Determining the New Solution

The procedure for determining the new solution tableau is the same as that of the simplex method of linear programming. First, each element of the pivot row is divided by the pivot element, that is, the element at the intersection of the pivot column and pivot row. The new value of each element in the other rows is calculated with the following formula:

$$\text{New value} = \text{Old value} - (\text{Row value} \times \text{New value in pivot row})$$

The row value is the element at the intersection of the given row and the pivot column. The new $z_j - c_j$ matrix is also computed in order to complete the tableau. The new tableau (second simplex tableau) of our example is shown in Table 8.2.

In our new tableau, x_2 is introduced with a value of 50, indicating that the company is producing 50 units of x_2. In fact, the negative deviational variable d_3^- is eliminated from the solution basis, which implies the achievement of that particular goal—the minimization of the sales capacity deviations for x_2. If we look at the z_j (solution) column and compare it with the old z_j (solution) column (new $= 30P_1 + 140P_3$ compared to the old one $= 80P_1 + 290P_3$), we find that the new z_j (solution) has a smaller numeric value. This indicates that a portion of the unattained goal has now been achieved.

Test the Optimality

To determine whether a solution is optimum, we inspect the $z_j - c_j$ matrix. If the z_j (solution) value is zero, the solution is reached. If positive values are in the $z_j - c_j$ matrix, and for every positive value in the $z_j - c_j$ matrix at least one negative value exists at its higher-priority level in the same column, then the final solution is attained.

Table 8.3 The third tableau

c_b \ c_j	Basis	Solution	0 x_1	0 x_2	P_1 d_1^-	$2P_3$ d_2^-	$3P_3$ d_3^-	0 d_4^-	0 d_1^+	P_2 d_4^+	
0	x_1	30	1	0	1	0	−1	0	−1	0	
$2P_3$	d_2^-	40	0	0	−1	1	1	0	1	0	
0	x_2	50	0	1	0	0	1	0	0	0	
0	d_4^-	20	0	0	−1	0	−1	1	(1)	−1	←Pivot row
$z_j - c_j$	P_3	80	0	0	−2	0	−1	0	2	0	
	P_2	0	0	0	0	0	0	0	0	−1	
	P_1	0	0	0	−1	0	0	0	0	0	
									↑ Pivot column		

When we inspect the $z_j - c_j$ matrix of the second tableau, neither case is true. Therefore, the solution has not been reached yet. The pivot column (x_1) and pivot row (d_1^-) are determined and the third tableau is completed. It is shown in Table 8.3. In this new tableau, it is found that with $x_1 = 30$ and $x_2 = 50$, the z_j (solution) decreases to $80P_3$. Both P_1 and P_2 are dropped from the z_j (solution) column. This implies that the two most important goals are achieved completely, leaving only a portion of the third goal unattained. We can also observe that there is an underachievement of the second goal constraint ($d_2^- = 40$) and under-achievement of the fourth goal constraint ($d_4^- = 20$).

Computation continues for two more tableaux before the optimum solution is found. The fourth tableau is shown in Table 8.4 while the final tableau is shown in Table 8.5. (See p. 184.) Notice in the fourth tableau, column d_4^+ has a $z_j - c_j$ value of $2P_3 - P_2$. This column is not chosen as the pivot column because if the variable d_4^+ is introduced, we are simply trying to achieve the P_3 goal at the expense of P_2. For this reason, column d_4^+ is not chosen; d_3^- is selected as the entering variable.

Let us study the last tableau. First, we notice that in the $z_j - c_j$ matrix, every positive value has at least one negative value at its higher priority levels. This indicates that the optimum solution has been reached. The solution shows that the company should produce 70 units of x_1 and 40 units of x_2. There is an underutilization of 10 units in the sales capacity of x_2 and an overutilization of 30 hours of the production capacity.

The unattained portion of the goal of our example is shown by the nonzero z_j (solution) value, which is $30P_3$. This is further verified by the positive value (3/2) in column d_4^+ at the $z_j - c_j$ matrix. The positive value implies that these are conflicting goals. The conflict occurs between the goals P_3 and P_2. Actually,

Table 8.4 The fourth tableau

c_b \ c_j	Basis	Solution	0 x_1	0 x_2	P_1 d_1^-	$2P_3$ d_2^-	$3P_3$ d_3^-	0 d_4^-	0 d_1^+	P_2 d_4^+	
0	x_1	50	1	0	0	0	−2	1	0	−1	
$2P_3$	d_2^-	20	0	0	0	1	(2)	−1	0	1	←Pivot row
0	x_2	50	0	1	0	0	1	0	0	0	
0	d_1^+	20	0	0	−1	0	−1	1	1	−1	
$z_j - c_j$	P_3	40	0	0	0	0	1	−2	0	2	
	P_2	0	0	0	0	0	0	0	0	−1	
	P_1	0	0	0	−1	0	0	0	0	0	
							↑ Pivot column				

Table 8.5 The final tableau

c_b \ c_j	Basis	Solution	0 x_1	0 x_2	P_1 d_1^-	$2P_3$ d_2^-	$3P_3$ d_3^-	0 d_4^-	0 d_1^+	P_2 d_4^+
0	x_1	70	1	0	0	1	0	0	0	0
$3P_3$	d_3^-	10	0	0	0	1/2	1	−1/2	0	1/2
0	x_2	40	0	1	0	−1/2	0	1/2	0	−1/2
0	d_1^+	30	0	0	−1	1/2	0	1/2	1	−1/2
$z_j - c_j$	P_3	30	0	0	0	−1/2	0	−3/2	0	3/2
	P_2	0	0	0	0	0	0	0	0	−1
	P_1	0	0	0	−1	0	0	0	0	0

Optimum solution reached: $x_1 = 70$, $x_2 = 40$, $d_1^+ = 30$, and $d_3^- = 10$.

goal conflicts could serve as a warning device to the decision maker for the evaluation of the soundness of the priority structure of the goals. The decision maker may wish to minimize the degree of conflict by rearranging the priority of the goals.

The decision maker should study the optimum solution carefully. In our example, the optimum solution shows an overutilization of 30 hours of production capacity. The decision maker should decide if that is possible or not. If it is not possible, the decision maker must revise the goal levels or their priorities.

Some Complications

In applying goal programming to multiple-objective decision problems, we may face a number of complicated situations. We will discuss some of these complications.

A Negative Right-Hand Side Value

If a goal constraint has a negative right-hand side value, we must multiply both sides of the constraint by -1 to make the right-hand side value positive. Then, we introduce the deviational variables to the goal constraint. If we want to minimize the positive deviation in the original constraint, we must minimize the negative deviational variable in the new goal constraint, and vice versa.

A Tie in Selecting the Incoming Variable

In selecting the pivot column, we look for the largest $z_j - c_j$ value at the highest-priority level. If two or more columns have the same largest $z_j - c_j$ value and the tie cannot be broken even at lower-priority levels, then we can select one of the tied columns as the pivot column on an arbitrary basis.

A Tie in Selecting the Outgoing Variable

In selecting the pivot row, we divide solution values by the associated positive coefficients in the pivot column. The row with the minimum nonnegative quotient is selected as the pivot row. If two or more rows have the same minimum nonnegative quotient, we can select the row that has the highest c_b (priority factor) as the pivot column.

Multiple-Optimum Solutions

If one or more of the nonbasic variable columns have zero $z_j - c_j$ values in the final simplex tableau, we have a situation of multiple-optimum solutions. Such a situation usually does not occur when conflicts exist among the goals.

An Infeasible Problem

When we have system constraints in a goal-programming model, we need to assign the superpriority (P_0) for these constraints. If a conflict exists among the system constraints, z_j values at the P_0 priority level will be positive in the final simplex tableau. Unless the conflict among system constraints can be resolved, the problem will remain an infeasible problem.

Advanced Topics

During the past decade, a number of important advances have been made in the area of goal programming. Some of the prominent new developments include sensitivity analysis, integer programming, zero–one programming, interactive systems, decomposition goal programming, chance-constrained goal programming, and nonlinear goal programming. If you are interested, consult the references at the end of this chapter.

Application of the *Micro Manager*

This section contains an example of an application of the *Micro Manager* to a multiple objective decision problem. The program diskette provides the complete information about goal programming, including the purpose of the technique, the solution of a sample problem, interactive input instructions, and the batch input procedure. This section presents only the information (purpose of the technique and the batch input data format) and the solution of a sample problem using the interactive input format of Goal Programming I and Goal Programming II.

```
<< PURPOSE >>

GOAL PROGRAMMING determines a satisficing solution for a decision-making
problem with multiple objectives.  This program can handle GP problems with up
to 50 decision variables and 40 constraints.  Initial and final tableaus will
be given, in addition to the final solution.

<<  BATCH INPUT DATA FORMAT  >>

Type in the values of the following input data requirements, after creating a
new file.  You may enter as many values as you want in a line, separating them
by commas for alphabetic characters and by commas or blank spaces for numeric
values.  However, the input data must be exactly in the following order:

1. Number of decision variables (maximum 50)
2. Number of constraints (maximum 40)
3. Number of priorities
4. Number of deviational variables in the objective function
5. Type of each constraint:
     For goal constraint type:
        B   :  d- and d+ (minimize d- and/or d+)
        L   :  d-        (minimize d-)
        G   :  d- and d+ (minimize d+)
     For system constraint type:
        E   :  equal to                 ( = )
        L   :  less than or equal to    ( <= )
        G   :  greater than or equal to ( >= )
6. Information for the priority structure
     6.1. N for negative or P for positive
     6.2. constraint number
     6.3. priority
     6.4. weight
7. Coefficient of each decision variable for each constraint
8. Right-hand side value of each constraint
```

```
** Sample Batch Input Data Set (Example 8.1) **

2                    ; two variables
4                    ; four constraints
4                    ; four priorities
5                    ; five deviational variables in the objective function
B,B,B,B              ; types of constraints
N,1,1,1              ; information for priority 1
N,2,2,1              ; information for priority 2
N,3,2,1              ; information for priority 2
P,2,3,1              ; information for priority 3
N,4,4,1              ; information for priority 4
1,0                  ; coefficients of variables in constraint 1
8,4                  ; coefficients of variables in constraint 2
3,4                  ; coefficients of variables in constraint 3
100,60               ; coefficients of variables in constraint 4
400,3600,2400,60000 ; right-hand side values of constraints

PROGRAM: Goal Programming

Enter number of decision variables: 2
Enter number of constraints: 4
Enter number of priority levels: 4
Enter number of deviational variables in the objective function: 5

Type of each constraint:
   Goal constraint type:   L (<=), G (>=), or B
   System constraint type: L (<=), G (>=), or E (=)
Enter type of constraint 1 : b
Enter type of constraint 2 : b
Enter type of constraint 3 : b
Enter type of constraint 4 : b

* Information for the priority structure *

Enter 'N'(neg.) OR 'P'(pos.), constraint number, priority, weight: n,1,1,1
Enter 'N'(neg.) OR 'P'(pos.), constraint number, priority, weight: n,2,2,1
Enter 'N'(neg.) OR 'P'(pos.), constraint number, priority, weight: n,3,2,1
Enter 'N'(neg.) OR 'P'(pos.), constraint number, priority, weight: p,2,3,1
Enter 'N'(neg.) OR 'P'(pos.), constraint number, priority, weight: n,4,4,1

Enter coefficient of decision variable  1  in constraint  1 : 1
Enter coefficient of decision variable  2  in constraint  1 : 0

Enter coefficient of decision variable  1  in constraint  2 : 8
Enter coefficient of decision variable  2  in constraint  2 : 4

Enter coefficient of decision variable  1  in constraint  3 : 3
Enter coefficient of decision variable  2  in constraint  3 : 4

Enter coefficient of decision variable  1  in constraint  4 : 100
Enter coefficient of decision variable  2  in constraint  4 : 60

Enter right-hand side value (RHS) of constraint 1 : 400
Enter right-hand side value (RHS) of constraint 2 : 3600
Enter right-hand side value (RHS) of constraint 3 : 2400
Enter right-hand side value (RHS) of constraint 4 : 60000
```

```
PROGRAM: Goal Programming

***** INPUT DATA ENTERED *****

Min  Z = P 1 dn 1  + P 2 dn 2  + P 2 dn 3  + P 3 dp 2  + P 4 dn 4

Subject to:

C 1    1 x 1 + dn 1 - dp 1  =  400
C 2    8 x 1 + 4 x 2 + dn 2 - dp 2  =  3600
C 3    3 x 1 + 4 x 2 + dn 3 - dp 3  =  2400
C 4    100 x 1 + 60 x 2 + dn 4 - dp 4  =  60000

*****   PROGRAM OUTPUT   *****

Initial tableau
```

C#	Cb	Basis	Bi
C 1	1P 1	-d 1	400.00
C 2	1P 2	-d 2	3600.00
C 3	1P 2	-d 3	2400.00
C 4	1P 4	-d 4	60000.00

\Cj C#	1P 1 -d 1	1P 2 -d 2	1P 2 -d 3	1P 4 -d 4	0 +d 1	1P 3 +d 2
C 1	1.00	0.00	0.00	0.00	-1.00	0.00
C 2	0.00	1.00	0.00	0.00	0.00	-1.00
C 3	0.00	0.00	1.00	0.00	0.00	0.00
C 4	0.00	0.00	0.00	1.00	0.00	0.00
P 4	0.00	0.00	0.00	0.00	0.00	0.00
P 3	0.00	0.00	0.00	0.00	0.00	-1.00
P 2	0.00	0.00	0.00	0.00	0.00	-1.00
P 1	0.00	0.00	0.00	0.00	-1.00	0.00

\Cj C#	0 +d 3	0 +d 4	0 x 1	0 x 2
C 1	0.00	0.00	1.00	0.00
C 2	0.00	0.00	8.00	4.00
C 3	-1.00	0.00	3.00	4.00
C 4	0.00	-1.00	100.00	60.00
P 4	0.00	-1.00	100.00	60.00
P 3	0.00	0.00	0.00	0.00
P 2	-1.00	0.00	11.00	8.00
P 1	0.00	0.00	1.00	0.00

Final tableau (iteration 4)

C#	Cb	Basis	Bi
C 1	0	x 1	400.00
C 2	0	x 2	300.00
C 3	1P 3	+d 2	800.00
C 4	1P 4	-d 4	2000.00

\Cj	1P 1	1P 2	1P 2	1P 4	0	1P 3
C#	-d 1	-d 2	-d 3	-d 4	+d 1	+d 2
C 1	1.00	0.00	0.00	0.00	-1.00	0.00
C 2	-0.75	0.00	0.25	0.00	0.75	0.00
C 3	5.00	-1.00	1.00	0.00	-5.00	1.00
C 4	-55.00	0.00	-15.00	1.00	55.00	0.00
P 4	-55.00	0.00	-15.00	0.00	55.00	0.00
P 3	5.00	-1.00	1.00	0.00	-5.00	0.00
P 2	0.00	-1.00	-1.00	0.00	0.00	0.00
P 1	-1.00	0.00	0.00	0.00	0.00	0.00

\Cj	0	0	0	0
C#	+d 3	+d 4	x 1	x 2
C 1	0.00	0.00	1.00	0.00
C 2	-0.25	0.00	0.00	1.00
C 3	-1.00	0.00	0.00	0.00
C 4	15.00	-1.00	0.00	0.00
P 4	15.00	-1.00	0.00	0.00
P 3	-1.00	0.00	0.00	0.00
P 2	0.00	0.00	0.00	0.00
P 1	0.00	0.00	0.00	0.00

Analysis of deviations

Constraint	RHS Value	d+	d-
C 1	400.00	0.00	0.00
C 2	3600.00	800.00	0.00
C 3	2400.00	0.00	0.00
C 4	60000.00	0.00	2000.00

Analysis of decision variables

Variable	Solution value
x 1	400.00
x 2	300.00

Analysis of the objective function

Priority	Nonachievement
P 1	0.00
P 2	0.00
P 3	800.00
P 4	2000.00

Summary

Most managerial problems involve multiple, conflicting objectives. In this chapter, we have examined the concept, application areas, model formulations, and solution methods of goal programming as a "satisficing" approach. Goal programming captures a rich set of properties of a real-world decision environment by incorporating the decision-maker's judgment about organizational goals and their priorities. The *Micro Manager* in an interactive mode makes goal programming a truly flexible decision-making tool for problems with multiple objectives.

References

Charnes, A., and W. W. Cooper. 1961. *Management models and industrial applications of linear programming.* New York: John Wiley & Sons.

Ignizio, J. P. 1976. *Goal programming and extensions.* Lexington, MA: Lexington Books.

Ijiri, Y. 1965. *Management goals and accounting for control.* Chicago: Rand McNally.

Lee, S. M. 1971. Decision analysis through goal programming. *Decision Sciences* 2, 172–180.

———. 1972. *Goal programming for decision analysis.* Philadelphia: Auerback Publishers.

———. 1979. *Goal programming methods for multiple objective integer programs.* Atlanta: American Institute of Industrial Engineers.

———. 1981. *Management by multiple objectives.* Princeton, NJ: Petrocelli Books.

———. 1983. *Introduction to management science.* Chicago: Dryden.

Lee, S. M., and E. R. Clayton. 1972. A goal programming model for academic resource allocation. *Management Science* 18, 395–408.

Lee, S. M., and R. Morris. 1977. Integer goal programming methods. In *Multiple criteria decision making,* ed. M. Starr and M. Zeleny, 273–89. TIMS Studies in the Management Sciences, 6. Amsterdam: North-Holland.

Lee, S. M., and J. Wynne. 1981. Separable goal programming. In *Multiple criteria analysis,* ed. P. Nijkamp and J. Spronk, 117–36. Hampshire, England: Gower.

Simon, H. A. 1955. A behavioral model of rational choice. *Quarterly Journal of Economics* 69, 99–118.

Spronk, J. 1981. *Interactive multiple goal programming.* Boston: Martinus Nijhoff Publishing.

Zeleny, M. 1982. *Multiple criteria decision making.* New York: McGraw-Hill.

Problems

1. Solve the following goal-programming problem by using the graphical method.

$$\begin{aligned} \text{Minimize } Z &= P_1d_1^- + P_2(d_2^- + d_2^+) + P_3d_3^- \\ \text{subject to } 2x_1 + 4x_2 + d_1^- - d_1^+ &= 100 \\ x_1 \qquad + d_2^- - d_2^+ &= 15 \\ x_2 + d_3^- - d_3^+ &= 20 \\ x_j, d_i^-, d_i^+ &\geq 0 \end{aligned}$$

2. Solve the following goal-programming problem by using the graphical method.

$$\begin{aligned} \text{Minimize } Z &= P_1d_1^+ + P_2d_2^- + P_3d_3^- \\ \text{subject to } x_1 + x_2 + d_1^- - d_1^+ &= 20 \\ x_1 \qquad + d_2^- - d_2^+ &= 10 \\ 40x_1 + 30x_2 + d_3^- - d_3^+ &= 900 \\ x_j, d_i^-, d_i^+ &\geq 0 \end{aligned}$$

3. Solve the following goal-programming problem by using the *Micro Manager.*

$$\begin{aligned} \text{Minimize } Z &= P_1d_1^+ + P_2d_3^+ + 2P_3d_2^- + P_3d_4^- + P_4d_5^+ + 8P_5d_2^+ \\ &\quad + 4P_5d_4^+ \\ \text{subject to } 2x_1 + 3x_2 + 5x_3 + d_1^- - d_1^+ &= 4{,}000 \\ x_1 \qquad + d_2^- - d_2^+ &= 1{,}800 \\ x_2 + x_3 + d_3^- - d_3^+ &= 5{,}000 \\ x_3 + d_4^- - d_4^+ &= 800 \\ 15x_1 + 9x_2 - 6x_3 + d_5^- - d_5^+ &= 26{,}000 \\ x_j, d_i^-, d_i^+ &\geq 0 \end{aligned}$$

4. The Super-Star Company produces three models of microcomputers—SS100, SS150, and SS250. Most of the components are imported from the Far East and the company only assembles the microcomputers. The operation hours required to produce one unit of the microcomputers are 2 hours for SS100, 3 hours for SS150, and 4 hours for SS250. The normal capacity of the assembly line is 400 hours per month. The profits per unit are \$100 for SS100, \$150 for SS150, and \$250 for SS250. The president of the company has set the following goals according to their order of importance:

   (a) Avoid the underutilization of production capacity.
   (b) Meet the outstanding orders—30 units for SS100, 20 units for SS150, and 50 units for SS250.
   (c) Avoid the overutilization of the production capacity.
   (d) Maximize total profit as much as possible.

   Formulate a goal-programming model for the problem and solve it by using the *Micro Manager.*

5. A company produces two products—products A and B. The resources requirements and selling prices are as follows.

	Material (units)	Labor (hr)	Selling price ($)
Product A	2	3	12
Product B	6	3	20

It has available 80 units of materials and 60 hours of labor per day at normal capacity. The president of the company wishes to achieve the following goals:

(a) Avoid the underutilization of both resources.

(b) Limit overtime operation of labor to 20 hours.

(c) Achieve a sales goal of $800.

Formulate a goal-programming model and solve it by using the *Micro Manager*.

6. The Colony-Center Shopping Mall is planning its advertising for the next year. The total budget is set at $100,000. One spot of TV advertising costs $500 and reaches 8,000 audiences. One spot of radio advertising costs $100 and reaches 2,000 audiences. One insertion of local newspaper advertising costs $200 and reaches 5,000 audiences. The president of the company has established the following goals for the advertising campaign in the order of their importance:

(a) The total budget should not exceed $100,000.

(b) Meet the contract with the TV station that requires the company to spend at least $20,000 in TV advertising.

(c) The newspaper advertising expenditures should not exceed $20,000.

(d) Maximize the audience for the advertising campaign.

Formulate a goal-programming model for this problem and solve it by using the *Micro Manager*.

7. A shoe manufacturer produces hiking boots and ski boots. Its manufacturing process consists of sewing and stretching. It has available 60 hours per week for the sewing process and 80 hours per week for the stretching process at normal capacity. The firm realizes profits of $15 per pair on hiking boots and $10 per pair on ski boots. It requires 2 hours of sewing and 5 hours of stretching to produce one pair of hiking boots, and

3 hours of sewing and 2 hours of stretching to produce one pair of ski boots. The president of the company wishes to achieve the following goals, listed in the order of their importance:

(a) Achieve the profit goal of $525 per week.
(b) Limit the overtime operation of the sewing center to 30 hours.
(c) Meet the sales goal for each type of boot—25 hiking boots and 20 ski boots.
(d) Avoid any underutilization of regular operation hours of the sewing center.

Formulate a goal-programming model and solve it by using the *Micro Manager*.

8. The Pinocchio Nut Company wishes to market two special nut mixes during the holiday season. Mix 1 contains ½ pound of peanuts and ½ pound of cashews. Mix 2 contains ½ pound of peanuts, ¼ pound of cashews, and ¼ pound of almonds. Mix 1 sells for $2 per pound, and mix 2 sells for $3 per pound. In its warehouse, Pinocchio has 3,000 pounds of peanuts, 1,200 pounds of cashews, and 600 pounds of almonds. The company has set the following goals in the order of their importance:

(a) Eliminate the stock of peanuts in the warehouse.
(b) Avoid new purchases of cashews and almonds.
(c) Achieve the following sales goals: Mix 1—2,000 lb; mix 2—1,200 lb. Assign differential weights to these two goals based on their sales prices.
(d) Minimize the leftovers of cashews and almonds in the warehouse.

Formulate a goal-programming model and solve it by using the *Micro Manager*.

9. General Caster, who is chief of an ordinance department, has a problem allocating rifles to fortresses. Two armories produce the rifles and then distribute them to five fortresses. The estimated distribution costs for shipping a rifle from an armory to a fortress are shown in the following table.

Armory	**Fortresses**				
	1	2	3	4	5
1	$0.03	$0.02	$0.01	$0.03	$0.04
2	0.06	0.05	0.03	0.02	0.02

Production capacity at each armory is 3,000 units at normal capacity. The general has established the following goals according to their importance:

(a) Supply at least 1,000 units to fortress 2.
(b) Avoid the overutilization of both armories.
(c) Supply at least 2,000 units to the northwest area, which includes fortresses 1 and 4, and at least 2,000 units to the southwest area, which includes fortresses 3 and 5.
(d) Avoid the underutilization of armory 1.
(e) Minimize the total distribution cost.

Formulate a goal-programming model and solve it by using the *Micro Manager.*

10. A university plans to expand its sporting facilities. The total budget available for this project is $900,000. The students need four different types of facilities: tennis courts, swimming pools, gymnasiums, and athletic fields. The detailed data concerning this project are shown in the following table.

Facility	Estimated demand	Cost ($)	Required acres	Expected usage (individuals/week)
Tennis court	8	$ 20,000	2	500
Swimming pool	3	100,000	5	1,000
Athletic field	3	80,000	8	2,000
Gymnasium	2	200,000	4	1,500

Although 50 acres of land are available for this project, this amount can be increased if necessary. The university has set the following goals in the order of their importance:

(a) Total budget should not exceed $900,000.
(b) The university desires that the facilities be used by more than 14,000 individuals per week.
(c) The university wishes to meet the estimated demand for each facility. Differential weights should be assigned to these goals based on the expected usage.
(d) The university does not want to allocate more than 50 acres to the project.

Formulate a goal-programming model and solve it by using the *Micro Manager.*

11. Tele-Bell Corporation has a scheduling problem. Operators needed and their wages are shown in the following table.

	Time period	Operators needed	Wage ($/hour)
Morning	Midnight to 4 A.M.	20	16
	4 A.M. to 8 A.M.	40	16
Daytime	8 A.M. to noon	200	8
	Noon to 4 P.M.	160	8
Evening	4 P.M. to 8 P.M.	120	12
	8 P.M. to midnight	60	16

Operators work 8-hour shifts and begin work at midnight, 4 A.M., 8 A.M., noon, 4 P.M., or 8 P.M. The personnel manager has set the following goals in the order of their importance:

(a) Secure the required number of operators in the daytime to maintain a 100% service level.

(b) Secure at least 80% of the operators needed in the morning and evening.

(c) Minimize the labor cost.

Formulate a goal-programming model and solve it by using the *Micro Manager.*

12. The Osburn Company faces a production-planning problem for the next year. The estimated demands and the capacity per quarter are shown in the following table.

Quarter	Demands (in units)	Capacities (in units)
1	80	140
2	170	140
3	220	150
4	120	100

The production manager has set the following goals in the order of their importance:

(a) Avoid any underutilization of regular time operations.
(b) Meet the estimated demand in each quarter.
(c) Limit the overtime operation to 20 units in the third and fourth quarters.
(d) Limit the overtime operation to 40 units in the first and second quarters.

Formulate a goal-programming model and solve it by using the *Micro Manager.*

13. Mayor Taylor recently named Robert Anderson to be the campaign director for the mayor's upcoming reelection campaign. Mayor Taylor thinks that he has a good chance to be reelected if he can reach a half million people in the city. A marketing-research firm supplied the following information.

Medium	Exposure/insertion	Cost/ insertion	Maximum insertion by law
Television	10,000 individuals	$1,000	30
Radio	6,000 individuals	$ 600	50
Newspaper	5,000 individuals	$ 400	60

The total campaign fund is limited to $100,000 by the city election law. Furthermore, the maximum number of insertions of each medium is restricted to 30, 50, and 60 units, respectively, by the law. The campaign team has set the following goals in the order of their importance:

(a) Obtain exposure to 759,000 individuals.
(b) Avoid spending over $70,000.
(c) Limit the newspaper ads to 40 units.

Robert Anderson is attempting to formulate the campaign strategies for Mayor Taylor. The limitations imposed by the city election law should be treated as system constraints and be observed in advance. Formulate a goal-programming model and solve it by using the *Micro Manager.*

14. A production manager faces the problem of job allocation between two assembly lines. The production rate of assembly line 1 is 10 units per hour and the production rate of assembly line 2 is 12 units per hour. The normal working period for both lines is 8 hours per day. The production manager has set the following goals for the next day, listed in order of their importance:

(a) Avoid any underachievement of the production level, which is set at 200 units of product.
(b) Avoid any overtime operation of line 2 beyond 4 hours.
(c) Avoid any underutilization of regular working hours (assign differential weights according to the relative productivity of the two lines).
(d) Minimize overtime in both assembly lines.

Formulate a goal-programming model and solve it by using the *Micro Manager.*

15. You are planning to invest $100,000 in four alternatives: stock options, bonds, diamonds, and real estate. Each dollar invested in stock options returns an average of $1.20 a year later. Each dollar invested in bonds at the beginning of each year will return $1.08 a year later. Each dollar invested in real estate will return $1.10 a year later. Since diamonds are risky, you cannot assume they will have any yield. You have established the following goals, in the order of their importance:

(a) To minimize risks, no more than 30% of the total investment should be put into stock options and at least 30% of the total investment should be put into bonds.
(b) Since diamonds are rumored to be profitable, at least $30,000 should be invested in this alternative.
(c) The amount invested in stock options and diamonds should not exceed the amount invested in bonds and real estate.
(d) Maximize the amount of money you have after one year.

Formulate a goal-programming model and solve it by using the *Micro Manager.*

16. Pamela Stein is a dealer of home-heating oil in a medium-sized city. She owns a storage tank with a capacity of 10,000 gallons of oil that initially has 4,000 gallons in it. Stein can purchase oil each month either for distribution during the month or for storage for later use. The selling price and purchasing cost and expected demand during each month are shown in the following table.

	Months		
Home heating oil	*1*	*2*	*3*
Selling price (cents/gal)	47	50	52
Purchasing cost (cents/gal)	40	42	45
Expected demand (gallons)	6,000	8,000	7,000

Pamela Stein has set the following goals, listed in the order of their importance.

(a) Avoid purchasing over 5,000 gallons each month.
(b) Meet the demand each month.
(c) Maximize total profit during the entire three-month period.

The oil is assumed to be available for purchase at the beginning of each month, but can be sold throughout the month. Formulate a goal-programming model and solve it by using the *Micro Manager.*

17. The Spring Brewing Company brews an extremely popular brand of beer. However, to preserve quality, it produces beer in only three plants where spring water is available. The weekly production capacity at each plant is: plant A—4,000 cases; plant B—2,000 cases; and plant C—3,000 cases. The company ships to three wholesalers. The weekly demands and transportation costs (in dollars per 100 cases) are as follows.

	Wholesaler		
Plant	***1***	***2***	***3***
A	\$8	\$6	\$4
B	\$4	\$7	\$5
C	\$5	\$8	\$6
Demand (cases)	2,000	4,000	5,000

The president of the firm has established the following goals in the order of their importance:

(a) Avoid any shipment from plant B to wholesaler 3, because of road conditions.
(b) Because wholesaler 3 covers a new marketing area, it is extremely important to satisfy the demand of wholesaler 3 completely.
(c) Avoid the overutilization of the production capacity in each plant.
(d) Meet the demands of wholesaler 1 and 2.
(e) Minimize the total transportation cost.

Formulate a goal-programming model and solve it by using the *Micro Manager.*

18. The Dandy Cosmetic Company has three plants. Plant 1 produces after-shave lotion, plant 2 cologne, and plant 3 soap. The company wishes to sell three kinds of gift sets for the upcoming Christmas season. The gift set Prince includes only an after-shave lotion, which is produced and packed in plant 1. The gift set King, which is packed in plant 2, includes a lotion and cologne. The gift set Emperor, which is packed in plant 3, includes a lotion, a cologne, and a soap. The company can either produce soap internally or purchase it from an outside company. A schematic reproduction of the problem is shown in the following diagram.

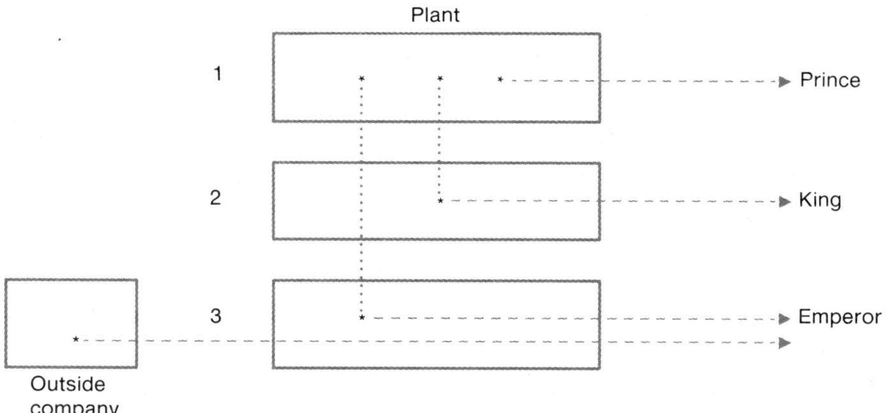

The capacities and estimated costs for manufacturing and packing these products are shown below.

	Manufacturing		Packing	
	Cost	Capacity	Cost	Capacity
Plant 1	$5	10,000 bottles	$0.2	5,000 sets
Plant 2	$4	5,000 bottles	$0.5	3,000 sets
Plant 3	$3	2,000 pieces	$1	5,000 sets

The soap can be purchased at $2.50 from the outside company without any limitation of quantity. The selling prices of the gift sets are: Prince—$8, King—$15, and Emperor—$20. The president of the firm has established the following multiple goals, in the order of their importance:

(a) Avoid any underutilization of the capacity of plant 3 (both packing and manufacturing).

(b) Satisfy the estimated demands—4,000 sets of Prince, 3,000 sets of King, and 3,000 sets of Emperor.

(c) Limit the overtime operation of plants 1 and 2 (both packing and manufacturing).

(d) Generate at least $80,000 profit.

Formulate a goal-programming model and solve it by using the *Micro Manager*.

19. Gold Star Electronics produces radios, tape recorders, and televisions. The production cost, the selling price, and the capacity for each product are shown in the table below.

Product	Cost	Price	Capacity
Radio	$21	$30	500 units
Tape recorder	$70	$100	2,000 units
Television	$230	$300	1,500 units

The company pays its costs as they occur but sells the products by either cash or credit, with 60% of the customers paying by cash and 40% by credit. The balance sheet of the company at the end of period zero is shown in the table below.

Assets		Liabilities	
Cash	$100,000	Short-term bank loan	$100,000
Accounts receivable	$150,000	Long-term debts	$200,000
Inventories	$0		
Plant and equipment	$450,000	Equity	$400,000
Total	$700,000	Total	$700,000

The accounting department reports that 50% of the accounts receivable will be collected during period 1. There is no schedule to repay the bank loan and the long-term debts. The president of the company has set the following goals for period 1, in the order of their importance:

(a) Avoid any overutilization of the production capacity for each of the products.

(b) Have at least $50,000 cash at the end of period 1.

(c) Have a net working capital of at least $200,000 at the end of period 1. (The excess of the current assets over the current liabilities is called working capital.)

Formulate a goal-programming model and solve it by using the *Micro Manager*.

20. Cornhusker Foods, Inc. specializes in the sale of corn. The company has three grain elevators in which it stores corn. The business of this company is restricted by the storage capacity of the elevators. The normal capacity of a grain elevator is 1,000 bushels (an overloading of 300 bushels is allowed in an emergency). The purchasing cost and selling price during each month are shown in the following table.

	Month			
	1	*2*	*3*	*4*
Cost ($/bushel)	3	3	5	6
Price ($/bushel)	4	5	6	5

The quantity of the purchase is assumed to be based entirely upon the revenue generated from sales. It is also assumed that sales are made at the beginning of the month, followed by purchases. At the beginning of the first month, there are 2,000 bushels of corn in the elevators. The president of the firm has set the following multiple goals, in the order of their importance:

(a) In the first month, only the normal capacity of the elevators should be used.

(b) The firm should reserve at least $1,500 each month for emergency purposes.

(c) The firm should have at least $40,000 for purchasing at the beginning of the fourth month.

(d) The firm should maximize total profit during the entire four-month period.

Formulate a goal-programming model and solve it by using the *Micro Manager.*

C H A P T E R 9

Decision Making under Risk

The type of scientific technique we use for decision making is often based on the nature of the decision environment. Basically, there are three different states of the decision environment: certainty, risk, and uncertainty. The certainty state exists when the information required to make a decision is known and available. The risk condition exists when the probabilities of certain decision outcomes occurring are known. The uncertainty state refers to the environment where the probabilities of decision outcomes occurring are not known.

In chapters 3 to 8, we have discussed various techniques that are useful under certainty. In this chapter we will discuss concepts of probabilities and their applications to decision making under the condition of risk.

Basics

For a decision-making problem under risk, we must first identify the alternative courses of action that are available and are feasible. Then, we should determine the possible events or states of nature that can occur and their probabilities. Next, we must determine the conditional consequence (either a payoff or loss) for a given event. Then, we can compute the expected payoff or monetary value for each course of action. The optimum decision alternative is the one that has the maximum expected monetary value or the minimum expected loss.

Decision making under risk involves the concept of probability. Although *probability* is part of our daily vocabulary, it is not easy to define it properly. A commonly accepted definition of probability is the frequency with which an event occurs, given a certain number of experimental trials. This definition is often referred to as an *objective* probability.

Probabilities are not always based on experiments. For example, an economic forecaster states that there is a 10 percent chance of higher-inflation rates; a weatherman says there is a 20 percent chance of snow tomorrow; or Jimmy the Greek states that the Washington Redskins have a 60 percent chance to win the

Super Bowl. Such probabilities are not based on actual experiments. But these *subjective* probabilities are based on specific information, knowledge, past experiences, or personal feelings about circumstances surrounding the events that could possibly occur.

The theory of probabilities is a field in itself. In this section, we will simply discuss several properties that are relevant to decision making under the condition of risk.

1. The probability of a possible event, say A, to occur cannot be negative. Also, it cannot exceed one.

   $$0 \leq P(A) \leq 1$$

2. The sum of the probabilities of all possible events must equal one.

   $$\sum_{i=1}^{n} P_i = 1$$

3. If possible events A and B are mutually exclusive, the probability of *A or B*'s occurring is the sum of their independent probabilities.

   $$P(A \text{ or } B) = P(A) + P(B)$$

4. If possible events A and B are not mutually exclusive, the probability of *A or B*'s occurring is the sum of their independent probabilities minus their joint probability.

   $$P(A \text{ or } B) = P(A) + P(B) - P(A \text{ and } B)$$

Illustrative Problems

Although decision making under risk always involves the concept of probability, a number of different factors might need to be considered as shown in the following examples. In the first example, the decision of whether to operate ski and racquet condos depends on the expected payoff of the proposed venture. The second example utilizes an opportunity-loss table to estimate the value of perfect information. The final example shows how expected profit can vary as different assumptions are applied.

Example 9.1 Ski Country, USA

Ski Country, USA, specializes in managing condominium rentals in a ski resort town in Colorado. The success of the company's annual operation is based on the weather, more specifically the snowfall during the ski season, November 25 to April 10. Recently, Ski & Racquet, Inc., has requested Ski Country, USA, to manage 70 condominiums during the upcoming ski season.

Ski Country, USA, can either manage the Ski & Racquet condos itself or it can subcontract the units to another management firm. Summit Country Rentals has offered \$150,000 to have an exclusive contract to manage the Ski & Racquet condos for the ski season. Based on past experience, Ski Country, USA, believes that its expected payoffs from the Ski & Racquet operation would be \$250,000 in a good season (over 70 inches of snow), \$175,000 in a normal season (40 to 70 inches of snow), and \$20,000 in a poor season (less than 40 inches of snow). The local U. S. Weather Bureau has predicted that there is a 30% chance of a good ski season, a 40% chance of a normal season, and a 30% chance of a poor ski season.

To determine which option to take, Ski Country, USA, has decided to use expected payoff as the decision-making criteria. The expected payoff is simply the sum of each conditional payoff multiplied by its associated probability. Thus, the expected payoff of operating Ski & Racquet condos is as follows:

$$\begin{aligned} E\text{ (Operate)} &= (0.3 \times \$250{,}000) + (0.4 \times \$175{,}000) \\ &\quad + (0.3 \times \$20{,}000) \\ &= 75{,}000 + 70{,}000 + 6{,}000 \\ &= \$151{,}000. \end{aligned}$$

Since the expected payoff of operating Ski & Racquet condos is \$1,000 more than the subcontract amount suggested by Summit Country Rentals, Ski Country, USA, decided to operate Ski & Racquet condos itself.

Example 9.2 Century Investments, Inc.

Century Investments is considering three investment alternatives: stocks, bonds, and real estate. The conditional payoff of each alternative depends upon economic conditions during the coming year. There are three possible economic conditions to consider: slow growth, normal growth, and fast growth. The best economic forecasting estimates indicate the following probabilities: slow growth—30%; normal growth—50%; and fast growth—20%. The conditional payoffs of each alternative under different economic conditions are listed below.

	Economic Conditions		
Alternative	**$P_1 = 0.3$ Slow growth**	**$P_2 = 0.5$ Normal growth**	**$P_3 = 0.2$ Fast growth**
Stocks	−\$100,000	\$70,000	\$120,000
Bonds	−40,000	50,000	90,000
Real estate	−150,000	40,000	180,000

Century Investments has decided to use expected value as the decision-making criterion for this investment problem. Consequently, the expected values for each investment alternative are computed as follows:

$$E(\text{Stocks}) = (-100{,}000 \times 0.3) + (70{,}000 \times 0.5) + (120{,}000 \times 0.2) = 29{,}000$$

$$E(\text{Bonds}) = (-40{,}000 \times 0.3) + (50{,}000 \times 0.5) + (90{,}000 \times 0.2) = 31{,}000$$

$$E(\text{Real estate}) = (-150{,}000 \times 0.3) + (40{,}000 \times 0.5) + (180{,}000 \times 0.2) = 11{,}000$$

Based on the above computations, Century Investments selects the investment alternative of bonds.

The same approach can be used when we apply the *expected opportunity-loss* criterion. The opportunity losses can be computed for each state of nature (the economic condition in this example). We can first identify the best conditional payoff. If the given state of nature occurs and the best conditional payoff is realized because we selected the particular decision alternative, the opportunity loss will be zero. In our example, the best outcome for the slow economic condition is −\$40,000 when we select bonds. If we selected stocks as our investment alternative and the slow economic condition occurred, the conditional payoff would be −\$100,000. The opportunity loss of this payoff is \$60,000, the difference between −\$100,000 and −\$40,000.

Now we can easily construct the opportunity-loss table for the problem as below.

	Economic Conditions		
Alternative	**$P_1 = 0.3$ Slow growth**	**$P_2 = 0.5$ Normal growth**	**$P_3 = 0.2$ Fast growth**
Stocks	\$60,000	\$0	\$60,000
Bonds	0	20,000	90,000
Real estate	110,000	30,000	0

The expected opportunity loss (EL) for each alternative is computed as follows:

$$EL(\text{Stocks}) = (60{,}000 \times 0.3) + (0 \times 0.5) + (60{,}000 \times 0.2) = \$30{,}000$$

$$EL(\text{Bonds}) = (0 \times 0.3) + (20{,}000 \times 0.5) + (90{,}000 \times 0.2) = \$28{,}000$$

$$EL(\text{Real estate}) = (110{,}000 \times 0.3) + (30{,}000 \times 0.5) + (0 \times 0.2) = \$48{,}000$$

Since we are trying to minimize the total expected opportunity loss, our choice once again will be bonds. As a matter of fact, the same optimum choice is always selected whether we use the expected value or the expected opportunity loss criterion.

Another interesting point we should discuss here is the *value of perfect information.* If we have perfect information, there is no need to compute the expected value or the expected opportunity loss to identify the optimum course of action. Thus, the value of perfect information is the difference between the expected value of the best alternative and the expected payoff under certainty.

If perfect information is available, the opportunity loss should always be zero since we will always choose the optimum alternative. Thus, the value of perfect information is exactly the same as the expected opportunity loss of the optimum alternative. In our example, the value of perfect information is $28,000, the expected opportunity loss of the bonds.

Example 9.3 The Airport Giftshop

The Airport Giftshop sells various gift items, paperback books, magazines, and newspapers. The shop began to sell the *Wall Street Journal* on a trial basis. The shop buys the *Journal* for 20 cents a copy and sells it for 50 cents. Any copies remaining unsold have no value. Based on the past several days' experience, the number of copies demanded and their associated probabilities are as follows:

Daily demand	Probability
1	0.1
2	0.3
3	0.4
4	0.1
5	0.1

The store is trying to determine the optimum number of copies to stock to maximize the expected payoff from selling the *Wall Street Journal.* Before we construct the conditional payoff table for analysis, we should determine the conditional payoff associated with stocking a certain number of copies of the *Journal.*

When Demand is Equal to or Greater Than Quantity Stocked ($D \geq Q$) When there is sufficient demand to sell the entire quantity stocked, the net profit will be as follows:

$$\begin{aligned} \text{Net Profit} &= \text{Total Revenue} - \text{Total Cost} \\ &= \$0.50 \times Q - \$0.20 \times Q \\ &= \$0.30Q. \end{aligned}$$

When Demand Is Less Than Quantity Stocked ($D < Q$) When demand is not sufficient to sell all of the *Journal* copies stocked, the net profit will be as follows:

$$\begin{aligned} \text{Net Profit} &= \text{Total Revenue} - \text{Total Cost} \\ &= \$0.50D - \$0.20Q. \end{aligned}$$

Table 9.1 Conditional and expected profits for stocking various copies

Quantity stocked (Q)	Demand (D) $P_1 = 0.1$ 1	$P_2 = 0.3$ 2	$P_3 = 0.4$ 3	$P_4 = 0.1$ 4	$P_5 = 0.1$ 5	Expected profit
1	\$0.30	\$0.30	\$0.30	\$0.30	\$0.30	\$0.30
2	0.10	0.60	0.60	0.60	0.60	0.55
3	−0.10	0.40	0.90	0.90	0.90	0.65
4	−0.30	0.20	0.70	1.20	1.20	0.55
5	−0.50	0	0.50	1.00	1.50	0.40

Based on the above computations, we can prepare a conditional profit table for the problem as shown in Table 9.1. The expected profit for stocking a certain quantity can be computed in the usual manner. For example, the expected profit for stocking three copies of the *Wall Street Journal* will be as follows:

$$\begin{aligned} E(Q = 3) &= (-0.10 \times 0.1) + (0.40 \times 0.3) + (0.90 \times 0.4) \\ &\quad + (0.90 \times 0.1) + (0.90 \times 0.1) \\ &= \$0.65. \end{aligned}$$

Based on the expected profit for stocking a certain copy of the *Journal,* the Airport Giftshop decided to stock three copies. The expected profit is \$0.65.

There are two possible additional costs that need our attention. The first is the salvage value. If the leftover items can be sold for less than the regular price, a certain salvage value exists. For example, let us suppose that the leftover *Wall Street Journal* can be sold to a fish market for five cents a copy. In that case, the net profit when demand is less than the quantity stocked ($D < Q$) will be as follows:

$$\begin{aligned} \text{Net Profit} &= \text{Total Revenue} - \text{Total Cost} \\ &= 0.50D + 0.05(Q - D) - 0.20Q \\ &= 0.50D + 0.05Q - 0.05D - 0.20Q \\ &= 0.45D - 0.15Q. \end{aligned}$$

The second possible cost is the goodwill cost. Goodwill cost involves costs that result due to ill effects caused by the failure to stock sufficient copies of the *Journal.* Goodwill cost exists only when demand is greater than the quantity stocked ($D > Q$). Let us suppose that the goodwill cost is ten cents per copy that is short. In such a case, the net profit will be as follows:

$$\begin{aligned} \text{Net Profit} &= \text{Total Revenue} - \text{Total Cost} \\ &= 0.50Q - [0.20Q + 0.10\,(D - Q)] \\ &= 0.50Q - 0.20Q - 0.10D + 0.10Q \\ &= 0.40Q - 0.10D. \end{aligned}$$

If demand is exactly equal to the quantity stocked ($Q = D$), the net profit remains \$0.30Q. Now we can develop the conditional profit table for the problem in the same manner as shown in Table 9.1.

Application of the *Micro Manager*

This section presents an application example of the *Micro Manager* to a decision making problem under risk. There are many different approaches we can use for decision making under risk; the program diskette provides you with the complete information, including the purpose of the techniques, solutions of various example problems, interactive input instructions, and the batch input procedure. Therefore, in this section we will present only the information (purpose of the technique and the batch input data format) and the solution of a sample problem using the interactive input mode.

```
<< PURPOSE >>

DECISION MAKING UNDER RISK determines the expected payoff or monetary value for
each course of action when certain probabilities are given for possible events
or states of nature.  The output presents the maximum expected monetary value
or minimum expected loss of the best course of action.  This program can handle
problems with up to 20 courses of action and 20 possible states of nature.

<<  BATCH INPUT DATA FORMAT  >>

Type in the values of the following input data requirements, after creating a
new file.  You may enter as many values as you want in a line, separating them
by commas for alphabetic characters and by commas or blank spaces for numeric
values.  However, the input data must be exactly in the following order:

1. Number of alternatives
2. Number of events
3. Probability of each event
4. Payoff input type
        1  :  Cost and revenue
        2  :  Payoff
If payoff input type is 1
     5. Cost of each alternative
     6. Revenue of each alternative and event combination
If payoff input type is 2
     5. Payoff of each alternative and event combination

** Sample Batch Input Data Set (Example 9.2) **

3,3             ; three alternatives and three events
.3,.5,.2        ; probabilities of three events
2               ; payoff input type 2
-100,70,120     ; payoff of row 1
-40,50,90       ; payoff of row 2
-150,40,180     ; payoff of row 3

PROGRAM: Decision Making Under Risk

Enter number of alternatives: 3
Enter number of events:       3

Enter probability of event  1 : .3
Enter probability of event  2 : .5
Enter probability of event  3 : .2
```

```
Payoff input type:

   1. Cost and Revenue
   2. Payoff

Enter a number (1 or 2): 2

Enter payoff of alternative 1 and event 1 : -100
Enter payoff of alternative 1 and event 2 : 70
Enter payoff of alternative 1 and event 3 : 120

Enter payoff of alternative 2 and event 1 : -40
Enter payoff of alternative 2 and event 2 : 50
Enter payoff of alternative 2 and event 3 : 90

Enter payoff of alternative 3 and event 1 : -150
Enter payoff of alternative 3 and event 2 : 40
Enter payoff of alternative 3 and event 3 : 180

PROGRAM: Decision Making Under Risk

***** INPUT DATA ENTERED *****

-----------------------------------------------
                       Events
              ---------------------------------
                  1         2         3
Alternative   p = 0.30 p = 0.50 p = 0.20
-----------------------------------------------
     1          -100.00     70.00    120.00
     2           -40.00     50.00     90.00
     3          -150.00     40.00    180.00
-----------------------------------------------

*****   PROGRAM OUTPUT   *****

----------------------------------
  Alternative    Expected Value
----------------------------------
      1               29.00
      2               31.00 *
      3               11.00
------------------------------

* indicates optimal solution
```

Summary

Many real-world decision problems exist in the condition of risk. Under the condition of risk, the probabilities of certain decision outcomes or states of nature are known. Thus, if we can estimate the conditional consequences for various possible events, then we can determine the expected payoff or loss for each course of action. In this chapter, we have examined many different approaches to decision making under risk. The *Micro Manager* is extremely useful when a problem can be analyzed in many different ways.

References

Hillier, F. S., and G. T. Lieberman. 1980. *Introduction to operations research.* 3d ed. San Francisco: Holden-Day.

Lee, S. M. 1983. *Introduction to management science.* Chicago: Dryden.

Lee, S. M., L. J. Moore, and B. W. Taylor. 1985. *Management science.* 2d ed. Dubuque, IA: Wm. C. Brown Publishers.

Luce, R. D., and J. Paiffa. 1957. *Games and decisions.* New York: John Wiley & Sons.

Schlaiffer, R. 1969. *Analysis of decisions under uncertainty.* New York: McGraw-Hill.

Problems

1. The activities and probabilities of Mrs. Robinson's Friday afternoon schedule are as follows:

Activity	Probability
A. Go to a movie	0.3
B. Go to the library	0.1
C. Go to a tea party	0.2
D. Go shopping	0.3
E. Stay at home	0.1

If all activities are mutually exclusive, what is the probability of Mrs. Robinson's going to a movie or to the library?

2. In the above problem, if activities A (go to a movie) and D (go shopping) are not mutually exclusive and the probability of Mrs. Robinson's going to a movie and shopping Friday afternoon is 0.1, what is the probability of Mrs. Robinson's going to a movie or shopping?

3. You have just bought a lottery ticket. The Grand Prize is $100,000. In addition, there are two $50,000 prizes, ten $10,000 prizes, one hundred $1,000 prizes, and one thousand $100 prizes. The odds of winning the respective prizes are as follows:

Prize	Odds
Grand Prize	One chance in 1,000,000
$50,000	One chance in 500,000
$10,000	One chance in 100,000
$ 1,000	One chance in 10,000
$ 100	One chance in 1,000

What is the expected payoff of your lottery ticket?

4. New Standard Oil is attempting to decide whether to drill for oil on Ben Johnson's farm. The company believes there is a 0.15 probability of finding oil. If oil is found, the project will return $3 million worth of oil. The cost of drilling is estimated at $300,000 including the $100,000 fee for drilling rights paid to Ben Johnson. Structure the problem and draw a table in terms of decision alternatives, nature of states, and so on.

5. Northumberland Machinery Works Ltd. plans to purchase a new pressing machine. It is considering two machines. The purchase prices are $10,000 for machine *A* and $15,000 for machine *B*. The operating costs per unit processed are $1 for machine *A* and $0.60 for machine *B*. The expected usage of the machine in its lifetime is not clear. However, the management believes that it may be 20,000, 40,000, or 30,000 units processed with probabilities of 0.2, 0.5, and 0.3, respectively. Between machines *A* and *B*, which one do you recommend purchasing?

6. Given the following information, determine the expected payoff for each of the alternatives and select the optimum alternative.

	State of Nature		
Alternatives	$E_1(p = 0.3)$	$E_2(p = 0.5)$	$E_3(p = 0.2)$
A	$200	$200	$200
B	$160	$220	$230
C	$220	$180	$250

7. Given the following payoff information, construct the conditional loss table and determine the optimum alternative by the expected loss criterion.

	State of Nature		
Alternatives	$E_1(p = 0.2)$	$E_2(p = 0.5)$	$E_3(p = 0.3)$
A	$5,000	$2,000	$4,000
B	$3,000	$4,000	$6,000
C	$2,000	$6,000	$5,000

8. Given the following payoff matrix:

   a. Determine the best strategy using the expected payoff criterion.
   b. Determine the best strategy using the expected loss criterion.
   c. What is the value of perfect information?

	State of Nature		
Strategy	$E_1(p = 0.4)$	$E_2(p = 0.4)$	$E_3(p = 0.2)$
S_1	\$50,000	−\$40,000	−\$10,000
S_2	−135,000	140,000	−30,000
S_3	0	0	0

9. Richman Real Estate Company is considering a condominium project in Colorado Springs, Colorado. The company is considering three different scales of the development. Currently, the uncertain state of the economy makes it difficult to ascertain the expected demand for new condominiums. If there would be a low demand after a large-scale development project is completed, it would result in a great loss to the company. The management of the company has prepared the following payoff table.

	Demand		
Alternative	**Low($p = 0.3$)**	**Medium($p = 0.4$)**	**High($p = 0.3$)**
Small-scale development	\$2 million	\$2.5 million	\$2.5 million
Medium-scale development	−1	4	4.5
Large-scale development	−2	3	6

   a. What is the best decision alternative under the expected payoff criterion?
   b. What is the value of perfect information?

10. White Mountain Resort Company in Vermont has just opened a new ski slope. The potential for a successful ski business in the area appears great because it can draw customers from all over the East. However, the key factor for success is the snowfall. If the winter brings an average of 60 or more inches of snow, the season could be a financial success. If the snowfall is between 40 and 60 inches, the firm can operate artificial snowmakers and still manage a moderate financial gain. However, if the snowfall is less than 40 inches, as was the case during the past two years,

the firm will be operating in the red. Recently, a large firm in New York has offered $250,000 to lease the ski slope from White Mountain Resort Company. A decision needs to be made either to operate the ski slope or lease it for the coming season. The conditional payoffs for operating the ski slope under the three snowfall conditions are below.

	Snowfall		
	60 in. or more	**40–60 in.**	**40 in. or less**
Operate	$750,000	$300,000	−$200,000

a. Should the company operate or lease the ski slope, if the probabilities of snowfalls are 0.4 for 60 in. or more, 0.2 for 40–60 in., and 0.4 for 40 in. or less?

b. If we assume that the National Weather Bureau can only predict the probability of snowfall of 40 in. or less as 0.4, what kind of probability must the management assign to 60 or more inches before the firm would decide to operate the ski slope?

11. Master Arts Production Company has proposed a comedy series to a major TV network. Once Master Arts produces the series, the major network has three options—to reject the series, broadcast the series for one year, or broadcast the series for two years. The profit that Master Arts can expect from producing the series under each state of nature and the associated probabilities are below.

	State of Nature		
	Reject	**1 year**	**2 year**
Produce a run	−$100,000	$100,000	$280,000
Probability	0.3	0.2	0.5

However, there is an opportunity for Master Arts to produce only the pilot and to transfer the rights for the series to another production company with the profit of $120,000. Which one is the better decision, to produce a series or to sell the rights?

12. Teresa Blum has farmland consisting of 200 acres in Orange County, California, in which she has citrus trees. Today, a food-processing company in Los Angeles offered a contract of $20,000 for the coming winter's crop. If the weather is nice and warm this winter, the crop should be worth $35,000. However, if there is a hard freeze, Teresa can expect only $10,000 profit. What kind of a probability must Teresa assign to the hard freeze to determine if the decision to sell her crop to the food-processing company is the best choice?

13. Shearson Holding Company plans to invest $1,000,000 in a new plant. If business conditions remain unchanged or improve, the investment will return 20 percent a year. However, if there is an economic recession, the investment is expected to return only 2 percent a year. Alternatively, the firm can invest the money in government bonds for a sure return of 8 percent per year. What would the probability be of an economic recession for the company to be indifferent between the two alternatives?

14. Juan Chavez is a merchant who deals with a perishable good. He purchases the food from farmers in batches of 100 units for $20 each. The sale is a one-time event and the sale price is $50 per batch. If items are not sold, the salvage value of the leftovers is half of the purchased price. The demand for the good has the following probabilities:

Demand	Probability
200	0.15
300	0.15
400	0.35
500	0.20
600	0.15

Construct a conditional payoff table and determine the optimum quantity to purchase.

15. Rochelle Atlas is the manager of the sporting goods department of Alexander Department Store, Inc. The store sells golf sets that can be purchased from a manufacturer at the price of $150 per set. The golf set sells for $250. If golf sets are not available, customers will go elsewhere. The goodwill cost is estimated to be $50. Unsold items retain 100 percent salvage value and can be sold in the next week. The weekly demand for the golf sets has the following probability distribution.

Weekly demand	Probability
6	0.2
7	0.3
8	0.4
9	0.1

a. Construct the conditional payoff table.

b. What is your recommendation to the manager about the quantity to purchase per week?

16. Rainbow Baker, Inc., has collected its past operating records and found that the demand for its product during the past six months has varied as follows.

Daily demand (units)	Probability
1,000	0.1
1,100	0.3
1,200	0.3
1,300	0.2
1,400	0.1

If production cost is $0.30 per unit, sale price is $0.40 per unit, and any leftover units at the end of the day are sold for $0.10 per unit, what is the optimum daily output for the bakery? Assume that the possible decision alternatives are producing the product in batches of 1,000, 1,100, 1,200, 1,300, or 1,400 units.

17. Clear Water Fish Market, Inc., sells fresh trout. Trout is bought in Denver for $2.00 (including the transportation costs) and sold for $3.00. Any trout not sold at the end of a week can be sold to a cat food plant for $0.20 per fish. According to the past 60-week experience, the weekly demand for trout has been as follows.

Demand	Number of weeks
20	6
21	12
22	24
23	12
24	6
	60 weeks

a. Construct a payoff table for the various demand and stocking quantities and determine the optimum quantity to stock per week by the expected payoff criterion.
b. Using the expected loss criterion, construct the conditional loss table and determine the optimum stock quantity.
c. Determine the value of perfect information.

18. A seasonal item can be purchased at the price of $40 per piece and sold for $80 per piece in retail. The goodwill cost is estimated at $20 per piece. If the items are not sold during the season, they will be sold wholesale at $35 per piece. The demand for the product during the season has varied as follows.

Seasonal demand (piece)	Probability
100	0.3
200	0.5
300	0.2

a. How many pieces should be purchased under the expected payoff criterion?

b. What is the value of perfect information?

19. *Popular Computing* is one of the best-selling weekly magazines at the local university. The university newsstand purchases *Popular Computing* for $1.50 a copy and sells it for $2.00. Any copies not sold are returned to the publisher for $0.20 per copy. For the past 100 weeks, the demand has varied as follows.

Weekly demand	Number of weeks
10	5
11	15
12	20
13	30
14	15
15	10
16	5

a. Construct a conditional loss table and then identify the proper quantity to stock.

b. What is the loss due to overstocking?

c. What is the loss due to understocking?

d. What is the value of perfect information?

20. Chip Wright is a farmer who grows roses and sells them to florists. Chip sells the roses for $2 per dozen; they cost $1.50 per dozen to grow and distribute to the florists. If the demand is greater than his capacity to supply, it is assumed that lost sales cost $0.50 per dozen. If there are any leftovers at the end of the day, Chip can sell them to the neighbors and nearby restaurants at $0.75 per dozen. The daily demand for roses is below.

Daily demand	Probability
10 dozen	0.1
11	0.1
12	0.2
13	0.3
14	0.2
15	0.1

a. Construct the conditional payoff table and determine the best alternative. Assume that the possible decision alternatives are 10, 11, 12, 13, 14, or 15 dozen.

b. Develop the opportunity-cost table for this problem.

c. Compute the expected value of perfect information.

CHAPTER 10

Decision Tree Analysis

Decision making under the condition of risk that we discussed in chapter 9 involved only a single stage or time period. For example, we analyzed an investment problem under risk, based on the expected value criterion without any consideration about the future consequences of the decision alternatives. However, many real-world problems involve not only probabilities associated with possible states of nature but also frequently involve multiple-stage or time periods. In this chapter we will discuss decision tree analysis, which is useful for sequential or multiperiod decision making under risk.

Basics

In many real-world problems, a decision made at a given time period or stage may have a lasting impact on future outcomes. Thus, determining what the optimum decision is requires an analysis of an entire series of decisions over the planning horizon. Decision tree analysis involves a schematic analysis of a multiperiod or sequential decision-making problem under risk.

Decision tree analysis is a useful tool for sequential decision-making problems for several reasons. First, a schematic presentation of the sequential decision process facilitates an easy understanding of a complex process. Second, a decision tree makes it easy to derive the expected value because the computation work can be done right on the tree diagram. Third, decision tree analysis can accommodate a group decision-making process.

Figure 10.1 A Typical Decision Tree

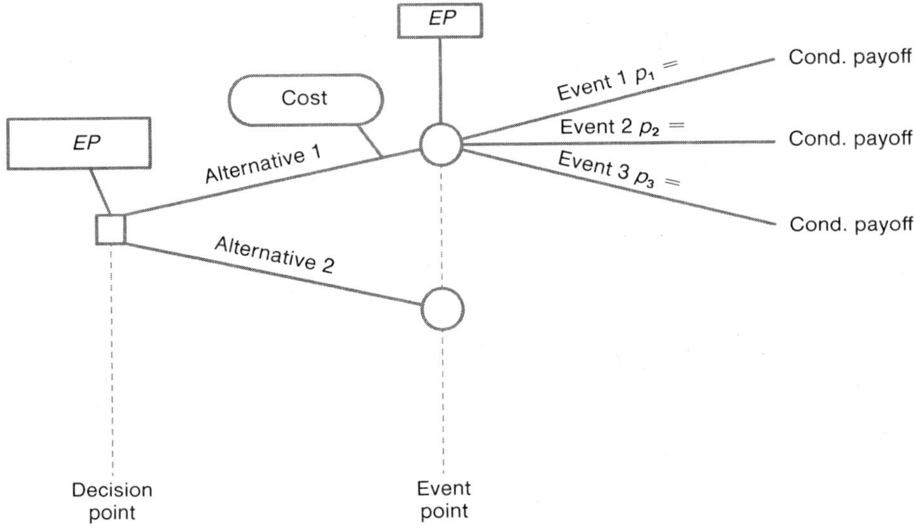

Decision tree analysis provides a pictorial representation of the sequential decision process by using the following elements:

1. Decision point. Decision points, often represented by squares (□), are specific points of time (or stages) when a certain decision must be made. Alternative decision options can branch out from a decision point.
2. Event point. Event points, often represented by circles (○), are possible states of nature that can occur. A number of possible events can branch out from an event point.
3. Probabilities. The known or best-estimated probabilities of events (states of nature) are listed above each of the possible event branches.
4. Conditional outcome. The known or best-estimated conditional outcome (payoff, loss, and so on) of each eventual branch is listed at the end of each branch.

A typical decision tree is presented in Fig. 10.1. A decision tree usually starts from the left side with one or more decision points to the right side with all possible decision alternatives and event branches. Each decision branch is evaluated by computing its expected consequence (payoff, loss, and so on).

The following two examples illustrate how decision trees are developed and analyzed.

Example 10.1 Sprint Print, Inc.

Sprint Print, Inc., specializes in printing and binding professional and legal documents for various organizations. Recently, the state legislature has requested that Sprint submit a bid to print all of the legislative proceedings. Currently, State Documents Company prints the legislative proceedings. State Documents has indicated that it would also bid to keep the state job.

Sprint Print has the option of either preparing to bid or not preparing to bid for the state printing job. The cost of bid-preparation work is estimated to be $10,000. State Documents Company has the option of bidding a lower amount, about the same amount, or a higher amount than its contracted amount last year. If Sprint Print gets the contract after the bid, the conditional payoff is $100,000. Based on reliable sources, the probability of State Documents' bidding a higher amount than the last year's contract is 0.3; it is 0.5 for about the same amount, and 0.2 for bidding a lower amount than last year's contract amount. The probability of Sprint Print's getting the contract with its bid when State Documents bid a higher amount than the last year's contract amount is 0.6; it is 0.4 when State Documents bids about the same amount, and 0.2 when State Documents bids a lower amount than the last year's contract amount.

Figure 10.2 presents the entire decision tree analysis for the Sprint Print problem. The expected payoff of preparing and actually bidding for the state printing job is $32,000. Thus, the firm should bid for the legislative proceedings job.

Example 10.2 UN Peacekeeping Forces

The United States is seriously considering participating in a United Nations' peacekeeping force with several other UN member nations in a troubled spot in the Middle East. The U. S. government believes that at least a moderate number of peacekeeping troops, with appropriate support from naval forces, should be sent to support the fragile local government. However, the hostile neighboring state, *A*, has formally announced that any UN forces will be countered by an increased number of its own troops in the territory. The experts in the Department of State believe that the probability of Country *A*'s actually increasing its own troops in the area as a response to the UN forces is 0.7.

Many experts believe that Country *A* will wait to see the size of UN peacekeeping forces before it will actually counter with its own military actions. The UN peacekeeping force size, the most likely reactions of Country *A*, the probability associated with each of Country *A*'s reactions, and the expected stability rating of the troubled local government are presented on page 223.

Figure 10.2 The Decision Tree for the Sprint Print Problem. SP = Sprint Print. SD = State Documents.

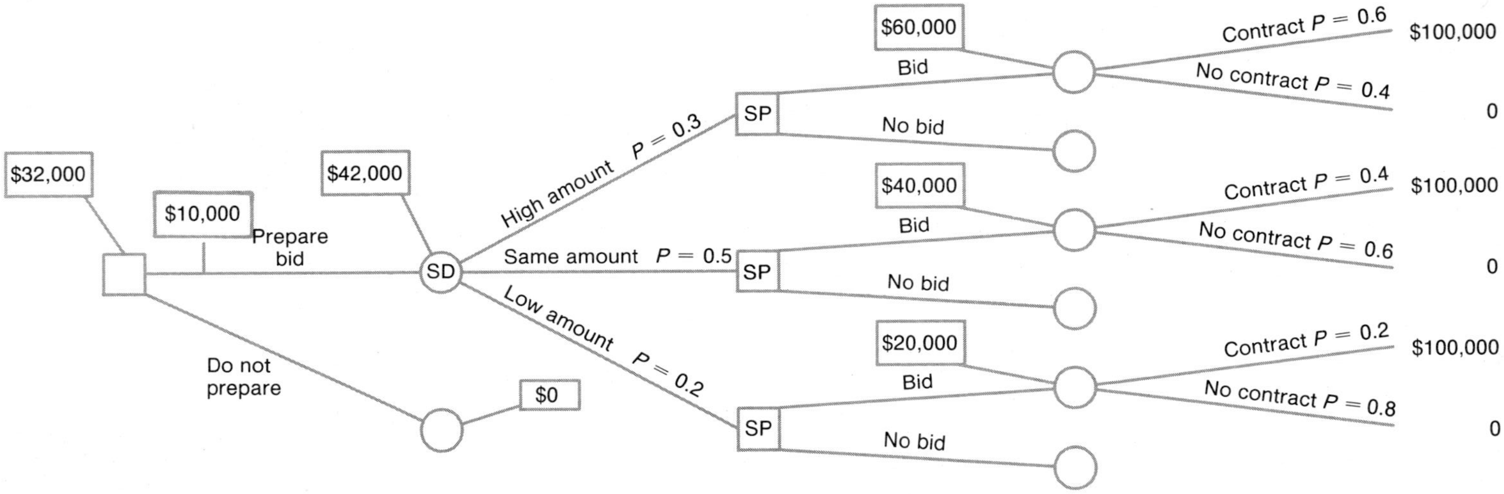

1,000 UN Forces

Country *A*'s reaction	Probability	Stability of local government
Send 3,000 troops	0.1	45%
Send 2,000 troops	0.5	50
Send 1,000 troops	0.4	60

2,000 UN Forces

Country *A*'s reaction	Probability	Stability of local government
Send 3,000 troops	0.2	40%
Send 2,000 troops	0.6	50
Send 1,000 troops	0.2	65

3,000 UN Forces

Country *A*'s reaction	Probability	Stability of local government
Send 3,000 troops	0.6	50%
Send 2,000 troops	0.3	60
Send 1,000 troops	0.1	70

As stated earlier, the probability of Country *A*'s not taking any military action is 0.3. In that case, the expected stability of the local government would be as follows.

UN forces	Stability of local government
1,000	60%
2,000	70
3,000	80

Several member states of the UN are trying to determine the most appropriate size of the peacekeeping forces in the area in order to improve the stability of the local government.

The entire decision tree analysis for the UN peacekeeping forces problem is presented in Fig. 10.3.

Figure 10.3 The UN Peacekeeping Forces Problem

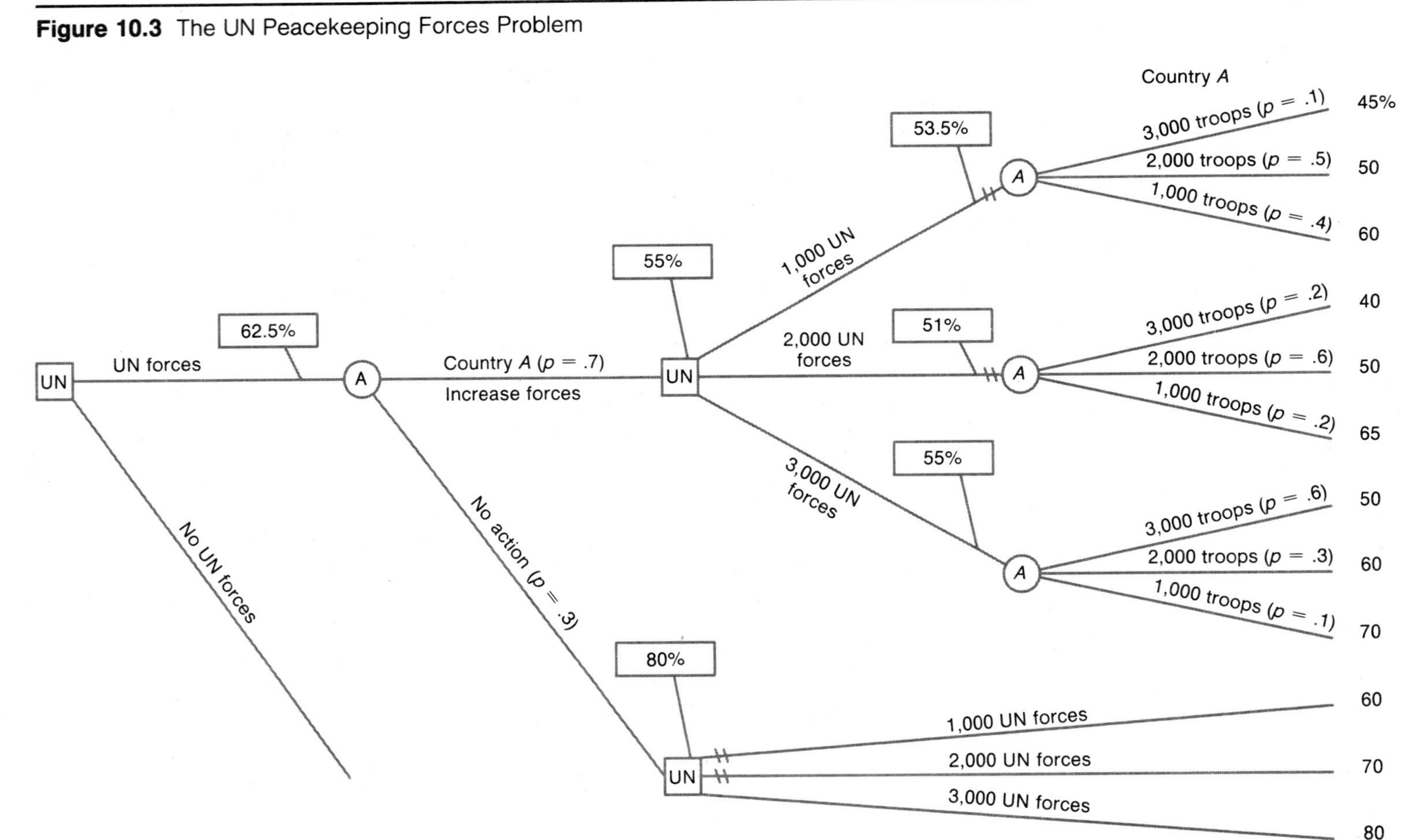

Application of the *Micro Manager*

In this section, an application example of the *Micro Manager* to a decision tree problem is presented. The program diskette provides the complete information about decision tree analysis, including the purpose of the technique, solution of an example problem, interactive input instructions, and the batch input procedure. Thus, in this section we will present only the information (purpose of the technique and the batch input data format) and the solution of a sample decision tree problem using the interactive input mode.

```
<< PURPOSE >>

DECISION TREE determines the optimum alternative that should be selected among
various paths of a decision tree.  It also computes the expected value of the
optimum alternative.  The program can handle up to 100 nodes in a decision
tree.

<<  BATCH INPUT DATA FORMAT  >>

Type in the values of the following input data requirements, after creating a
new file.  You may enter as many values as you want in a line, separating them
by commas for alphabetic characters and by commas or blank spaces for numeric
values.  However, the input data must be exactly in the following order:

1. Number of branches
2. For each branch
     starting node number
     ending node number
     probability (0 at decision node)
     conditional payoff (0 if not available)

** Sample Batch Input Data Set (Example 10.1) **

17              ; seventeen branches
1,2,0,-10       ; start & end node, probability, and payoff at branch 1
1,3,0,0         ; start & end node, probability, and payoff at branch 2
2,4,.3,0        ; start & end node, probability, and payoff at branch 3
2,5,.5,0        ; start & end node, probability, and payoff at branch 4
2,6,.2,0        ; start & end node, probability, and payoff at branch 5
4,7,0,0         ; start & end node, probability, and payoff at branch 6
4,8,0,0         ; start & end node, probability, and payoff at branch 7
5,9,0,0         ; start & end node, probability, and payoff at branch 8
5,10,0,0        ; start & end node, probability, and payoff at branch 9
6,11,0,0        ; start & end node, probability, and payoff at branch 10
6,12,0,0        ; start & end node, probability, and payoff at branch 11
7,13,.6,100     ; start & end node, probability, and payoff at branch 12
7,14,.4,0       ; start & end node, probability, and payoff at branch 13
9,15,.4,100     ; start & end node, probability, and payoff at branch 14
9,16,.6,0       ; start & end node, probability, and payoff at branch 15
11,17,.2,100    ; start & end node, probability, and payoff at branch 16
11,18,.8,0      ; start & end node, probability, and payoff at branch 17
```

```
PROGRAM: Decision Tree

Enter number of branches: 17
For branch 1
Enter starting node number and ending node number: 1,2
Enter probability (enter 0 at decision node): 0
Enter conditional payoff (enter 0 if not available): -10

For branch 2
Enter starting node number and ending node number: 1,3
Enter probability (enter 0 at decision node): 0
Enter conditional payoff (enter 0 if not available): 0

For branch 3
Enter starting node number and ending node number: 2,4
Enter probability (enter 0 at decision node): .3
Enter conditional payoff (enter 0 if not available): 0

For branch 4
Enter starting node number and ending node number: 2,5
Enter probability (enter 0 at decision node): .5
Enter conditional payoff (enter 0 if not available): 0

For branch 5
Enter starting node number and ending node number: 2,6
Enter probability (enter 0 at decision node): .2
Enter conditional payoff (enter 0 if not available): 0

For branch 6
Enter starting node number and ending node number: 4,7
Enter probability (enter 0 at decision node): 0
Enter conditional payoff (enter 0 if not available): 0

For branch 7
Enter starting node number and ending node number: 4,8
Enter probability (enter 0 at decision node): 0
Enter conditional payoff (enter 0 if not available): 0

For branch 8
Enter starting node number and ending node number: 5,9
Enter probability (enter 0 at decision node): 0
Enter conditional payoff (enter 0 if not available): 0

For branch 9
Enter starting node number and ending node number: 5,10
Enter probability (enter 0 at decision node):0

For branch 10
Enter starting node number and ending node number: 6,11
Enter probability (enter 0 at decision node): 0
Enter conditional payoff (enter 0 if not available): 0

For branch 11
Enter starting node number and ending node number: 6,12
Enter probability (enter 0 at decision node): 0
Enter conditional payoff (enter 0 if not available): 0
```

```
For branch 12
Enter starting node number and ending node number: 7,13
Enter probability (enter 0 at decision node): .6
Enter conditional payoff (enter 0 if not available): 100

For branch 13
Enter starting node number and ending node number: 7,14
Enter probability (enter 0 at decision node):

For branch 14
Enter starting node number and ending node number: 9,15
Enter probability (enter 0 at decision node): .4
Enter conditional payoff (enter 0 if not available): 100

For branch 15
Enter starting node number and ending node number: 9,16
Enter probability (enter 0 at decision node): .6
Enter conditional payoff (enter 0 if not available): 0

For branch 16
Enter starting node number and ending node number: 11,17
Enter probability (enter 0 at decision node): .2
Enter conditional payoff (enter 0 if not available): 100

For branch 17
Enter starting node number and ending node number: 11,18
Enter probability (enter 0 at decision node): .8
Enter conditional payoff (enter 0 if not available): 0

PROGRAM: Decision Tree

***** INPUT DATA ENTERED *****
```

Branch	Nodes	Probability	Conditional Payoff
1	1 ---> 2	0.00	-10.00
2	1 ---> 3	0.00	0.00
3	2 ---> 4	0.30	0.00
4	2 ---> 5	0.50	0.00
5	2 ---> 6	0.20	0.00
6	4 ---> 7	0.00	0.00
7	4 ---> 8	0.00	0.00
8	5 ---> 9	0.00	0.00
9	5 --->10	0.00	0.00
10	6 --->11	0.00	0.00
11	6 --->12	0.00	0.00
12	7 --->13	0.60	100.00
13	7 --->14	0.40	0.00
14	9 --->15	0.40	100.00
15	9 --->16	0.60	0.00
16	11 --->17	0.20	100.00
17	11 --->18	0.80	0.00

***** PROGRAM OUTPUT *****

Evaluated Decision Tree

Branch	Nodes	Probability	Conditional Payoff
1	1 ---> 2	Decision	32.00 *
2	1 ---> 3	Decision	0.00
3	2 ---> 4	0.30	18.00
4	2 ---> 5	0.50	20.00
5	2 ---> 6	0.20	4.00
6	4 ---> 7	Decision	60.00 *
7	4 ---> 8	Decision	0.00
8	5 ---> 9	Decision	40.00 *
9	5 --->10	Decision	0.00
10	6 --->11	Decision	20.00 *
11	6 --->12	Decision	0.00
12	7 --->13	0.60	60.00
13	7 --->14	0.40	0.00
14	9 --->15	0.40	40.00
15	9 --->16	0.60	0.00
16	11 --->17	0.20	20.00
17	11 --->18	0.80	0.00

* indicates preferred decision branches and payoffs

Conditional payoff of the solution = 32.00

Summary

Decision tree analysis is a useful tool for problems that involve sequential decisions under the condition of risk. The schematic presentation of the sequential decision process makes decision tree analysis especially easy to use for complex multiperiod decision problems. The *Micro Manager* is very effective in analyzing even the most complex decision tree problems.

References

Lee, S. M. 1983. *Introduction to management science.* Chicago: Dryden.

Lee, S. M., L. J. Moore, and B. W. Taylor. 1985. *Management science.* 2d ed. Dubuque, IA: Wm. C. Brown Publishers.

Luce, R. D., and H. Raiffa. 1957. *Games and decisions.* New York: John Wiley & Sons.

Schlaiffer, R. 1969. *Analysis of decisions under uncertainty.* New York: McGraw-Hill.

Problems

1. Draw the decision tree for the following concession-stand payoff problem and solve it by using the *Micro Manager.*

Alternative \ Future	Sunny $p = 0.4$	Rainy $p = 0.6$
Coke	$1,000	400
Ice cream	600	800

2. Draw the decision tree for the following payoff decision problem and solve it by using the *Micro Manager.*

Alternative \ Future	Demand		
	Low($p = 0.3$)	Med.($p = 0.4$)	High($p = 0.3$)
Make	−$400	200	300
Buy	100	190	150

3. Draw the decision tree for the following investment problem and solve it by using the *Micro Manager.*

Alternative \ Future	Demand		
	Low($p = 0.2$)	Med.($p = 0.5$)	High($p = 0.3$)
Small	$300	300	300
Medium	100	400	400
Large	−200	200	500

4. Draw the decision tree for the following decision table and solve it by using the *Micro Manager.*

Alternative \ Future	State of Nature		
	$S_1(p = 0.3)$	$S_2(p = 0.4)$	$S_3(p = 0.3)$
Produce	−$150	100	200
Buy	200	200	200

5. Draw the decision tree for the following decision table and solve it by using the *Micro Manager.*

Alternative \ Future	State of Nature			
	S_1	S_2	S_3	S_4
D_1	$50	40	40	30
D_2	40	40	30	40
D_3	30	40	30	20
D_4	−10	100	10	10
Probability	0.30	0.15	0.35	0.20

6. Construct the equivalent table for the following decision tree and solve it by using the *Micro Manager.*

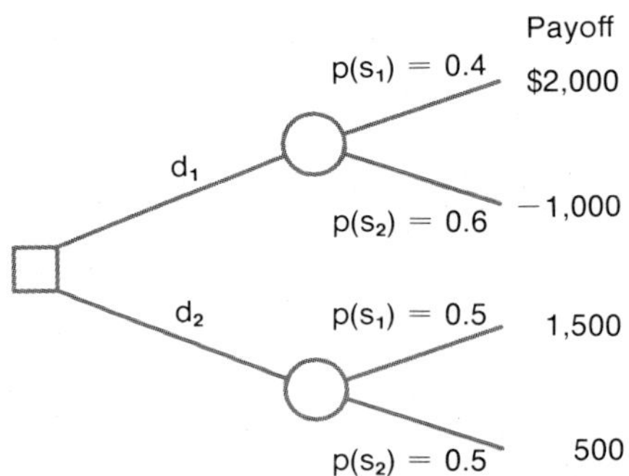

7. Construct the equivalent table for the following decision tree and solve it by using the *Micro Manager.*

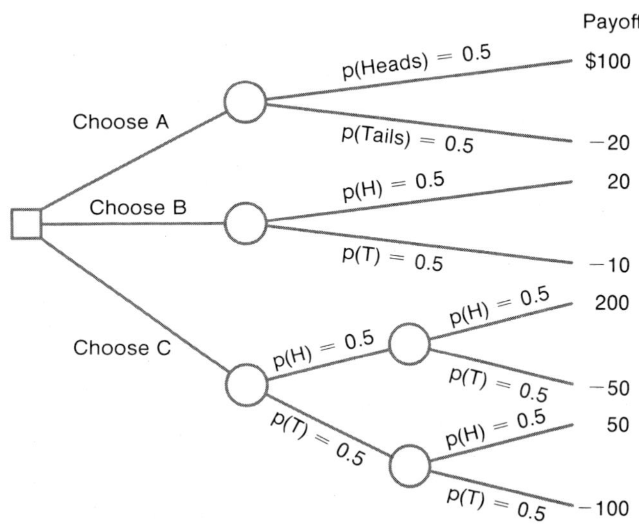

8. Construct the equivalent table for the following decision tree and solve it by using the *Micro Manager.*

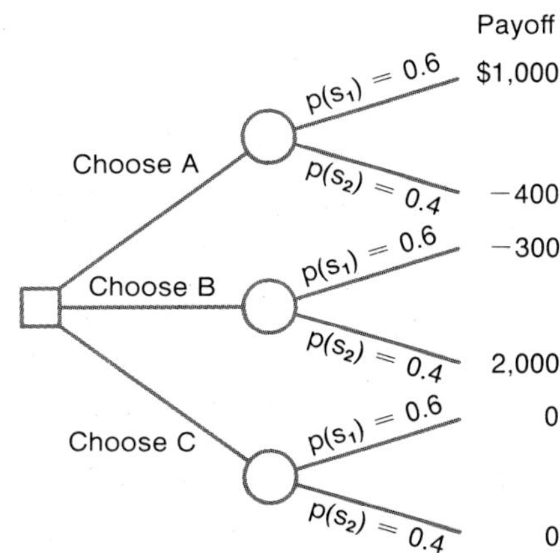

9. Construct the equivalent table for the following decision tree and solve it by using the *Micro Manager.*

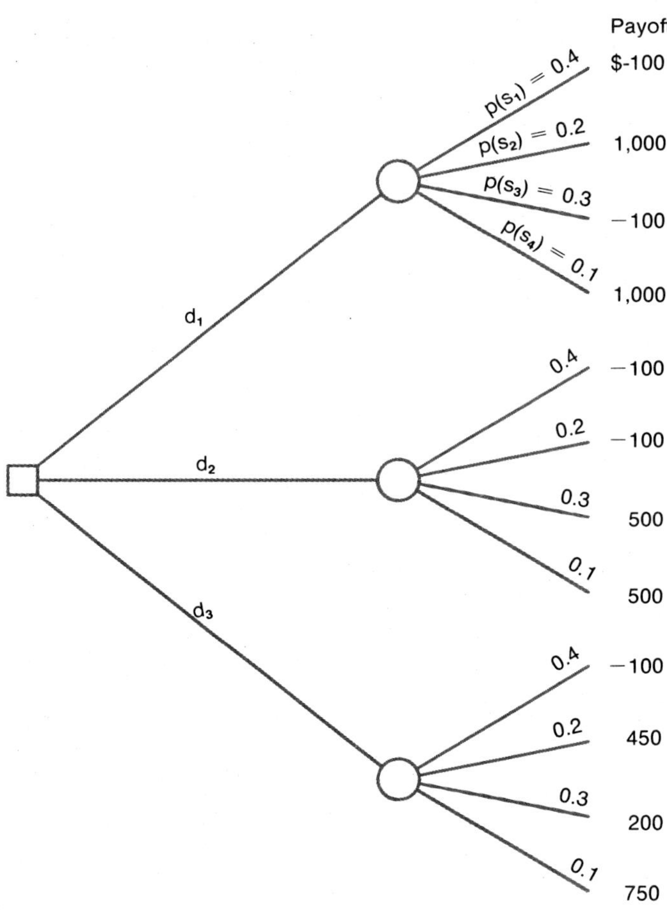

10. Construct the equivalent table for the following decision tree and solve it by using the *Micro Manager.*

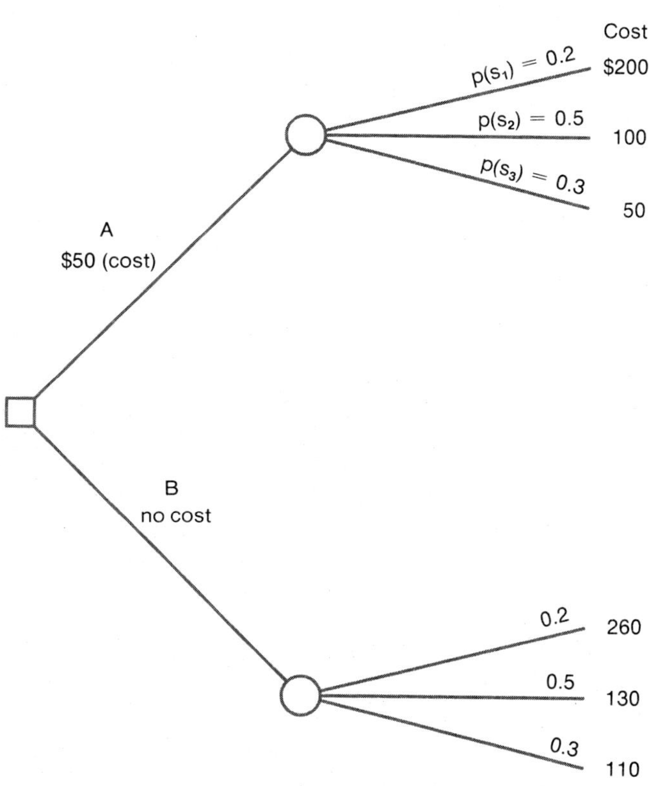

11. Given the following decision tree, find the best action by using the *Micro Manager*.

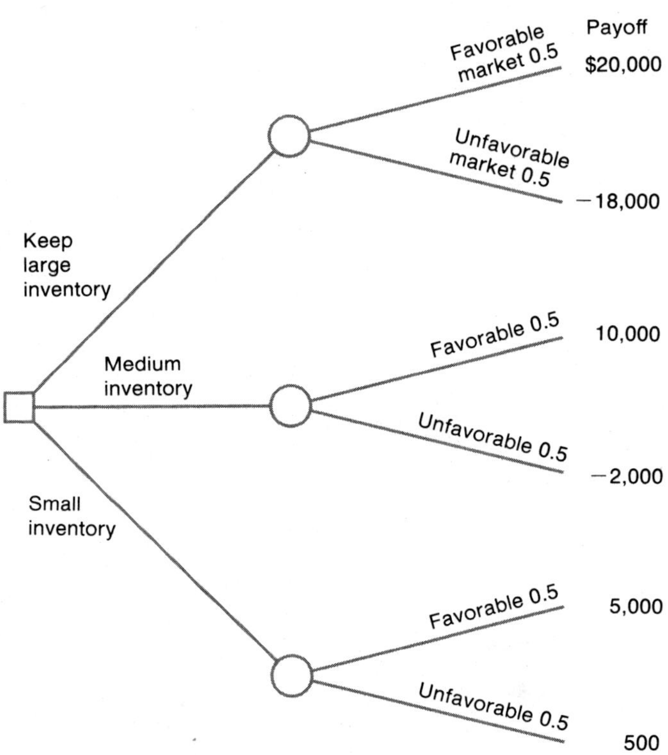

12. Given the following decision tree, find the best action by using the *Micro Manager.*

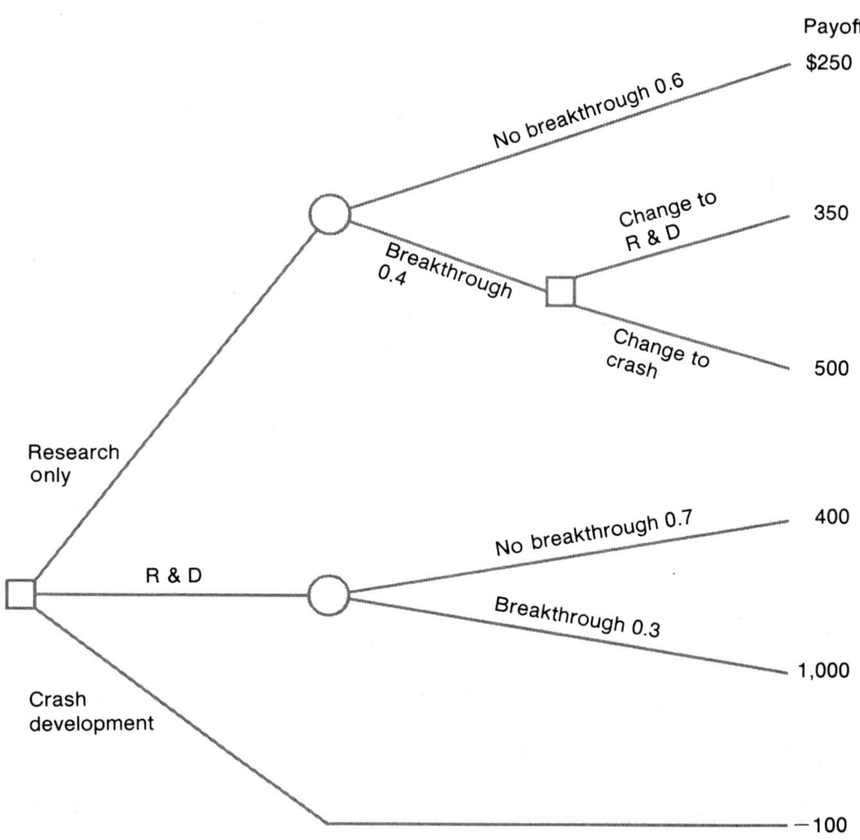

13. Given the following decision tree, find the best action by using the *Micro Manager.*

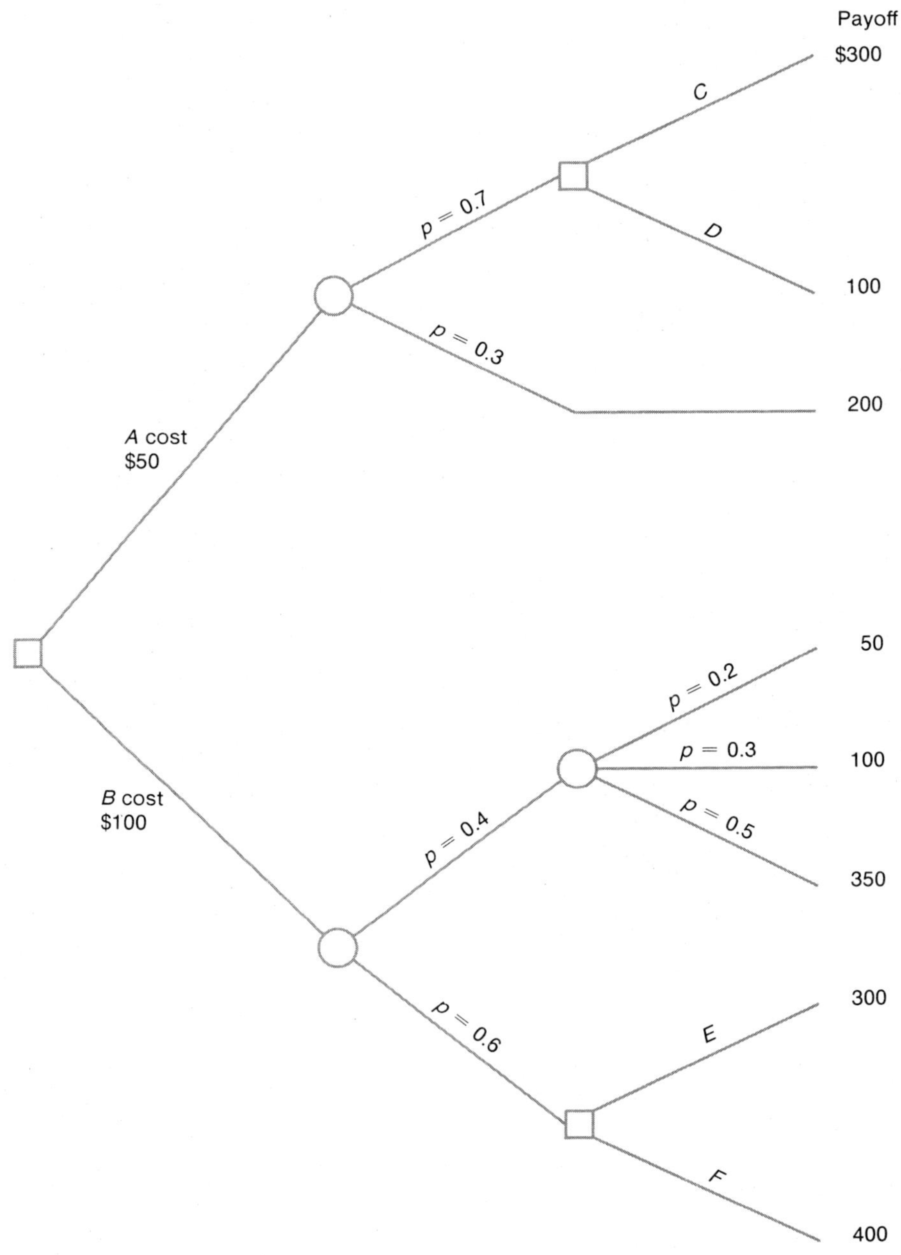

14. Given the following decision tree, find the best action by using the *Micro Manager*.

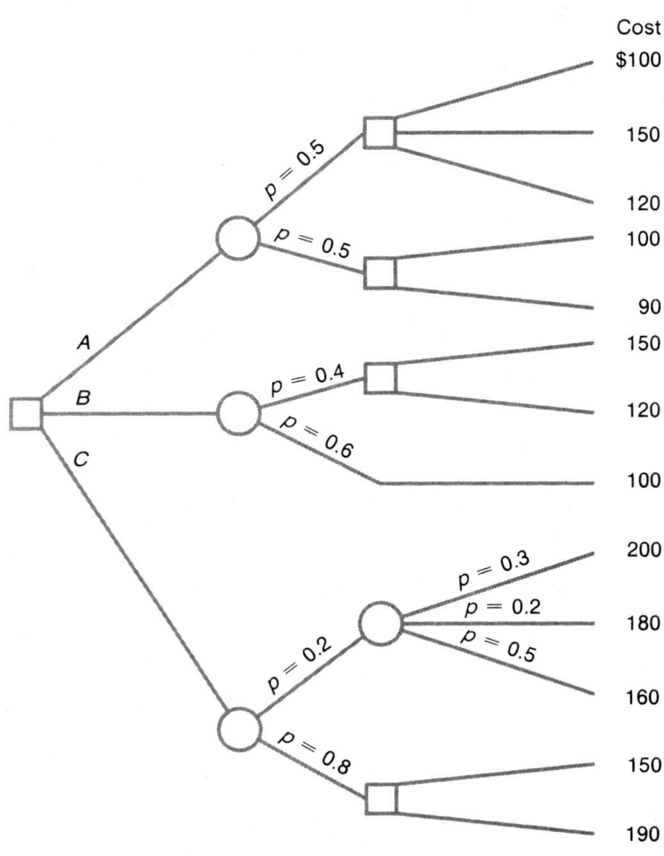

15. Given the following decision tree, find the best action by using the *Micro Manager*.

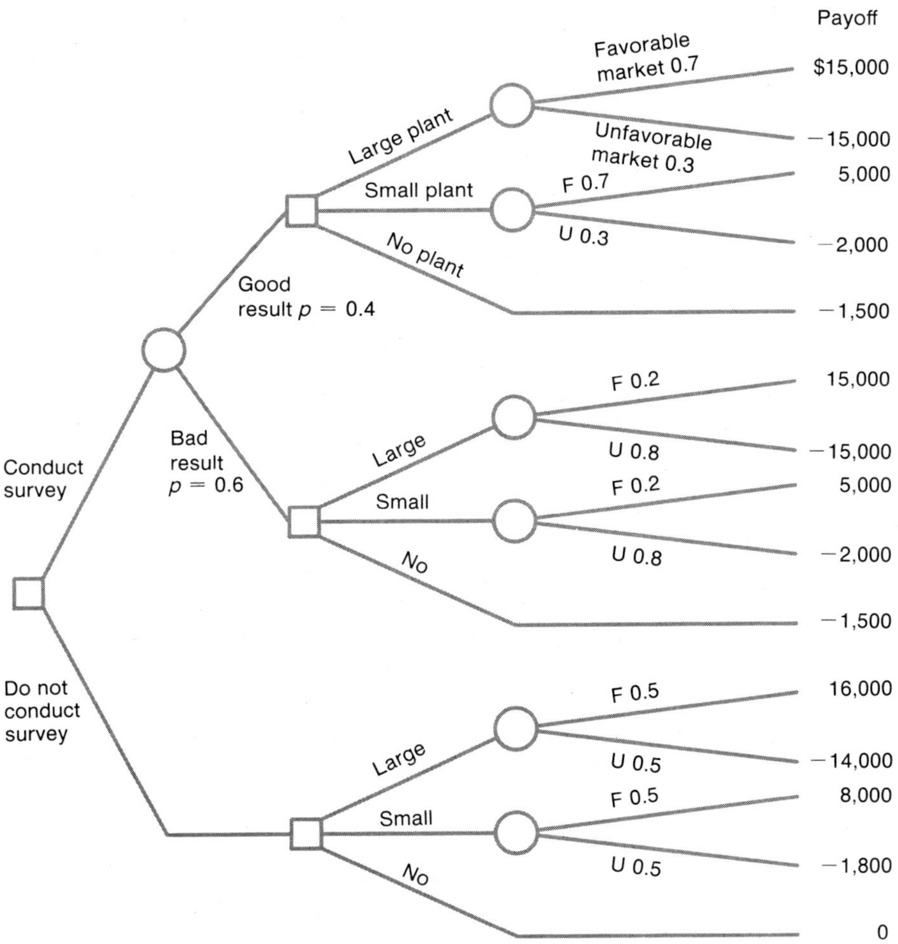

16. Luke Wagner is considering the construction of a new plant. If the market is favorable to him, he could realize a new profit of $10,000. If the market is not favorable, Luke could lose $4,000. If he does not construct the plant, there is no cost at all. He guesses the chance of success is 50–50, since he does not have market data.

    a. Draw a decision tree for this problem.
    b. Determine the best alternative by using the *Micro Manager*.

17. Luke (in Problem 16) found a consulting company that offered to perform a study of the market at a fee of $500. The consulting company gave Luke the following probability data.

p(favorable market/favorable research) = 0.8
p(unfavorable market/favorable research) = 0.2
p(favorable market/unfavorable research) = 0.1
p(unfavorable market/unfavorable research) = 0.9
p(favorable research) = 0.6
p(unfavorable research) = 0.4

a. Draw a decision tree for this problem.
b. Determine the best alternative by using the *Micro Manager.*

18. Micro Company is considering developing one of two possible home computers: Micro I and Micro II. The future of home computers depends on software prices. The anticipated profits as they relate to software prices are shown in the following table.

	Software Prices		
	Low(p = 0.2)	Med(p = 0.5)	High(p = 0.3)
Micro I	−$5,000	8,000	20,000
Micro II	10,000	−10,000	2,000

a. Draw a decision tree for this problem.
b. Determine the best alternative by using the *Micro Manager.*

19. The Auto Tire company is considering ordering a quantity of snow tires for this coming winter. If the company orders 1,000 pairs of snow tires, it forecasts a profit of $3,500 when snowfall is heavy, $1,000 when snowfall is moderate, and a $4,500 loss when snowfall is light. On the other hand, if the company orders 2,000 pairs of snow tires, it forecasts a profit of $9,000 if snowfall is heavy, $3,000 if it is moderate, and $10,000 loss if it is light. Based on the weather station's long-range forecast, Auto Tire company estimates P(heavy snow) = 0.4, p(moderate snow) = 0.4, and p(light snow) = 0.2.

a. Draw the decision tree for this problem.
b. Determine the best alternative by using the *Micro Manager.*

20. Pig Skin Sporting Company has an opportunity to buy footballs at a special price if it buys them before the football season begins. If Pig Skin buys early, it can buy the balls for $10 each. If Pig Skin buys during the season, the balls will cost $15 each. If Pig Skin overstocks, it must sell the balls after the season for $9 each. The balls retail for $20. They forecasted the demand for balls as:

Demand	Probability
50	0.20
60	0.30
70	0.30
80	0.20

a. Draw the decision tree for this problem.

b. Determine the best alternative by using the *Micro Manager.*

CHAPTER 11

Decision Making under Uncertainty

Decision making under risk assumes that the probabilities of certain events occurring are known and such information is available. However, in many real-world situations, such probabilities either are not known or such information is not available. Such a situation constitutes decision making under uncertainty. Decision making under uncertainty is extremely difficult since no clear-cut criterion can be used for decision making. Nevertheless, a number of criteria have been suggested for decision making under uncertainty. In this chapter, we will study these criteria and the ways to use them through the *Micro Manager*.

Basics

In a situation of uncertainty, the decision maker may have concrete information about conditional outcomes of various, alternative courses of action under possible states of nature, as in the decision-making situation under risk. However, in a situation of uncertainty, the probabilities of potential states of nature occurring are not known and must be estimated. Decision making under uncertainty involves the following elements: alternative courses of action, possible states of nature, conditional payoffs for alternatives under various states of nature, and unknown probabilities for the possible states of nature.

The following example shows five different decision rules that can be used for conditions of uncertainty.

Example 11.1 Financial Consultants, Inc.

Financial Consultants, Inc., specializes in estate planning and investments for professional clients. Currently, the firm has $500,000 to invest and is considering three investment alternatives: stocks, tax-free bonds, and real-estate. The firm intends to invest the entire amount in one alternative. The conditional payoffs of the investments are based on the future state of the economy. Three possible states of the economy exist: rapid growth, normal growth, and slow growth. The payoff matrix for Financial Consultants' problem is shown below.

	Economic Condition		
Alternative	**Rapid growth**	**Normal growth**	**Slow growth**
Stocks	$60,000	$30,000	−$10,000
Bonds	50,000	35,000	5,000
Real estate	40,000	30,000	20,000

As the payoff matrix indicates, no probabilities are listed for each of the possible economic conditions. Other than that, the payoff table is exactly the same as a decision problem table under risk. Here are several criteria that have been suggested for decision making under uncertainty.

Laplace Criterion

The Laplace criterion proposes that since complete uncertainty exists about the possible states of nature, we should assign an equal probability to each of the states of nature. In our problem, three possible states of nature (economic conditions) exist. Thus, a probability of one-third should be assigned to each economic condition. With the assigned probabilities, we can easily compute the expected value for each of the alternatives as follows:

$$E(\text{Stocks}) = \tfrac{1}{3}(60{,}000) + \tfrac{1}{3}(30{,}000) + \tfrac{1}{3}(-10{,}000) = \$26{,}667$$

$$E(\text{Bonds}) = \tfrac{1}{3}(50{,}000) + \tfrac{1}{3}(35{,}000) + \tfrac{1}{3}(5{,}000) = \$30{,}000$$

$$E(\text{Real Estate}) = \tfrac{1}{3}(40{,}000) + \tfrac{1}{3}(30{,}000) + \tfrac{1}{3}(20{,}000) = \$30{,}000$$

Thus, our choice will be either bonds or real estate.

Maximin Criterion

The maximin criterion, also known as the Wald criterion, is based on an extremely cautious or pessimistic outlook for the future. In this criterion, decision alternatives are compared based on their minimum conditional payoffs. The alternative that has the maximum amount among the minimum payoffs is selected as the best alternative. In our example, the minimum conditional payoffs of the alternatives are as follows:

Alternative	Minimum payoff
Stocks	−$10,000
Bonds	5,000
Real estate	20,000

Thus, real estate is selected as the best alternative according to the maximin criterion.

Maximax Criterion

The maximax criterion is the opposite of the maximin criterion. In this criterion, the decision maker is assumed to be totally optimistic about the future. Thus, the decision maker selects the alternative that has the maximum amount among the maximum conditional payoffs. In our example, the maximum payoffs of the alternatives are as follows:

Alternative	Minimum payoff
Stocks	$60,000
Bonds	50,000
Real estate	40,000

Thus, the alternative of stocks is selected as the best choice.

Hurwicz Criterion

This criterion, suggested by Leonid Hurwicz, is a compromise between the maximin and maximax criterion. The decision maker may not be totally pessimistic or optimistic but somewhere in between the extremes. Hurwicz suggested a measure called the "coefficient of optimism," which represents the degree of the decision maker's optimism. The coefficient of optimism α is like probability in that it has a scale from 0 to 1. If $\alpha = 1$, the decision maker is completely optimistic. On the other hand, if $\alpha = 0$, the decision maker is completely pessimistic as the coefficient of pessimism is $1 - \alpha$.

According to the Hurwicz criterion, each decision alternative is analyzed by finding the sum of the maximum conditional payoff multiplied by α and the minimum conditional payoff multiplied by $1 - \alpha$. If $\alpha = 1$, the Hurwicz criterion results in the same solution as the maximax criterion. On the other hand, if $\alpha = 0$, the Hurwicz criterion is exactly the same as the minimax criterion.

In our example, let us suppose that $\alpha = 0.7$. Then, our analysis is as follows:

Stocks:	$60{,}000 \times 0.7 + (-10{,}000) \times 0.3 = \$39{,}000$
Bonds:	$50{,}000 \times 0.7 + 5{,}000 \times 0.3 = \$36{,}500$
Real estate:	$40{,}000 \times 0.7 + 20{,}000 \times 0.3 = \$34{,}000$

The stocks are the best choice since they have the highest weighted payoff ($39,000).

Minimax Criterion

The minimax criterion, originally suggested by L. J. Savage, which is also referred to as the regret criterion, attempts to minimize the maximum opportunity loss. The opportunity loss or opportunity cost, as we studied in the transportation and assignment problem, represents the difference between the best possible outcome and the outcome of a given alternative.

In our example, the opportunity loss is determined by subtracting each conditional payoff from the maximum conditional payoff for each column or type of economic condition (state of nature). Thus, we can develop the following opportunity loss or regret matrix.

	Economic Condition		
Alternative	**Rapid growth**	**Normal growth**	**Slow growth**
Stocks	0	5,000	30,000
Bonds	10,000	0	15,000
Real estate	20,000	5,000	0

The maximum opportunity loss for each alternative is presented below.

Alternative	**Maximum opportunity loss**
Stock	$30,000
Bonds	15,000
Real estate	20,000

Since we attempt to minimize the maximum regret, our choice will be bonds.

Bayes' Theorem

Another important topic that is related to decision making under uncertainty is Bayes' theorem or Bayes' decision rule. Bayes was an eighteenth-century English Presbyterian minister and an outstanding mathematician. Bayes' decision rule is a powerful statistical tool for revising the prior probabilities of events or states of nature based on experiments or additional information. The basic principle behind Bayes' theorem is that the accuracy of event probabilities can be improved by using new information. Currently available probabilities are known as prior probabilities, while the revised probabilities are referred to as posterior probabilities.

When the college football season opens in the fall, the top twenty ratings are often based on the last season's record and returning lettermen. However, as the season progresses, the ratings are altered based on the win–loss records and actual performance of the teams. Decision making under uncertainty is quite similar to the football rating system.

The formula for revising probabilities based on Bayes' theorem is

$$P(A_i \mid B) = \frac{P(A_i)P(B \mid A_i)}{\sum_{i=1}^{n} P(A_i)P(B \mid A_i)},$$

where A_i = a set of mutually exclusive events; B = an outcome of an experiment; $P(A_i)$ = the prior probability for event i; and $P(B \mid A_i)$ = the conditional probability of outcome B, given the occurrence of A_i.

$P(A_i \mid B)$ is called a revised probability, a posterior probability, or a Bayesian probability. Using the above formula, it is possible to solve for $P(A_i \mid B)$ if $P(B \mid A_i)$ is known.

Example 11.2 Mississippi Electronics, Inc.

Mississippi Electronics, Inc., has three plants that produce random-access memory (RAM) boards for microcomputers. Plant A produces 55 percent of the total output, plant B produces 25 percent, and plant C produces the remaining 20 percent of the output. The production manager has been very concerned about the quality of products, since many customers are beginning to purchase Japanese RAM boards.

After evaluating the records that the quality-control department compiled, the following percentages of defective boards have been established:

Plant	% defective
A	3%
B	1
C	2

The production manager inspected one of the boards in the warehouse, whereupon the board was proved to be defective. The production manager has been extremely concerned about product quality at plant A. Thus, the manager would like to know the probability that the particular board he inspected came from plant A.

The prior and conditional probabilities for this problem are as follows:

$$\begin{aligned} P(A) &= 0.55 \qquad & P(D|A) &= 0.03 \\ P(B) &= 0.25 \qquad & P(D|B) &= 0.01 \\ P(C) &= 0.20 \qquad & P(D|C) &= 0.02 \end{aligned}$$

where $P(A)$, $P(B)$, and $P(C)$ represent the prior probability that a board came from each of the plants, and $P(D|A)$, $P(D|B)$, and $P(D|C)$ indicate the conditional probability that a defective part came from each of the plants.

Given the above probabilities, the manager attempts to determine the posterior probability that a defective board came from plant A. Applying Bayes' theorem, we can compute the following:

$$\begin{aligned} P(A|D) &= \frac{P(A)P(D|A)}{P(A)P(D|A) + P(B)P(D|B) + P(C)P(D|C)} \\ &= \frac{(0.55)(0.03)}{(0.55)(0.03) + (0.25)(0.01) + (0.20)(0.02)} \\ &= \frac{0.0165}{0.0230} \\ &= 0.717. \end{aligned}$$

The only information the production manager had previously was that 55 percent of the total production came from plant A and that 3 percent of its products were defective. After inspecting a RAM board and finding it to be defective, the production manager now knows there is a 0.717 probability that the defective board came from plant A. Thus, the inspection or sampling provides additional information that allows the production manager to revise the probability. Improved and more accurate information certainly will enhance the production manager's efforts to improve quality control.

Application of the *Micro Manager*

In this section we present an application example of the *Micro Manager* to a decision making problem under uncertainty. There are many different decision making criteria for decision making under uncertainty. The program diskette provides you with the complete information, including the purpose of the techniques, solutions of various example problems using different criteria, interactive input instructions, and the batch input procedure. Here we will present only the information (purpose of the technique and the batch input data format) and the solution of a sample problem using the interactive input mode of the Laplace Criterion and the Bayes' Decision Rule.

<< PURPOSE >>

DECISION MAKING UNDER UNCERTAINTY determines the optimum alternative among various courses of action available under uncertainty. This program utilizes various decision criteria such as Laplace, Maximin, Maximax, Hurwicz, and Minimax. The output will indicate either the maximum expected value or minimum expected loss by analyzing the alternatives under various states of nature.

<< BATCH INPUT DATA FORMAT >>

Type in the values of the following input data requirements, after creating a new file. You may enter as many values as you want in a line, separating them by commas for alphabetic characters and by commas or blank spaces for numeric values. However, the input data must be exactly in the following order:

1. Number of alternatives
2. Number of events
3. Payoff of each alternative and event combination
4. Coefficient of optimism (alpha: 0 to 1)

** Sample Batch Input Data Set (Example 11.1) **

```
3,3        ; three alternatives and three events
60,30,-10  ; payoffs of alternative 1
50,35,5    ; payoffs of alternative 2
40,30,20   ; payoffs of alternative 3
.5         ; coefficient of optimism
```

```
PROGRAM: Decision Making Under Uncertainty

Enter number of alternatives: 3
Enter number of events: 3

Enter payoff of alternative 1 and event 1 : 60
Enter payoff of alternative 1 and event 2 : 30
Enter payoff of alternative 1 and event 3 : -10

Enter payoff of alternative 2 and event 1 : 50
Enter payoff of alternative 2 and event 2 : 35
Enter payoff of alternative 2 and event 3 : 5

Enter payoff of alternative 3 and event 1 : 40
Enter payoff of alternative 3 and event 2 : 30
Enter payoff of alternative 3 and event 3 : 20

Enter coefficient of optimism (alpha: 0 to 1), if not available enter 0: .5
```

```
PROGRAM: Decision Making Under Uncertainty

***** INPUT DATA ENTERED *****

---------------------------------------------
                         Events
              -------------------------------
Alternative        1          2          3
---------------------------------------------
     1        60000.00   30000.00  -10000.00
     2        50000.00   35000.00    5000.00
     3        40000.00   30000.00   20000.00
---------------------------------------------

Coefficient of optimism:  .5

*****   PROGRAM OUTPUT   *****


Laplace
-----------------------------------------
Alternatives            Expected Value
-----------------------------------------
     1                    26666.67
     2                    30000.00*
     3                    30000.00*
-----------------------------------------

Maximin
-----------------------------------------
Alternatives            Maximin Payoff
-----------------------------------------
     1                   -10000.00
     2                     5000.00
     3                    20000.00*
-----------------------------------------

Maximax
-----------------------------------------
Alternatives            Maximax Payoff
-----------------------------------------
     1                    60000.00*
     2                    50000.00
     3                    40000.00
-----------------------------------------

Hurwicz
-----------------------------------------
Alternatives            Hurwicz Payoff
-----------------------------------------
     1                    25000.00
     2                    27500.00
     3                    30000.00*
-----------------------------------------
```

Mimimax

Alternatives	Maximum Regret
1	30000.00
2	15000.00*
3	20000.00

* indicates the best solution.

Decision Criterion	Optimum Alternative
Laplace	2 3
Maximin	3
Maximax	1
Hurwicz (alpha = .5)	3
Mimimax	2

<< PURPOSE >>

BAYES' DECISION RULE computes the marginal probabilities and posterior probabilities given once an event has taken place. This program can deal with up to 20 states of nature and 20 different predictors associated with these states of nature.

<< BATCH INPUT DATA FORMAT >>

Type in the values of the following input data requirements, after creating a new file. You may enter as many values as you want in a line, separating them by commas for alphabetic characters and by commas or blank spaces for numeric values. However, the input data must be exactly in the following order:

1. Number of alternatives
2. Number of events
3. Prior probability for each alternative
4. Conditional probability for each alternative and event combination

** Sample Batch Input Data Set (Example 11.2) **

```
3,2           ; three alternatives and two events
.55,.25,.2    ; prior probabilities for alternatives
.03,.97       ; conditional probabilities for events in alternative 1
.01,.99       ; conditional probabilities for events in alternative 2
.02,.98       ; conditional probabilities for events in alternative 3
```

PROGRAM: Bayes' Decision Rule

```
Enter number of alternatives (states): 3
Enter number of predicted events: 2

<< Prior Probability Information >>

Enter prior probability for alternative 1 :  .55
Enter prior probability for alternative 2 :  .25
Enter prior probability for alternative 3 :  .2
```

```
<< Conditional Probability Information >>

Enter conditional probability for alternative 1 and event  1 :  .97
Enter conditional probability for alternative 1 and event  2 :  .03
Enter conditional probability for alternative 2 and event  1 :  .99
Enter conditional probability for alternative 2 and event  2 :  .01
Enter conditional probability for alternative 3 and event  1 :  .98
Enter conditional probability for alternative 3 and event  2 :  .02

PROGRAM: Bayes' Decision Rule

***** INPUT DATA ENTERED *****

  State     Prior Probability
--------------------------------
    1           0.550
    2           0.250
    3           0.200
--------------------------------
  Total         1.000

        Conditional Probability of Prediction
  State         1        2
-------------------------------------
    1        0.970    0.030
    2        0.990    0.010
    3        0.980    0.020
-------------------------------------

*****   PROGRAM OUTPUT   *****


        Posterior Probability of Prediction
  State         1        2
-------------------------------------
    1        0.546    0.717
    2        0.253    0.109
    3        0.201    0.174
-------------------------------------
```

Summary

Many decision problems we face in real-world situations involve numerous possible events whose probabilities of occurrence are not known. Decision making under uncertainty, while quite prevalent, is not easy to analyze and consequently there are no clear-cut superior techniques to use. As a matter of fact, there are a number of different criteria suggested for decision making under uncertainty. In this chapter, we have examined these criteria and applied the *Micro Manager* for analyzing decision problems under uncertainty.

References

Halloway, C. A. 1979. *Decision making under uncertainty.* Englewood Cliffs, NJ: Prentice-Hall.

Lee, S. M. 1983. *Introduction to management science.* Chicago: Dryden.

Lee, S. M., L. J. Moore, and B. W. Taylor. 1985. *Management science.* 2d ed. Dubuque, IA: Wm. C. Brown Publishers.

Schlaiffer, R. 1969. *Analysis of decisions under uncertainty.* New York: McGraw-Hill.

Problems

1. A chief-executive officer (CEO) of a multinational corporation told a group of micro managers: "In inflation-prone countries, we utilize a flexible credit policy adjusted to the short-term outlook for inflation in the local currency. If inflation will be slight, a two-month credit limit is allowed to retailers, since this limit will generate the highest dollar profits. If inflation will be moderate, we cut this limit to one month, since a one-month limit will result in the highest profits in dollar terms, and so on down to a limit of one week if inflation is severe. Lately, the government of Brazil has told us that we have to declare a credit policy that will be fixed for the next year. I urge all of you to find an optimum credit policy in Brazilian subsidiary."

Identify the structural elements of the above decision-making problem under uncertainty and construct a payoff matrix format.

2. Based on the information about past sales volume and various credit policies, the following expected profits are estimated—in millions of dollars.

$$P_{11} = 100 \qquad P_{12} = 99 \qquad P_{13} = 80$$
$$P_{21} = 95 \qquad P_{22} = 105 \qquad P_{23} = 85$$
$$P_{31} = 85 \qquad P_{32} = 90 \qquad P_{33} = 95$$

Using the Laplace criterion, compute the expected value of each credit-limit alternative and choose the best alternative.

3. Given the decision situation in Problem 2, choose the best credit-limit alternative, based on the regret criterion.

4. With the imperfect international capital market integration, modern financial portfolio theories suggest that multinationality of a company's operations should make the firm more attractive than a similar domestic company. The existence of real barriers to trading securities internationally allows multinational corporations (MNCs) to provide diversification opportunities not otherwise available to individual investors. Table 1 provides information about the beta coefficients of three MNCs

Table 1

Company	Foreign sales ratio	Beta
IBM	0.53	0.9192
Exxon	0.74	0.7321
Royal Dutch	0.76	0.7000
GE	0.21	1.2000
RCA	0.19	1.7000
Zenith Radio	0.00	1.9800

Table 2 Security return from $100 investment under the different states of economy

	State of Economy		
Alternative	**Recession**	**Normal**	**Boom**
IBM	95	117	140
Exxon	90	112.5	135
Royal Dutch	97	121	145
GE	85	120	155
RCA	60	110	160
Zenith Radio	50	115	180

and three other companies with little or no foreign operations. The beta coefficient measures a particular stock's relative volatility in relation to a stock market index. Based on the beta coefficients in Table 1, the expected security return under different states of economy is summarized in Table 2. When solving Problems 4 through 8, assume that you are interested in choosing only a particular stock.

Based on most of the financial portfolio theories that are constructed on the assumption that the average investor is a risk avertor, answer the following questions.

a. Define "risk" and discuss how it can be measured.
b. Based on the beta coefficients in Table 1, select the securities of three companies in the order of minimum risk.

5. Using the Laplace criterion, compute the expected value of each investment alternative in Problem 4. Choose the best alternative investment for an investor who seeks risk neutrality.

6. a. In Problem 4, if you are pessimistic or conservative about next year's state of economy, what investment alternative would you choose?
b. As an optimistic decision maker, choose the best alternative.

7. Again, in Problem 4, choose an investment alternative based on the regret criterion.

8. a. In Problem 4, using the Hurwicz criterion, choose the best alternative. Assume $\alpha = 0.7$.
   b. Compute the coefficient of optimism (α) to be indifferent between investment in IBM and investment in RCA.

9. The primary business of Multinational Mining and Petroleum Corporation (MMPC), headquartered in Chicago, is to explore natural resources such as oil, gas, coal, nickel, and copper on a global basis. Tom Brown, vice president of the International Financial Management Department, faces an important decision in regard to selecting a new project. He must choose only one of three candidate projects. Brown believes that the net present value (NPV) of the future income stream from a foreign natural resources development project depends heavily on the political conditions of host countries. According to a news report, Nicaragua is one of ten countries with the highest political risks and Canada is one of ten countries with the least political risks. Considering all relevant information, the project analysis team provided Tom Brown with the following payoff matrix.

NPV of three investment alternatives (all in millions of dollars)

	Political Conditions		
Alternative	**Deteriorate**	**Normal**	**Improve**
Canada	85	90	95
Nicaragua	−50	85	220
Australia	80	100	120

   Using the Laplace criterion, compute the expected value of each investment alternative and choose the best alternative.

10. a. In Problem 9, if you are a pessimist about the political condition of each host country, which investment alternative would you choose?
    b. As an optimist, choose the best alternative.

11. In Problem 9, choose an investment alternative based on the regret (minimax) criterion.

12. In Problem 9, using the Hurwicz criterion, choose the best alternative ($\alpha = 0.2$).

13. Now compute the coefficient of optimism to be indifferent between an investment in Australia and an investment in Canada.

14. Janet Wagenar, financial officer in Transnational Business Machine Corporation (TBM), wants to choose the most desirable policy of short-term financing to meet the current financing requirements. Basically, Wagenar has three alternative, short-term financing strategies. They include aggressive, zero-exposure, and "do nothing" strategies under three possible scenarios. Each scenario describes future states of the currencies that are involved in the financing strategies.

"No change" indicates that there will be no changes in foreign-exchange rates from the present situation. "Opposite to likely" refers to the changes in foreign-exchange rates opposite to the one anticipated in the most likely scenario. The "do nothing" policy indicates that the company will accept any foreign-exchange losses by not covering. Under the aggressive policy, the company makes the best estimate of currency change and acts accordingly by aggressive hedging or covering through the money market and/or the forward market. "Zero-exposure policy" reduces exposure to the minimum level.

Cost of short-term financing strategies (all in thousand dollars)

Policy	Scenario		
	Most likely	**No change**	**Opposite to likely**
Aggressive	−12.2	−28.9	−34.8
Zero exposure	−19.6	−26.0	−30.6
Do nothing	−18.7	−25.6	−26.9

Using the above table, Wagenar has to reach a decision on which policy to follow. Determine the best policy based on the criteria listed below:

a. Laplace
b. Maximin
c. Maximax
d. Minimax

15. Referring to Problem 14, determine the best alternative based on the Hurwicz criterion ($\alpha = 0.3$).

16. Toy International of Japan has been engaged in the business of manufacturing and distributing highly advanced electronic toys to domestic and foreign markets. Recently, the company sold $10,000 worth of products to a U. S. company. Payment is due in 90 days. Toy International has three alternatives to reduce the transaction exposure due to fluctuating foreign-exchange rates between the U. S. dollar and

to fluctuating foreign-exchange rates between the U. S. dollar and Japanese yen. The Japanese firm may decide to take the transaction risk ("do nothing" strategy). Under this "do nothing" strategy, if the Japanese yen depreciates against U. S. dollars, Toy International would receive only ¥ 180 million. On the other hand, if the yen should strengthen even more rapidly, the Japanese firm could receive ¥ 220 million.

If Toy International wants to hedge its transaction exposure in either the forward market or the money market, this is a covered transaction in which the company has no foreign-exchange risk. Therefore, the amount of money to be received in 90 days is fixed, regardless of future foreign-exchange rates between U. S. dollars and Japanese yen. Assume that the current spot exchange rate is ¥ 200 per U. S. dollar and the 90-day forward rate is ¥ 195 per U. S. dollar.

a. Construct a payoff matrix for this problem.
b. Determine the best policy based on each of these criteria: Laplace, maximin, and maximax.

17. The management of Paradies Schönheitsprodukte GmbH, a German-based multinational company, decided to give serious consideration to undertaking a major plant expansion in South America. Paradies GmbH has been confronted with a series of fierce competitions primarily from Japanese competitors in the South American market. In an attempt to react to the Japanese invasion based on just-in-time (JIT) production and the total-quality-control (TQC) system, the company decided to install a flexible manufacturing system (FMS) in one of three South American subsidiaries, the one that has the lowest-posterior probability of producing a defective product. The following table presents the output and defective rate at each plant during 1983–85.

Output and defective rate of plants by subsidiaries in 1983, 1984, 1985 (in %)

	1983		1984		1985	
	Output	**Defective**	**Output**	**Defective**	**Output**	**Defective**
Brazil	60	5	63	6	65	8
Paraguay	25	3	26	?	23	3
Colombia	15	2	11	3	12	?
Annual total output			130,000 units		138,000 units	
Total defective rate			5.5%		7%	

Determine the posterior probability of a defective product that is coming from a plant in the Colombian subsidiary in 1983.

18. a. In Problem 17, compute the percentage of defective products produced from the subsidiary in Paraguay in 1984.

b. Compute the posterior probability that a defective product would come from a plant in the Paraguay subsidiary in 1984.

19. a. In Problem 17, compute the percentage of defective products coming from the subsidiary in Colombia in 1985.

b. Compute the posterior probability that a defective product would come from a plant in the Colombian subsidiary in 1985.

20. The probability of classifying a good item as defective is 0.06, and the probability that a quality-control inspector classifies a defective item as defective is 0.94. The probability of an item's being defective is 0.15. An item has been classified as defective. Obtain the revised probability that this item is actually defective.

CHAPTER 12

Network Models

Many real-world problems involve a series of activities and events that can be constructed in a network form. Thus, network analysis has become an important topic of management science. Network analysis has been applied to such management problems as transportation (chap. 6), assignment (chap. 7), location–allocation, product flow, project management, and travel systems. In this chapter, we will discuss the most widely applied network models: namely, shortest route, miminum spanning tree, maximum flow, and critical path method–program evaluation and review technique (CPM-PERT).

Basics

A network is an undertaking that has a clear beginning point and a definite ending point. Some of the networks in real-world situations include construction of a new airport, transportation of oil from Alaska to Los Angeles, and development of a new cancer-fighting drug. Many organizations use network models to plan activities or projects. Network models can be extremely useful in determining project-duration time, shortest route, maximum or minimum flows, probability of completing a project within the given amount of time or resources, and so on.

A network is simply a graphical presentation of a flow of events and activities. A network consists of two primary elements: activities and events. An activity typically represents an operation that requires resources and consumes time. An event represents a junction point in time, or a location, such as a beginning or ending point of an activity. A graphical model of a network is usually represented by nodes (circles) for events and arcs (branches) for activities. Arcs establish the relationship between two events by connecting them with a branch.

An arc simply indicates a relationship without showing the direction of flow. A directed arc, shown by an arrow, indicates a specified direction. A sequence of connecting branches between any two nodes is often referred to as a *chain*. If the chain has a specified direction, it is called a *path*. If a chain connects a node to itself, it is called a *cycle*. The originating point of a network is often referred to as the *source node* and the terminating point is usually called the *sink node*.

Shortest-Route Problem

As the name implies, the shortest-route problem is concerned with determining the shortest route from a point in space to a destination. The typical shortest-route problem is the traveling plan from an originating city to a destination city through various highways and connecting cities.

The basic solution approach for the shortest-route problem is to fan out from the originating node and successively identify the next node that is the shortest route from the origin. The procedure can be summarized as follows:

1. Designate the originating node as the permanent set and identify the adjacent set of nodes from the permanent set.
2. Identify the node in the adjacent set with the shortest distance from the origin.
3. Store this branch and its direction. Delete any other branches that connect the permanent set to the selected adjacent set node from further evaluation.
4. Add the selected adjacent node to the permanent set.
5. Identify the new adjacent set of nodes. If there is no further adjacent set, terminate the procedure. Otherwise, go to Step 2.

Example 12.1 International Van Lines, Inc.

International Van Lines, Inc., is a professional moving company that helps organizations or households move by land, sea, or air. The company has just received a contract from a government agency to move several truckloads of furniture from Los Angeles to Washington, D.C.

Looking over the map, the dispatching manager has tentatively selected the following cities as connecting points of various possible routes: Denver (2), Dallas (3), Chicago (4), St. Louis (5), and Atlanta (6). Figure 12.1 presents the network from Los Angeles (1) to Washington, D.C. (7) through connecting cities, with appropriate driving time in hours.

Figure 12.1 International Van Lines Network

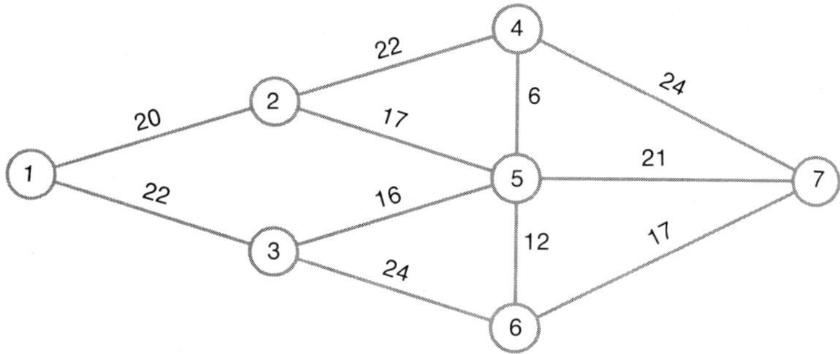

The solution procedure involves the following steps.

1. Designate the originating node 1 (Los Angeles) as the permanent set and identify adjacent nodes 2 (Denver) and 3 (Dallas).
2. Select node 2 (Denver) in the adjacent set as the node with the shortest route from node 1.
3. Store branch (1⟶2).
4. Add node 2 to the permanent set that now consists of nodes 1 and 2.
5. Identify the new adjacent set consisting of nodes 3, 4, 5, and 6.

In the initial permanent set, only node 1 is included. The first iteration identified node 2 as the shortest-route adjacent node. Thus, the permanent set after the first iteration includes nodes 1 and 2.

In the second iteration, we return to Step 2 and repeat the process again. To identify the adjacent node that is to enter the permanent set, the sum of the node value (distance accumulated for the node in the permanent set) and the connecting branch distance should be determined. The node with the minimum sum is selected and added to the permanent set. The computation procedure for the second iteration is as follows:

Permanent set node	Adjacent set node	Permanent set node value	+	Branch value	=	Total sum of distance
1	3	0	+	22	=	22 ⟵
2	4	20	+	22	=	42
2	5	20	+	17	=	37

After the second iteration, we select node 3 to be included in the permanent set. Also, we store branch (1⟶3).

Now we can proceed with the rest of the iterations as shown below.

Permanent set	Adjacent set	Connecting branch	Permanent set node value	+	Branch value	=	Total sum of distance	
Iteration 3								
1,2,3	4,5,6	(2,4)	20	+	22	=	42	
		(2,5)	20	+	17	=	37	←
		(3,5)*X*	22	+	16	=	38	
		(3,6)	22	+	24	=	46	
Store branch (2→5), delete branch (3,5)								
Iteration 4								
1,2,3,5	4,6,7	(2,4)	20	+	22	=	42	←
		(5,4)*X*	37	+	6	=	43	
		(5,7)	37	+	21	=	58	
		(3,6)	22	+	24	=	46	
Store branch (2→4), delete branch (5,4)								
Iteration 5								
1,2,3,4,5	6,7	(4,7)	42	+	24	=	66	
		(5,7)	37	+	21	=	58	
		(5,6)*X*	37	+	12	=	49	
		(3,6)	22	+	24	=	46	←
Iteration 6								
1,2,3,4,5,6	7	(4,7)*X*	42	+	24	=	66	
		(5,7)	37	+	21	=	58	←
		(6,7)*X*	46	+	17	=	63	

In the above iteration, we deleted from further consideration any branch that is inferior to the existing optimal route to a given permanent set node. The optimum solution found in iteration 6 indicates that the shortest route is given by branches (1→2), (2→5), and (5→7), with a total traveling time of 58 hours.

Minimum Spanning-Tree Problem

The minimum spanning-tree problem is quite similar to the shortest-route problem. The objective of the shortest-route problem is to determine the route from an originating point to a specific destination that minimizes the total distance (or time). On the other hand, the objective of the minimum spanning-tree problem is to determine the minimum total branch lengths that connect all of the network nodes. The solution forms a spanning tree that connects all points of the network. Many real-world problems can be solved by this approach. For example, connecting various computer terminals, telephones, and television sets while minimizing the length of cable required is a minimum spanning-tree problem. Also, sending out volunteer election campaign workers to cover all im-

Figure 12.2 Minimum Spanning-Tree Problem

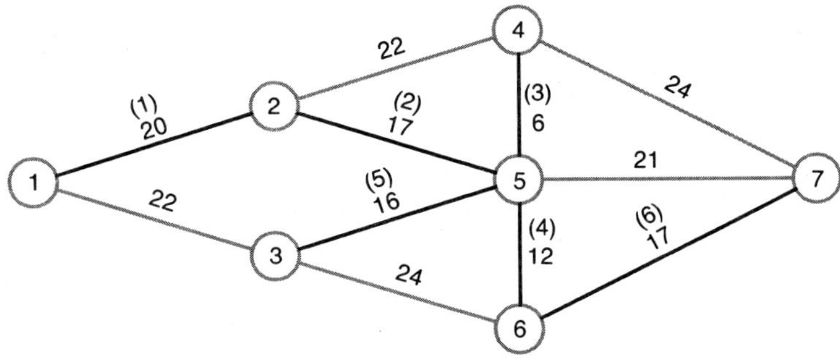

portant cities while minimizing the time required is another example of a minimum spanning-tree problem.

The solution procedure for the minimum spanning tree can be summarized as follows:

1. Select a node in the network arbitrarily and connect it to the node with the shortest distance (time or cost).
2. Identify the unconnected node with the shortest distance to a connected node. Connect these two nodes. In case of a tie, select one arbitrarily.
3. If all nodes of the network are connected, stop. Otherwise, go to Step 2.

Suppose that we are attempting to connect all cities involved in the network presented in Example 12.1 by electrical transmission lines. The distance is expressed in 100 kilometers (km). The solution procedure can be summarized as follows:

Iteration 1 We can begin the solution process with any node in the network. Let us select node 1 as the starting point. The closest unconnected node to node 1 is node 2 with the distance of 20.

Iteration 2 Since all nodes of the network are not connected, we identify the unconnected node with the shortest distance to either node 1 or node 2. Node 5 is the node with the shortest distance, in this case, to node 2.

Iteration 3 We repeat the process. The unconnected node with the shortest distance to a connected node is node 4. We connect node 4 to node 5.

Iteration 4 The next node we connect is node 6. This node has the shortest distance from any of the connected nodes. Node 6 is connected to node 5.

Iteration 5 The process is repeated. Node 3 is connected to node 5.

Iteration 6 The only unconnected node, node 7, is connected to node 6.

The entire solution process is shown in Fig. 12.2 with the numbers in parentheses corresponding with the iteration numbers. The total distance in terms of transmission lines in 100 km is 88.

Maximum Flow Problem

The maximum flow problem is concerned with determining a particular route through a network that would maximize the total flow from a source point to a specified destination. There are many real-world examples that can be analyzed by the maximum flow approach, such as the pipeline transportation of coal, oil, or natural gas; traffic flows through busy downtown streets; flow of information through telecommunication systems; flow of electricity through a complex network of transmission systems; and flow of water through irrigation systems.

The maximum flow problem may involve a network consisting of either directed or individual branches. For example, traffic on a one-way street is directed while transportation in a pipeline network is undirected. A convenient way to handle a simultaneous two-way flow problem is to treat it as two separate, directed branch problems.

The solution procedure for the maximum flow problem can be summarized as follows:

1. Determine a path from the source node to the destination (sink) node with *positive* flow capacity on each branch of the path. If no such path exists, terminate the process.
2. Determine the branch with the minimum current flow capacity on the selected path. This capacity, denoted as *C*, is allocated to each branch of the selected path.
3. Decrease the current flow capacity of each branch on the selected path by *C*.
4. Increase the flow capacity for each branch of the selected path by *C* in the *reverse* direction. This operation is necessary to compute the potential redirected flow for each branch on the selected path. Go back to Step 1.

Example 12.2 Gosper County Irrigation System

Gosper County Rural Planning District is responsible for operating the irrigation system in the county. The water system involves the source node at Johnson Lake and several canal systems with locks. Because of the size of the canals involved, the water-flow capacity varies for each of the branches. The sink node is at Plum Creek, which supplies water to various farms in the county. The irrigation system is shown in Fig. 12.3 as a network. All branches are directed in Fig. 12.3, as shown by possible flow capacities at one end and by zero capacities at the other end of each branch.

Figure 12.3 Gosper County Irrigation System

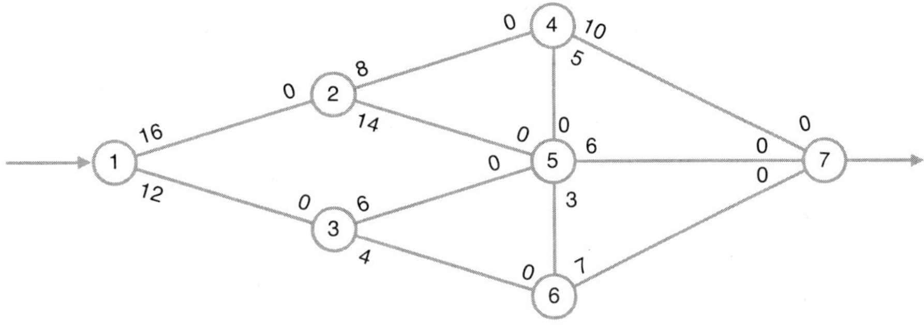

Iteration 1 The initial path arbitrarily selected is 1→2→4→7. The maximum flow possible on this path is 8, as $C = 8$, shown by branch (2,4). Figure 12.4 presents the revision of flow capacities on path 1→2→4→7.

Iteration 2 Path 1→3→5→7 is selected arbitrarily with $C = 6$, as shown by branches (3,5) and (5,7). Figure 12.5 presents this iteration.

Iteration 3 Path 1→3→6→7 is selected with $C = 4$, as shown in Fig. 12.6.

Iteration 4 The only remaining path is 1→2→5→6→7, with $C = 3$, as shown in Fig. 12.7.

The final network after the above four iterations is presented in Fig. 12.8, with the assigned flow amount in parentheses for each branch and the directions of flow. The table below presents the summary of flow for each canal branch. The total amount of flow from the source node to the sink node is 21.

	Branch										
Iteration	1→2	1→3	2→4	2→5	3→5	3→6	4→5	5→6	4→7	5→7	6→7
1	8		8						8		
2		6			6					6	
3		4				4					4
4	3			3				3			3
Total flow	11	10	8	3	6	4	0	3	8	6	7
Capacity	16	12	8	14	6	4	5	3	10	6	7
Unused capacity	5	2	0	11	0	0	5	0	2	0	0

Figure 12.4 Iteration One

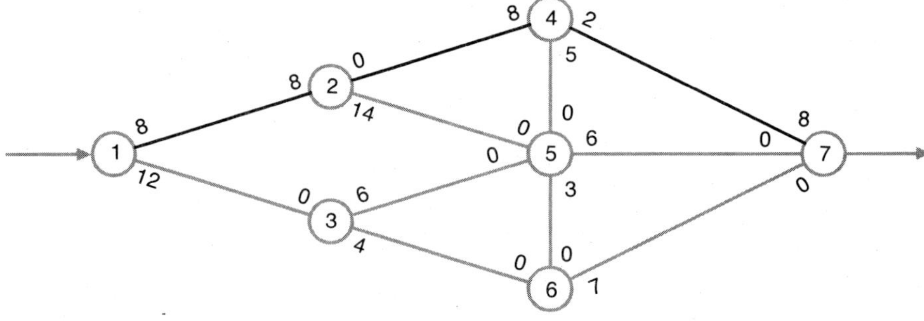

Figure 12.5 Iteration Two

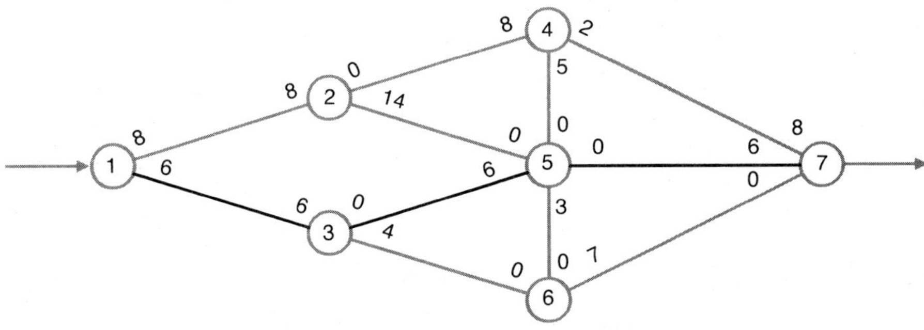

Figure 12.6 Iteration Three

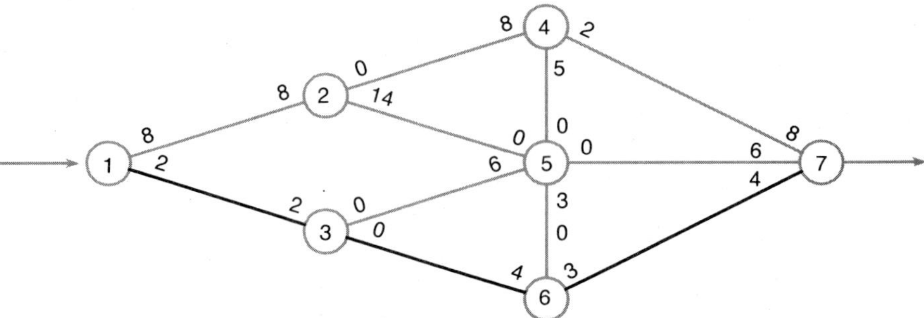

Figure 12.7 Iteration Four

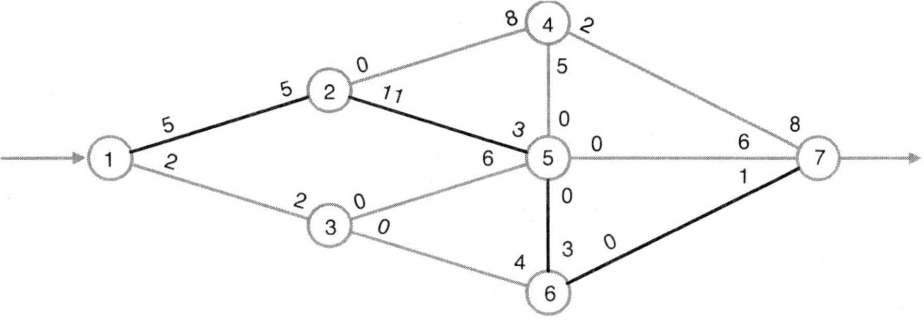

Figure 12.8 Final Solution Network

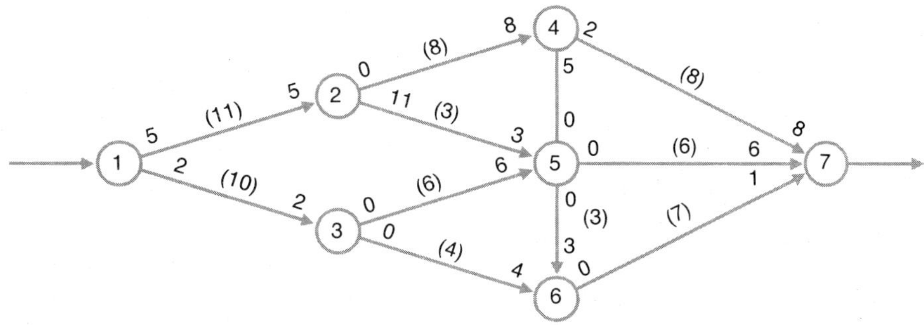

CPM/PERT Network

Critical path method (CPM) and program evaluation and review technique (PERT) are the two most widely known and applied network-modeling techniques. The DuPont Company and the Univac Division of Remington Rand Corporation developed CPM as a device to control the maintenance of chemical plants. The U.S. Navy developed PERT in 1958 for planning and scheduling the Polaris missile project.

In many respects, CPM and PERT are quite similar in their basic concepts and approaches. However, CPM emphasizes the analysis of trade-off between project cost and project completion time in an environment of certainty. PERT, on the other hand, focuses on analyzing the project completion time in an environment of uncertainty.

The CPM/PERT networks involve two basic elements: activities and events. An activity, or an arc, typically shown by an arrow, represents an operation of the project that requires time and other resources. An event, or a node, shown by a circle, represents a certain point in time, typically representing the beginning or ending of an activity. Thus, a network is graphically represented by a series of events and activities. We identify activities by event numbers at the beginning and ending points.

Each activity in a network should have its own unique event numbers. If two activities have the same beginning and ending events, we must introduce a dummy activity. In other words, if a doublet exists, we need to create a new event node to remove one activity and include a dummy activity.

The Critical Path

The critical path represents the path that has the longest time through a network from the starting node to the finishing node. Identifying the critical path is important because any delay of activities in this path will delay the entire project. To determine the critical path, we should determine the following areas.

The Earliest Expected Time

The earliest expected time (*ET*) represents the point in time at which an event can be realized. The *ET* for each event is computed in a forward or a left-to-right movement in the network.

$$ET_j = \max\,(ET_i + t_{ij})$$

where

ET_j = earliest expected time of event j
ET_i = earliest expected time of event i, which is a precedent of event j
t_{ij} = estimated duration of activity (i, j)

Latest Allowable Time

The latest allowable time (*LT*) for an event is the greatest amount of time that an event can be realized without delaying the project completion time. The *LT* for each event is computed in a backward or a right-to-left movement in the network. The *LT* for the final event is equal to its corresponding *ET*.

$$LT_i = \min\,(LT_j - t_{ij})$$

where

LT_i = latest allowable time of node i
LT_j = latest allowable time of node j, which is the descendant of event i
t_{ij} = estimated duration of activity (i, j)

The Critical Path

Once we have computed ET and LT values, we can easily identify the critical path of the network. If ET and LT values are identical for an event, this event is a critical event. The critical path is the path along the critical events.

Slack Time

The slack time at a noncritical event is simply the difference between its LT and ET. The slack time along the critical path will be zero. The slack time for a noncritical event represents the amount of time that we can delay the particular activity without risking the delay of the entire project.

The total slack time (TS) is the maximum additional amount of time available to complete an activity without delaying the entire project.

$$TS_{ij} = LT_j - ET_i - t_{ij}$$

where

TS_{ij} = total slack for activity (i, j)
LT_j = latest allowable time for event j
ET_i = earliest expected time for event i
t_{ij} = time duration for activity (i, j)

The total slack for a given activity may be valid only when other activities on the same path are completed during a certain time period. If two or more noncritical activities are in a given path, there may be shared or floating slack time. We can use the shared slack in any way we want among the noncritical activities in the path. Free slack (FS) is total slack minus shared slack. Free slack is the length of time an activity can be delayed without risking any delay of the entire project.

$$FS_{ij} = ET_j - ET_i - t_{ij}$$

where

FS_{ij} = free slack for activity (i, j)
ET_j = earliest expected time for event j
ET_i = earliest expected time for event i
t_{ij} = time duration for activity (i, j)

Example 12.3 A CPM Network

A construction firm has a project to construct a shopping center. The project involves the network as shown in Fig. 12.9. The company is attempting to determine the critical path and other relevant information about the project. Figure 12.10 presents the network with the computed ET, LT, TS, and FS values. The earliest expected time is listed on the left-hand side and the latest allowable time

Figure 12.9 A CPM Network

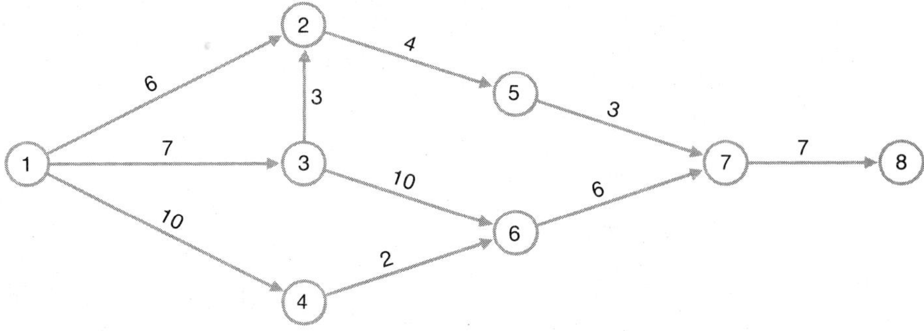

Figure 12.10 ET_j, LT_i, Critical Path, TS, and FS

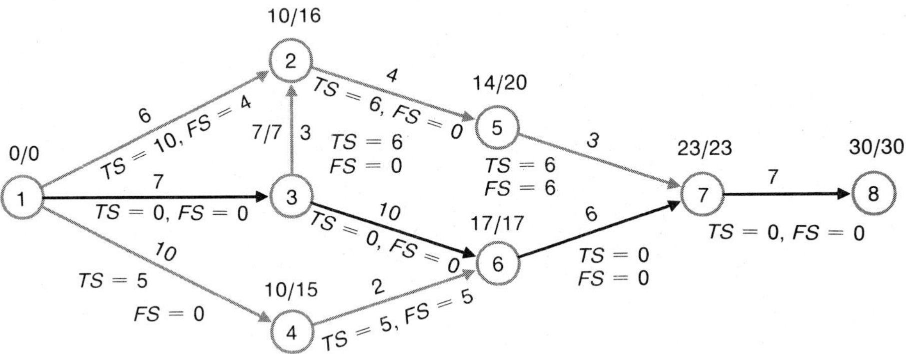

is shown on the right-hand side, right above each node. The critical path is identified as branches 1→3→6→7→8. The project analysis can be summarized as below.

Project summary

Critical path	Duration
1→3	7
3→6	10
6→7	6
7→8	7
	Total 30 days

Noncritical activities	Duration	Total slack	Free slack
1→2	6	10	4
1→4	10	5	0
2→5	4	6	0
4→6	2	5	5
5→7	3	6	6

CPM Time and Cost Trade-Offs

The critical-path method is effective in uncovering important information about the project under study. For example, CPM determines the critical activities, noncritical activities, total project completion time, and free slack times for noncritical activities. A critical aspect of any project is to expedite the project duration time. Usually, one can use a number of different alternatives to expedite some or all activities of the network. However, such expedition typically requires additional costs. Thus, an important aspect of CPM is to analyze the time–cost trade-offs.

Expediting activities to shorten the project duration time is often referred to as *project crashing*. The time–cost analysis is performed to determine which activities can be crashed and at what cost. Typically, the crash cost per unit of time (e.g., per day) for an activity can be determined as follows:

$$\text{Crash cost} = \frac{\text{Crash cost} - \text{Normal Cost}}{\text{Normal time} - \text{Crash time}}$$

The time–cost analysis involves the following two basic steps:

1. Identify the critical activity with the minimum crash cost per unit of time and crash it. If there are multiple critical paths, select the joint critical activity that has the minimum crash cost per unit of time. If there is no joint critical activity, select the minimum crash cost activity in each critical path. Compare the crashing times of these activities and select the minimum crash time. Each selected activity is crashed by this crashing time.
2. Revise the network by adjusting the time and cost of the crashed activity. Identify the critical path and compare its crashed-completion time with the normal project completion time. If they are the same, terminate the process. Otherwise, return to Step 1.

Example 12.4 Time–Cost Analysis of a CPM Network

Let us examine the CPM network that we studied previously. Suppose that the following network crashing information has been obtained.

	Completion time (days)		Completion cost ($)		
Activity	**Normal**	**Crash**	**Normal**	**Crash**	**Crash cost per Day**
1–2	6	4	$ 600	$ 900	$150
1–3*	7	4	840	1,050	70
1–4	10	5	1,500	2,000	100
2–5	4	3	400	440	40
3–2	3	2	450	600	150
3–6*	10	7	500	770	90
4–6	2	1	400	800	400
5–7	3	2	150	300	150
6–7*	6	4	600	750	75
7–8*	7	5	350	700	175

*Critical path

Normal project completion time = 30. Completely crashed completion time = 20.

Figure 12.11 presents the network with normal activity completion times and crashed activity completion times. The crashed times also show the same critical path $1 \rightarrow 3 \rightarrow 6 \rightarrow 7 \rightarrow 8$. The project completion time based on normal activity times is 30 days with a total cost of $5,790. If we crash all activities, the crashed project completion time is 20 days with a total cost of $8,310.

First Crashing

The critical activity with the minimum crash cost is activity 1–3 and its crash cost is $70 per day. This activity can be crashed by three days with a total cost of $210. The critical path is not altered. The new project completion time is 27 days, which is greater than the completely crashed completion time of 20 days. Therefore, we must continue the crashing procedure.

Second Crashing

Now the critical activity with the minimum crash cost is activity 6–7, with $75 crashing cost per day. We can crash this activity by two days at a total cost of $150. The new project completion time is 25 days, five days longer than the completely crashed completion time of 20 days. The critical path has not been changed. Thus, we continue the procedure.

Figure 12.11 The Network with Normal and Crashed Activity Times

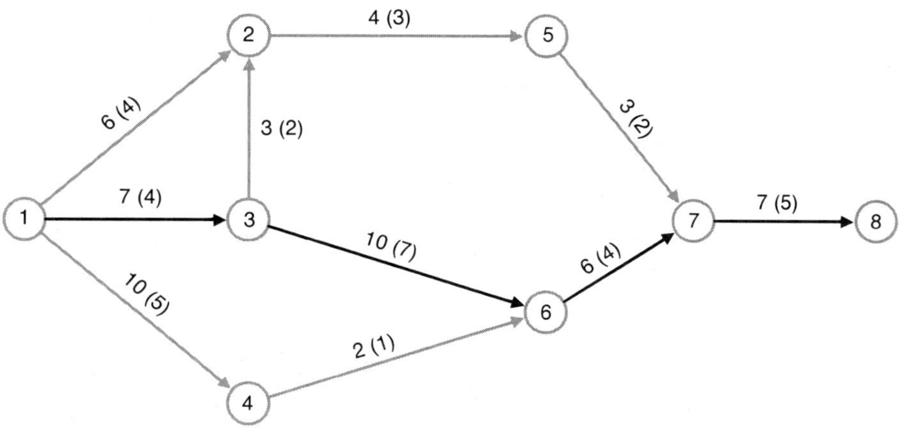

Figure 12.12 The Network with Two Critical Paths

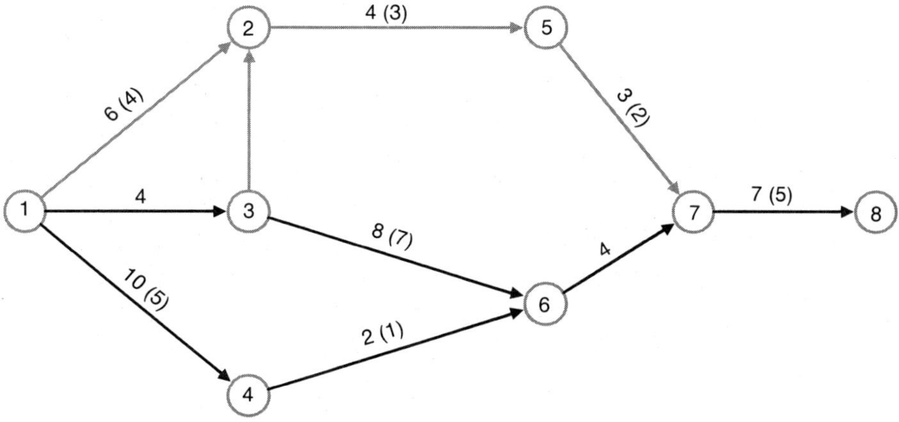

Third Crashing

Now we can crash activity 3–6 by three days at a total cost of $270. The new project completion time can be reduced to 22 days. However, this crashing will result in a new critical path 1⟶4⟶6⟶7⟶8. Thus, we should crash only two days at a total cost of $180. The new project completion time is 23 days. Since this completion time is longer than the completely crashed project completion time of 20 days, we must continue the process.

Fourth Crashing

Now there are two critical paths: 1⟶3⟶6⟶7⟶8 and 1⟶4⟶6⟶7⟶8, as shown in Fig. 12.12. We can crash a joint critical activity (activity 7–8 in this case) or crash two activities in each of the two critical paths. We will select the option that can reduce the project completion time for the least total cost. In our case,

Figure 12.13 Time-Cost Trade-offs during Crashing

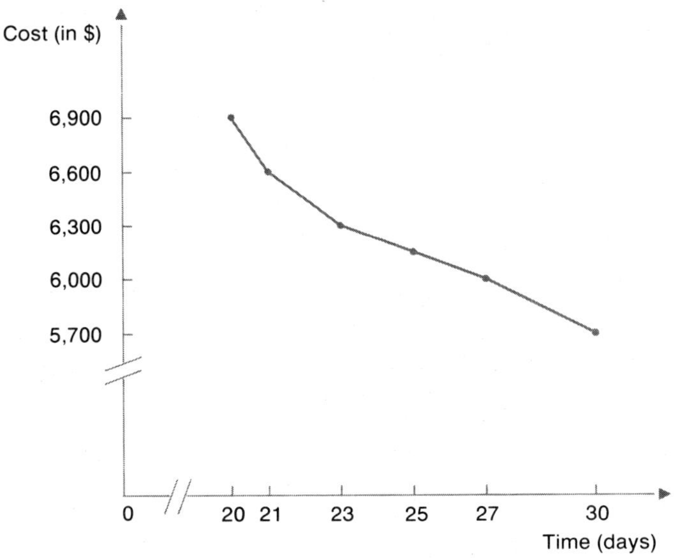

crashing activity 7–8 costs $175 per day. On the other hand, we can also crash activities 3–6 and 1–4 by one day at a total cost of $190 ($90 + $100). Thus, we select activity 7–8 for crashing. We can crash this activity by two days at a total cost of $350. The total project completion time is 21 days.

Fifth Crashing

The only remaining crashing possibility is crashing activities 3–6 and 1–4 by one day each at a total cost of $190. The completely crashed project completion time is 20 days. Thus, our crashing process is complete. We can summarize the crashing process below.

Crashing step	Activity crashed	Time reduced	Cost increased	Project completion time	Total project cost
0	—	—	—	30	$5,790
1	1-3	3	$210	27	6,000
2	6-7	2	150	25	6,150
3	3-6	2	180	23	6,330
4	7-8	2	350	21	6,680
5	3-6, 1-4	1	190	20	6,870

The entire project has been shortened by 10 days at a total extra cost of $1,080. Figure 12.13 presents the time–cost, trade-off relationship during the crashing process.

Estimating PERT Activity Times

In CPM-related analyses, we use a single deterministic duration time for each activity. In many real-world situations, such an assumption of certainty for the duration time of an activity is unrealistic. In PERT-related network analysis, we use three estimates of the activity duration—optimistic, most likely, and pessimistic times. The distribution of the three time estimates is often assumed to be a beta distribution. Thus, we can determine the mean and standard deviation for an activity duration as follows:

$$\text{Mean: } t_e = \frac{a + 4m + b}{6}$$

$$\text{Standard deviation: } T_t = \frac{b - a}{6},$$

where

a = optimistic (shortest) duration of an activity
m = most likely duration of an activity
b = pessimistic (longest) duration of an activity

Another important assumption we make in a PERT network is that the summed totals of activity times based on their means and variances are normally distributed. Thus, we can use the standardized random variate formula to determine the probability of completing a network within a specified period of time.

$$Z = \frac{X - E(t)}{\sigma_{cp}},$$

where

Z = number of standard deviation of a normal distribution (standardized random variate)
X = a specified project completion time
$E(t)$ = expected project completion time along the critical path
σ_{cp} = standard deviation of activities on the critical path

Example 12.5 Commonwealth Construction Company

Commonwealth Construction Company is in the process of developing a new shopping center. Although hundreds of activities are involved in the project, they can be grouped into the following nine activities (with precedence in parentheses). The time estimates for each of the activities are also provided.

Activity (precedence)	Time Estimates (months) Optimistic (a)	Most likely (m)	Pessimistic (b)
1–2	2	4	8
1–3	1	2	3
3–2 (1–3)	2	3	5
2–4 (1–2 and 3–2)	4	6	10
3–4 (1–3)	3	5	8
4–5 (2–4 and 3–4)	1	2	3
4–6 (2–4 and 3–4)	2	3	4
5–6 (4–5)	2	4	8
6–7 (4–6 and 5–6)	4	5	6

Based on the information provided above, we can compile the following relevant data.

Activity	Mean Time $\left(\frac{a + 4m + b}{6}\right)$	Standard Deviation $\frac{b - a}{6}$	Variance $\left(\frac{b - a}{6}\right)^2$
1–2	4.33	1	1
1–3*	2	0.33	0.11
3–2*	3.17	0.50	0.25
2–4*	6.33	1	1
3–4	5.17	0.83	0.69
4–5*	2	0.33	0.11
4–6	3	0.33	0.11
5–6*	4.33	1	1
6–7*	5	0.33	0.11

*Critical path

The expected project completion time is the sum of mean activities' times along the critical path. Thus, the project is expected to be completed in 22.83 months. Since we are assuming that the activity times are normally distributed, the probability of completing the project in 22.83 months is 0.5. By using the standardized random variate formula, we can determine the probability of completing the project in different time periods.

Figure 12.14 The Commonwealth Construction Company Problem

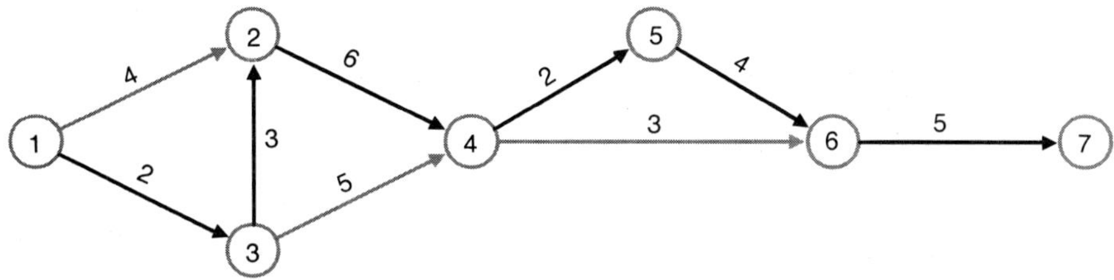

First, we must determine the standard deviation of activities on the critical path as below.

Critical activities	σ_e	σ_e^2
1–3	0.33	0.11
3–2	0.50	0.25
2–4	1	1
4–5	0.33	0.11
5–6	1	1
6–7	0.33	0.11
$\sigma_{cp} = \sqrt{\Sigma\sigma_e^2} = \sqrt{2.58} \simeq 1.61$		

Now let us suppose that Commonwealth Construction Company is interested in finding the probability of completing the project in 23 months. This probability can be computed as follows:

$$
\begin{aligned}
P\left(Z \leq \frac{23 - 22.83}{1.61}\right) &= P\left(Z \leq \frac{0.17}{1.61}\right) \\
&= P\,(Z \leq 0.1056) \\
&= 0.54005.
\end{aligned}
$$

In the above computation, the standard deviation 0.1056 corresponds to 0.54005 in probability when we look up the normal distribution table. We can determine the probability of completing the project in different time periods by using this approach. The network for the Commonwealth Construction Company problem is presented in Fig. 12.14.

Application of the *Micro Manager*

This section presents an application example of the *Micro Manager* to various network problems. The program diskette provides you with the complete information about each of the different network modeling techniques, including the purpose of the technique, the solution of an example problem, interactive input instructions, and the batch input procedure. Thus, in this section we will present only the information (purpose of the technique and the batch input data format) and the solution of a sample problem using the interactive input mode for the shortest route, minimum spanning tree, maximum flow, and CPM/PERT models.

```
<< PURPOSE >>

SHORTEST ROUTE determines the shortest route from an origin to a destination
through a connected network, given the distance associated with each branch of
the network.  The output shows the complete route from the starting node to the
ending node.  This program will handle problems with up to 40 nodes and 40
links.

<<  BATCH INPUT DATA FORMAT  >>

Type in the values of the following input data requirements, after creating a
new file.  You may enter as many values as you want in a line, separating them
by commas for alphabetic characters and by commas or blank spaces for numeric
values.  However, the input data must be exactly in the following order:

1. Graph type
     1   : directed graph
     2   : undirected graph
2. Number of nodes
3. Number of branches
4. For each branch
     starting node number
     ending node number
     value

** Sample Batch Input Data Set (Example 12.1) **

1        ; directed graph
7        ; seven nodes
11       ; eleven branches
1,2,20   ; starting and ending node number and value for branch 1
1,3,22   ; starting and ending node number and value for branch 2
2,4,22   ; starting and ending node number and value for branch 3
2,5,17   ; starting and ending node number and value for branch 4
3,5,16   ; starting and ending node number and value for branch 5
3,6,24   ; starting and ending node number and value for branch 6
4,5,6    ; starting and ending node number and value for branch 7
5,6,12   ; starting and ending node number and value for branch 8
4,7,24   ; starting and ending node number and value for branch 9
5,7,21   ; starting and ending node number and value for branch 10
6,7,17   ; starting and ending node number and value for branch 11
```

```
PROGRAM: Shortest Route

Enter 1 for directed graph or 2 for undirected one: 1
Enter number of nodes   : 7
Enter number of branches: 11

For branch 1
Enter starting node number and ending node number: 1,2
Enter value: 20

For branch 2
Enter starting node number and ending node number: 1,3
Enter value: 22

For branch 3
Enter starting node number and ending node number: 2,4
Enter value: 22

For branch 4
Enter starting node number and ending node number: 2,5
Enter value: 17

For branch 5
Enter starting node number and ending node number: 3,5
Enter value: 16

For branch 6
Enter starting node number and ending node number: 3,6
Enter value: 24

For branch 7
Enter starting node number and ending node number: 4,5
Enter value: 6

For branch 8
Enter starting node number and ending node number: 5,6
Enter value: 12

For branch 9
Enter starting node number and ending node number: 4,7
Enter value: 24

For branch 10
Enter starting node number and ending node number: 5,7
Enter value: 21

For branch 11
Enter starting node number and ending node number: 6,7
Enter value: 17
```

PROGRAM: Shortest Route

***** INPUT DATA ENTERED *****

Branch	Nodes	Value
1	1 ----> 2	20.0
2	1 ----> 3	22.0
3	2 ----> 4	22.0
4	2 ----> 5	17.0
5	3 ----> 5	16.0
6	3 ----> 6	24.0
7	4 ----> 5	6.0
8	5 ----> 6	12.0
9	4 ----> 7	24.0
10	5 ----> 7	21.0
11	6 ----> 7	17.0

***** PROGRAM OUTPUT *****

Branch	Nodes	Value
1	1 ----> 2	20.0
4	2 ----> 5	17.0
10	5 ----> 7	21.0

Total branch lengths : 58

<< PURPOSE >>

MINIMUM SPANNING TREE determines the best way to connect all the network nodes such that the total branch lengths required would be minimum (distance, time, or cost). The program output includes the total length of the minimum spanning tree and the branches that connect all of the nodes in the network. A network of up to 40 nodes and 40 branches can be solved by this program.

<< BATCH INPUT DATA FORMAT >>

Type in the values of the following input data requirements, after creating a new file. You may enter as many values as you want in a line, separating them by commas for alphabetic characters and by commas or blank spaces for numeric values. However, the input data must be exactly in the following order:

1. Number of nodes
2. Number of branches
3. For each branch
    - starting node number
    - ending node number
    - value

```
** Sample Batch Input Data Set (Example 12.1) **

7        ; seven nodes
11       ; eleven branches
1,2,20   ; starting and ending node number and value for branch 1
1,3,22   ; starting and ending node number and value for branch 2
2,4,22   ; starting and ending node number and value for branch 3
2,5,17   ; starting and ending node number and value for branch 4
3,5,16   ; starting and ending node number and value for branch 5
3,6,24   ; starting and ending node number and value for branch 6
4,5,6    ; starting and ending node number and value for branch 7
5,6,12   ; starting and ending node number and value for branch 8
4,7,24   ; starting and ending node number and value for branch 9
5,7,21   ; starting and ending node number and value for branch 10
6,7,17   ; starting and ending node number and value for branch 11

PROGRAM: Minimum Spanning Tree

Enter number of nodes   : 7
Enter number of branches: 11

For branch 1
Enter starting node number and ending node number: 1,2
Enter value: 20

For branch 2
Enter starting node number and ending node number: 1,3
Enter value: 22

For branch 3
Enter starting node number and ending node number: 2,4
Enter value: 22

For branch 4
Enter starting node number and ending node number: 2,5
Enter value: 17

For branch 5
Enter starting node number and ending node number: 3,5
Enter value: 16

For branch 6
Enter starting node number and ending node number: 3,6
Enter value: 24

For branch 7
Enter starting node number and ending node number: 4,5
Enter value: 6

For branch 8
Enter starting node number and ending node number: 5,6
Enter value: 12

For branch 9
Enter starting node number and ending node number: 4,7
Enter value: 24
```

For branch 10
Enter starting node number and ending node number: 5,7
Enter value: 21

For branch 11
Enter starting node number and ending node number: 6,7
Enter value: 17

PROGRAM: Minimum Spanning Tree

***** INPUT DATA ENTERED *****

Branch	Nodes	Value
1	1 <---> 2	20.0
2	1 <---> 3	22.0
3	2 <---> 4	22.0
4	2 <---> 5	17.0
5	3 <---> 5	16.0
6	3 <---> 6	24.0
7	4 <---> 5	6.0
8	5 <---> 6	12.0
9	4 <---> 7	24.0
10	5 <---> 7	21.0
11	6 <---> 7	17.0

***** PROGRAM OUTPUT *****

Branch	Nodes	Value
1	1 <---> 2	20.0
4	2 <---> 5	17.0
4	5 <---> 4	6.0
8	5 <---> 6	12.0
8	5 <---> 3	16.0
11	6 <---> 7	17.0

Total branch lengths : 88

<< PURPOSE >>

MAXIMUM FLOW determines a route which maximizes the total flow from a specified source to a specified destination in a network. This program will handle problems with up to 40 nodes and 40 branches.

<< BATCH INPUT DATA FORMAT >>

Type in the values of the following input data requirements, after creating a new file. You may enter as many values as you want in a line, separating them by commas for alphabetic characters and by commas or blank spaces for numeric values. However, the input data must be exactly in the following order:

1. Number of nodes
2. Number of branches
3. For each branch
   - starting node number
   - ending node number
   - capacity from starting node to ending node
   - capacity from ending node to starting node

** Sample Batch Input Data Set (Example 12.2) **

```
7       ; seven nodes
11      ; eleven branches
1,2     ; starting and ending node number for branch 1
16,0    ; capacity from 1 to 2 and capacity from 2 to 1
1,3     ; starting and ending node number for branch 2
12,0    ; capacity from 1 to 3 and capacity from 3 to 1
2,4     ; starting and ending node number for branch 3
8,0     ; capacity from 2 to 4 and capacity from 4 to 2
2,5     ; starting and ending node number for branch 4
14,0    ; capacity from 2 to 5 and capacity from 5 to 2
3,5     ; starting and ending node number for branch 5
6,0     ; capacity from 3 to 5 and capacity from 5 to 3
3,6     ; starting and ending node number for branch 6
4,0     ; capacity from 3 to 6 and capacity from 6 to 3
4,5     ; starting and ending node number for branch 7
5,0     ; capacity from 4 to 5 and capacity from 5 to 4
5,6     ; starting and ending node number for branch 8
3,0     ; capacity from 5 to 6 and capacity from 6 to 5
4,7     ; starting and ending node number for branch 9
10,0    ; capacity from 4 to 7 and capacity from 7 to 4
5,7     ; starting and ending node number for branch 10
6,0     ; capacity from 5 to 7 and capacity from 7 to 5
6,7     ; starting and ending node number for branch 11
7,0     ; capacity from 6 to 7 and capacity from 7 to 6
```

PROGRAM: Maximum Flow

```
Enter number of nodes    : 7
Enter number of branches: 11

For branch 1
Enter starting node number and ending node number: 1,2
Enter capacity from 1 to 2 : 16
Enter capacity form 2 to 1 : 0

For branch 2
Enter starting node number and ending node number: 1,3
Enter capacity from 1 to 3 : 12
Enter capacity form 3 to 1 : 0
```

```
For branch 3
Enter starting node number and ending node number: 2,4
Enter capacity from 2 to 4 : 8
Enter capacity form 4 to 2 : 0

For branch 4
Enter starting node number and ending node number: 2,5
Enter capacity from 2 to 5 : 14
Enter capacity form 5 to 2 : 0

For branch 5
Enter starting node number and ending node number: 3,5
Enter capacity from 3 to 5 : 6
Enter capacity form 5 to 3 : 0

For branch 6
Enter starting node number and ending node number: 3,6
Enter capacity from 3 to 6 : 4
Enter capacity form 6 to 3 : 0

For branch 7
Enter starting node number and ending node number: 4,5
Enter capacity from 4 to 5 : 5
Enter capacity form 5 to 4 : 0

For branch 8
Enter starting node number and ending node number: 5,6
Enter capacity from 5 to 6 : 3
Enter capacity form 6 to 5 : 0

For branch 9
Enter starting node number and ending node number: 4,7
Enter capacity from 4 to 7 : 10
Enter capacity form 7 to 4 : 0

For branch 10
Enter starting node number and ending node number: 5,7
Enter capacity from 5 to 7 : 6
Enter capacity form 7 to 5 : 0

For branch 11
Enter starting node number and ending node number: 6,7
Enter capacity from 6 to 7 : 7
Enter capacity form 7 to 6 : 0
```

PROGRAM: Maximum Flow

***** INPUT DATA ENTERED *****

Branch	Nodes	Value	Nodes	Value
1	1 ----> 2	16.0	2 ----> 1	0.0
2	1 ----> 3	12.0	3 ----> 1	0.0
3	2 ----> 4	8.0	4 ----> 2	0.0
4	2 ----> 5	14.0	5 ----> 2	0.0
5	3 ----> 5	6.0	5 ----> 3	0.0
6	3 ----> 6	4.0	6 ----> 3	0.0
7	4 ----> 5	5.0	5 ----> 4	0.0
8	5 ----> 6	3.0	6 ----> 5	0.0
9	4 ----> 7	10.0	7 ----> 4	0.0
10	5 ----> 7	6.0	7 ----> 5	0.0
11	6 ----> 7	7.0	7 ----> 6	0.0

***** PROGRAM OUTPUT *****

Branch	Nodes	Value	Flow
1	1 ----> 2	16.0	16.0
2	1 ----> 3	12.0	5.0
3	2 ----> 4	8.0	8.0
4	2 ----> 5	14.0	8.0
5	3 ----> 5	6.0	1.0
6	3 ----> 6	4.0	4.0
9	4 ----> 7	10.0	8.0
8	5 ----> 6	3.0	3.0
10	5 ----> 7	6.0	6.0
11	6 ----> 7	7.0	7.0

Total maximum flow : 21

<< PURPOSE >>

PERT/CPM determines the minimum time required to complete a project. The minimum time required for project completion is equal to the longest time path (the critical path) of a sequence of connected activities. The program output includes the variance of the expected project completion time, slack, critical path, the earliest start and latest finish times for each activity, and the probability of completing a project within a certain time period. This program can handle project problems which have up to 40 activities.

<< BATCH INPUT DATA FORMAT >>

Type in the values of the following input data requirements, after creating a new file. You may enter as many values as you want in a line, separating them by commas for alphabetic characters and by commas or blank spaces for numeric values. However, the input data must be exactly in the following order:

```
1. Problem type
      1   : CPM
      2   : CPM with Crashing
      3   : PERT
2. Number of Activities
3. Information for each activity
   3.1. Starting node
   3.2. Ending node
   3.3. Number of predecessors (NP)
   If NP is not equal to 0 then
      3.4. Predecessor nodes as many as NP
   For CPM
      3.5. Activity duration (time)
   For CPM with Crashing
      3.5. Normal time
      3.6. Crashing time
      3.7. Normal cost
      3.8. Unit crashing cost
   For PERT
      3.5. Optimistic time
      3.6. Most likely time
      3.7. Pessimistic time
```

** Sample Batch Input Data Set (Example 12.3) **

```
2               ; CPM with Crashing
10              ; ten activities
1,2,0           ; 1 -> 2 (activity 1) with no predecessor
6,4,600,150     ;   normal and crash time and normal and unit crash cost
1,3,0           ; 1 -> 3 (activity 2) with no predecessor
7,4,840,70      ;   normal and crash time and normal and unit crash cost
1,4,0           ; 1 -> 4 (activity 3) with no predecessor
10,5,1500,100   ;   normal and crash time and normal and unit crash cost
2,5,2           ; 2 -> 5 (activity 4) with two predecessors
1,5             ;   two predecessor activities 1 and 5
4,3,400,40      ;   normal and crash time and normal and unit crash cost
3,2,1           ; 3 -> 2 (activity 5) with one predecessor
2               ;   one predecessor activity 2
3,2,450,150     ;   normal and crash time and normal and unit crash cost
3,6,1           ; 3 -> 6 (activity 6) with one predecessor
2               ;   one predecessor activity 2
10,7,500,90     ;   normal and crash time and normal and unit crash cost
4,6,1           ; 4 -> 6 (activity 7) with one predecessor
3               ;   one predecessor activity 3
2,1,400,400     ;   normal and crash time and normal and unit crash cost
5,7,1           ; 5 -> 7 (activity 8) with one predecessor
4               ;   one predecessor activity 4
3,2,150,150     ;   normal and crash time and normal and unit crash cost
6,7,2           ; 6 -> 7 (activity 9) with two predecessors
6,7             ;   two predecessor activities 6 and 7
6,4,600,75      ;   normal and crash time and normal and unit crash cost
7,8,2           ; 7 -> 8 (activity 10) with two predecessors
8,9             ;   two predecessor activities 8 and 9
7,5,350,175     ;   normal and crash time and normal and unit crash cost
```

```
PROGRAM: PERT/CPM

         1   CPM
         2   CPM with Crashing
         3   PERT


       Enter a number: 2

  ****   CPM with Crashing   ****

Enter number of activities: 10

For activity 1
Enter starting node number and ending node number: 1,2
Enter number of predecessor activities:           0
Enter normal time:     6
Enter crashed time:    4
Enter normal cost:     600
Enter unit crash cost: 150

For activity 2
Enter starting node number and ending node number: 1,3
Enter number of predecessor activities:           0
Enter normal time:     7
Enter crashed time:    4
Enter normal cost:     840
Enter unit crash cost: 70

For activity 3
Enter starting node number and ending node number: 1,4
Enter number of predecessor activities:           0
Enter normal time:     10
Enter crashed time:    5
Enter normal cost:     1500
Enter unit crash cost: 100

For activity 4
Enter starting node number and ending node number: 2,5
Enter number of predecessor activities:           2
   Enter predecessor activity number (given by system): 1
   Enter predecessor activity number (given by system): 5
Enter normal time:     4
Enter crashed time:    3
Enter normal cost:     400
Enter unit crash cost: 40

For activity 5
Enter starting node number and ending node number: 3,2
Enter number of predecessor activities:           1
   Enter predecessor activity number (given by system): 2
Enter normal time:     3
Enter crashed time:    2
Enter normal cost:     1450
Enter unit crash cost: 150

For activity 6
Enter starting node number and ending node number: 3,6
Enter number of predecessor activities:           1
   Enter predecessor activity number (given by system): 2
Enter normal time:     10
Enter crashed time:    7
Enter normal cost:     500
Enter unit crash cost: 90
```

```
For activity 7
Enter starting node number and ending node number: 4,6
Enter number of predecessor activities:            1
   Enter predecessor activity number (given by system): 3
Enter normal time:     2
Enter crashed time:    1
Enter normal cost:     400
Enter unit crash cost: 400

For activity 8
Enter starting node number and ending node number: 5,7
Enter number of predecessor activities:            1
   Enter predecessor activity number (given by system): 4
Enter normal time:     3
Enter crashed time:    2
Enter normal cost:     150
Enter unit crash cost: 150

For activity 9
Enter starting node number and ending node number: 6,7
Enter number of predecessor activities:            2
   Enter predecessor activity number (given by system): 6
   Enter predecessor activity number (given by system): 7
Enter normal time:     6
Enter crashed time:    4
Enter normal cost:     600
Enter unit crash cost: 75

For activity 10
Enter starting node number and ending node number: 7,8
Enter number of predecessor activities:            2
   Enter predecessor activity number (given by system): 8
   Enter predecessor activity number (given by system): 9
Enter normal time:     7
Enter crashed time:    5
Enter normal cost:     350
Enter unit crash cost: 175
```

PROGRAM: PERT/CPM

***** INPUT DATA ENTERED *****

CPM with Crashing

Activity	Nodes	Predecessor Activities	Normal Time	Crashed Time	Normal Cost	Unit Crash Cost
1	1 -> 2		6.0	4.0	600.00	150.00
2	1 -> 3		7.0	4.0	840.00	70.00
3	1 -> 4		10.0	5.0	1500.00	100.00
4	2 -> 5	1 5	4.0	3.0	400.00	40.00
5	3 -> 2	2	3.0	2.0	1450.00	150.00
6	3 -> 6	2	10.0	7.0	500.00	90.00
7	4 -> 6	3	2.0	1.0	400.00	400.00
8	5 -> 7	4	3.0	2.0	150.00	150.00
9	6 -> 7	6 7	6.0	4.0	600.00	75.00
10	7 -> 8	8 9	7.0	5.0	350.00	175.00

***** PROGRAM OUTPUT *****

** Analysis of CPM **

Activity	Nodes	Activity Duration	Early Start	Late Finish	Total Slack	Free Slack
1	1 -> 2	6.0	0.0	16.0	10.0	4.0
2	1 -> 3	7.0	0.0	7.0	0.0	0.0
3	1 -> 4	10.0	0.0	15.0	5.0	0.0
4	2 -> 5	4.0	10.0	20.0	6.0	0.0
5	3 -> 2	3.0	7.0	16.0	6.0	0.0
6	3 -> 6	10.0	7.0	17.0	0.0	0.0
7	4 -> 6	2.0	10.0	17.0	5.0	5.0
8	5 -> 7	3.0	14.0	23.0	6.0	6.0
9	6 -> 7	6.0	17.0	23.0	0.0	0.0
10	7 -> 8	7.0	23.0	30.0	0.0	0.0

The Critical Path (nodes) 1 -> 3 -> 6 -> 7 -> 8
The Critical Path (activities) 2 - 6 - 9 - 10

The Normal Completion Time = 30
The Completely Crashed Completion Time = 20

** Summary of the Crashing Procedure **

Step	Activities Crashed	Time Reduced	Revised Completion Time	Additional Cost	Revised Project Cost
0			30		6790
1	2 (1 -> 3)	3	27	210	7000
2	9 (6 -> 7)	2	25	150	7150
3	6 (3 -> 6)	2	23	180	7330
4	10 (7 -> 8)	2	21	350	7680
5	6 (3 -> 6)	1	20	190	7870
	3 (1 -> 4)				
Total		10		1080	

** Summary of the Critical Path (Nodes) **

Step	Project Completion Time	Critical Path (Nodes)
0	30	1 -> 3 -> 6 -> 7 -> 8
1	27	1 -> 3 -> 6 -> 7 -> 8
2	25	1 -> 3 -> 6 -> 7 -> 8
3	23	1 -> 3 -> 6 -> 7 -> 8
4	21	1 -> 3 -> 6 -> 7 -> 8
		1 -> 4 -> 6 -> 7 -> 8
5	20	1 -> 3 -> 6 -> 7 -> 8
		1 -> 4 -> 6 -> 7 -> 8

Summary

Many decision problems involve a series of activities and events that can be constructed as a network. Network models, thus, have become important topics of management science. In this chapter, we have examined the shortest-route, minimum spanning-tree, maximum flow, and CPM/PERT models, and their applications. These models have one important commonality—complexity. Thus, the *Micro Manager* is especially useful in analyzing network models.

References

Cleland, D. I., and W. R. King. 1975. *Systems analysis and project management.* 2d ed. New York: McGraw-Hill.

Elmaghraby, S. B. 1977. *Activity networks: Project planning and control by network models.* New York: John Wiley & Sons.

Ford, L. R., Jr., and D. R. Fulkerson. 1962. *Flows in networks.* Princeton, N.J.: Princeton University Press.

Lee, S. M. 1983. *Introduction to management science.* Chicago: Dryden.

Lee, S. M., L. J. Moore, and B. W. Taylor. 1985. *Management science,* 2d ed. Dubuque, IA: Wm. C. Brown Publishers.

Wiest, J. D., and F. K. Levy. 1977. *A management guide to PERT/CPM.* 2d ed. Englewood Cliffs, N.J.: Prentice-Hall.

Problems

1. Marian Rogers, the sales manager of Pony Auto Parts Company, Los Angeles, is planning to deliver auto parts ordered by one of its chain stores located in St. Louis. The nodes of the network below represent connecting cities of various possible routes. Determine the shortest-route distances from Los Angeles to St. Louis (the branch distances are in hundreds of miles).

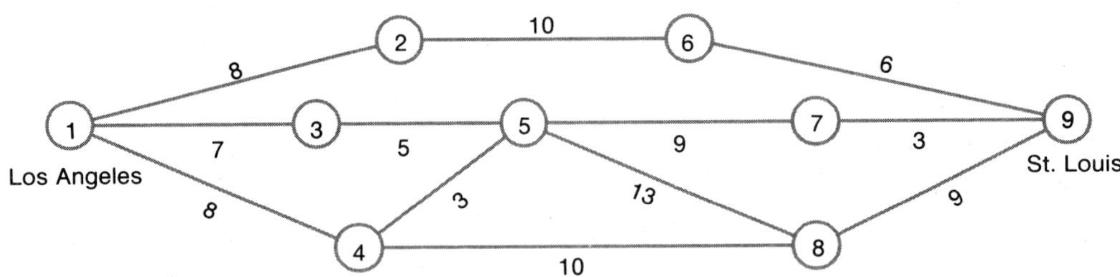

2. Eagle Commuter Airline Company operates a fleet of small airplanes to provide commuter flights between a number of small midwestern cities. The flight times between these cities are shown below (in hours).

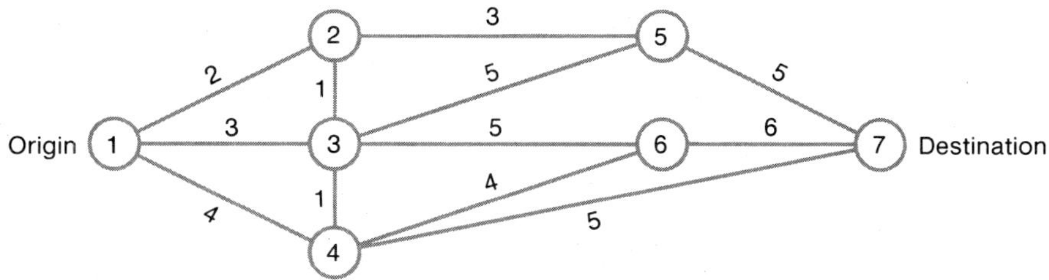

Determine the shortest route for the commuter service from the origin to destination.

3. Find the shortest route from the origin to the destination for the following electrical transmission network. The branch distances are in hundreds of miles.

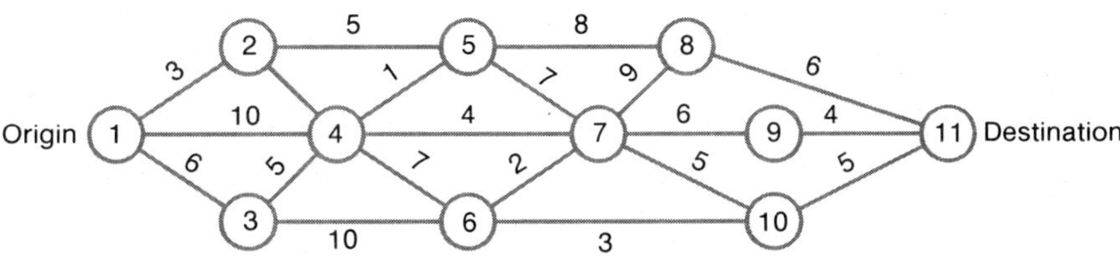

4. Heinz is planning to hike through the Mark Twain National Park in as few days as possible. The network below shows the possible branches between various ranger stations. Branch numbers represent the number of days required to hike between nodes of that branch. Determine the shortest route for Heinz.

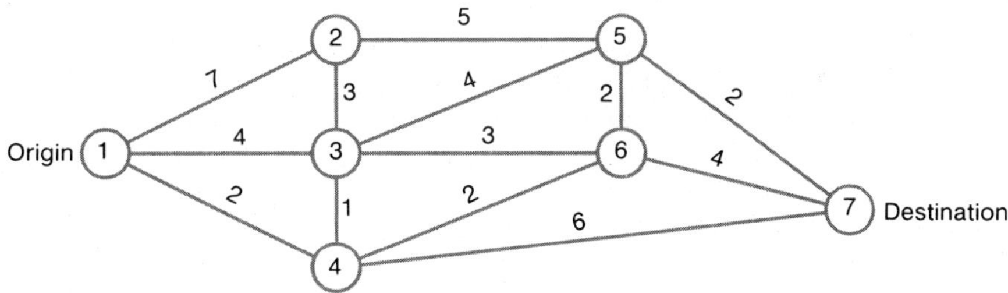

5. Midwestern Telephone Company is planning to install telephone switch stations around a city. The locations for the switch stations are represented by the nodes of the network below. The branches of the network represent distances in miles. Determine the minimum length of telephone lines required to connect all switch stations.

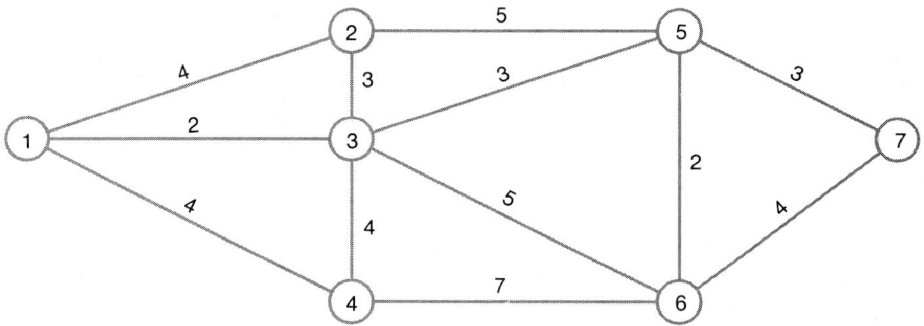

6. Lone Star Recreation Company has recently purchased a tract of land for a new amusement park. It has a single entrance and a single exit to and from the park. There are eight major amusement areas within the park that are represented by the nodes of the network below. The branches of the network represent possible road alternatives in the park. If the park designer wants to minimize the total road miles that must be constructed in the park and still permit access to all facilities, how should the roadway be constructed?

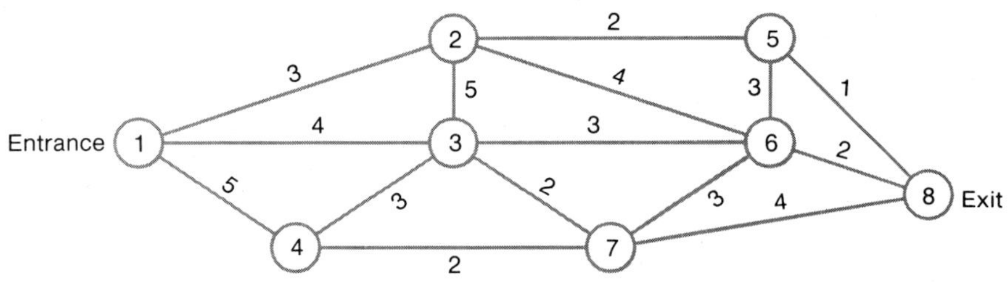

7. The Computing Resource Center of State University has purchased special computer communication lines to be installed for connecting computer labs, located around the campus, with the central mainframe computer. Since the installation is an expensive project, the business manager wants to minimize the total length of the new communication line. The network with possible connection alternatives and distances in miles is shown on p. 291. Determine the minimal spanning-tree solution.

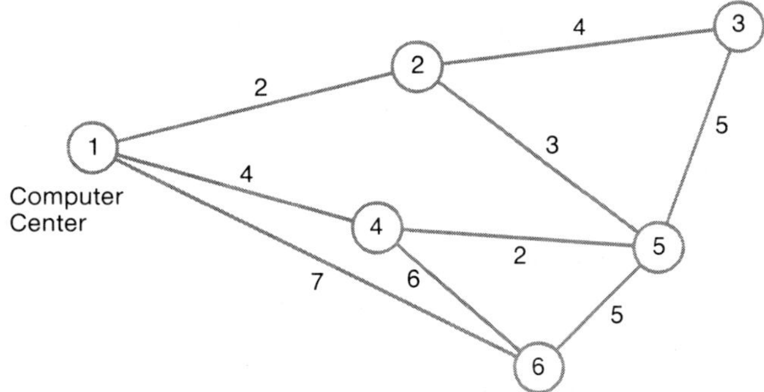

8. Challenge Oil Company owns a network of pipelines that transmit oil from its source to several storage locations. The oil-flow capacity from a node to connecting nodes (in barrels per minute) is provided below. Determine the solution quantity and direction of flow for each branch of the pipeline network.

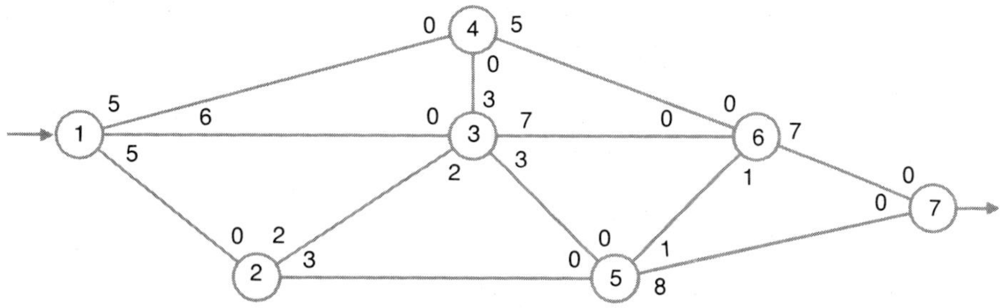

9. The road system passing through Omaha, Nebraska, can accommodate limited traffic, based on the road capacities (thousands of vehicles per hour) shown in the network below. Determine the maximum vehicle flow per hour through the system.

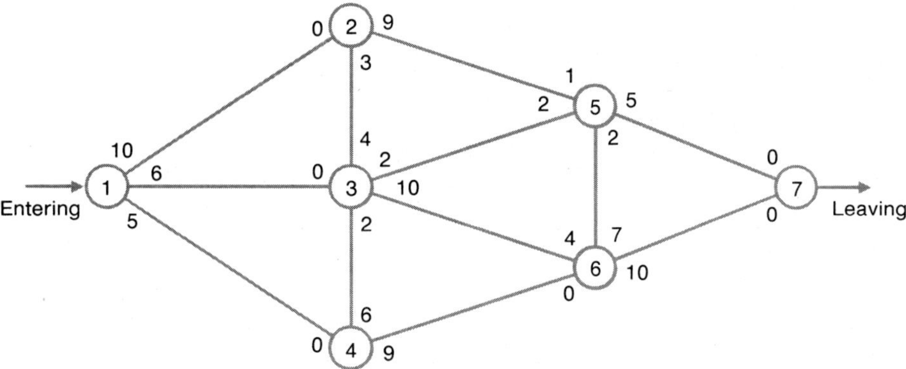

10. Lancaster Power & Light Company owns an electrical transmission network as shown below. Find the maximum energy flow from the source to sink, given that the flow capacity from node i to node j is the number along branch (i,j) nearest i.

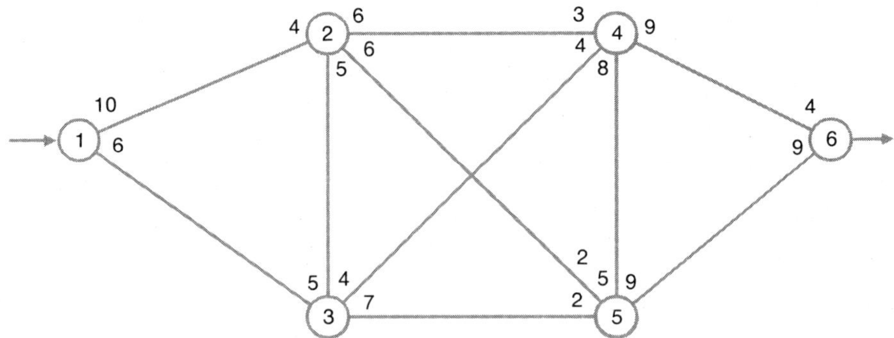

11. A student is in the process of selecting a university in which to enroll. The durations for the activities are estimated as follows:

Activity	Predecessor	Duration (days)
A. Select universities	—	10
B. Obtain application materials	A	20
C. Take necessary tests and send results	A	60
D. Complete and send applications	B	10
E. Visit universities	C, D	20
F. Wait for answer	E	30
G. Make the final choice	F	10

a. Construct a network and determine the following information: *ET, LT, TS,* and *FS.*

b. Determine the critical path and the expected project completion time.

12. Consider the following project network:

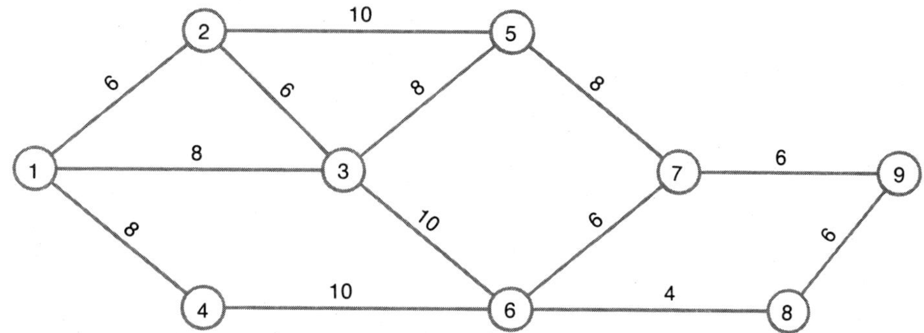

a. Compute ET and LT at each of the events.
b. Determine TS and FS for each activity.
c. Identify the critical path and determine the expected project completion time.

13. A project being planned involves the following activities:

Activity	Durations (weeks)
1–2	2
1–3	4
2–3	3
2–5	5
3–4	4
3–5	3
4–6	6
5–6	2

a. Construct a network and determine the following: ET, LT, TS, and FS.
b. Determine the critical path and the expected project completion time.

14. Refer to Problem 13. The following project description provides estimates of normal activity completion times and crashed activity completion times, together with their associated costs.

	Time Estimates		Cost Estimates	
Activity	**Normal**	**Crash**	**Normal**	**Crash**
1–2	2 weeks	1 week	$300	$400
1–3	4	2	300	600
2–3	3	1	200	350
2–5	5	3	600	780
3–4	4	3	500	560
3–5	3	2	200	320
4–6	6	3	600	750
5–6	2	1	400	600

a. Determine the crashing cost per week for each activity.
b. Compute the minimum cost required to crash the project.
c. Illustrate with a table and a graph the time–cost trade-off for the problem.

15. A class project has been assigned for designing an information system to keep track of students' credit hours earned in the Executive MBA program. The following activity table provides estimates of normal activity completion times (and associated costs) and crashed activity completion times (and associated costs).

		Time Estimates (days)		Cost Estimates (dollars)	
Activity	**Predecessor**	**Normal**	**Crash**	**Normal**	**Crash**
A. Feasibility study	—	5	5	50	50
B. Interview	A	6	3	50	110
C. Gather documents	B	4	3	60	80
D. Analyze data	C	6	4	200	300
E. Select hardware	A	6	4	200	280
F. Develop system specification	D, E	6	4	300	470
G. Select software	B	10	6	400	700
H. Programming	F, G	10	8	800	1,200
I. Test system	H	5	4	400	460
J. Training	H	7	4	500	710
K. Install the system	I	4	2	200	250
L. Evaluation	J, K	6	6	300	300

a. Determine the crashing cost per day for each activity.
b. Determine the minimum cost required to crash the project.
c. Identify the project's critical path for crashing the project by 10 days.

16. Consider a PERT network that has the following activity time estimates:

Activity	Time (days)		
	a	*m*	*b*
1–2	2	6	12
2–3	12	20	30
3–4	4	8	12
4–5	6	12	20

a. Compute the mean time, standard deviation, and variance of each activity.

b. Compute the expected project completion time and its standard deviation.

17. Consider a project having the following activities, and their time estimates:

Activity	Time (weeks)		
	a	*m*	*b*
1–2	2	8	10
1–3	4	8	12
1–4	5	9	15
2–3	4	12	16
2–5	4	8	14
3–5	5	11	15
3–6	2	7	9
3–7	4	8	16
4–3	4	6	10
4–6	4	7	9
5–7	3	9	12
6–7	3	5	9

a. Construct a PERT network for the project.

b. Compute the mean time of each activity.

c. Compute the expected project completion time and its standard deviation.

d. Determine the probability of project completion within 48 or fewer weeks.

18. Consider the following network that has three activity time estimates:

Activity	Predecessor	Time (weeks)		
		a	*m*	*b*
A	—	8	12	14
B	—	4	6	10
C	A	16	20	28
D	B	8	10	18
E	A	14	18	24
F	C, D	9	12	15
G	B	14	16	20
H	E	16	22	30
I	G	8	14	18
J	F, H, I	2	4	8

a. Construct a PERT network for the project.
b. Compute the mean time of each activity.
c. Compute the expected project completion time.
d. Compute the standard deviation of the project completion time.
e. Determine the 95 percent confidence interval estimate of project completion time.

19. Suppose that a PERT network has the expected project completion time of 180 days and a standard deviation of 24 days.

a. What is the probability of completing the project within 150 days?
b. What is the probability of completing the project between 160 days and 200 days?

20. Consider a project having the following activities, and their time estimates:

Activity	Predecessor	Time (days)		
		a	*m*	*b*
A	—	16	22	24
B	A	30	40	48
C	—	20	24	30
D	C	24	30	36
E	B, D	40	54	60
F	C	24	36	42
G	C	42	60	66
H	E, F	32	46	54
I	G	8	12	30
J	H, I	18	24	36

a. Construct a PERT network for the project.

b. Compute the expected project completion time and its standard deviation.

C H A P T E R 13

Inventory Models

Inventory control is an important aspect of operations management, since virtually every organization maintains inventories of some kind. The level of inventory to carry must be determined very carefully for two basic reasons: (1) to meet the demand to maximize sales and (2) to minimize the total inventory cost.

Successful inventory management requires answering two critical questions: (1) what is the timing of inventory replacement and (2) what quantity should be ordered each time. To answer the two questions, we need to develop inventory models. There is virtually an unlimited number of variations of inventory models, each suitable for a specific situation. In this chapter, we will discuss the most widely used inventory models and their solutions by using the *Micro Manager.*

Basics

In its simplest form, inventory is a resource we set aside for future use. Inventory is needed because demand and supply are never perfectly balanced in real-world situations. The typical mentality about inventory is the "just-in-case" approach. We would like to keep inventories just in case they would be needed or demanded at a future date. However, maintaining a high level of inventory costs a great deal of money as inventories are unearning, idle resources. Thus, inventories are often referred to as the graveyard of many failing organizations.

The basic motivation for developing inventory models is to minimize the total inventory cost by determining when items are to be replenished and how much of each item should be ordered. The total inventory cost is the sum of total holding costs, ordering costs, and shortage costs.

Holding Costs

Holding costs, sometimes referred to as *carrying costs,* represent costs that are required to store and maintain a certain level of inventory. The total holding costs are a function of the number of units of a product stored and the duration of storage. The holding cost is measured either by a dollar cost associated with carrying one unit of inventory per unit of time or by a percentage of the average inventory value.

Ordering Costs

Ordering costs represent costs associated with replenishing inventories. Typically, ordering costs are based on the number of orders prepared rather than the quantity ordered at a time. Thus, ordering costs are usually expressed by dollar cost per order.

Shortage Costs

Shortage costs, also referred to as stock-out costs, are costs that result when demand is not satisfied due to the shortage of inventory. Shortage costs are expressed by dollar cost per unit short to meet the demand per unit of time. These costs may include the lost profit and goodwill cost due to unsatisfied demand.

The *EOQ* Model

The economic order quantity (*EOQ*) model is the basic model that is the simplest of all inventory models. The objective of the *EOQ* model is to determine the optimum order quantity that minimizes the total inventory cost. The *EOQ* model is based on the following assumptions: (1) certainty of the demand quantity; (2) certainty of the lead time; (3) instantaneous replenishment of inventory; (4) no need for inventory shortage; and (5) the constancy of unit holding cost and ordering costs, regardless of the quantity involved.

Based on the above assumptions, we can plot the inventory level over time as shown in Fig. 13.1. To develop the *EOQ* model, let us define the following variables and parameters:

TIC = total annual inventory cost
THC = total annual holding cost
TOC = total annual ordering cost
C_h = holding cost per unit per year
C_o = ordering cost per order
Q = quantity per order
D = total annual demand for items

Figure 13.1

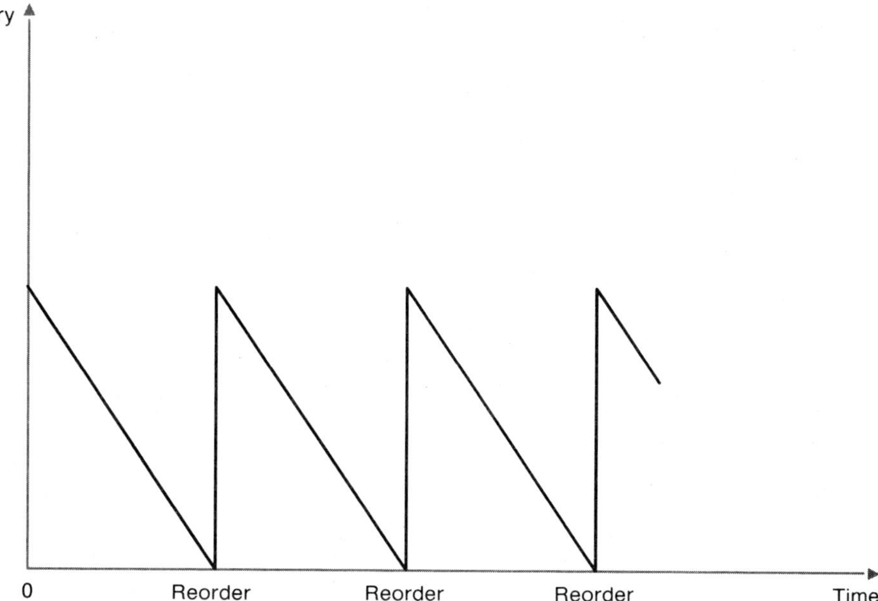

The objective of developing an *EOQ* model is to determine the optimum order quantity (Q^*) that will minimize the total annual inventory cost. Inventory shortage costs are not considered in the *EOQ* model as we assume an environment of certainty.

We can now proceed to formulate the *EOQ* model.

Total Inventory Cost

Since there is no stock-out cost involved, the total annual inventory cost is simply the sum of total annual holding cost and total annual ordering cost.

$$TIC = THC + TOC$$

Total Annual Holding Cost

The total annual holding cost is determined by multiplying the holding cost per unit per year (C_h) by the average inventory level. Since the demand rate is assumed to be constant and inventory replenishment is instantaneous, the inventory level fluctuates between Q and zero, as shown in Fig. 13.1. Thus, the average inventory level throughout the year is $\frac{1}{2}Q$. Now we can formulate *THC* as

$$THC = C_h \cdot \frac{Q}{2}.$$

Total Annual Ordering Cost

The cost per order is assumed to be constant regardless of the quantity involved. Thus, *TOC* is simply the cost per order (C_o) times the number of orders per year. Since the annual demand (D) is assumed to be known, the number of orders we must prepare will be D divided by the quantity per order (Q).

$$TOC = C_o \cdot \frac{D}{Q}$$

Optimum Order Quantity

Figure 13.2 is a graphic illustration of relationships among *TIC, THC,* and *TOC.* The total inventory cost is minimum at the point where *THC* and *TOC* intersect. In other words, if we determine that Q is where $THC = TOC$, then this quantity will be the optimum order quantity (Q^*).

$$THC = TOC$$

$$C_h \cdot \frac{Q}{2} = C_o \cdot \frac{D}{Q}$$

$$\frac{C_h \cdot Q}{2} = \frac{C_o \cdot D}{Q}$$

$$C_h \cdot Q^2 = 2C_o \cdot D$$

$$Q^2 = \frac{2C_o \cdot D}{C_h}$$

$$Q^* = \left(\frac{2C_o \cdot D}{C_h}\right)^{1/2}$$

Figure 13.2

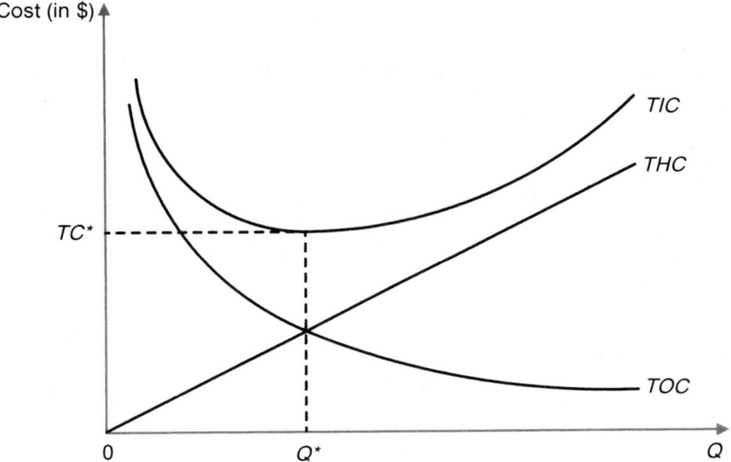

Example 13.1 Micros R Us, Inc.

Micros R Us is a microcomputer retail store that specializes in sales and service of Star Personal Computer sets. The manager is extremely concerned about ordering the optimum quantity of microcomputers to minimize the total inventory cost. Information currently available indicates the following:

Annual demand (D) = 180 computers
Holding cost (C_h) = \$100 per set
Ordering cost (C_o) = \$40 per order

The demand for microcomputers is assumed to be constant, one unit for every two days during 360 business days per year. Also, inventory replenishment can be assumed as instantaneous, since the primary warehouse is located only 40 miles away. By accepting all of the assumptions required for the *EOQ* model, the manager has computed the optimum order quantity as follows:

$$\begin{aligned} Q^* &= \left(\frac{2C_o \cdot D}{C_h}\right)^{1/2} \\ &= \left(\frac{2 \cdot 40 \cdot 180}{100}\right)^{1/2} \\ &= (144)^{1/2} \\ &= 12. \end{aligned}$$

Thus, we can obtain inventory costs as follows:

$$\begin{aligned} THC &= C_h \cdot \frac{Q}{2} \\ &= 100 \cdot \frac{Q}{2} \\ &= 50Q \\ &= 50 \cdot 12 \\ &= \$600. \\ TOC &= C_o \cdot \frac{D}{Q} \\ &= 40 \cdot \frac{180}{Q} \\ &= \frac{7{,}200}{Q} \\ &= \frac{7{,}200}{12} \\ &= \$600. \\ TIC &= THC + TOC \\ &= \$1{,}200. \end{aligned}$$

Based on the above computation, the manager was able to derive additional information about the inventory behavior.

Figure 13.3 Inventory Behavior of Micros R Us

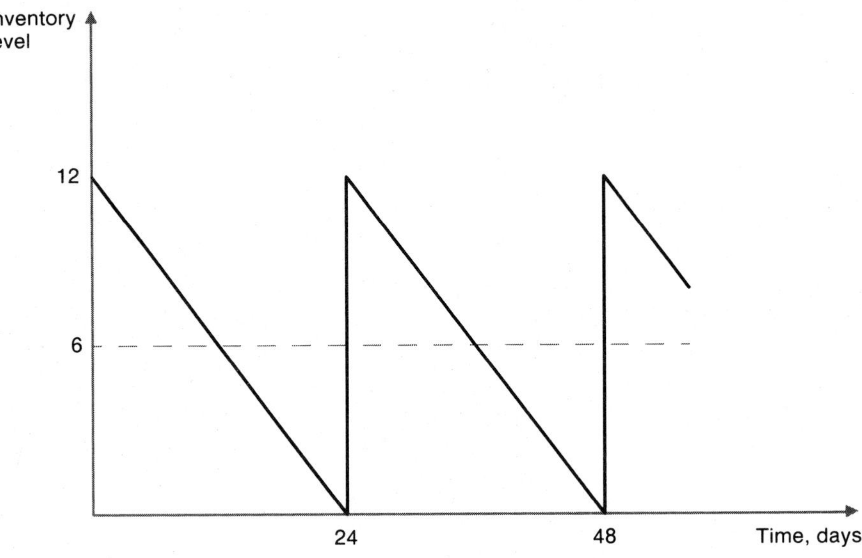

Inventory Cycle

The inventory cycle represents the time lapse (in days) from the time of order receipt to the time when the inventory level reaches zero.

Business days per year = 360

Demand rate per day = 1/2 unit

Number of orders per year $= \dfrac{D}{Q^*} = \dfrac{180}{12} = 15$

Inventory cycle = Business days ÷ 15 = 24 days

The manager was able to determine the following additional information:

Maximum inventory level $= Q^* = 12$

Average inventory level $= \dfrac{Q^*}{2} = 6$

The behavior of the inventory level is presented in Fig. 13.3.

Beyond *EOQ* Models

The *EOQ* model is based on strict assumptions. We need to make a number of modifications once we begin to relax some of the assumptions. Then the model parameters need different definitions.

Holding Cost as a Percentage of Inventory Value

Sometimes it is difficult to measure the holding cost of every item in inventory. In that case, it may be more practical to use C_h as a percentage of the average dollar value of inventory. For example, public utility firms often use 25 percent as the typical holding cost of items in inventory. The only change we need, then, is the following:

$$C_h = C_{hp} \cdot P$$

where C_{hp} = holding cost percentage
P = price or value of inventory item

Inventory Time Horizon

If the inventory analysis is for a specified time horizon, then the total demand and holding cost should also be further defined only for that specific time horizon. Thus, we need to modify our definition of the following parameters:

T = time horizon specified for analysis
D = total demand during T
C_{ht} = holding cost per unit of time during T

The only change that is required in the *EOQ* model is to redefine C_h as follows:

$$C_h = C_{ht} \cdot T.$$

Reorder Point

One of the most unrealistic assumptions of the *EOQ* model is instantaneous replenishment. Typically, some time lag exists between the time of order and the time of receipt. This time lag is referred to as *lead time*. When a known lead time exists, orders must be placed before the inventory level reaches zero. The reorder point is simply the inventory-level point at which an order is placed.

To compute the reorder point, we must use the following assumptions: (1) the demand rate per time period (e.g., per day) is known and constant, and (2) the lead time is known and constant.

Let us define the following parameters:

R = reorder point
DR = demand rate per unit of time (e.g., per day)
LT = lead time

Now we can compute the demand rate and the reorder point as follows:

$$DR = \frac{D}{360}, \text{ assuming 360 business days per year}$$

$$R = LT \cdot DR.$$

For example, in the Micros R Us case, if the lead time is four days and the demand rate is one-half unit per day, we can compute the reorder point as follows:

$$R = LT \cdot DR$$

$$R = 4 \times 0.5 = 2 \text{ units}.$$

Incremental Receipt Model

In the *EOQ* model, we typically assume that the entire quantity is received instantaneously. In many real-world situations, the delivery of ordered quantity may be incremental rather than in one shot. Let us assume that the inventory receipt rate is greater than the demand rate. Then, we can define the following:

IR = inventory receipt rate, assumed to be constant

DR = demand rate per unit of time, assumed to be constant

$\frac{Q}{IR}$ = number of days required to receive the entire order (order receipt period)

$\frac{Q}{IR} \cdot DR$ = number of units demanded during the order receipt period

$Q - \left(\frac{Q}{IR} \cdot DR\right)$ = maximum inventory level during an order cycle

The average inventory level can be obtained as follows:

$$\text{Average inventory level} = 1/2\left[Q - \left(\frac{Q}{IR} \cdot DR\right)\right]$$

$$= \frac{Q}{2}\left(1 - \frac{DR}{IR}\right)$$

$$THC = C_h \cdot \frac{Q}{2}\left(1 - \frac{DR}{IR}\right).$$

Thus, the optimum order quantity, Q^*, can be computed as follows:

$$Q^* = \left\{\frac{2C_o \cdot D}{C_h\,[1 - (DR/IR)]}\right\}^{1/2}.$$

Example 13.2 Microwave Oven Shop

The Microwave Oven Shop sells Gold Star Microwave Ovens. The shop purchases ovens from the distributor for \$200. It is estimated that the holding cost per unit per year is about 25 percent of the cost. The average ordering cost is estimated to be \$40 per order. The expected annual demand is 720 units for 360 working days, or the demand rate of two units per day. When an order is placed, the average inventory receipt rate is four units per day. The manager is trying to determine the optimum order quantity.

$$
\begin{aligned}
C_h &= \$200 \times 0.25 = 50 \\
C_o &= \$40 \\
D &= 720 \text{ units} \\
DR &= 2 \text{ units per day} \\
IR &= 4 \text{ units per day} \\
Q^* &= \left(\frac{2 \cdot 40 \cdot 720}{50(1 - 2/4)}\right)^{1/2} \\
&= \left(\frac{57{,}600}{25}\right)^{1/2} \\
&= (2{,}304)^{1/2} \\
&= 48
\end{aligned}
$$

Economic Lot Size Model

The economic lot size (*ELS*) model is an extension of the *EOQ* model to the production area. In this model, the ordering process is replaced by the production process to satisfy demand. Thus, the ordering cost is replaced by the setup cost. Setup cost represents the total costs incurred in preparing the production setup for the next run.

We can define the following variables and parameters:

C_h = holding cost per unit per year
C_s = setup cost per production lot
PR = production rate over time on an annual basis
DR = demand rate over time on an annual basis
Q = production lot size
TPC = total production cost

Now we are ready to develop relationships that are needed to determine the optimum lot size.

1. Length of the production phase = Q/PR
2. The maximum inventory level

During the production phase, the inventory level increases by $(PR - DR)$, assuming $PR > DR$.

Since the length of production phase is Q/PR, we can determine the following:

$$\text{Maximum inventory level} = (PR - DR)\,\frac{Q}{PR}$$

3. The average inventory level $= \dfrac{(PR - DR)Q}{2 \cdot PR}$
4. Length of inventory depletion phase

Once production stops, the maximum inventory level will be decreased gradually at the rate of DR.

$$\text{Length of inventory depletion phase} = \frac{(PR - DR)Q}{PR \cdot DR}$$

5. Number of annual inventory cycles $= \dfrac{DR}{Q}$
6. $THC = \dfrac{C_h \cdot (PR - DR) \cdot Q}{2 \cdot PR}$
7. Total annual setup cost, $TUC = \dfrac{C_s \cdot DR}{Q}$
8. Optimum production lot size

$$THC = TUC$$

$$\frac{C_h \cdot (PR - DR)Q}{2 \cdot PR} = \frac{C_s \cdot DR}{Q}$$

$$Q^* = \left[\frac{2 \cdot PR \cdot C_s \cdot DR}{C_h(PR - DR)}\right]^{1/2}$$

Example 13.3 Continental Upholstery Company

Continental Upholstery Company is the exclusive producer of motorcycle seats for several motorcycle producers in the United States. The expected demand per year, based on currently outstanding orders and past records, is 100,000 or 500 per day for 200 operation days per year. The expected setup cost is $4,000. The annual holding cost per seat is $10. The production rate during the production phase is 750 seats per day.

Based on the above information, we can determine the following:

$DR =$ 100,000 seats

$PR =$ 150,000 seats

$C_h =$ \$10

$C_s =$ \$4,000

$$Q^* = \left[\frac{2 \cdot PR \cdot C_s \cdot DR}{C_h\,(PR - DR)}\right]^{1/2}$$
$$= \left[\frac{2 \cdot (150{,}000) \cdot (4{,}000) \cdot (100{,}000)}{10(150{,}000 - 100{,}000)}\right]^{1/2}$$
$$= \left[\frac{(300{,}000)\ (400{,}000{,}000)}{500{,}000}\right]^{1/2}$$
$$= (240{,}000{,}000)^{1/2} \cong 15{,}492 \text{ per lot}$$

$$\text{Length of production phase} = \frac{Q^*}{PR} = \frac{15{,}492}{150{,}000} = 0.103 \text{ year}$$

200 working days per year $\times$ 0.103 = 20.6 $\cong$ = 21 days

$$\text{Maximum inventory level} = (PR - DR)\frac{Q^*}{PR}$$
$$= (150{,}000 - 100{,}000)\frac{15{,}492}{150{,}000}$$
$$= 5{,}164$$

$$\text{Average inventory level} = \frac{5{,}164}{2} = 2{,}582$$

$$\text{Length of inventory depletion phase} = \frac{(PR - DR)Q^*}{DR \cdot PR}$$
$$= \frac{(150{,}000 - 100{,}000)\ (15{,}492)}{(100{,}000)\ (150{,}000)}$$
$$= \frac{15{,}492}{300{,}000} = 0.052 \text{ year}$$
$$\cong 10 \text{ days}$$

Length of inventory cycles = production phase + inventory depletion phase
= 21 days + 10 days = 31 days

$$\text{Number of inventory cycles} = \frac{DR}{Q^*} = \frac{100{,}000}{15{,}492} \cong 6.45$$

$$\text{Total annual holding cost} = \frac{C_h \cdot (PR - DR) \cdot Q^*}{2 \cdot PR}$$
$$= \frac{10 \cdot (150{,}000 - 100{,}000)(15{,}492)}{2(150{,}000)}$$
$$= \$25{,}820$$

$$\text{Total annual setup cost} = \frac{C_s \cdot DR}{Q^*}$$
$$= \frac{(4{,}000)(100{,}000)}{15{,}492}$$
$$= \$25{,}820$$

$$TIC = THC + TUC$$
$$= 25{,}820 + 25{,}820$$
$$= \$51{,}640.$$

Figure 13.4 presents the inventory behavior of the Continental Upholstery Company case.

Figure 13.4 Continental Upholstery Company Production and Inventory Behavior

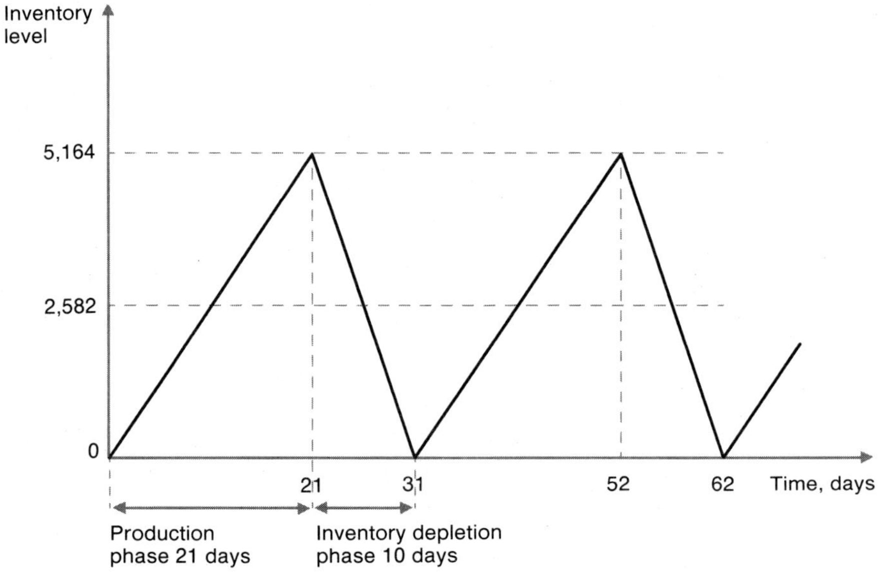

Quantity Discount Situation

Many manufacturers or wholesalers offer price discounts for orders of large quantities. To determine whether the order quantity should be increased beyond Q^*, we can simply compare the total cost with Q^* and the total cost with the price discount quantity. We will choose the alternative that yields the minimum total cost.

Let us define the following variables and parameters:

C_{hp} = holding cost as a percentage of inventory value
P_1 = purchase price without discount
Q^* = EOQ
P_2 = discount purchase price
Q = price discount quantity

Then we can compute the optimum order quantity without discount as

$$Q^* = \left(\frac{2 \cdot C_o \cdot D}{C_{hp} \cdot P_1}\right)^{1/2}.$$

The total inventory cost, including the purchase cost for the two alternatives, will be

$$TC_1 = C_{hp} \cdot P_1 \frac{Q^*}{2} + C_o \frac{D}{Q^*} + P_1 \cdot D$$

$$TC_2 = C_{hp} \cdot P_2 \frac{Q}{2} + C_o \frac{D}{Q} + P_2 \cdot D.$$

Inventory Models with Shortages

In many real-world situations, inventory shortages occur frequently. If inventory shortages are allowed to occur and they can be back-ordered, we need to modify the previously presented models. The typical inventory behavior with allowed shortages is presented in Fig. 13.5. We can define the following variables and parameters.

C_{so} = stock-out cost per unit per year
S = shortage quantity back-ordered per order
I = maximum inventory level $(Q - S)$
TSC = total annual shortage cost
T = inventory cycle time period $(t_i + t_s)$
t_i = time period when inventory is available
t_s = time period when there are shortages in a cycle

Although the process for developing various relationships is too involved to describe here, the optimum solutions for the model variables are presented here. The *Micro Manager* solves problems based on these formulas:

$$Q^* = \left(\frac{2 \cdot C_o \cdot D}{C_h}\right)^{1/2} \cdot \left(\frac{C_h + C_{so}}{C_{so}}\right)^{1/2}$$

$$I^* = \left(\frac{2 \cdot C_o \cdot D}{C_h}\right)^{1/2} \cdot \left(\frac{C_{so}}{C_h + C_{so}}\right)^{1/2}$$

$$S^* = Q^* - I^*$$

$$T^* = \left(\frac{2 \cdot C_o}{C_h \cdot D}\right)^{1/2} \cdot \left(\frac{C_h + C_{so}}{C_{so}}\right)^{1/2}$$

$$TC^* = (2 \cdot C_h \cdot C_o \cdot D)^{1/2} \cdot \left(\frac{C_{so}}{C_h + C_{so}}\right)^{1/2}$$

Figure 13.5 Inventory Model with Allowed Shortages

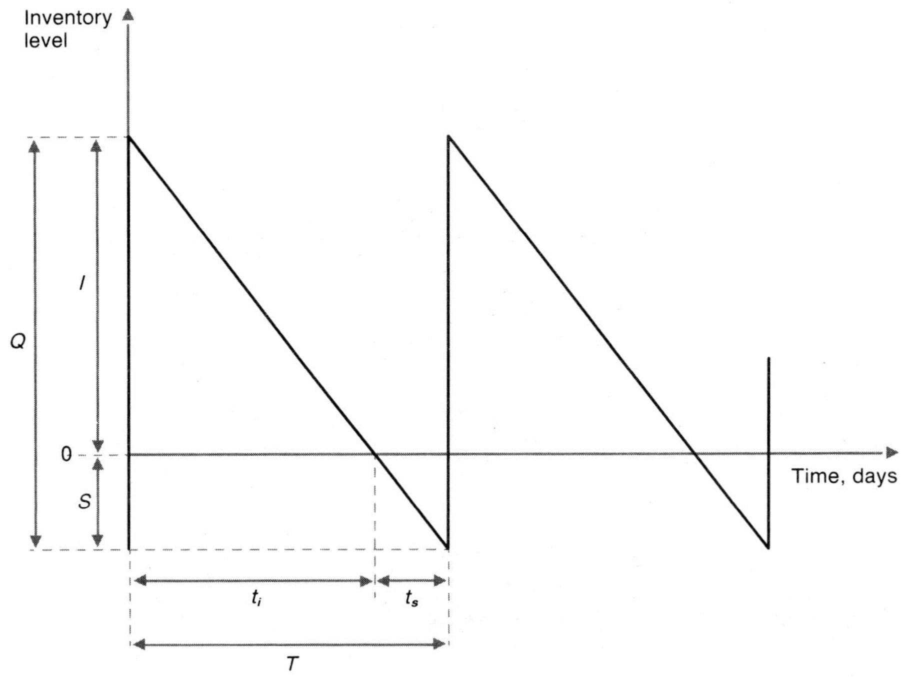

Inventory Model under Uncertainty

In the case of inventory models under uncertainty, two parameters are uncertain: demand rate per unit of time (e.g., per day) and lead time. We cannot determine the optimum order quantity (Q^*) and the optimum reorder point (R^*). With uncertain demand rate and lead time, stock-outs or shortages are quite possible. Thus, total inventory cost will be: $TIC = THC + TOC + TSC$. Figure 13.6 presents inventory behavior, without showing the shortage possibilities for simplicity, under the condition of uncertainty.

Now we can define the following variables and parameters.

$$R = \text{reorder point}$$
$$D_{lt} = \text{demand during lead time}$$
$$E(D_{lt}) = \text{expected demand during lead time}$$
$$E(D_{lt} > R) = \text{expected shortage during lead time}$$
$$C_{so} = \text{stock-out cost per unit per year}$$
$$TSC = \text{total shortage cost}$$
$$LT = \text{lead time}$$
$$SS = \text{average safety stock } [R - E(D_{lt})]$$

Figure 13.6 Average Inventory Pattern with Uncertain Demand Rate and Lead Time (No Shortage Assumption)

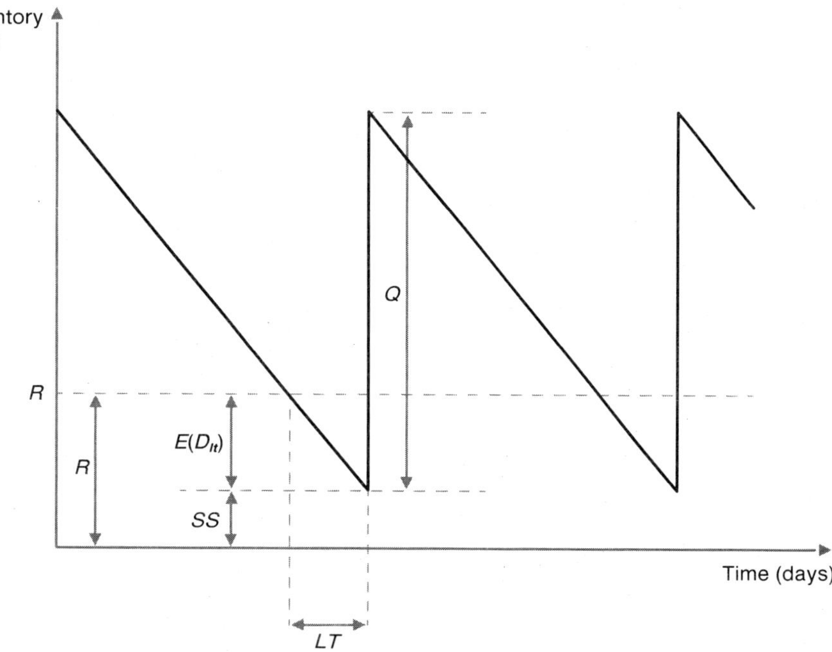

$$\text{Total holding cost, } THC = C_h\left(\frac{Q}{2} + SS\right) \text{ or}$$

$$= C_h\left[\frac{Q}{2} + R - E(D_{lt})\right]$$

$$\text{Total ordering cost, } TOC = C_o \cdot \frac{D}{Q}$$

$$\text{Total storage cost, } TSC = E(D_{lt} > R) \cdot C_{so} \cdot \frac{D}{Q}$$

$$TIC = THC + TOC + TSC$$

$$TIC = C_h \cdot \left[\frac{Q}{2} + R - E(D_{lt})\right] + C_o \cdot \frac{D}{Q} + C_{so} \cdot \left(\frac{D}{Q}\right) \cdot E(D_{lt} > R)$$

By using the partial derivation procedure, we obtain

$$Q^* = \left\{\frac{2 \cdot D[C_o + C_{so} \cdot E(D_{lt} > R)]}{C_h}\right\}^{1/2}.$$

Thus, if we select a certain reorder point R, we can determine the optimum order quantity for the given R. For each set of R and Q^*, we can easily compute the TIC. As we increase R, TOC may gradually decrease and then again gradually increase. The optimum reorder point, R^*, and the optimum order quantity, Q^*, are identified by selecting the corresponding minimum TIC.

Example 13.4 Modern Medical Equipment, Inc.

Modern Medical Equipment, Inc., is a pioneer in developing and selling innovative medical and health-care delivering equipment. The company has just introduced a new line of birthing chairs that have been proved medically to be much more efficient than the traditional birthing beds.

The company has compiled the following information:

$C_h = \$200$
$C_o = \$40$
$C_{so} = \$80$
$D = 200$ chairs for 200 working days per year

Shortage units are back-ordered.

Daily demand rate (*DR*): uncertain

DR	**Probability**
0	.3
1	.4
2	.3
	1.0

Lead time (*LT*): uncertain

LT	**Probability**
1	.25
2	.50
3	.25
	1.00

Demand during Lead Time, Probabilities, and Shortages

To analyze the demand behavior, we must compute the joint probabilities associated with demand during lead time $[P(D_{lt})]$. For example, since the maximum lead time is three days and the maximum demand rate is two units per day, the maximum demand during a lead time will be six birthing chairs. The probability of having six birthing chairs demanded during a lead time will require $LT = 3$ and $DR = 2$ for all three lead-time days. Thus, we can compute this probability as follows:

$$\begin{aligned} P(D_{lt} = 6) &= P(LT = 3)\,[P(DR = 2) \times P(DR = 2) \\ &\quad \times P(DR = 2)] \\ &= 0.25 \times 0.30 \times 0.30 \times 0.30 \\ &= 0.00675. \end{aligned}$$

Once we obtain each possible $P(D_{lt})$, we can also find the cumulative probability that demand during lead time will be greater than a certain unit, $P(D_{lt} > Z)$. We can also compute the expected shortage during lead time, $E(D_{lt} > P)$, which is simply a cumulation of the cumulative probability $[P(D_{lt} > Z)]$, as shown below.

D_{lt}	$P(D_{lt})$	$P(D_{lt} > Z)$	$E(D_{lt} > R)$
0	0.12675	0.87325	2.00000
1	0.24700	0.62625	1.12675
2	0.30125	0.32500	0.50050
3	0.19000	0.13500	0.17550
4	0.10125	0.03375	0.04050
5	0.02700	0.00675	0.00675
6	0.00625	0.00000	0.00000

Expected Demand during Lead Time

The expected demand during lead time, $E(D_{lt})$, can be obtained simply by multiplying the expected lead time and the expected demand rate. Given the probability distributions for the lead time and demand rate, we can compute the following:

$$\begin{aligned} E(LT) &= (1 \times .25) + (2 \times .5) + (3 \times .25) \\ &= 2 \text{ days} \\ E(DR) &= (0 \times .3) + (1 \times .4) + (2 \times .3) \\ &= 1 \text{ unit} \\ E(D_{lt}) &= E(LT) \times E(DR) \\ &= 2 \text{ units.} \end{aligned}$$

Optimum Order Quantity for a Given R

Once we set our reorder point at a given number, we can determine the optimum order quantity for this given R. Then we can obtain the TIC for this R and Q combination. For example, if we set $R = 3$, $E(D_{lt} > 3) = 0.17550$.

$$\begin{aligned} Q^* &= \left\{\frac{2 \cdot D[C_o + C_{so} \cdot E(D_{lt} > 3)]}{C_h}\right\}^{1/2} \\ &= \left[\frac{2 \cdot 200\ (40 + 80 \times 0.17550)}{200}\right]^{1/2} \\ &= \left[\frac{400\ (40 + 14.04)}{200}\right]^{1/2} \\ &= 10.4 \\ &\cong 10. \end{aligned}$$

Total Inventory Cost for Selected R and O

Once we set a reorder point and determine its corresponding Q^*, we can compute the TIC. For example, if $R = 3$ and $Q = 10$, TIC will be

$$TIC = C_h \cdot \left[\frac{Q}{2} + R - E(D_{lt})\right] + C_o \cdot \frac{D}{Q} + C_{so} \cdot \left(\frac{D}{Q}\right) \cdot E(D_{lt} > R)$$

$$= 200\left[\frac{10}{2} + (3 - 2)\right] + 40 \cdot \frac{200}{10} + 80 \cdot \left(\frac{200}{10}\right) \cdot 0.17550$$
$$= 1{,}200 + 800 + 280.80$$
$$= \$2{,}280.80.$$

The total inventory cost for selected R and Q is presented below

R	*Q*	*THC*	*TOC*	*TSC*	*TIC*
3	10	$1,200.00	$800.00	$280.80	$2,280.80
4	9	1,300.00	888.89	72.00	2,260.89
5	9	1,500.00	888.89	12.00	2,400.89

Since the TIC decreased from $R = 3$ to $R = 4$, and increased when $R = 5$, we can easily conclude that the optimum combination of R and Q is: $R = 4$ and $Q = 9$. We should note here that THC increases when the reorder point increases, while TSC decreases.

Determination of the Optimum R and Q**

The procedure we used in determining the optimum R^* and Q^* is as follows:

1. Set R at a low number.
2. Determine the optimum Q^* for the set R.
3. Compute TIC for the R and Q combination.
4. List this TIC. If this TIC is smaller than the previous TIC, go to Step 5. Otherwise, go to Step 6.
5. Increase R by one and go to Step 2.
6. Stop.

Application of the *Micro Manager*

In this section we present an application example of the *Micro Manager* to an inventory problem. The program diskette provides you with the complete information about the many different inventory models, including the purpose of the techniques, solutions of example problems, interactive input instructions, and the batch input procedure. This section presents only the information (purpose of inventory models and the batch input data format) and the solution of a sample problem using the interactive input format.

<< PURPOSE >>

INVENTORY MODELS determines the economic order quantity (EOQ) (either with or without shortage) and the optimum lot size. The output will present the order quantity (either with or without a discount situation), order frequency, reorder point, inventory cycle, total inventory cost, and/or the maximum required inventory level. For the inventory problem with uncertain demand rates and lead times, a simulation program is presented in SIMULATION.

<< BATCH INPUT DATA FORMAT >>

Type in the values of the following input data requirements, after creating a new file. You may enter as many values as you want in a line, separating them by commas for alphabetic characters and by commas or blank spaces for numeric values. However, the input data must be exactly in the following order:

1. Model type
   - 1 : Basic economic order quantity (EOQ) model
   - 2 : Receipt model
   - 3 : Economic lot-size (ELS) model
   - 4 : Quantity Discount Model
   - 5 : Inventory model with planned shortages
   - 6 : Inventory model with safety stocks
2. Annual demand
3. Annual working days

For model type = 1
   4. Ordering cost
   5. Holding cost

For model type = 2
   4. Ordering cost
   5. Holding cost
   6. Receipt rate per day

For model type = 3
   4. Setup cost
   5. Production rate
   6. Holding cost

For model type = 4
   4. Holding cost as percentage
   5. Number of price levels
   6. For each price level
      - minimum quantity
      - price

For model type = 5
   4. Ordering cost
   5. Holding cost
   6. Shortage cost

For model type = 6
   4. Ordering cost
   5. Holding cost
   6. Shortage cost
   7. Number of demand during lead time (DDLT)'s
   8. for each DDLT
      - Demand during lead time (DDLT)
      - Probability
   9. Number of Orders per year

```
** Sample Batch Input Data Set (Example 13.3) **

3             ; ELS model
100000        ; annual demand
200           ; annual working days
4000          ; setup cost
150000        ; annual production rate
10            ; unit annual holding cost

Inventory Models

    1   Basic economic order quantity (EOQ) model
    2   Receipt  model
    3   Economic lot-size (ELS) model
    4   Quantity discount model
    5   Inventory model with planned shortages
    6   Inventory model with safety stocks


Enter a model number (1 TO 6): 3

Economic lot-size (ELS) model

Enter annual demand (units/year): 100000
Enter annual working days (360 by default): 200
Enter setup cost ($/production lot): 4000
Enter production rate (units/year): 150000
Enter holding cost ($/unit/year): 10

PROGRAM: Inventory Models

***** INPUT DATA ENTERED *****

Economic lot-size (ELS) model

Demand (annual)       :   100000 units/year
Annual working days   :   200 days/year
Setup cost            : $ 4000 /production lot
Production rate       :   150000 units/year
Holding cost          : $ 10 /unit/year

*****   PROGRAM OUTPUT   *****

Optimum production lot size        :   15491.9 units per lot
Maximum inventory level            :    5164.0 units
Average inventory level            :    2582.0 units
Length of inventory depletion phase :     10   days
Demand rate (DR)                   :     500.0 units per day
Number of inventory cycles         :       6.5 per year
Total annual inventory cost        :  $51639.78 per year
```

Summary

Inventory management has been an important aspect of operations management because virtually every organization maintains inventories of some kind. Recently, inventory management has received a renewed attention due to the popularity of the Japanese just-in-time manufacturing system. In this chapter, we have reviewed various inventory-related models under certainty and uncertainty. The *Micro Manager* is extremely effective and user-friendly for analyzing complex inventory models.

References

Buffa, E. S., and W. H. Taubert. 1972. *Production-inventory systems: Planning and control.* rev. ed. Homewood, IL: Irwin.

Lee, S. M. 1983. *Introduction to management science.* Chicago: Dryden.

Lee, S. M., L. J. Moore, and B. W. Taylor. 1985. *Management science.* 2d ed. Dubuque, IA: Wm. C. Brown Publishers.

Schonberger, R. J. 1985. *Operations management.* 2d. ed. Dallas: Business Publications.

Turban, E., and J. R. Meredith. 1981. *Fundamentals of management science.* 2d ed. Dallas: Business Publications.

Problems

1. Pan American Hydraulic Supply Company is a distributor of hydraulic supplies in the Gulf states area. Pan American handles standard hydraulic fittings, tubing, and similar items. Recently, the company has been experiencing increasing difficulty with out-of-stock situations and unbalanced inventories. The annual demand for tubing is estimated to be 18,000 units. The ordering cost is $20 per order, and the annual unit holding cost is $15. Assume 260 working days.

a. Determine the optimum order quantity.

b. Determine the number of orders.

c. What is the total inventory cost per year?

d. Describe the inventory pattern graphically.

2. Refer to the Pan American problem. Janet Schwartz, the purchasing manager of Pan American, insists that the unit holding costs of tubing are difficult to measure. Therefore, she suggests modifying the above inventory problem by replacing the estimated per unit annual holding cost as a percentage of the price.

$$C_{hp} = .20$$
$$P = \$35$$

a. Determine the optimal order quantity.
b. Determine the optimal number of orders.
c. What is the total inventory cost per year?

3. Ernest Mayer, the vice president of production and the inventory control department of Pan American, ordered a detailed analysis of the costs for a small hydraulic fitting. The fitting was purchased for \$14.00 and sold for \$19.50. The costs of preparing a purchase order and making the necessary record change were estimated to be \$10.50 per order. The inspection of shipments, preparation of receiving reports, and related activity were estimated to cost Pan American \$13.25 per order. An analysis of company records indicated that the following were reasonable estimates of the annual cost of carrying inventories (as a percentage of the dollar value of an average inventory):

Cost category	% of total
Capital cost	15
Obsolescence	8
Insurance and taxes	3
Storage and handling	12
Total	38

Purchase orders are prepared once each week. The lead time between the preparation of the purchase order and receipt of the fitting is assumed to be eight days with certainty. Customer orders filled for one year (260 working days) are estimated to be 3,500 orders without demand rate variation.

a. Determine the optimum order quantity.
b. Determine the optimum reorder point.
c. Determine the number of orders.
d. What is the total inventory holding cost, total ordering cost, and total inventory cost per year?

4. Referring to Problem 3, the manufacturer from whom Pan American procured the fitting does not offer any quantity discount on the fitting, but will not fill orders for less than 200 fittings without adding a flat charge of \$5.00.

a. Describe the inventory cost behavior graphically.

b. Determine the optimal order quantity.

c. Determine the optimal reorder point.

d. What are the total inventory costs, total ordering cost, and total annual inventory cost?

5. Referring to Problem 3, suppose that the manufacturer from whom Pan American procures the fittings offers a quantity discount (according to the following schedule) without adding a flat charge.

Schedule of Quantity Discount

Quantity	Unit purchase
Under 180	\$14.00
181–200	\$13.00
201 or more	\$12.00

a. Determine the optimal order quantity with quantity discounts.

b. Compute the total inventory cost for each optimal order quantity.

c. Compare the total inventory cost and total purchase cost between with and without discounts. Assume that unit holding costs are obtained by $C_{hp} * P$.

6. Refer to Problem 3. Recently, George Howard, the president of Pan American, has been impressed by the "just-in-time" concept of the Japanese management system. Also, a representative from a consulting company emphasized that just-in-time purchasing is often able to undercut the average order-processing cost. Thus, George Howard requested that Margaret Gisberg, a recent college graduate, conduct preliminary research regarding cost reduction in the order-processing process under just-in-time purchasing. A few days later, Margaret estimated that a 60% and a 40% reduction of the order-processing cost can be achieved under the once-a-day and once-a-week ordering system, respectively.

a. Determine the total inventory holding cost under the once-a-week and once-a-day ordering system. Assume that under a once-a-week and once-a-day order system, C_{hp} are .20 and .10, respectively.

b. What are the possible benefits of just-in-time?

7. Refer to Problem 3. Agatha King, a new graduate from the local college with an MBA degree, mentioned that her analysis of procurement lead time showed a variation ranging from 5 to 11 working days. The historical record of lead-time variations is shown in the following table.

Analysis of procurement lead time
(Working days between order issue and delivery of fittings)

10	6	7	7	9	5	8	10	9	6	8
10	9	6	9	8	7	6	8	7	7	7
9	7	9	7	8	5	7	6	6	8	5
8	11	7	9	9	10	8	8	9	6	5
9	9	10	8	8	7	9	9	8	6	9

Determine the optimal quantity of safety stock to cover 90% of the lead-time variations.

8. Refer to Problem 3. According to new information about the analysis of orders for one year, the average variations of demand rates are shown in the following table. Assume that shortages costs are $10.

D_{lt}	$P(D_{lt})$
10	.10
12	.20
13	.40
14	.20
16	.10

a. Determine the expected (average) demand during lead time.
b. Determine the total annual shortage cost (*TSC*).
c. Determine the total expected cost.

9. Refer to Problem 3. Simulate this problem with the same assumptions of procurement lead-time variation and demand-rate variations as in Problems 7 and 8.

10. Chalton Hoston, vice president of the production and inventory control division of Lester Manufacturing Company (LMC), is reviewing the optimality of the current inventory policy on power transformers.

The LMC uses six large transformers each working day of the month in manufacturing passenger elevators. LMC operated on a 250-day-per-year schedule. Chalton Hoston asked Brenda Stark to evaluate the current purchasing policy on power transformers by using the following information:

Total annual demand	1,500 units
Annual requisitions	48 times (weekly)
Units per requisition	30 units
Annual inventory holding cost	20% of purchase price
Order-processing cost per requisition	\$30
Warehouse capacity	80 units
Outside warehouse costs	\$20 per unit per year
Purchase price	\$490
Lead time	Instantaneous delivery

Evaluate the optimality of the current requisition policy. If it is optimal, then solve only Problem 11(c). If not, solve Problems 11(a)–(c).

11. Refer to Problem 10. Answer the following questions.

a. Determine the optimum order quantity.
b. Determine the optimum number of orders.
c. What is the total inventory cost per year?

12. Refer to Problem 10. Several months later, Chalton Hoston was informed that the LMC supplier could not deliver the product instantaneously because of a heavy work load. Therefore, the supplier could only deliver with an average lead time of four days. The demand during this lead time is assumed to be fixed. Identify any required changes in the current purchasing policy.

13. Refer to Problem 10. Assume that the supplier did not offer any quantity discount on the power transformer and would not fill orders for less than 150 units without adding a flat charge of \$50.

a. Determine the optimum order quantity.
b. Determine the optimum number of orders.
c. Determine the total inventory cost per year.

14. Refer to Problem 13. If the company decides to order 150 units to avoid the flat charge, determine the total inventory cost per year.

15. Refer to Problem 10. Several weeks later, the supplier informed Chalton Hoston about a new price structure.

Units per order	Unit price
First 20	$490
Next 20	$450
All over 40	$410

a. Describe inventory cost behavior graphically.

b. Determine the optimum order quantity with quantity discounts.

c. Compare the total inventory cost and total purchase cost between with and without discounts. Assume that unit holding costs are obtained by $C_{hp} \cdot P$.

16. Refer to Problem 10. Recently, Helena Dangerfield, the president of LMC, returned from Tokyo, Japan, after attending the Japan–U.S. Business Conference. Dangerfield now firmly believes that just-in-time (*JIT*) and total quality control (*TQC*) can be effectively transferred and implemented in the United States. As a first step, she ordered a comparison of the once-a-week ordering system with the once-a-day ordering system. Assume that the once-a-day ordering system can reduce the ordering cost by 35% and that C_{hp} is .10. Determine the total inventory carrying cost under the once-a-day ordering system.

17. Referring to the LMC problem, James Hawkins, a production and inventory control clerk, insists that his analysis of procurement lead time showed a wide variation ranging from 3 to 8 working days with the following probabilities:

LT	Prob.	Cumulative prob.
3	.1	.1
4	.2	.3
5	.2	.5
6	.2	.7
7	.2	.9
8	.1	1.0

a. Determine the expected (average) lead time.

b. Determine the optimum quantity of safety stock to cover 90% of the lead-time variation.

18. Referring to the LMC problem, according to new information about the analysis of orders for one year, the average variation of demand rates is shown in the following table. Assume that the shortage cost is \$20 and that the lead time is fixed.

D_{lt}	$P(D_{lt})$
5	.05
6	.15
7	.20
8	.20
9	.20
10	.15
11	.05

a. Determine the expected (average) demand during lead time.

b. Determine the total annual shortage cost (*TSC*).

c. Determine the total expected cost.

19. The Lester Manufacturing Company (see Problem 10) also uses medium transformers in manufacturing different sizes of passenger elevators. Inventory information for the medium transformer is as follows:

Total annual demand = 750 units

Purchase price = \$380 per unit

Annual inventory carrying cost = 15% of purchase price per unit per year

Order-processing cost = 10% of purchase price per unit per year.

LT	*P(LT)*	*DR*	*P(DR)*
1	.30	1	.25
2	.40	2	.50
3	.30	3	.25

D_{lt}	$P(D_{lt})$	$P(D_{lt} > Z)$
0	.0000	1.0000
1	.0613	.9387
2	.1520	.7867
3	.2011	.5856
4	.2188	.3668
5	.1718	.1950
6	.1101	.0849
7	.0578	.0271
8	.0232	.0039
9	.0039	.0000

a. Assuming that you have complete certainty about the lead time and the demand rate, compute EOQ.

b. Under the condition of certainty, the order-processing cost is not known (while other cost information is known), but EOQ is known to be 35. What will be the order-processing cost?

20. Referring to Problem 19, under the condition of uncertainty, if the optimum R is assumed to be 5, what should the optimum Q be?

C H A P T E R 14

Dynamic Programming

Many real-world problems involve sequential or multistage decision making. For example, typical investment problems involve sequential decisions over several time periods. For such problems, we cannot use a single-stage optimization technique that attempts to solve a given problem in a single assault. For instance, in chapter 10, we discussed decision-tree analysis that applied a sequential decision-making approach. Dynamic programming is somewhat similar to decision-tree analysis to the extent that the problem under consideration is decomposed into smaller subproblems and a sequential decision-making approach is applied. Dynamic programming is based on a multistage decision process where a decision at one stage will affect the decision at a subsequent stage. In this chapter, we will briefly walk through the fundamentals of dynamic programming and discuss how the *Micro Manager* can be used to solve sequential decision problems.

Basics

Many practical decision problems are very complex; however, they can be solved easily by breaking them down into smaller interrelated subproblems that can then be solved sequentially. Dynamic programming is a convenient way to solve complex problems through decomposition or segmentation.

The pioneer of dynamic programming is Richard Bellman. Bellman's work began in the late 1940s and his contribution culminated with the publication of his 1957 book, *Dynamic Programming.* Since then, a large number of studies dealing with methodological and application aspects of dynamic programming have been published.

In dynamic programming, there is no universal solution algorithm, such as the simplex method for linear programming. Dynamic programming makes use of a variety of methods to solve multistage decision problems. Consequently, dynamic programming has been applied to a variety of real-world problems, including production planning, sales and marketing strategies, inventory control, equipment replacement and maintenance, manpower scheduling, network flow and allocation, and investment planning.

Dynamic programming involves several unique concepts. In this section, we will discuss these concepts and basic features of dynamic programming.

Decomposition and Sequential Decision

The first fundamental concept of dynamic programming is decomposition or subdivision of the problem under analysis into a sequence of smaller subproblems. Each subproblem is referred to as a stage. Thus, the problem becomes a sequence of stages and the solution process involves multistage, sequential decision making.

The Backward Approach

The typical way to analyze a sequence of subproblems is by arranging stages linked from left to right. Thus, the flow of information required for sequential decision making is based on this backward approach. For example, Fig. 14.1 presents a manpower-planning problem for a three-year period with its segmentation and sequential decision-making flows.

Recursive Relations

The sequential decision making at each stage must be tied together in a particular way. The recursive relation function serves this purpose and allows the sequential decision making to optimize the entire operation.

Features of Dynamic Programming

A. State—A state is the condition or status of a particular problem in a given stage.
B. Stage—A stage is a decision point in a sequence of subproblems.
C. Policy decision—A policy decision represents a decision alternative that can be selected based on a predetermined policy at each stage.
D. Return—A return is the value (profit, cost, distance, and so on) at each stage.
E. Total return—Total return is represented by a function generated from the initial state to the current state. The total return function could be a sum, a multiplication, a series of recursive operations, or a more complex process.
F. The principle of optimality—The basic optimality approach used in dynamic programming is that, with the given current state, the optimum policy decision for the remaining stages is independent of prior decision.

Figure 14.1 A Three-Year, Manpower-Planning Problem

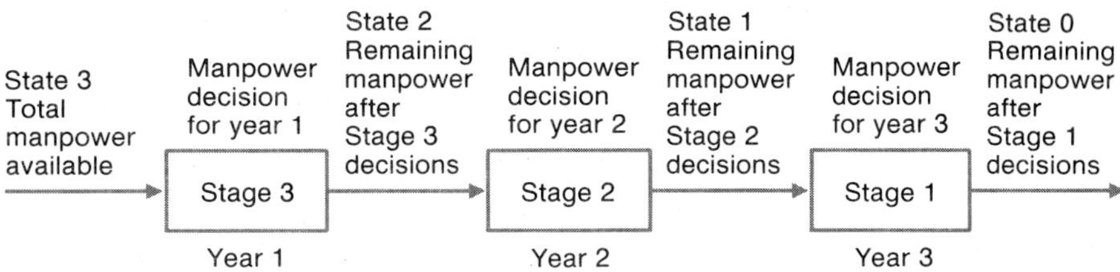

The Dynamic-Programming Model

In this section, we will discuss the basic structure of the dynamic-programming model. As we discussed earlier, the basic features of dynamic programming involve decomposition, sequential decision making, and recursive relations. The basic structure of dynamic programming involves the following variables, parameters, and functions:

n	: stage
s_n	: state
x_n	: policy decision
c_{x_n}	: return incurred by x_n
$f_n(s_n)$	: total return
x_n^*	: the optimum policy decision
$f_n^*(s_n)$	: the optimum total return

The general recursive function can be expressed as follows:

$$f_n^*(s_n) = \text{max or min } [f_n^*(s_n, x_n)].$$

If the problem is a shortest-route type, sequential problem, the recursive function will be a summation operation as shown below.

$$f_n^*(s_n) = \min\ [c_{x_n} + f_{n-1}^*(s_{n-1})]$$

The general structure of dynamic programming is shown in Fig. 14.2.

Example 14.1 Elizabeth Anderson Cosmetics, Inc.

Elizabeth Anderson Cosmetics, Inc., distributes cosmetics through personal selling on home visits by salespeople. Cathy regularly visits six neighborhood areas throughout the year. Because of the characteristics of the neighborhood (e.g., income, residence types, working homemakers, traffic patterns, distance between neighborhoods, and so on), the net profit for each route differs significantly.

Figure 14.2

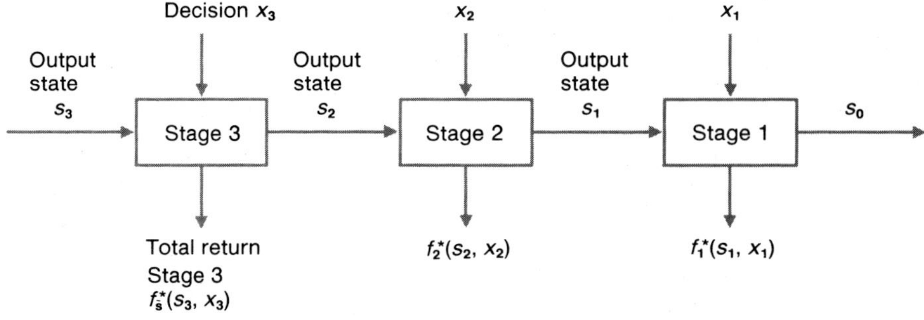

Figure 14.3 Elizabeth Anderson Cosmetics Problem

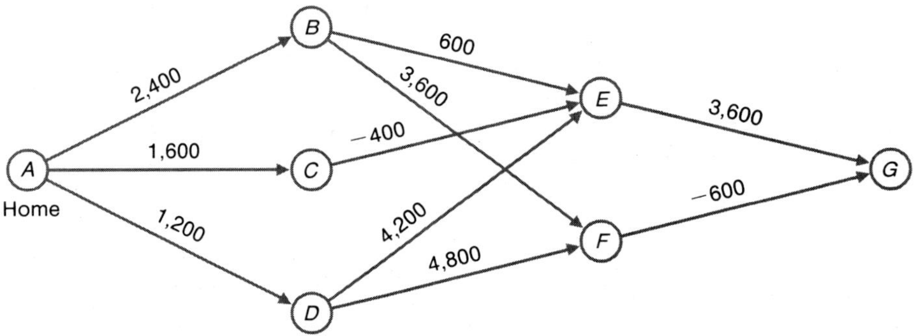

Figure 14.3 presents Cathy's typical travel patterns with associated profits from each trip. Cathy is required to travel in the direction of the arrows as shown in the figure. Cathy is trying to determine the optimum path to travel from home to neighborhood G to maximize total profit.

There are three decision points in determining the travel routes. Thus, we have three stages as shown in Fig. 14.4. We can define the stage and states as follows:

Stage	State
1	E,F
2	B,C,D
3	A

Figure 14.4 Elizabeth Anderson Cosmetics Problem States and Stages

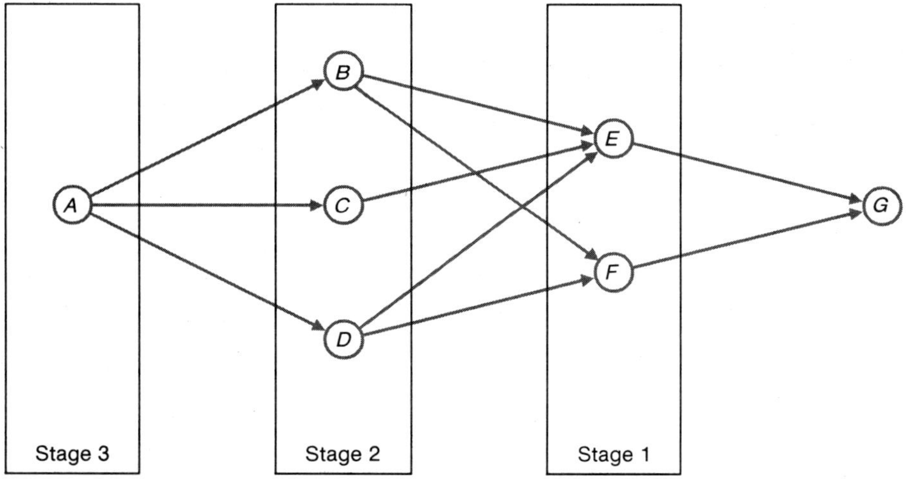

By employing the backward approach, we can compute the total returns at each stage as follows:

Stage 1

$$f_1(E) = \$3{,}600$$
$$f_1(F) = -\$600$$

Stage 2

The general backward recursive relation is

$$f_n(s_n) = \max\,[c_{x_n} + f^*_{n-1}(s_{n-1})].$$

The second stage function to maximize profit is

$$f_2(s_2) = \max\,[c_{x_2} + f^*_1(s_1)].$$

Thus, we obtain the following functions:

$$\begin{aligned}
f_2(B) &= \max\,[c_{B\to E} + f^*_1(E)] = \$600 + \$3{,}600 = \$4{,}200^* \\
&[c_{B\to F} + f^*_1(F)] = \$3{,}600 - \$600 = \$3{,}000 \\
f_2(C) &= \max\,[c_{C\to E} + f^*_1(E)] = -\$400 + \$3{,}600 = \$3{,}200^* \\
f_2(D) &= \max\,[c_{D\to E} + f^*_1(E)] = \$4{,}200 + \$3{,}600 = \$7{,}800^* \\
&[c_{D\to F} + f^*_1(F)] = \$4{,}800 - \$600 = \$4{,}200
\end{aligned}$$

Stage 3

$$f_3(s_3) = \max\,[c_{x_3} + f_2^*\,(s_2)]$$

Thus, we obtain the following functions:

$$\begin{aligned} f_3(A) = \max\,& [c_{A\to B} + f_2^*(B)] = \$2{,}400 + \$4{,}200 = \$6{,}600 \\ & [c_{A\to C} + f_2^*(C)] = \$1{,}600 + \$3{,}200 = \$4{,}800 \\ & [c_{A\to D} + f_2^*(D)] = \$1{,}200 + \$7{,}800 = \$9{,}000^* \end{aligned}$$

Now we can determine the optimum traveling path for Cathy as follows: $A \to D \to E \to G$. The total expected profit from this trip is $9,000.

Example 14.2 Old Father Brewing Company

Old Father Brewing Company specializes in bottling Scotch whiskey. The company imports original Scotch whiskey concentrate from Scotland twice a year and dilutes it with water and several other ingredients. Then the company bottles the Scotch whiskey into elegant ceramic bottles. Today, Scotland notified the company that 20 tons of the concentrate were shipped from Southampton, England.

The company plans to produce three types of Scotch whiskey: Passport, VIP, and Gold. Each type of Scotch whiskey requires a certain amount of concentrate. The allocation of concentrate is critical in this business because the company receives the shipments from Scotland only twice a year. The probable returns from the three types of Scotch whiskey, as shown below, depend on the quantity of concentrate allocated. Notice that the allocation of concentrate is made in units of 5 tons.

	Expected Profit		
Concentrate (5-ton unit)	**Passport**	**VIP**	**Gold**
5	$40,000	$24,000	$32,000
10	$70,000	$70,000	$44,000
15	N/A	N/A	$76,000

The objective of this problem is to determine the optimum allocation plan of concentrate for the company to maximize the total return.

Let us first define the following:

Stage: Each type of Scotch whiskey (1 = Gold, 2 = VIP, 3 = Passport)

State: The amount of concentrate used for each type of whiskey (in units of 5 tons)

Return: The estimated profit

Decision: The allocation of concentrate to each type of whiskey (in units of 5 tons)

The recursive function is

$$f_n(s_n) = \max\ [c_{x_n} + f^*_{n-1}(s_{n-1})].$$

Now, we can analyze the problem as follows:

Stage (n)	State (s_n)	Return (c_{x_n})	Total Return $[f_{n-1}(s_n)]$
1	0	$c_0 = 0$	0*
	5	$c_5 = 32$	$32 + f^*_0(s_0) = 32$*
	10	$c_{10} = 44$	$44 + f^*_0(s_0) = 44$*
	15	$c_{15} = 76$	$76 + f^*_0(s_0) = 76$*
2	10	$c_0 = 0$	$0 + f^*_1(10) = 44$
		$c_5 = 24$	$24 + f^*_1(5) = 56$
		$c_{10} = 70$	$70 + f^*_1(0) = 70$*
	15	$c_0 = 0$	$0 + f^*_1(15) = 76$
		$c_5 = 24$	$24 + f^*_1(10) = 68$
		$c_{10} = 70$	$70 + f^*_1(5) = 102$*
	20	$c_5 = 24$	$24 + f^*_1(15) = 100$
		$c_{10} = 70$	$70 + f^*_1(10) = 114$*
3	20	$c_0 = 0$	$0 + f^*_2(20) = 114$
		$c_5 = 40$	$40 + f^*_2(15) = 142$*
		$c_{10} = 70$	$70 + f^*_2(10) = 140$

(Unit: $1,000)

Thus, the optimum allocation of concentrate is as follows:

Passport = 5 tons
VIP = 10 tons
Gold = 5 tons
Total Return = $142,000

Application of the *Micro Manager*

In this section, an application example of the *Micro Manager* to a dynamic programming problem will be presented. There are several different models of dynamic programming that we can apply. The program diskette provides the complete information about dynamic programming, including the purpose of the technique, solutions of example problems, interactive input instructions, and the batch input procedure. In this section, therefore, we will present only the information (purpose of dynamic programming and the batch input data format) and the solution of a sample problem using the interactive input format.

<< PURPOSE >>

DYNAMIC PROGRAMMING determines the optimum time, cost, or return for complex problems through a sequential decision-making approach. The output will include a description of the complete route from the starting state to the ending state. This program can handle problems with up to 10 stages and 10 states.

<< BATCH INPUT DATA FORMAT >>

Type in the values of the following input data requirements, after creating a new file. You may enter as many values as you want in a line, separating them by commas for alphabetic characters and by commas or blank spaces for numeric values. However, the input data must be exactly in the following order:

```
1. Problem type 1
      1    : maximization
      2    : minimization
2. Problem type 2
      1    : Network
      2    : Nonnetwork
3. Number of stages

For network
   4. Information for each state in each stage
        4.1. Starting node
        4.2. Ending node
        4.3. Return value
   5. Type of recursion function
        1  : f(n) = R(n) + f(n-1)
        2  : f(n) = R(n) - f(n-1)
        3  : f(n) = R(n) * f(n-1)
        4  : f(n) = a(n) * R(n) + b(n) * f(n-1) + c(n)
   For recursion function type 4
      6. coefficients a, b, and c for each stage (from last stage)

For nonnetwork type
   4. Type of transition function
        1  : S(n-1) = S(n) - D(n)
        2  : S(n-1) = S(n) + D(n)
        3  : S(n-1) = S(n) * D(n)
        4  : S(n-1) = D(n)
        5  : S(n-1) = a(n) * S(n) + b(n) * D(n) + c(n)
   For transition function type 1 or 3
      5.1.  maximum value of decisions
            (decision values should be incremented by 1 from 0)
   For transition function type 2 or 4
      5.1.  maximum value of decisions
            (decision values should be incremented by 1 from 0)
      5.2.  Maximum value of states
   For transition function type 5
      5.1.  coefficients a, b, and c for each stage
      5.2.  maximum value of decisions
            (decision values should be incremented by 1 from 0)
      if coefficient b > 0 then
         5.3.  maximum value of states
```

```
6. Value of state in last stage
7. Type of recursion function
     1  : f(n) = R(n) + f(n-1)
     2  : f(n) = R(n) - f(n-1)
     3  : f(n) = R(n) * f(n-1)
     4  : f(n) = a(n) * R(n) + b(n) * f(n-1) + c(n)
For recursion function type  4
   8. coeffients a, b, c for each stage (from last stage)
   9. Type of return function
        1  : R(n) = constant
        2  : R(n) = a(n) * S(n) + b(n) * D(n) + c(n)
   For return function type 1
      11. Return value of each decision in each stage
          (from decision 0 in last stage
           to maximum decision in first stage)
   For return function type 2
      11. Number of return function (NF)
      If NF = 1 then for each stage (from last stage)
         12. coefficents a, b, and c
      If NF > 1 then for each stage (from last stage)
         12.1. decision range (lower limit, upper limit)
         12.2. coefficients a, b, and c

** Sample Batch Input Data Set (Example 14.2) **

1       ; maximization problem
2       ; nonnetwork
3       ; three stages
1       ; transition function type 1
3       ; maximum decision value (15 tons divided by 5-tons unit)
4       ; value of state in last stage
1       ; recursion function type 1
1       ; return function type 1
0       ; return value of decision 0 in stage 3
40      ; return value of decision 1 in stage 3
70      ; return value of decision 2 in stage 3
0       ; return value of decision 3 in stage 3
0       ; return value of decision 0 in stage 2
24      ; return value of decision 1 in stage 2
70      ; return value of decision 2 in stage 2
0       ; return value of decision 3 in stage 2
0       ; return value of decision 0 in stage 1
32      ; return value of decision 1 in stage 1
44      ; return value of decision 2 in stage 1
76      ; return value of decision 3 in stage 1
          (each decision value should be divided by 5-tons unit)
```

```
PROGRAM: Dynamic Programming

Enter 1 for maximization or 2 for minimization: 1
Enter 1 for network or 2 for nonnetwork problem: 2
Enter number of stages: 3

    1.   S(n-1) = S(n) - D(n)
    2.   S(n-1) = S(n) + D(n)
    3.   S(n-1) = S(n) * D(n)
    4.   S(n-1) = D(n)
    5.   S(n-1) = a(n)*S(n) + b(n)*D(n) + c(n)
```

```
To define the transition function, enter a number: 1

Enter maximum value of decisions (should be integer): 3
Enter value of state in stage 3  (should be integer): 4

    1.   f(n) = R(n) + f(n-1)
    2.   f(n) = R(n) - f(n-1)
    3.   f(n) = R(n) * f(n-1)
    4.   f(n) = a(n)*R(n) + b(n)*f(n-1) + c(n)


To define the recursion function, enter a number: 1

    1.   R(n) = known value
    2.   R(n) = a(n)*S(n) + b(n)*D(n) + c(n) ; function value


To define the return function, enter a number: 1

Enter return value for decision 0 in stage 3 : 0
Enter return value for decision 1 in stage 3 : 40
Enter return value for decision 2 in stage 3 : 70
Enter return value for decision 3 in stage 3 : 0

Enter return value for decision 0 in stage 2 : 0
Enter return value for decision 1 in stage 2 : 24
Enter return value for decision 2 in stage 2 : 70
Enter return value for decision 3 in stage 2 : 0

Enter return value for decision 0 in stage 1 : 0
Enter return value for decision 1 in stage 1 : 32
Enter return value for decision 2 in stage 1 : 44
Enter return value for decision 3 in stage 1 : 76

PROGRAM: Dynamic Programming

***** INPUT DATA ENTERED *****

Nonnetwork/Maximization problem

Maximum value of decisions:  3
Value of state in stage 3 :  4

Transition function: S(n-1) = S(n) - D(n)

Recursion function:  f(n) = R(n) + f(n-1)

Return function
------------------------------------------------
                                         Stages
 Decisions            3          2          1
------------------------------------------------
      0            0.00       0.00       0.00
      1           40.00      24.00      32.00
      2           70.00      70.00      44.00
      3            0.00       0.00      76.00
------------------------------------------------
```

***** PROGRAM OUTPUT *****

Stage 1

S(n)	D(n)	R(n)	S(n-1)	f(n-1)	f(n)
0	0	0.000	0	0.000	0.000
1	0	0.000	0	0.000	0.000
1	1	32.000	0	0.000	32.000
2	0	0.000	0	0.000	0.000
2	1	32.000	0	0.000	32.000
2	2	44.000	0	0.000	44.000
3	0	0.000	0	0.000	0.000
3	1	32.000	0	0.000	32.000
3	2	44.000	0	0.000	44.000
3	3	76.000	0	0.000	76.000
4	0	0.000	0	0.000	0.000
4	1	32.000	0	0.000	32.000
4	2	44.000	0	0.000	44.000
4	3	76.000	0	0.000	76.000

Stage 2

S(n)	D(n)	R(n)	S(n-1)	f(n-1)	f(n)
0	0	0.000	0	0.000	0.000
1	0	0.000	1	32.000	32.000
1	1	24.000	0	0.000	24.000
2	0	0.000	2	44.000	44.000
2	1	24.000	1	32.000	56.000
2	2	70.000	0	0.000	70.000
3	0	0.000	3	76.000	76.000
3	1	24.000	2	44.000	68.000
3	2	70.000	1	32.000	102.000
4	0	0.000	4	76.000	76.000
4	1	24.000	3	76.000	100.000
4	2	70.000	2	44.000	114.000

Stage 3

S(n)	D(n)	R(n)	S(n-1)	f(n-1)	f(n)
4	0	0.000	4	114.000	114.000
4	1	40.000	3	102.000	142.000
4	2	70.000	2	70.000	140.000

Final Solution

Stage	Optimal Dn	Optimal Rn
3	1.000	40.000
2	2.000	70.000
1	1.000	32.000
Total	4.000	142.000

Summary

Dynamic programming is primarily concerned with deriving an optimum solution to a multistage decision problem. There are many different approaches and objective criteria in dynamic programming. Thus, a number of different models need to be developed based on the nature of the problems under consideration. In this chapter, we have examined the nature, modeling process, and solution approaches of dynamic programming. The *Micro Manager* presents a user-friendly dynamic-programming program that can handle various types of multistage decision problems.

References

Bellman, R. 1957. *Dynamic programming.* Princeton, NJ: Princeton University Press.

Bellman, R., and S. E. Dreyfus. 1962. *Applied dynamic programming.* Princeton, NJ: Princeton University Press.

Hillier, F. S., and G. J. Lieberman. 1980. *Operations research.* 3rd ed. San Francisco: Holden-Day.

Howard, R. A. 1960. *Dynamic programming and Markov processes.* New York: John Wiley & Sons.

Lee, S. M. 1983. *Introduction to management science.* Chicago: Dryden.

Lee, S. M., L. J. Moore, and B. W. Taylor. 1985. *Management science.* 2d ed. Dubuque, IA: Wm. C. Brown Publishers.

Nemhauser, G. L. 1966. *Introduction to dynamic programming.* New York: John Wiley & Sons.

Wagner, H. M. 1969. *Principles of operations research.* Englewood Cliffs, NJ: Prentice-Hall.

Problems

1. Modern Technology Company has budgeted $3 million to be allocated among three plants for capital investment next year. The president has decided to allocate the budget in block amounts of $1 million. The company has estimated the probability of failure for the three plants as follows:

	Probability of Failure		
Amount Invested (in $ millions)	**Plant *A***	**Plant *B***	**Plant *C***
0	.6	.5	.4
1	.4	.3	.3
2	.2	.2	.15
3	.1	.05	.1

Determine the funds to be allocated to each plant in order to minimize the probability of failure by dynamic programming.

2. Beauty Cosmetics Company has four sales teams to cover three territories. The company has estimated the following weekly profit of each team assigned to each territory:

	No. of Sales Teams Allocated				
Territory	**0**	**1**	**2**	**3**	**4**
1	0	1	2	2.5	3
2	0	1.5	1.8	2	2.8
3	0	2	2.4	3.2	4

Determine the best way to assign the four sales teams to maximize the weekly profit by using dynamic programming.

3. The capacity of a cargo plane is six tons. There are four types of machines that may be carried on the plane. The estimated profit and weight of a unit of each type of machine are given as follows:

Machine	Weight (ton)	Profit
A	1	4
B	3	7
C	4	10
D	2	6

Determine the optimum cargo that will maximize total profit and also satisfy the weight limit of six tons.

4. A firm wants to determine a production schedule to meet the following demands:

Month	Demand
Sept.	4
Oct.	5
Nov.	3
Dec.	3

The estimated costs are given as follows:

Setup cost	Variable cost	Inventory holding cost
$10	4	$2

In addition, there are two units of beginning inventory and the company wishes to have one unit in inventory at the end of the year. The company can produce a maximum of five units and has the maximum storage capacity of three units. Determine the optimum production schedule by using dynamic programming.

5. Barra Moris Computer Manufacturing Company distributes its product to three stores. The company has produced six computers. Based on the past sales records, the minimum number of computers needed at each of stores X, Y, and Z is 2, 3, and 1, respectively. In addition, the maximum number of computers allocated to any one store is four. The profit at each store, as a function of the number of computers allocated to it, is shown as follows:

	Store Profit (in $1,000)		
No. of computers	***X***	***Y***	***Z***
0	0	0	0
1	1	2	1.5
2	2	3.5	3
3	3	5	3.5
4	5	6	5

Determine the best allocation scheme of computers to each of the stores to maximize total profit by using dynamic programming.

6. Carol is the purchasing manager of a medium-sized department store. She is considering visiting the suppliers in several areas. Carol classified the geographically scattered suppliers into three groups, based on the characteristics of their products, and wants to visit only one supplier in each product group. She made the following chart for her traveling. Carol's major concern is to minimize the traveling cost. Determine the best route to take from point A to point I by using dynamic programming.

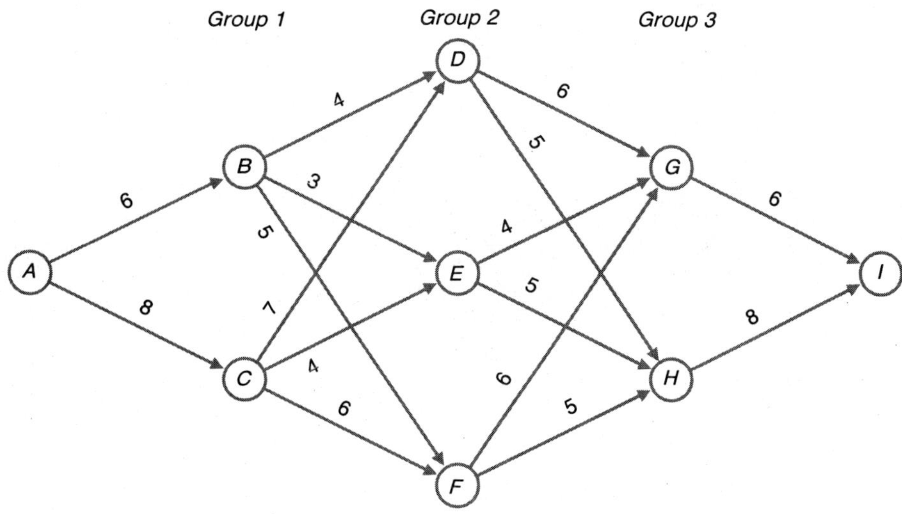

7. James Smith is a salesman at a hardware store. He is considering visiting important customers in several areas. He has classified the customers into three groups, based on the characteristics of consumers' preferences, and would like to visit only one customer in each group. James prepared the following chart for his traveling, along with the estimated profit as a result of his visits. Determine the best traveling route that will maximize total profit by using dynamic programming.

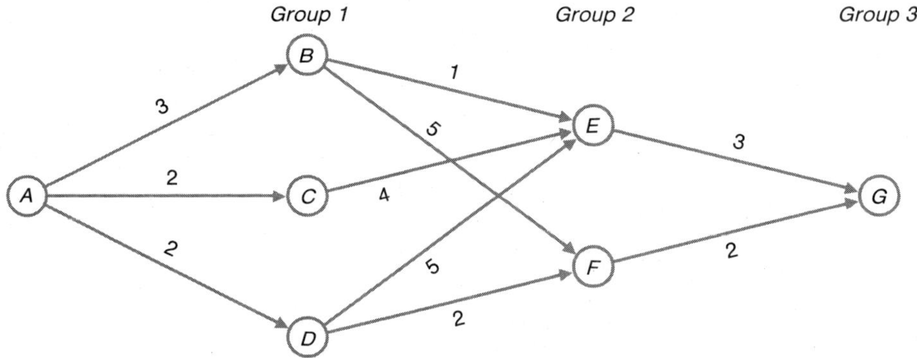

8. Julia Joffrey has $160,000 and is planning to invest this amount to maximize her return. She has decided to invest some of the money among three stocks in block amounts of $10,000. Due to the market uncertainty, a maximum of $30,000 is to be allocated to any one stock. Julia has estimated the following expected returns:

	Return (in $10,000)		
Investment (in $10,000)	**Stock *A***	**Stock *B***	**Stock *C***
0	0	0	0
1	2	3	2.5
2	4	4	5
3	5	6	7

Determine the best investment plan by using dynamic programming.

9. Three medical research teams are formed to develop a new medicine for cancer. The probability of success for each team is 0.2, 0.5, and 0.3, respectively. The overall probability of total success is (.2) (.5) (.3) = .03. To increase the probability of success, three prominent scientists will be added to the teams. The estimated probability of success for each team, if zero, one, two, or three scientists are allocated, is given as follows:

	Probability of Success Team		
No. of scientists	***A***	***B***	***C***
0	.2	.5	.3
1	.4	.6	.4
2	.5	.75	.6
3	.7	.9	.75

Determine the best staffing scheme that will maximize the probability of success.

10. Jane owns three stores. She has purchased four boxes of apples. She does not wish to split boxes among the stores but wants to allocate at least one box to each store. The profit at each store as a function of the number of boxes distributed to it is determined as follows:

	Profit (in $1,000) Stores		
No. of boxes	***A***	***B***	***C***
0	0	0	0
1	3	1	5
2	5	3	7
3	7	6	8
4	8	7	9

How many boxes should be allocated to each store to maximize total profits?

11. BGL Manufacturing Company has decided to produce a newly designed automatic cutting machine for the next month, April. The firm currently has orders for 20 units of the machine for the next five months and wishes to have a plan for zero-ending inventory in August. The following table illustrates the various production-related information: delivery schedule, production and storage capacity, and other cost data. Determine the optimal production and inventory schedule to minimize the total cost by using dynamic programming.

Delivery schedule	No. of units
April	4
May	2
June	6
July	5
August	3

Production capacity per month = 6 units
Storage capacity per month = 5 units
Variable production cost per unit = $5,000
Fixed-setup cost = $20,000
Inventory holding cost per unit per month = $3,000

12. In Problem 11, assume that BGL Company has two units of machines at the end of March. Determine the optimal production and inventory schedule.

13. The following network diagram shows alternative highway routes and travel times from Los Angeles to New York. Using dynamic programming, determine the shortest route from L. A. to N. Y.

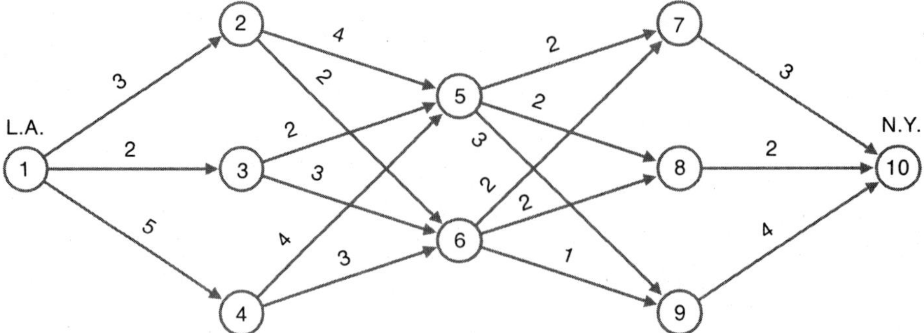

14. XYZ Company has considered three investment plans for the coming fiscal year and has retained \$5 million for the investment. The following table indicates the expected return of each investment plan with each of the proposed levels of capital investment. Assume that the capital is allocated in block amounts of \$1 million. Find the optimum allocation of funds among the three investment plans by using dynamic programming.

	Total revenue per year (in \$ millions)		
Proposed levels of capital investment (in \$ millions)	**Plan *A***	**Plan *B***	**Plan *C***
0	0	0	0
1	0.20	—	—
2	0.33	0.30	—
3	0.50	0.60	0.55
4	0.87	0.70	0.75
5	0.90	0.90	0.93

15. Young Company has budgeted \$600,000 for the next year to be allocated among three promotional plans for expanding its market share drastically. The marketing manager has decided to allocate the budget in block amounts of \$100,000. The minimum amount required for each of three plans is \$200,000. There is no maximum limit for budget allocation to plan *A* and plan *B*. However, the amount allocated to plan *C* cannot exceed \$400,000. Each of the plans has the following expected returns (in terms of the percentage of market share) associated with each of the proposed levels of budget allocation:

Decision Alternative	**Evaluation Criterion**		
	Return associated with allocation (market share increase in %)		
Amount allocated (in \$100,000)	**Plan *A***	**Plan *B***	**Plan *C***
2	6	2	3
3	7	3	4
4	8	8	7
5	10	10	—
6	12	13	—

a. Using dynamic programming, illustrate the problem graphically.

b. Determine the optimum allocation of the \$600,000 budgeted amount among the three plans.

16. Refer to Problem 14. If an additional \$1 million can be borrowed from a bank at an annual interest rate of 20%, which can be invested in plan *A*, what decision should be made in terms of profit maximization and why? Assume that the revenue gained from an additional \$1 million of investment in plan *A* amounts to \$200,000.

17. ABC Company plans to send three types of machines by truck to Data Systems Company in New York. The truck's weight capacity is five tons. Thus, management attempts to determine the way in which the value of the shipment can be maximized. The weight and value for each of the three types of machines are as follows. Solve the problem by using the *Micro Manager*.

Item	Unit weight (in tons)	Unit value (in \$1,000)
A	3	95
B	1	30
D	2	75

18. In Problem 17, if a cargo can be loaded to the weight of seven tons, how many units for each of the three types of machines should be shipped on the truck to maximize the total value of the shipment?

19. K's Manufacturing Company has prepared three new product promotion plans to compete effectively with the major leading brands in the domestic market. Each of three promotion plans has the following estimated probability of success (Table 1). The probability of success can be raised to some extent with an increase of the promotion budget (Table 2). Determine the optimum budget allocation among the three plans to maximize the total probability of success if an additional budget of \$4 million is available for these plans. Assume that the budget should be allocated in the block amount of \$1 million.

Table 1

Promotion Plans		
A	**B**	**C**
.80	.75	.60

Total probability of success: .36

Table 2

The amount of additional budget allocation	Probability of Success—Promotion Plans		
	A	*B*	*C*
0	.80	.75	.60
1	.85	.80	.80
2	.87	.85	.83
3	.89	.90	.90
4	.90	.95	.95

20. In Problem 19, determine the resource allocation scheme if the additional budget available is reduced to $3 million.

C H A P T E R 15

Queuing Models

Life consists of preparing for and waiting for opportunities. We all have experienced waiting for traffic lights, telephone operators, doctors, and bank-teller services. Waiting lines, or queues, occur primarily because the arrival time of someone who needs a service and the time for someone to provide the service vary from a predetermined schedule. Waiting lines not only are inconvenient to individuals in the lines but also they have a profound impact on business operations.

Almost an unlimited number of real-world situations exist in which we wait in lines. Thus, there are numerous variations of queuing models. In this chapter, we will walk through the basic concepts of queuing systems and then discuss how the *Micro Manager* can be used to solve some of the most commonly used queuing models.

Basics

Almost everyone experiences some waiting situation every day. Queues may consist of people, automobiles, airplanes, assembly parts, animals, and myriad others. Queues are necessary evils in any organized society. Thus, queuing theory is one of the oldest topics of management science. The pioneering work of queuing theory was done by A. K. Erlang, a Danish mathematician. His 1913 study was about telephone service delays due to varying demands. Since then, queuing theory has become an important topic of management science.

Many queuing systems are clearly observable, such as people waiting at a grocery store, bank, or a hamburger eatery. However, there are many invisible or subtle queues as well. For example, inventories at an assembly plant, restaurant customers waiting in the bar, standby passengers assigned to the first-class section of an airplane, and others.

Some of the most prevalent queue situations are: airplanes stacked in holding patterns, customers at the grocery check-out counter, automobiles at the car wash, students in the registration line, service telephone calls on hold in a police department, ships waiting to be unloaded at the dock, cars waiting at the intersection for traffic lights, stacked computer programs at a computer center, and so on.

The Queuing System

A queuing system has the following basic components: arrivals, waiting lines, queue discipline, service facility, and departures. The above components are self-explanatory, with a possible exception of queue discipline. Queue discipline is simply the rule that determines how arrivals will be served in the service facility. Typically, arrivals are served on a first-come, first-served basis. Other possible decision rules are: last-come first-served, random service, or other priority-based rules.

Queuing systems can be classified into four basic structures, as shown in Figure 15.1. If a service facility has parallel service stations, the stations are referred to as *channels*. If a service facility, on the other hand, involves a number of sequential steps, the steps are known as *phases*.

Queuing Decision Problems

At first glance, it may appear that eliminating the waiting line is a good idea. However, in actuality, it may be extremely costly. Thus, we must balance the cost associated with providing a certain level of service and the costs involved in waiting. The service costs include personnel, facilities, equipment, and other related expenses required for providing the service. The waiting costs include many implicit goodwill costs involved with waiting customers.

The total expected cost of a queuing system is the sum of service costs and waiting costs as follows:

$$\text{Minimize } TC(s) = IC_i + WC_w,$$

where

$TC(s)$ = expected total cost for the service levels
I = expected total server idle time for a specified period of time
C_i = cost associated with a unit of server idle time
W = expected total waiting time for all arrivals for a specified period of time
C_w = cost associated with customer waiting per unit of time

Figure 15.2 presents the relationship of the decision variable—level of service—to costs. The total system cost is minimized at the point where the increase of service cost equals the decrease of waiting cost.

Figure 15.1 Basic Queuing System Structures

(1) Single-channel, single-phase

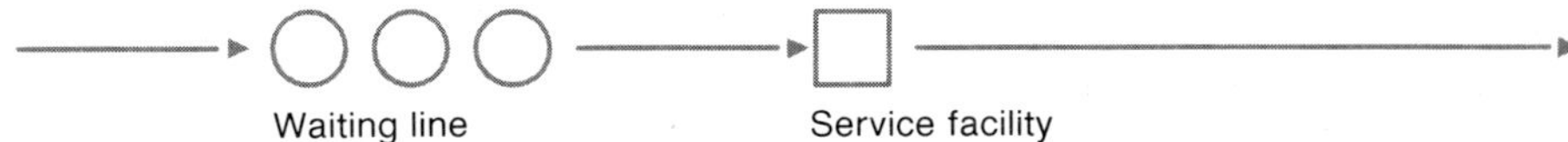

(2) Multiple-channel, single-phase

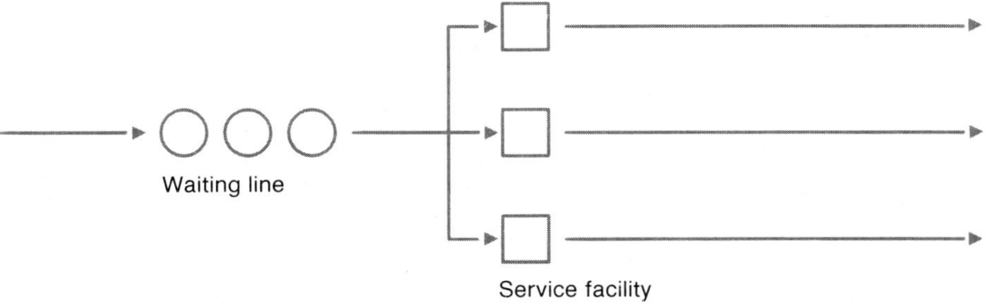

(3) Single-channel, multiple-phase

Waiting line

Service facility

(4) Multiple-channel, multiple-phase

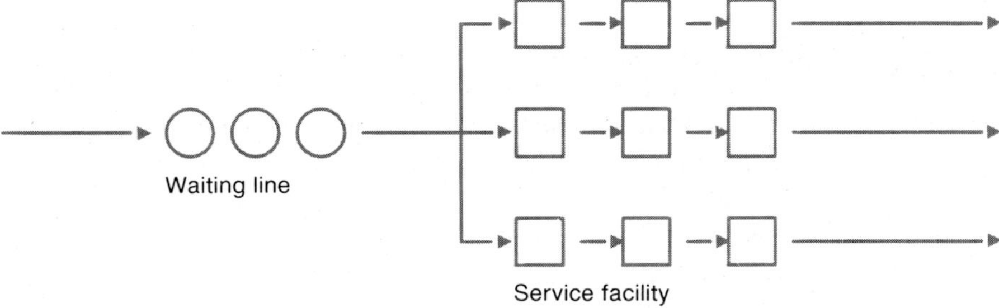

Figure 15.2 Relationship of Level of Service to Typical Waiting and Service Cost

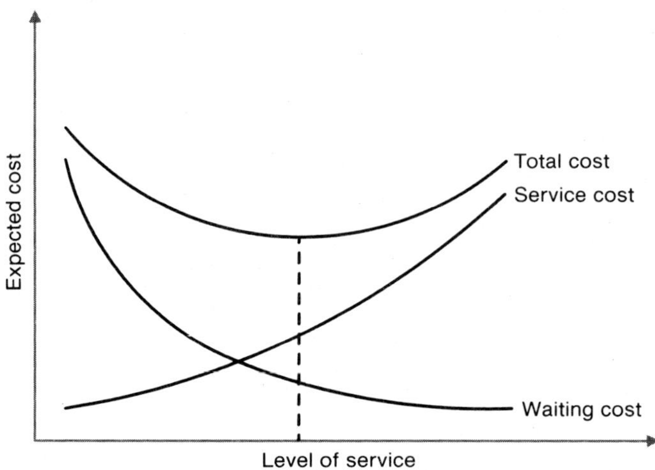

Queuing Model Assumptions

In queuing analysis, we attempt to determine a number of operating characteristics. Some of the most frequently obtained operating characteristics are: (1) probability of a specific number of customers in the system; (2) mean waiting time for each customer; (3) expected (mean) length of the queue; (4) expected (mean) time in the system for each customer; (5) mean number of customers in the system; and (6) probability of the service facility's being idle.

To determine the above operating characteristics, we need to make certain assumptions about queuing parameters. Here we will discuss the most important assumptions that affect the operating characteristics of the queuing system.

Distribution of Arrivals

Queuing models are probabilistic, or stochastic, models since certain elements of the process are random variables. In general, both the arrivals and service times are described as random variables. These random variables are described by their associated probability distribution.

The most frequently assumed distribution in regard to customer arrivals is the Poisson distribution, as shown below.

$$P(r) = \frac{e^{-\lambda}(\lambda)^r}{r!},$$

where

r = number of arrivals
$P(r)$ = probability of r arrivals
λ = mean arrival rate
e = the base of natural logarithms, 2.71828
$r! = r(r-1)(r-2)\ldots(3)(2)(1)$

The arrivals can be described as a Poisson distribution, assuming random independent arrivals and also assuming that the arrivals are independent of the state of the system. The unique feature of the Poisson distribution is that its mean is equal to the variance. Thus, once we determine the mean, we can define the entire Poisson distribution. The Poisson distribution is a discrete distribution and, consequently, we need to deal only with whole numbers.

If the arrivals can be described as a Poisson distribution, with a mean rate of λ, the time between arrivals is distributed as a negative exponential probability distribution with a mean of $1/\lambda$. The relationship between the arrival rate and the time between arrivals is as follows:

Arrival rate	**Time between arrivals**
Poisson	Negative exponential
Mean $= \lambda$	Mean $= 1/\lambda$

Another important distribution is the Erlang distribution. The Erlang distribution is often appropriate for arrivals or service times. The Erlang distribution density function is

$$f(t) = \frac{(\mu k)^k}{(k-1)!} t^{k-1} e^{-k\mu t},$$

where

$t =$ service time
$f(t) =$ probability density function associated with t
$k =$ number of service phases
$\mu =$ mean service rate
$e =$ natural number, 2.71828

In the Erlang distribution density function above, μ is the mean and k is the parameter that determines the dispersion of the distribution. A good explanation of k can be described by a multiphase queuing system. In a multiphase queuing system, a server can perform several functions, such as a grocer's cutting the meat, taking care of the check-out counter, stocking the shelves, and so on. If a server performs several functions during one service operation, and all of the k-service functions are assumed to have identical exponential distributions with a mean of $1/k\mu$, the aggregate service distribution will be $1/\mu$ and the variance σ^2 will be $1/k^2$.

The arrival distribution symbols are as follows:

Symbols	**Arrival distribution**
M	Poisson
D	Deterministic
E_k	Erlang with parameter k
GI	General independent

Distribution of Service Times

We can also describe service times in a queuing system by any one of a number of different probability distributions. The most commonly assumed distribution for service times is the negative exponential distribution. If the service times are described by a negative exponential distribution, then the service rate follows a Poisson distribution.

The general formula for the negative exponential density function is as follows:

$$f(t) = \mu e^{-\mu t},$$

where

t = service time
$f(t)$ = probability density function associated with t
μ = mean service rate
$1/\mu$ = mean service time
e = natural number, 2.71828

The area under the curve of the negative exponential distribution can be obtained from the cumulative distribution function. The area under the curve to the left of T (T is any time selection) is described by

$$F(T) = f(t < T) = 1 - e^{-\mu t}.$$

Service time distribution can take the following forms:

Symbol	**Distribution description**
M	Negative exponential
D	Constant
E_k	Erlang with parameter k
GS	General distribution

Number of Servers

Servers in a queuing system can be people, equipment, or a combination of both. Servers can be arranged in a parallel, sequential, or other combination of arrangements. In a queuing system, the service rate must exceed the arrival rate. Otherwise, the queue will grow indefinitely long. To shorten or eliminate queues, parallel servers will be needed. For a queuing system to attain equilibrium, the rate of service time multiplied by the number of parallel servers must exceed the rate of arrival.

Queue Discipline

The queue discipline, as we discussed earlier, is a decision rule that determines the order in which customers are selected for service. Normally, customers are accommodated on a first-come, first-served basis. However, other decision rules are possible. The symbols and descriptions of queue discipline are presented below:

Symbol	***Description***
FCFS	First-come first-served
LCFS	Last-come first-served
SIRO	Served in random order
GD	General distribution (other rules)

Infinite vs. Finite Queue Length

Many queuing models may assume that waiting lines could build up to an infinite length. However, in reality, queues can build up only to finite lengths because of physical limitations or because people do not like to wait. For example, automobiles waiting to enter a bank's drive-in window may be limited to the space capacity. Customers often do not enter a waiting line if the queue length is unusually long. Such behavior—the decision not to enter a waiting line—is referred to as balking. Infinite queues are easier to work with, mathematically speaking, but balking can often result in only finite queue lengths. The maximum queue length is indicated by the appropriate integer or by the infinity sign (∞).

Maximum Calling Population

The calling population represents the source of arrivals to be serviced. If the calling population is very large, we can assume that it is infinite in size. However, if the sources of arrivals are small enough that removal of one member of that population would affect the probability of arrival, it would be more appropriate to assume a finite population. The calling population is indicated by the appropriate integer or by the infinity sign (∞).

Queuing Models

In this section, we will discuss the most widely used queuing models and their required assumptions. Queuing systems are in a transient state at the beginning stage of operations, then they approach steady-state conditions or equilibrium. In this section, we will only discuss steady-state models.

The queuing models are usually categorized on the basis of their required assumptions. In 1953, D. G. Kendall introduced a compact notational scheme to describe the characteristics of queuing systems. The Kendall notation is used as a succinct and systematic means of describing queuing models. The six parameters or assumptions are placed in the appropriate position in the following format:

(Arrival distribution/Service distribution/Number of servers):
(Queue discipline/Queue length/Calling population)

Eight different queuing systems are explained below through the use of examples.

Model 1 (*D/D/1*) : (*FCFS*/∞/∞)

The first waiting-line model we will examine is a deterministic queuing model. This model assumes the following: (1) deterministic arrival; (2) deterministic service time; (3) one server or a single-channel system; (4) queue discipline is first-come, first-served; (5) infinite queue length; and (6) infinite calling population.

Example 15.1 Pay Less Groceries, Inc.

Pay Less Groceries, Inc., is a family-owned, corner grocery store. Customers arrive at the constant rate of 12 per hour, with an arrival every five minutes. It is also assumed that customers are checked out at a constant rate of 15 per hour. In this situation, a waiting line will not form. As a matter of fact, the customer check-out counter will be idle 3/15 or 20 percent of the time. The customers use the check-out facility only 12/15 or 80 percent of capacity.

From this example, it is clear that there will be no queue and no idle check-out time if the arrival rate equals the service rate. Also, if the arrival rate exceeds the service rate, there will be no idle check-out time but the waiting line will grow infinitely.

Model 2 (*M/M/1*) : (*FCFS*/∞/∞)

This queuing model assumes the same basic conditions as the first model except that it assumes a Poisson distribution for arrival rates and a negative exponential distribution for service times. This model has the following operating characteristics:

λ = mean arrival rate ($1/\lambda$ = mean time between arrivals)

μ = mean service rate ($1/\mu$ = mean service time)

n = number of customers (units) in the system (including those waiting and in service)

L = mean number in the system

L_q = mean number in the waiting line (queue length)

W = mean time in the system

W_q = mean waiting time (in the queue)
ρ = service facility utilization factor
I = percentage of server idle time

By assuming Poisson distribution arrival rates and exponential service times, we can determine the parameters of the model as follows:

The percentage of time the service facility is operating,

$$\rho = \frac{\lambda}{\mu}$$

The probability of no units in the system,

$$P_0 = 1 - \frac{\lambda}{\mu}$$

The probability of n units in the system,

$$P_n = \left(\frac{\lambda}{\mu}\right)^n \left(1 - \frac{\lambda}{\mu}\right)$$

The probability of k or more units in the system,

$$P_{n > k} = \left(\frac{\lambda}{\mu}\right)^k$$

Mean (expected) number of units in the system,

$$L = \frac{\lambda}{\mu - \lambda}$$

Mean number of units in the queue,

$$L_q = \frac{\lambda^2}{\mu\,(\mu - \lambda)}$$

Mean time in the system,

$$W = \frac{1}{\mu - \lambda}$$

Mean waiting time,

$$W_q = \frac{\lambda}{\mu\,(\mu - \lambda)}$$

Percentage of server idle time,

$$I = P_0 = 1 - \frac{\lambda}{\mu}$$

Sometimes we may be able to obtain only part of the above information. To determine information on other parameters, the following relationships can assist us in completing our information:

$$P_n = P_0 \left(\frac{\lambda}{\mu}\right)^n$$

$$P_0 = 1 - \rho$$

$$L_q = L - \frac{\lambda}{\mu} = \lambda \cdot W_q$$

$$L = L_q + \frac{\lambda}{\mu} = \lambda \cdot W$$

$$W_q = W - \frac{1}{\mu} = \frac{L_q}{\lambda}$$

$$W = W_q + \frac{1}{\mu} = \frac{L}{\lambda}$$

Example 15.2 Dragon Palace, Inc.

Dragon Palace, Inc., is a fast-food, Chinese restaurant in a shopping center. Peter Cheng, the owner and cook, has computed an average of 10 customers per hour, randomly distributed. Determine the total clients waiting, average client waiting time, and the probability of 0, 1, 2, or more than two clients waiting, given the following cooking time.

a. Average cooking time of six minutes
b. Average cooking time of five minutes
c. Average cooking time of four minutes

We can solve the Dragon Palace problem as follows:

$$\text{(a) } L = \frac{\lambda}{\mu - \lambda} = \frac{10}{10 - 10} = \infty,\ W = \frac{1}{\mu - \lambda} = \frac{1}{10 - 10} = \infty$$

$$P_0 = 1 - \rho = 1 - 1 = 0,\ P_n = (1 - \rho)\ \rho^n = 0\rho^n = 0$$

When the mean arrival rate equals the mean service rate, this model does not work properly.

$$\text{(b) } L = \frac{10}{12 - 10} = 5,\ W = \frac{1}{\mu - \lambda} = \frac{1}{12 - 10} = .5$$

$$P_0 = 1 - \rho = 1 - \frac{10}{12} = 1/6$$

$$P_1 = (1 - \rho)\rho^n = (1/6)(5/6)^1 = 5/36$$

$$P_2 = (5/36)(5/6) = 25/216$$

$$P > 2 = 1 - \frac{36 + 30 + 25}{216} = 125/216$$

(c) $L = \dfrac{10}{15 - 10} = 2,\ W = \dfrac{1}{15 - 10} = .2$

$P_0 = 1 - \rho = 1 - 2/3 = 1/3$

$P_1 = (1 - \rho)\rho = (1/3)(2/3) = 2/9$

$P_2 = (2/9)(2/3) = 4/27$

$P > 2 = 1 - \dfrac{9 + 6 + 4}{27} = 8/27$

Model 3 (*M*/*GS*/1) : (*FCFS*/∞/∞)

In this model, arrival rates are assumed to have a Poisson distribution, but the service rates can take on a normal, beta, or any other type of distribution. If the service times are independent with a mean of $1/\mu$ and standard deviation of σ, we can describe the system performance as follows:

$$\rho = \frac{\lambda}{\mu}$$

$$P_0 = 1 - \frac{\lambda}{\mu}$$

$$L_q = \frac{\lambda^2\sigma_\mu^2 + (\lambda/\mu)^2}{2(1 - \lambda/\mu)}$$

$$L = L_q + \frac{\lambda}{\mu}$$

$$W_q = \frac{L_q}{\lambda}$$

$$W = W_q + \frac{1}{\mu}$$

Example 15.3 Galloping Accountants, Inc.

Galloping Accountants, Inc., specializes in income tax returns and estate plans. The most precious resource the company has is accountants' time consulting with each client or prospective clients. The client's degree of satisfaction is often determined by the amount of service time that an accountant provides. However, a longer service time can result in longer waiting times for the clients.

The estimated arrival rate is four clients per hour, distributed randomly. The company's average service rate is six clients per hour. The distribution of service times can best be described by a variance of 1/144 hours or a standard deviation of 1/12 hours (5 minutes). Determine the number of clients waiting in the office, average waiting time, average time in the system, and the probability of no clients in the office.

We can analyze this queuing problem as follows:

$$\rho = \frac{\lambda}{\mu} = 4/6 = 2/3$$

$$L_q = \frac{\lambda^2\sigma_\mu^2 + \rho^2}{2(1-\rho)} = \frac{(4)^2(1/144) + (2/3)^2}{2(1-2/3)} = 5/6$$

$$L = L_q + \rho = 5/6 + 4/6 = 1.5$$

$$W_q = \frac{L_q}{\lambda} = \frac{5/6}{4} = 5/24$$

$$W = W_q + \frac{1}{\mu} = 5/24 + 1/6 = 9/24$$

$$P_0 = 1 - \rho = 1 - 2/3 = 1/3$$

Model 4 ($M/D/1$) : ($FCFS/\infty/\infty$)

In this model, we assume Poisson arrival rates and constant service times. Many queuing problems involving automatic service facilities, e.g., automatic bank tellers, automatic car washers, self-service stamp dispensers, and so on, may have this model. In this model, the parameters can be determined in the same way as in the case of ($M/GS/1$) : ($FCFS/\infty/\infty$) with $\sigma^2 = 0$.

$$\rho = \frac{\lambda}{\mu}$$

$$P_0 = 1 - \frac{\lambda}{\mu}$$

$$L_q = \frac{(\lambda/\mu)^2}{2(1-\lambda/\mu)}$$

$$L = L_q + \frac{\lambda}{\mu}$$

$$W_q = \frac{L_q}{\lambda}$$

$$W = W_q + \frac{1}{\mu}$$

Example 15.4 Zippy Car Wash, Inc.

Zippy Car Wash, Inc., is the largest car-wash operation in town. The entire car-wash process requires three minutes, regardless of the size or model of the automobile. The automatic washing and drying process is complemented by three workers who provide extra services (cleaning the interior, waxing, or vacuuming) and making necessary adjustments for the type of automobile in the system during the three-minute period.

The company charges \$5 for the car wash and \$2 extra for waxing or interior cleaning and vacuuming. However, the company sells the car-wash coupons to local car dealers at 40 percent discount. The car dealers, in turn, give out the coupons to their customers who have service bills of over \$75. Thus, Zippy Car Wash has a built-in flow of customers. Customers arrive in a random manner at the average rate of 10 per hour. Compute the expected number of automobiles in the system and the average amount of time each customer is expected to spend at Zippy Car Wash.

This queuing problem can be solved as follows:

$$\lambda = 10,\ \mu = 20,\ \rho = .5,\ \sigma_\mu^2 = 0$$
$$L = L_q + \rho,\ L_q = \frac{\rho^2}{2(1-\rho)} = \frac{(.5)^2}{2(.5)} = .25$$
$$L = .25 + .50 = .75$$
$$W = W_q + 1/\mu,\ W_q = L_q/\lambda = .25/10 = 1/40$$
$$W = 1/40 + 1/20 = 3/40 = 4.5 \text{ minutes}$$

Model 5 $(M/E_k/1) : (FCFS/\infty/\infty)$

In this queuing model, service times are assumed to be an Erlang distribution. This model has been proven to be very practical because of its flexibility of the service distribution. As a matter of fact, the negative exponential and constant service distributions are special cases of the Erlang distribution with k parameters of 1 and 0, respectively. The operating characteristics for the Erlang service time model can be analyzed by setting $\sigma^2 = 1/k\mu^2$ and using arbitrary service times.

$$\rho = \frac{\lambda}{\mu}$$
$$P_0 = 1 - \rho$$
$$L_q = \frac{\lambda^2\sigma^2 + (\lambda/\mu)^2}{2(1-\lambda/\mu)} = \frac{(k+1)\,\rho^2}{2k(1-\rho)}$$
$$\sigma^2 = \frac{1}{k\mu^2}$$
$$L = L_q + \frac{\lambda}{\mu}$$
$$W_q = \frac{(k+1)\,\rho}{2k(\mu-\lambda)} = \frac{L_q}{\lambda}$$
$$W = W_q + \frac{1}{\mu}$$

Example 15.5 State Savings and Loan Association

State Savings and Loan processes mortgage applications through two steps. At the first step, the customer prepares an application blank for the mortgage with the assistance of the receptionist. At the second step, the customer prepares his or her personal and financial information with the help of a loan officer. Each step requires an average service time of 10 minutes. If the customer arrival rate is every 30 minutes on average, compute the average time a customer applying for a mortgage would spend in the State Savings and Loan office filling out applications, the number of customers expected to be in the office, and the probability that no one is in the office to apply for a mortgage.

This queuing problem can be analyzed as follows:

$$\lambda = 2,\ \mu = 3,\ \rho = \frac{\lambda}{\mu} = 2/3$$

$$L = L_q + \rho,\ L_q = \frac{(k+1)\rho^2}{2k(1-\rho)} = \frac{3(2/3)^2}{2(2)(1/3)} = \frac{4/3}{4/3} = 1$$

$$L = 1 + 2/3 = 5/3$$

$$W = W_q + 1/\mu,\ W_q = \frac{k+1}{2k} \cdot \frac{\rho}{(\mu - \lambda)} = \frac{3}{4} \cdot \frac{2/3}{1} = 1/2$$

$$W = 1/2 + 1/3 = 5/6$$

$$P_0 = 1 - \rho = 1/3$$

Model 6 (*M*/*M*/1) : (*FCFS*/*m*/∞)

This queuing model is exactly the same as the classical queuing model presented earlier, except for the limited queue. Many real-world queuing situations can be analyzed by this model when a limited physical facility for a queue or a high-balking rate exists on the part of the customers. In this model, to reach a steady state, the service rate is not required to exceed the arrival rate ($\mu > \lambda$). The operating characteristics of this queuing system are as follows:

m = maximum number of customers in the system

$$P_0 = \frac{1 - \lambda/\mu}{1 - (\lambda/\mu)^{m+1}}$$

$$P_n = (P_0)\left(\frac{\lambda}{\mu}\right)^n \quad (\text{for } n < m)$$

$$L = \frac{\lambda/\mu}{1 - \lambda/\mu} - \frac{(m+1)(\lambda/\mu)^{m+1}}{1 - (\lambda/\mu)^{m+1}}$$

$$L_q = L - \frac{\lambda(1 - P_m)}{\mu}$$

$$W = \frac{L}{\lambda(1 - P_m)}$$

$$W_q = W - \frac{1}{\mu}$$

P_m (the value of P_n for $n = m$) is the probability that customers are lost from the system.

Example 15.6 Kwik Stop Mufflers, Inc.

Kwik Stop Mufflers, Inc., specializes in providing speedy muffler repair and replacement service. The company's past records indicate that the arrival rate is an average of six customers per hour and an average service time is 7 minutes and 30 seconds (eight customers per hour). The management believes that if three customers are in the system, the customers tend not to wait for service and leave. The management is interested in knowing the probabilities of the system's being idle, having one customer, two customers, or three customers in the system.

This queuing problem can be analyzed as follows:

$$\lambda = 6,\ \mu = 8,\ \rho = \frac{\lambda}{\mu} = 3/4$$

$$P_0 = \frac{1 - \rho}{1 - (\rho)^{m+1}},\ \text{where } m = 3,\ P_0 = \frac{1 - (3/4)}{1 - (3/4)^4}$$

$$= \frac{1/4}{1 - (81/256)} = \frac{64}{175}$$

$$P_1 = P_0(\rho)^1 = (64/175) \cdot (3/4) = \frac{48}{175}$$

$$P_2 = P_0(\rho)^2 = (64/175) \cdot (9/16) = \frac{36}{175}$$

$$P_3 = P_0(\rho)^3 = (64/175) \cdot (27/64) = \frac{27}{175}$$

$$P_0 + P_1 + P_2 + P_3 = \frac{64 + 48 + 36 + 27}{175} = 1$$

Model 7 $(M/M/1) : (FCFS/\infty/m)$

In this queuing model, we consider the case in which there is a limited calling population. Thus, the probabilities of arrivals depend upon the number of customers in the system. Let us assume that both the service times and the time spent outside the system between services are in the form of exponential distributions with means of $1/\lambda$ and $1/\mu$, respectively. Then, the operating characteristics of this queuing model can be described as follows:

$$P_0 = \frac{1}{\sum_{n=0}^{N} \frac{N!}{(N-n)!}\left(\frac{\lambda}{\mu}\right)^n} \quad \text{(where } N = \text{population size)}$$

$$P_n = \frac{N!}{(N-n)!}\left(\frac{\lambda}{\mu}\right)^n P_0 \quad \text{(where } n = 1, 2, \ldots, N)$$

$$L_q = N - \frac{\lambda + \mu}{\lambda}(1 - P_0)$$

$$L = L_q + (1 - P_0) \text{ or } L = N - \frac{\mu}{\lambda}(1 - P_0)$$

$$W_q = \frac{L_q}{(N - L)\lambda}$$

$$W = W_q + \frac{1}{\mu}$$

Example 15.7 Metro Express, Inc.

Metro Express, Inc., provides a limousine service between the airport and the downtown hotel district. The company currently has five vans. The company's vans break down an average of two per day. The World Motors, Inc., has the contract to repair the vans on a top-priority basis. The average service rate is five per day. Past experience indicates that the arrivals are in the Poisson distribution and the service times are in the negative exponential distribution. The company is interested in determining P_0, P_1, P_2, P_3, P_4, P_5, L, and W.

This queuing problem can be analyzed in the following manner:

$$\lambda = 2, \mu = 5, \rho = \frac{\lambda}{\mu} = 2/5$$

$$P_0 = \frac{1}{\sum_{n=0}^{N} \frac{N!}{(N-n)!}\left(\frac{\lambda}{\mu}\right)^n}$$

$$= \frac{1}{1 + 5(.4) + 20(.16) + 60(.064) + 120(0.0256) + 120(0.01024)}$$

$$= .069731$$

$$P_1 = \frac{N!}{(N-n)!} \cdot \rho^n \cdot P_0 = \frac{5!}{4!}(.4)(.069731) = .139462$$

$$P_2 = \frac{5!}{3!}(.4)^2(.069731) = .223140$$

$$P_3 = \frac{5!}{2!}(.4)^3(.069731) = .267767$$

$$P_4 = \frac{5!}{1!}(.4)^4(.069731) = .214214$$

$$P_5 = \frac{5!}{0!}(.4)^5(.069731) = .085686$$

$$L = L_q + (1 - P_0),\ L_q = N - \frac{\lambda + \mu}{\lambda}(1 - P_0) = 1.744$$

$$L = 1.744 + .930 = 2.674$$

$$W = W_q + \frac{1}{\mu},\ W_q = \frac{L_q}{(N-L)\lambda} = \frac{1.744}{(5 - 2.674)2} = .375$$

$$W = .375 + .2 = .575$$

Model 8 $(M/M/s) : (FCFS/\infty/\infty)$

In this queuing model, we can consider multichannel servers (s). Thus, it is possible to analyze the impact of adding servers to the system. We are still assuming Poisson arrivals and exponential service times distributions. The mean service rate is determined by $s(\mu)$, where s = number of servers. We are assuming the mean service rate $s\mu$ exceeds the arrival rate λ. We will further assume that the service time distribution for each server is virtually the same. The operating characteristics of this queuing system are:

$$P_0 = \frac{1}{\sum_{n=0}^{s-1} \frac{(\lambda/\mu)^n}{n!} + \frac{(\lambda/\mu)^s}{s!(1 - \lambda/s\mu)}}$$

$$P_n = \frac{(\lambda/\mu)^n}{n!} P_0 \qquad \text{(if } n < s\text{)}$$

$$P_n = \frac{(\lambda/\mu)^n}{s!s^{(n-s)}} P_0 \qquad \text{(if } n > s\text{)}$$

$$\rho = \frac{\lambda}{s\mu}$$

$$L_q = \frac{P_0(\lambda/\mu)^s \rho}{s!(1 - \rho)^2}$$

$$L = L_q + \frac{\lambda}{\mu}$$

$$W_q = \frac{L_q}{\lambda}$$

$$W = W_q + \frac{\lambda}{\mu}$$

Example 15.8 Duplicat, Inc.

Duplicat, Inc., is a quick duplicating-service company. The company's downtown operation currently has two Smart 1000X machines. The company's record indicates that the average demand for duplicating has been eight jobs per hour, varying randomly from single-page copying to manuscripts involving extensive copying time. The average copying time per job is six minutes.

The operating costs for each Smart 1000X is \$30 per hour. The cost of waiting for the operating personnel is estimated to be \$8 per hour.

The company is considering a new, larger piece of duplicating equipment, Smart XT, which is twice as fast as the Smart 1000X. The operating costs for Smart XT are believed to be \$65. The company is trying to decide whether to continue operating with two Smart 1000X machines or to purchase a new Smart XT. The company is not concerned about the salvage value for Smart 1000X's because they can be shipped to another Duplicat franchise.

This decision problem can be analyzed as follows:

Two Smart 1000X Machines

$$\lambda = 8,\ \mu = 10,\ s = 2,\ (M/M/2) : (FCFS/\infty/\infty)$$

$$P_0 = \frac{1}{\sum_{n=0}^{s-1} \frac{(\lambda/\mu)^n}{n!} + \frac{(\lambda/\mu)^s}{s!(1 - \lambda/s\mu)}}$$

$$= \frac{1}{\sum_{n=0}^{1} \frac{(8/10)^n}{n!} + \frac{(8/10)^2}{2![1 - (8/10 \times 2)]}}$$

$$= \frac{1}{1 + .8 + .5333} = .42857$$

$$P_n = \frac{(\lambda/\mu)^n}{n!} P_0, \text{ if } n < s$$

$$P_n = \frac{(\lambda/\mu)^n}{s!s^{(n-s)}} P_0, \text{ if } n > s$$

$$P_1 = \frac{(8/10)}{1} (.42857) = .34286$$

$$P_2 = \frac{(8/10)^2}{2} (.42857) = .13714$$

$$P_3 = \frac{(8/10)^3}{2!2} (.42857) = .05486$$

$P_4 = .02194$
$P_5 = .00878$
$P_6 = .00351$
$P_7 = .00140$
$P_8 = .00056$
$P_9 = .00022$
$P_{10} = .00009$

$$\text{The cost of waiting} = \sum_{n=1}^{10} (\text{Prob}_n \times \text{waiting cost/hr})$$
$$= (.42857 \times 0) + (.34286 \times 8) + (.13714 \times 16) + \ldots + (.00009 \times 80)$$
$$= \$7.62/\text{hour}$$

Total cost = operating cost + cost of waiting
= ($30 × 2) + $7.62 = $67.62

One Smart XT Machine

$$\lambda = 8, \mu = 20, (M/M/1) : (FCFS/\infty/\infty)$$

$P_0 = 1 - \rho = 1 - .4,$

$P_n = (1 - \rho)\rho^n$

Cost of Waiting

P_0	= .60000 ×	$ 0	=	$0
P_1	= .24000 ×	8	=	1.92
P_2	= .09600 ×	16	=	1.54
P_3	= .03840 ×	24	=	.92
P_4	= .01536 ×	32	=	.49
P_5	= .00614 ×	40	=	.25
P_6	= .00246 ×	48	=	.12
P_7	= .00098 ×	56	=	.05
P_8	= .00039 ×	64	=	.02
P_9	= .00016 ×	72	=	.01
P_{10}	= .00006 ×	80	=	0
				$5.32

Total cost = operating cost + cost of waiting
= $65.00 + 5.32 = $70.32

Thus, the company decided to keep the two Smart 1000X machines for the time being.

Application of the *Micro Manager*

This section presents an application example of the *Micro Manager* to queuing problems. There are a number of queuing models that require different approaches. The program diskette provides the complete information about queuing models, including the purpose of waiting-line analysis, solutions of example problems, interactive input instructions, and the batch input procedure. Therefore, in this section we will present only the information (purpose of queuing analysis and the batch input data format) and the solution of a sample problem using the interactive input mode.

```
<< PURPOSE >>

QUEUING MODEL determines the mean value (time or number of persons, etc.) in a
system and in a queue under various conditions.  The output will include an
economic analysis of the solution.  Economic analysis involves computation of
the operating costs, waiting cost, and total costs.
```

<< BATCH INPUT DATA FORMAT >>

Type in the values of the following input data requirements, after creating a new file. You may enter as many values as you want in a line, separating them by commas for alphabetic characters and by commas or blank spaces for numeric values. However, the input data must be exactly in the following order:

```
1. Queue type
     1  : M/M/1
     2  : M/M/C
     3  : M/E(K)/1
     4  : M/G/1
     5  : M/D/1
     6  : D/D/1
2. Average service rate
3. Average customer arrival rate
For Type 2
   4. Number of servers
For Type 3
   4. Erlang parameter
For Type 4
   4. Variance of service distribution
```

** Sample Batch Input Data Set (Example 15.3) **

```
 4       ; M/G/1 type
 6       ; average service rate
 4       ; average customer arrival rate
 .00694  ; variance of service distribution
```

```
PROGRAM: Queuing Models

Queuing Models

1.   M/M/1
2.   M/M/C
3.   M/E(K)/1
4.   M/G/1
5.   M/D/1
6.   D/D/1

Enter queue type (1 to 6): 4

Enter average service rate: 6
Enter average customer arrival rate: 4
Enter variance of service distribution: .00694

PROGRAM: Queuing Models

***** INPUT DATA ENTERED *****

M/G/1    type

Average service rate:  6
Average customer arrival rate:  4

Variance of service distribution:  .00694
```

```
*****  PROGRAM OUTPUT  *****

Average number of customers in system :     1
Average number of customers in queue  :     1
Average wait time to complete service :     0.21
Average wait time in waiting line     :     0.37
Traffic intensity ratio               :     0.67
Probability of zero customer in system:     0.33
```

Summary

Waiting lines, or queues, occur every day because of the variation of the arrival time of someone who needs a service and the time required to provide the service. Thus, queuing models have been important topics of management science. This chapter has presented various queuing models and their applications. Perhaps the two most important characteristics of queuing models are the variety and complexity. The *Micro Manager* has a convenient menu system where the appropriate model can be selected to analyze the queuing problem under consideration. Thus, the *Micro Manager* is very useful for analyzing any type of queuing problem.

References

Hillier, F., and G. J. Lieberman. 1980. *Operations research.* 3d ed. San Francisco: Holden-Day.

Kendall, D. G. 1953. Stochastic processes occurring in the theory of queues and their analysis by means of the embedded Markov chain. *The Annals of Mathematical Statistics* 24, 338–54.

Kleinrock, L. 1975. *Queuing systems* (2 vols.). New York: John Wiley & Sons.

Lee, S. M. 1983. *Introduction to management science.* Chicago: Dryden.

Lee, S. M., L. J. Moore, and B. W. Taylor. 1985. *Management science.* 2d ed. Dubuque, IA: Wm. C. Brown Publishers.

Problems

1. $(D/D/1) : (FCFS/\infty/\infty)$
Dr. James Brown is a physician who has his office in his hometown. His secretary usually schedules three patients per hour (one patient every 20 minutes). Because he is a general practitioner, Dr. Brown typically spends 15 minutes with each patient.

a. What is the average number of patients waiting to be served?
b. What is the average waiting time for the patient?
c. What is the mean time in the system (waiting plus being served) for the patient?

2. $(M/D/1) : (FCFS/\infty/\infty)$
Cornhusker Car Wash uses a fixed-time assembly line requiring five minutes to wash a car, including drying time. Customers arrive at the average rate of six per hour, and the distribution of arrival is described by the Poisson distribution.

a. How many customers on the average are waiting to be served?
b. What is the average time in the system (waiting plus being served) for each customer?
c. What is the expected number of cars in the system?

3. $(M/M/1) : (FCFS/\infty/\infty)$
Mary Hart is a ticket seller in the university ticket booth. She can serve 20 customers per hour, and the distribution of service time is negative exponential. An average of 15 customers arrive to purchase tickets every hour. The customer arrivals are described by the Poisson distribution.

a. What is the average time a customer should wait in line to buy a ticket?
b. What portion of the time is Mary not busy?
c. What is the average number of customers in the waiting line?

4. $(M/M/1) : (FCFS/\infty/\infty)$
Tomas Anderthal is an up-and-coming young CPA. Usually, he wants to spend as much time as possible with a client to maximize the client's satisfaction. However, longer consulting times may result in other clients having to wait longer. If clients wait too long, they are likely to consult other public accountants. The mean arrival time of clients is three clients per hour and the arrivals can be described by the Poisson distribution. Anderthal wishes to obtain information on each of three possible average consulting times—20 minutes, 15 minutes, and 10 minutes. Determine the following for each consulting time:

a. Total clients in the office
b. Average client time in the office
c. The probabilities of 0, 1, 2, and more than two clients in the office

5. $(M/GS/1) : (FCFS/\infty/\infty)$
Tomas Anderthal (see Problem 4) decided on an average service rate of four clients per hour and later determined that distribution of consulting times was described by a variance of 1/64 hour (a 7.5-minute standard deviation). What effect does this added information have on the expected number of clients in the office, the average time a client spends in the office, and the probability of no clients in the office?

6. $(M/GS/1):(FCFS/\infty/\infty)$
Trucks arrive at the dock of Green Grocery Company, a wholesaler of grocery goods in Manhattan, with a mean arrival rate of one every 10 minutes. The distribution of arrival is described by the Poisson model. The loading and/or unloading time averages four minutes, and an estimate of the standard deviation of service time is five minutes. Truckers are complaining that they spend more time waiting than loading/unloading. Are the truckers' complaints justified? Verify your answer.

7. $(M/GS/1):(FCFS/\infty/\infty)$
Cathy is a secretary in the management department. She services five faculty members, performing a variety of stenographic and other clerical duties. On the average, faculty members bring her three jobs per hour and the average job takes 10 minutes. Both arrival and service processes are described by the Poisson distribution.

a. What is the average number of faculty members waiting to be served?
b. What is the average waiting time?
c. What percentage of the time is the secretary idle?
d. What is the probability that a faculty member bringing work to the secretary will find her busy?

8. $(M/M/1):(FCFS/\infty/\infty)$
Customers arrive at a service facility at the rate of four per hour. The distribution of arrival is described by the Poisson model. The distribution of service time is negative exponential with the average service rate of five customers per hour.

a. What is the average number of customers waiting to be served?
b. What is the expected number of customers in the system?
c. What is the average time a customer spends in the system?
d. What is the average time a customer spends waiting?

9. $(M/M/1):(FCFS/m/\infty)$
For Problem 8, let us assume that the maximum queue length allowed is three customers, while the calling population is infinitely large.

a. What percentage of the arriving customers is lost due to the queue-length limitation?
b. What is the probability that 0, 1, or 2 customers are in the system?

10. $(M/E_k/1) : (FCFS/\infty/\infty)$
During registration in a university, each student must pass two stations. The first station checks a student's I.D., receives the registration fee of \$25, and issues receipts. The second station examines the registration documents and files them properly. Students arrive at the first station every five minutes. Both service stations require an average service time of two minutes, randomly varying.

a. What is the average time students would spend for registration?
b. What is the average number of students in the system?
c. What is the probability that no students are registering?

11. $(M/E_k/1) : (FCFS/\infty/\infty)$
The university (refer to Problem 10) plans to add a third station to perform some of the work required at stations 1 and 2. This will result in all three stations requiring an average of 1.33 minutes for registration. The arrival rate is still 12 students per hour.

a. What is the average time students would spend to register?
b. What is the average number of students in the system?
c. What are the differences from the solutions of Problem 10?

12. $(M/M/1) : (FCFS/\infty \text{ or } m/\infty)$
Crazy Monkey provides speedy oil changes and chassis lubrications for automobiles. From past experience, the company knows that the service time varies exponentially with an average of six minutes. Customers arrive at the rate of six per hour. Both rates are randomly distributed. The company fears that if three customers are in the system, potential customers will leave. What are the probabilities of the system's being idle, having only one customer in the system, having two customers in the system, and having three customers in the system? Use the formulas for an unlimited queue length to identify probabilities, and compare the results with the formulas for a limited queue length of 3.

13. $(M/M/1) : (FCFS/\infty/\infty)$
Wahou Airport has a single runway for light aircraft landings and one air traffic controller to guide the landings. It takes an airplane an average of 15 minutes to land and clear the runway. The landing rate varies exponentially. Planes arrive at the runway according to a Poisson distribution at the rate of two per hour. According to an FAA rule, the controller must have an average of 15 minutes idle time out of every hour to relieve tension.

a. What is the average number of planes that will stack up waiting to land?
b. What is the average time a plane must circle before it can land?
c. Will this airport have to hire an extra air traffic controller to abide by the FAA rule?

14. $(M/E_k/1) : (FCFS/\infty/\infty)$
Lester Electrical manufactures generators for the commercial market. One of the key operations in the total manufacturing process is the pressing process, which consists of two pressing operations. Units arrive at the press area with an average rate of 8 units per hour. The distribution of operator-processing times are Erlang with the parameter $k = 2$, with the total average rate of 12 units per hour.

a. What is the average number of units waiting to be worked on?
b. What is the average time a unit spends in the system?
c. What is the percentage of time the operator is working?

15. $(M/M/1) : (FCFS/\infty \text{ or } m/\infty)$
York Company is a stevedoring and warehousing company in the port of Newark, New Jersey. Forklifting trucks are crucial to the business of the company. The maintenance department provides service to forklift trucks, and forklifts are supposed to check in for service every 720 operating hours. Service time averages 15 minutes. Forklift arrivals occur two times an hour on the average. Because forklift operators are paid incentive wages, they tend to skip service when two other forklifts are at the service station. This has led to an increase in the rate of mechanical failures of forklifts. The maintenance department manager would like to know the probability of 0, 1, 2, or more than two forklifts being at a maintenance station, as well as the average number of forklifts and the average time spent by a forklift at the maintenance station. Identify these parameters for a model with an unlimited queue and for a model with a maximum queue length of 2.

16. $(M/M/1) : (FCFS/\infty/m)$
Marc Spaey is a mechanic in a company whose job is to repair the broken-down cranes. The company has five cranes that periodically break down and require services. The average time between breakdowns is five days, distributed according to an exponential distribution. The average time to repair a crane is three days, distributed according to an exponential distribution.

a. What is the probability that two cranes are not operating (being repaired or waiting to be repaired)?
b. What is the average number of cranes waiting to be repaired?
c. What is the average waiting time?

17. $(M/M/s) : (FCFS/\infty/\infty)$
The Internal Revenue Service is considering opening a temporary office to help taxpayers fill out tax reports. Service time varies exponentially with an average of 15 minutes. Taxpayers will arrive at the rate of eight per hour. The office will have a small waiting room, where people wait for the next available consultant. The IRS is planning to staff the office with four tax consultants. Due to the space limitation of the room, the IRS wants to know what is the probability that more than three taxpayers are in the waiting room (more than seven taxpayers in the office)?

18. $(M/M/1) : (FCFS/\infty/\infty)$
A multinational petroleum company has an unloading facility at its Brazilian crude-oil refinery. Due to random variations in weather and other factors, the mean arrival rate of tankers at the refinery is one every six hours and the distribution of arrival is Poisson. The distribution of unloading time is described by a negative exponential with the average unloading rate of one tanker every four hours.

a. Determine the average number of ships waiting to deliver crude oil.
b. Determine the average time a ship must wait before beginning to deliver its cargo to the refinery.
c. Determine the average total time (waiting plus actual delivery) that a ship spends at the refinery.

19. $(M/M/s) : (FCFS/\infty/\infty)$
Refer to Problem 18. The company has under consideration a second unloading facility that could be rented for $5,000 per week. The service time for this facility would also be negative exponential with the same average service rate as the company's own facility. The tankers charge demurrage of $600 per hour for idle waiting time.

a. If the second facility is rented, what will be the average number of ships waiting?
b. What is the average time a ship would wait?
c. Is the benefit of reduced waiting time worth (in dollars) the rental cost for the new facility?

20. $(M/E_k/1$ or $M/M/s) : (FCFS/\infty/\infty)$
The Internal Revenue Service is considering two alternative configurations for its temporary office to help taxpayers file their complaints. Taxpayers arrive randomly at the rate of eight per hour. Design 1 would have two separate consultants. Each consultant would discuss problems and help taxpayers fill out forms at the rate of six customers per hour. Design 2 would have one line, but two stations. Each station would have one consultant and have the same service rate of six customers per hour. In the first station, a consultant discusses the problems; in the second station the other consultant helps taxpayers fill out the forms. Which plan should the IRS adopt, using the average number of taxpayers waiting to be served as a major consideration for selecting a plan? Verify your recommendation.

C H A P T E R 16

Markov Analysis

Markov analysis, a widely used tool in management science, is concerned with the analysis of current movements of certain variables in an effort to forecast their future trends. For example, marketing researchers are keenly interested in predicting the future market share of various products based on customer preference. Although the technique has some unrealistic assumptions, it is very useful in the study of marketing, finance, management, accounting, and so on. In fact, Markov analysis provides useful information to assist the individual in his or her decision-making processes. In this chapter, we will discuss the most interesting and useful Markov analysis technique and the ways to apply it through the *Micro Manager.*

Basics

Markov analysis is a *stochastic* analysis that describes and attempts to explain the evolution of dynamic systems controlled by sequences of decisions. It has been widely used as a research technique in the field of brand switching, credit management, financial analysis, and so forth. For example, brand switching, a marketing decision problem, is concerned with the examination and forecast of the behavior of customers from the standpoint of their loyalty to one particular brand and their switching patterns to other brands.

Markov analysis, as a mathematical approach, was originally introduced by A. A. Markov. It was further refined as a distinct management science technique through the efforts of many scholars. Some of the typical Markov analysis problems in real-world situations are as follows:

Marketing area

Analysis of market share

Analysis of brand switching

Finance area

Analysis of credit management

Analysis of accounts receivable

Management area

Analysis of employee productivity

Analysis of personnel administration

Analysis of hospital administration

Others

Analysis of computer maintenance

Analysis of equipment repair

The objective of Markov analysis is to provide probabilistic information about a problematic situation to a decision maker. Markov analysis is based on the following assumptions: (1) a finite number of discrete states; (2) dependence of the state in the most recent period; and (3) constant transition probabilities.

The following example shows the use of Markov analysis in a service operation.

Example 16.1 PC Warehouse, Inc.

PC Warehouse, Inc., is a store that specializes in selling microcomputer software. Currently, the store has three types of credit customers, namely: (1) those who are prompt in their payments; (2) those who pay only after the store has initiated considerable action for collection; and (3) those whose balances are written-off as losses. The store's credit manager intends to examine and accurately predict in advance which bad debts the store would be expected to incur over an extended period of time as well as which credit customers have the potential of becoming delinquent payers.

Based on past behavioral characteristics of the credit customers in each of these three classifications, one can easily establish the transition probabilities that would be encountered from one group to the other. Table 16.1 presents the movement of credit customers from one group to another over an observation period of one month from January 1 to February 1; the initial number of credit customers is 15,000.

Table 16.1 Flow of credit customers

		Gains from Jan. 1			Losses to Feb. 1			
Classification	**Jan. 1 credit customers**	**Paid**	**Delinquent**	**Bad debts**	**Paid**	**Delinquent**	**Bad debts**	**Feb. 1 credit customers**
1. Paid	3,000	0	200	100	0	100	50	3,150
2. Delinquent	7,500	100	0	500	200	0	300	7,600
3. Bad debts	4,500	50	300	0	100	500	0	4,250

Table 16.2 Matrix of transition probabilities

	Paid	Delinquent	Bad debts
Paid	2,850/3,000 = .950	100/3,000 = .033	50/3,000 = .017
Delinquent	200/7,500 = .027	7,000/7,500 = .933	300/7,500 = .040
Bad debts	100/4,500 = .022	500/4,500 = .111	3,900/4,500 = .867

Matrix of Transition Probabilities

By accepting all of the assumptions required for Markov analysis, the credit manager has converted Table 16.1 into a more concise form, wherein all the gains and losses take the form of transition probabilities. However, a more convenient form would be the use of a matrix of transition probabilities. This will be found in Table 16.2, with the probabilities calculated to three decimal points. (The rows in the matrix show the retention and the loss of credit customers while the columns show the retention and gain of credit customers.)

Forecasting Future Periods

Several advantages accrue to the credit manager through the utilization of the data shown in Table 16.2. It can help the manager analyze the department store's ultimate gain or loss in its credit collections. These data can help forecast the rate at which each group will gain or lose its relative credit position in the future and can show the possibilities of a future equilibrium.

From our discussions thus far, it should be clear that the percentages of credit customers for each category—paid, delinquent, and bad debts—are now 21, 51, and 28 percent, respectively, for the February 1 period compared with 20, 50, and 30 percent for the January 1 period. The credit manager would benefit considerably by knowing where and what percentage of the credit customers in each group would be at in some future point in time. Calculating the probable percentage of credit customers for each category in the period of March 1 is merely a matter of multiplying the matrix of transition probabilities by the percentage of credit customers in each group in the period of February 1.

Let us now denote each of the groups—paid, delinquent, and bad debts—as X, Y, and Z, respectively:

$$\begin{matrix}\text{February 1}\\\text{percentage of}\\\text{credit customers}\end{matrix} \times \begin{matrix}\text{Matrix of}\\\text{transition probabilities}\end{matrix} = \begin{matrix}\text{March 1}\\\text{percentage of}\\\text{credit customers}\end{matrix}$$

$$(.21 \;\; .51 \;\; .28) \times \begin{matrix} & (X) & (Y) & (Z) \\ (X) & .950 & .033 & .017 \\ (Y) & .027 & .933 & .040 \\ (Z) & .022 & .111 & .867 \end{matrix} = (.219 \;\; .514 \;\; .267)$$

Calculation of Group X [Paid] (row 1 × col. 1):

X's propensity to retain its credit customers	= .950
(times)	×
X's percentage of credit customers	.210
	.200

X's propensity to attract Y's credit customers	= .027
(times)	×
Y's percentage of credit customers	.510
	.014

X's propensity to attract Z's credit customers	= .022
(times)	×
Z's percentage of credit customers	.280
	.006

.200 + .014 + .006 = .219 = X's percentage of credit customers on March 1. (Difference due to rounding.)

Similar calculations can now be made by using the same methods for groups Y and Z.

Calculation of Group Y [Delinquent] (row 1 × col. 2):

Y's propensity to attract X's credit customers	= .033
(times)	×
X's percentage of credit customers	.210
	.007

Y's propensity to retain its credit customers	= .933
(times)	×
Y's percentage of credit customers	.510
	.476

Y's propensity to attract Z's credit customers	= .111
(times)	×
Z's percentage of credit customers	.280
	.031

.007 + .476 + .031 = .514 = Y's percentage of credit customers on March 1.

Calculation of Group Z [Bad Debts] (row 1 × col. 3):

Z's propensity to attract X's credit customers	= .017
(times)	×
X's percentage of credit customers	.210
	.004

Z's propensity to attract Y's credit customers	= .040
(times)	×
Y's percentage of credit customers	.510
	.020

Z's propensity to retain its credit customers	$= .867$
(times)	$\times$
Z's percentage of credit customers	$\underline{.280}$
	$.243$

$.004 + .020 + .243 = .267 = Z$'s percentage of credit customers on March 1.

If the credit manager desired the percentage of credit customers for each category after six periods, i.e., August 1, he or she would set up the problem as follows:

February 1 percentage of credit customers	$\times$	Matrix of transition probabilities	$=$	Probable percentage of credit customers on August 1

Calculating Steady-State Conditions (Equilibrium)

With the information we discussed earlier, it is reasonable to assume that a state of equilibrium might be reached in the future in regard to the percentage of credit customers. The exchange of credit customers in terms of retentions, gains, and losses would be static at the moment equilibrium is reached. To find out what the equilibrium percentage of credit customers will be, let us proceed as follows:

Matrix of Transition Probabilities

		Paid (X)	Delinquent (Y)	Bad debts (Z)
Paid	(X)	.950	.033	.017
Delinquent	(Y)	.027	.933	.040
Bad debts	(Z)	.022	.111	.867

Now, X's percentage of credit customers in the equilibrium period is derived by multiplying .950 by the percentage of credit customers X had in the equilibrium $_{-1}$ period, plus .027 multiplied by the percentage of credit customers Y had in the equilibrium $_{-1}$ period, plus .022 multiplied by the percentage of credit customers Z had in the equilibrium $_{-1}$ period. This equation can be written as follows:

$$X_{\text{equilibrium}} = (.950)\ X_{\text{eq}\ -1} + (.027)\ Y_{\text{eq}\ -1} + (.022)\ Z_{\text{eq}\ -1}$$

This same type of equation can also be developed for both the Y and Z groups as follows:

$$Y_{\text{equilibrium}} = (.033)\ X_{\text{eq}\ -1} + (.933)\ Y_{\text{eq}\ -1} + (.111)\ Z_{\text{eq}\ -1}$$
$$Z_{\text{equilibrium}} = (.017)\ X_{\text{eq}\ -1} + (.040)\ Y_{\text{eq}\ -1} + (.867)\ Z_{\text{eq}\ -1}$$

In most Markovian problems, the gains and losses are usually of a high magnitude in the early periods, but as equilibrium is approached, they become very small. To put it another way, the changes in the percentage of credit customers between the equilibrium period and the period immediately preceding it are so slight that they have been treated mathematically as equals. In the equation above, "*equilibrium*" = "$equilibrium_{-1}$." Accordingly, the three equations above can be written as follows:

$$X = .950X + .027Y + .022Z$$
$$Y = .033X + .933Y + .111Z$$
$$Z = .017X + .040Y + .867Z$$
$$X + Y + Z = 1.0$$

A fourth equation is used to show that the total of these three percentages of credit customers equals 100 percent. Having four equations, and three unknowns, it is very easy to calculate these equations through the use of simultaneous equation solving. So the resulting equilibrium percentage of credit customers for groups *X, Y,* and *Z* are, respectively, 33.9%, 47.5%, and 18.6% (totaling 100%). The solution is based on the assumption that the matrix of transition probabilities is constant over time.

Application of the *Micro Manager*

In this section we present an application example of the *Micro Manager* to Markov analysis. There are several different approaches available for Markov analysis. The program diskette provides the complete information about Markov analysis, including the purpose of Markov analysis, the solution of an example problem, interactive input instructions, and the batch input procedure. This section will present only the information (purpose of Markov analysis and the batch input data format) and the solution of a sample problem using the interactive input format.

```
<< PURPOSE >>

MARKOV ANALYSIS provides probabilistic information about a future decision
situation.  The program determines the future probabilities of certain
conditions based on a transition probability matrix.  It also provides the
equilibrium state probabilties.  This program can handle up to 5 by 5 matrix
for an infinite number of periods.

<<  BATCH INPUT DATA FORMAT  >>

Type in the values of the following input data requirements, after creating a
new file.  You may enter as many values as you want in a line, separating them
by commas for alphabetic characters and by commas or blank spaces for numeric
values.  However, the input data must be exactly in the following order:

1. Number of states
2. Probability from each state to each state
3. Number of iterations (periods)
4. Initial vector: probability or any other numeric value of
                   state for each state
```

```
** Sample Batch Input Data Set (Example 16.1) **

3       ; three states
.950    ; probability from state 1 to state 1
.033    ; probability from state 1 to state 2
.017    ; probability from state 1 to state 3
.027    ; probability from state 2 to state 1
.933    ; probability from state 2 to state 2
.040    ; probability from state 2 to state 3
.022    ; probability from state 3 to state 1
.111    ; probability from state 3 to state 2
.867    ; probability from state 3 to state 3
30      ; thirty iterations (periods)
3000    ; initial value of state 1
7500    ; initial value of state 2
4500    ; initial value of state 3

PROGRAM: Markov Models

Enter number of states: 3

Transition probability table

Enter probability from state 1 to state 1 (0 to 1): .95
Enter probability from state 1 to state 2 (0 to 1): .033
Enter probability from state 1 to state 3 (0 to 1): .017

Enter probability from state 2 to state 1 (0 to 1): .027
Enter probability from state 2 to state 2 (0 to 1): .933
Enter probability from state 2 to state 3 (0 to 1): .040

Enter probability from state 3 to state 1 (0 to 1): .022
Enter probability from state 3 to state 2 (0 to 1): .111
Enter probability from state 3 to state 3 (0 to 1): .867


Enter number of iterations (periods) you want to run: 30

Enter initial vector: state 1 : 3000
Enter initial vector: state 2 : 7500
Enter initial vector: state 3 : 4500

PROGRAM: Markov Models

***** INPUT DATA ENTERED *****

Transition probability table

---------------------------------------
States:  to      1      2      3
from
 1             0.950  0.030  0.020
 2             0.030  0.930  0.040
 3             0.020  0.110  0.870
---------------------------------------
```

```
Number of iterations (periods):  30

    Initial vector
    States          Value
    -------------------------

      1              3000
      2              7500
      3              4500
    -------------------------

*****   PROGRAM OUTPUT   *****


-----------------------------------------------------------
States    Steady state probability   Steady state Value
-----------------------------------------------------------
   1               0.35                    5261.19
   2               0.46                    6828.36
   3               0.19                    2910.45
-----------------------------------------------------------

After 30 iterations steady state is not approached.

Transition probability table after period  30

---------------------------------------
States:  to       1       2       3
from
 1              0.410   0.410   0.180
 2              0.320   0.480   0.200
 3              0.310   0.480   0.200
---------------------------------------
```

Summary

Markov analysis is concerned with forecasting future trends of certain variables based on an analysis of their current movements. It is a stochastic analysis that attempts to explain the evolution of dynamic systems controlled by sequences of decisions. The basic objective of Markov analysis is to provide probabilistic information about a problematic situation to a decision maker. This chapter has presented the basic nature, analysis process, and applications of Markov analysis. Markov analysis can be performed very simply and conveniently on the *Micro Manager*.

References

Dannenbring, D. G., and M. K. Starr. 1981. *Management science: An introduction.* New York: McGraw-Hill.

Derman, C. 1970. *Finite state Markovian decision process.* New York: Academic Press.

Hillier, F. S., and G. J. Lieberman. 1980. *Introduction to operations research.* 3d ed. San Francisco: Holden-Day.

Levin, R. I., C. A. Kirkpatrick, and D. S. Rubin. 1982. *Quantitative approaches to management.* 5th ed. New York: McGraw-Hill.

Problems

1. Given the following transition matrix, determine the steady-state probabilities.

$$\begin{array}{cc} & \begin{array}{cc} A & B \end{array} \\ \begin{array}{c} A \\ B \end{array} & \begin{pmatrix} .65 & .35 \\ .45 & .55 \end{pmatrix} \end{array}$$

2. Given the following transition matrix, determine the steady-state probabilities.

$$\begin{array}{cc} & \begin{array}{cc} X & Y \end{array} \\ \begin{array}{c} X \\ Y \end{array} & \begin{pmatrix} .6 & .4 \\ .5 & .5 \end{pmatrix} \end{array}$$

3. Given the following transition matrix, determine the steady-state probabilities.

$$\begin{array}{cc} & \begin{array}{ccc} X & Y & Z \end{array} \\ \begin{array}{c} X \\ Y \\ Z \end{array} & \begin{pmatrix} .65 & .25 & .10 \\ .15 & .45 & .4 \\ .3 & .2 & .5 \end{pmatrix} \end{array}$$

4. Given the following transition matrix, determine the steady-state probabilities.

$$\begin{array}{cc} & \begin{array}{ccc} X & Y & Z \end{array} \\ \begin{array}{c} Y \\ X \\ Z \end{array} & \begin{pmatrix} .80 & .08 & .12 \\ .06 & .84 & .10 \\ .06 & .07 & .87 \end{pmatrix} \end{array}$$

5. Given the following transition matrix, determine the steady-state probabilities.

$$\begin{array}{cc} & \begin{array}{ccc} A & B & C \end{array} \\ \begin{array}{c} A \\ B \\ C \end{array} & \begin{pmatrix} .5 & .3 & .2 \\ .1 & .7 & .2 \\ .1 & .1 & .8 \end{pmatrix} \end{array}$$

6. Given the following transition matrix, determine the equilibrium market share of companies X, Y, and Z.

$$\begin{array}{cc} & \begin{array}{ccc} X & Y & Z \end{array} \\ \begin{array}{c} Y \\ X \\ Z \end{array} & \begin{pmatrix} .80 & .15 & .05 \\ .05 & .85 & .10 \\ .05 & .05 & .90 \end{pmatrix} \end{array}$$

7. Given the following transition probabilities for the market share among three companies, determine the equilibrium market share.

$$\begin{array}{cc} & \begin{array}{ccc} X & Y & Z \end{array} \\ \begin{array}{c} X \\ Y \\ Z \end{array} & \begin{pmatrix} .90 & .06 & .04 \\ .10 & .85 & .05 \\ .10 & .10 & .80 \end{pmatrix} \end{array}$$

8. Suppose that the market share is currently 30 percent for brand X, 20 percent for brand Y, and 50 percent for brand Z. What will be their market shares in two years, given the following transition matrix?

$$\begin{array}{cc} & \begin{array}{ccc} X & Y & Z \end{array} \\ \begin{array}{c} X \\ Y \\ Z \end{array} & \begin{pmatrix} .90 & .05 & .05 \\ .10 & .80 & .10 \\ .30 & .20 & .50 \end{pmatrix} \end{array}$$

9. Oldstyle, a light beer sold on a national basis, currently holds 20 percent of the market, and the other 80 percent is divided among a number of competing brands. A market analysis has shown that from one month to the next, Oldstyle has managed to retain 80 percent of its customers while gaining 15 percent of the customers of competing brands. What share of the market will Oldstyle have after one month?

10. The LaCrosse Handicapped Pioneer Club, which is a nonprofit organization dependent upon volunteer help, is divided into three departments and allows free movement of personnel between any two. Between March and June, personnel movement was as indicated in the table below.

		Gains			
Dept.	**March**	**From *A***	**From *B***	**From *C***	**June**
A	150	135	15	20	170
B	300	10	285	20	315
C	200	5	0	160	165

What percentage of the volunteers will be working for each department in September?

11. The Credit Department of the Morningside Department Store has secured a breakdown on the transition among three categories of accounts receivable by its customers.

Category	**March 1**	**From paid**	**From delinquent**	**From bad debts**	**April 1**
Paid	1,500	1,425	100	50	1,575
Delinquent	3,750	50	3,500	250	3,800
Bad debts	2,250	25	150	1,950	2,125

What percentage of credit customers will be classified in each category on June 1? Assume that no new credit customers are added.

12. Beatrice has three gas stations: Amoco, Phillips, and Citgo. The residents of Beatrice buy gasoline on a weekly basis. Historical data have shown the following patterns. In a typical week, Amoco retains 50 percent of its customers while losing 30 percent to Phillips and 20 percent to Citgo. Phillips retains 70 percent of its customers while losing 10 percent to Amoco and 20 percent to Citgo. Citgo retains 80 percent while losing 10 percent each to Amoco and Phillips. If the current pattern continues, what will be Amoco's equilibrium share of the market?

13. Hinky Brewing Company is one of the largest breweries in the midwestern United States. An M.B.A. class in management science at the university is currently investigating the loyalty to Hinky brands in relation to the loyalty of its major competitor, Old Madison, and to all other breweries considered as a single group. A questionnaire filled out by 1,000 beer drinkers indicates the following patterns. In a typical month, Hinky retains 80 percent of its customers while losing 8 percent to Old Madison and 12 percent to all other breweries. Old Madison retains 85 percent of its customers while losing 6 percent to Hinky and 9 percent to all other breweries. All other breweries, taken as a group, retain 86 percent while losing 7 percent each to Hinky and Old Madison. What can Hinky expect for an equilibrium share of the market?

14. Omaha Airport has three car-rental agencies: Hertz, Budget, and Alamo. In the past month, Hertz retained 85 percent of its customers from the previous month, lost 5 percent of its business to Budget, and lost 10 percent to Alamo. Budget retained 90 percent of its customers while losing 10 percent to Alamo. Alamo retained 75 percent of its customers, while losing 10 percent to Hertz, and 15 percent to Budget. What will be the equilibrium share of the market for each car-rental agency?

15. The marketing vice president of the *Omaha Herald* would like to estimate the equilibrium share of the Sunday newspaper market for his *Herald* in a certain area. He has broken the market into three categories and has estimated the transition as follows:

	Omaha Herald	*Lincoln Star*	Others
Omaha Herald	.80	.10	.10
Lincoln Star	.10	.70	.20
Others	.05	.10	.85

What will be the *Omaha Herald* equilibrium share of the Sunday newspaper market?

16. Etc., a 5¼ floppy diskette sold on a national basis, currently holds one-third (⅓) of the market. Its major competitor, Max, and all others hold an equal share of the remaining market. During the year, the following purchasing pattern took place:

Etc. retained 80 percent of its customers and lost 16 percent to Max and 4 percent to all others.

Max retained 76 percent of its customers and lost 18 percent to Etc. and 6 percent to all others.

All others retained 84 percent of their customers and lost 12 percent to Etc. and 4 percent to Max.

If the floppy diskette market does not expand, what share of the total market would be held by each brand at the end of the year?

17. Brennen Department Store would like to analyze the payment behavior of credit customers. Historical data from the credit department have shown the following patterns:

		This month	
		Paid	Delinquent
Last Month	Paid	.8	.2
	Delinquent	.9	.1

What percentage of the credit customers eventually will be in each category?

18. A computer center at the local state university has developed a transition matrix on the probabilities of its computer system's status in terms of up or down for operation in the following month, given its condition in the present month.

		This month	
		Up	Down
Last Month	Up	.8	.2
	Down	.4	.6

Determine the probabilities that the system will be up or down in the next month.

19. The local telephone company is well known for the unreliable nature of its equipment on heavy, snowy days. This spring break began with a heavy snowstorm in the area served by the telephone company. An M.B.A. student, who was working part-time for the company, quickly formulated the following matrix showing the likelihood of the trunk lines being "Open," "Busy," or "Down" from one minute to the next. The manager of the telephone company wants to know what the equilibrium state of the system will be.

	Open	Busy	Down
Open	.3	.2	.5
Busy	.2	.6	.2
Down	.5	.3	.2

20. The College of Business at a university is considering the purchase of 100 more microcomputers to expand its microcomputer lab to meet the students' demand for microcomputer education. The director of the microcomputer lab has been unhappy with the reliability of their current microcomputer. The past month's data have shown the following results:

	Working	Nonworking
Working	.8	.2
Nonworking	.4	.6

Determine the probabilities whether the microcomputer will be or will not be operating in the next month.

CHAPTER 17

Computer-Based Simulation

Many real-world decision problems are complex, dynamic, and probabilistic in nature. Such problems cannot be analyzed neatly by applying an optimization algorithm such as linear programming, goal programming, or other solution methods. Many decision problems are characterized by a complex set of interrelationships among the decision variables, random changes of parameters, and large-scale models.

When analytical models are not appropriate to analyze the problem, one possible way open to us is to conduct an experiment. Simulation is such an experimental technique. Simulation is usually performed on a computer to analyze the behavior of many real-world operating systems, such as inventory, production, research and development, sales, financial transactions, manpower, and others. In this chapter, we will discuss the application of the *Micro Manager* for computer-based simulations.

Basics

The simulation technique was briefly introduced in discussing inventory control (chap. 13) and queuing problems (chap. 15). Simulation represents a major departure from other management science techniques that are typically based on analytical modeling approaches. Many complex problems are not easily analyzed by algorithmic approaches. Thus, simulation has been a popular way to conduct an experiment by analyzing the behavior of a problem under various conditions.

We are most familiar with a physical simulation, where a physical system is replaced by an analogous physical system. For example, a complex mechanical system can be represented by an equivalent electrical system. We are familiar with such simulation systems as the ground flight simulator for training pilots, the space simulation of the manned space-flight programs of NASA, and games such as Monopoly, Acquire, Life, and others.

In many ways, simulation is quite similar to a model. A model, as we discussed in chapter 2, is a representation of reality. Simulation, on the other hand, simply imitates reality. Therefore, the simulation process typically involves running the model to generate operational information about the real system that is useful for decision making.

Today, the term *simulation* refers to a computer-based simulation. Thus, simulation is a numerical experimentation used on a computer to analyze the dynamic behavior of a management system. The typical simulation approach attempts to obtain descriptive information through computer-based experimentation. In fact, it is possible to include a search routine in the simulation process in such a way that the optimum solution to the decision problem can be identified.

Today, we have easy access to powerful computers in terms of speed, computational capacity, and space requirements. Also, the advent of powerful microcomputers at affordable costs makes even more sense for us to apply computer-based simulation techniques. But, the simulation of a large-scale system is extremely difficult on an independent microcomputer. However, with the availability of networking or interfacing technologies between a mainframe computer and a set of microcomputers, we can use the microcomputer as a dedicated, smart terminal for various simulation projects.

Simulation has been applied to a wide range of management problems. Some of the typical areas of applying simulation are queuing, inventory control, network analysis, production scheduling, system maintenance, financial planning, marketing strategies, public service operations, environmental management, and health-care planning.

The Simulation Process

The simulation process for a system consists of several phases, as shown in Fig. 17.1. The initial phase is quite similar to the first step of the management science process—problem formulation. In this phase, we must identify important performance criteria, decision rules, and model variables and parameters. Once we have identified all components of the model, we develop the model itself in such a way that we can analyze it on the computer. When we use a mainframe computer system, a model may be required to be written in a specific simulation language such as GPSS, Dynamo, GASP, Simscript, and others. Then, we must validate the model to check its reliability.

The next phase involves the design of the model experiments. This preparatory phase provides a further opportunity to check the appropriateness of the model to study the behavior of a particular system. Once this stage is finished, we can actually run the model on the computer. The model's results are often in the form of operating statistics, such as cost, and other input requirements, output, time requirements, and so on. If the results of the simulation obtained are satisfactory, the process is completed and we can analyze the results further for decision making. On the other hand, if the model's results are not satisfactory, we make the necessary changes and repeat the simulation run.

Figure 17.1 The Simulation Process

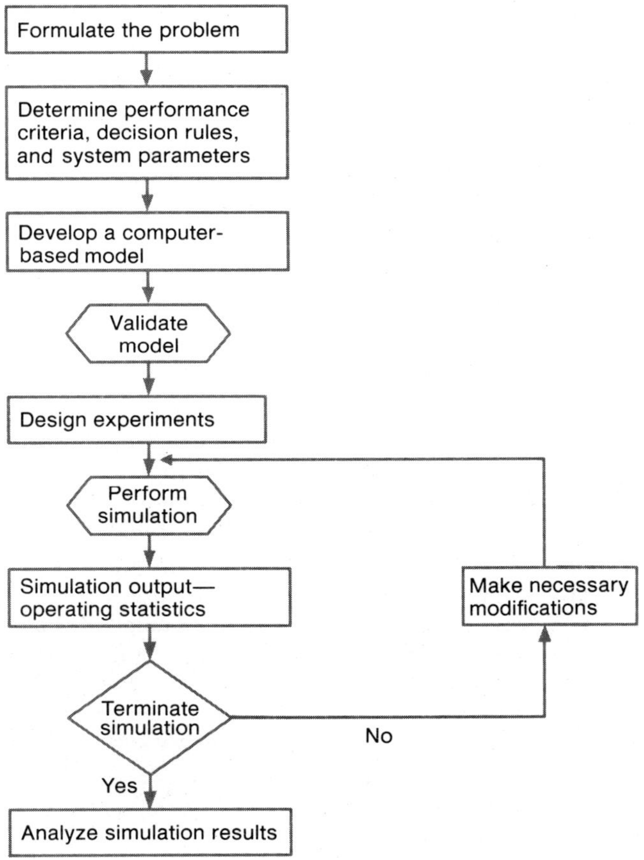

Monte Carlo Simulation

The Monte Carlo simulation is generally used for stochastic simulation. In certain systems, model parameters are best represented as random variables. Such random variables can be described by appropriate probability distributions and the model is referred to as a *probabilistic,* or *stochastic, model.*

The Monte Carlo technique is basically a sampling technique for selecting numbers randomly from a given probability distribution for simulation. The original use of the Monte Carlo technique is generally attributed to von Neumann and Ulan who used the technique as an experimental tool in the development of the atom bomb during World War II.

The basic objective of the stochastic simulation is to reproduce closely the randomness of the system's behavior. Let us consider the following example.

Example 17.1 Milkyway Electronics Company

Milkyway Electronics Company specializes in sales and service of Milkyway products. One of the most popular products that the company carries is the Milkyway VCR. The daily demand for VCR units is random with the following probability distribution.

Daily demand for VCR, (*D*)	Probability, *P* (*D*)
0	0.1
1	0.2
2	0.4
3	0.2
4	0.1

We can use the Monte Carlo simulation to generate the daily demand for VCR's by sampling from the probability distribution. We can apply the Monte Carlo technique in many different ways to generate the random number to determine the demand. However, the tabular method is perhaps the easiest way to transform a random number to a daily demand. This tabular method is based on the cumulative probability function, as shown below.

Demand (*D*)	*P*(*D*)	Cumulative prob.	Random-number interval
0	0.1	0.1	00–09
1	0.2	0.3	10–29
2	0.4	0.7	30–69
3 ←	0.2 ←	0.9 ←	70–89 ←
4	0.1	1.0	90–99

In the above table, the random-number interval column represents the two-digit random-number distributions that correspond to the cumulative probability distribution of demand. Suppose that we generated a two-digit random number and found it to be 78. Then, we can easily determine that the corresponding daily demand for VCR is three units, as shown in the above table.

In the typical computer-based simulation process, the random-number generator subroutine generates pseudorandom numbers. If we generate enough random numbers (*RN*) to determine the daily demand, the average, daily demand obtained from this process will be very close to the actual, expected, daily demand.

Example 17.2 Student Union Hair Style Shop

The Student Union Hair Style Shop has discrete random arrival intervals and service times. The formation of a queue depends upon the above two random events. The Hair Style Shop has two stylists with equal skills. Suppose that the probability distributions for arrival intervals and service times are as follows:

Arrival interval, (*A*)	**Probability, *P*(*A*)**	**Cumulative prob.**	**Range of *RN***
1 minute	0.2	0.2	00–19
2	0.5	0.7	20–69
3	0.3	1.0	70–99

Service time, (*S*)	**Probability, *P*(*S*)**	**Cumulative prob.**	**Range of *RN***
2.5 minutes	0.3	0.3	00–29
3	0.5	0.8	30–79
3.5	0.2	1.0	80–99

A simulation of the operation of the Hair Style Shop requires two random-number generations—first, the arrival interval and second, the service time. Suppose that we are interested in simulating five customer arrivals. The following table illustrates the simulation runs that describe the customers' activities.

Customer	***RN* 1**	**Arrival interval**	**Waiting time**	**Customers in queue**	***RN* 2**	**Service time**	**Time in system**
1	48	2	0	0	16	2.5	2.5
2	08	1	1.5	1	54	3	4.5
3	39	2	2.5	1	72	3	5.5
4	41	2	3.5	2	91	3.5	7.0
5	82	3	4.0	2	62	3	7.0

Optimization in Simulation

Simulation does not usually generate an optimum solution to a problem. Instead, simulation merely provides information about the behavior of the system under consideration. Nevertheless, we can obtain a quasi-optimum solution through a simulation model by employing search routines. For example, in an inventory problem under uncertainty, we may wish to determine the optimum combination of order quantity (Q) and reorder point (R). The simulation process involves generating random numbers to determine the lead time and demand rate. Each run with predetermined Q and R will generate the total inventory cost. Through a search routine, we can determine the optimum combination of Q and R.

Example 17.3 *Lincoln Tractor Company*

Lincoln Tractor Company specializes in the sales and service of ABC Farm Equipment Company's products. One of the main products that the company stocks is tractors. The monthly demand and the lead time for tractors are random with the following probability:

Demand, (Q)	Probability, $P(Q)$	Cumulative prob.	Range of *RN*
1 tractor	.25	.25	00–24
2 tractors	.50	.75	25–74
3 tractors	.25	1.00	75–99

Lead time, (LT)	Prob., $P(LT)$	Cumulative prob.	Range of *RN*
1 month	.25	.25	00–24
2 months	.50	.75	25–74
3 months	.25	1.00	75–99

Simulation of the Lincoln Tractor Company operations requires two random-number generations, that is, for the demand and the lead time. The following table shows the simulation results using the input data described below.

Input Data

Holding cost per unit: $300
Total annual working months: 12
Initial inventory: 5 tractors
Maximum order qty: 8 tractors
Maximum reorder point: 4 tractors

Ordering cost per order: $1,000
Stock-out cost per unit: $500
Minimum order qty: 5 tractors
Minimum reorder point: 1

Simulation Results

Q \ R	1	2	3	4
5	16,212	14,388	14,028	22,572
6	14,580	13,092	14,412	15,480
7	14,004	14,616	15,624	19,116
8	13,680	14,340	18,180	19,344

Based on the simulation results, we can determine the best inventory policy, which is ordering six tractors at the reorder point of two tractors, resulting in the minimum total inventory cost of $13,092.

Application of the *Micro Manager*

This section presents an application example of the *Micro Manager* to a simulation problem. Because there are a variety of simulation models, there is no one unified modeling approach to simulation. The program diskette provides you with the complete information about computer-based simulation, including the purpose of simulation models, solutions of example problems, interactive input instructions, and the batch input procedure. This section will present only the information (purpose of the computer-based simulation and the batch input data format) and the solution of a sample problem using the interactive input format.

```
<< PURPOSE >>

SIMULATION simulates the following three categories of problems by generating
random numbers: (1) Monte Carlo simulation; (2) Inventory simulation; and
(3) Queuing simulation.

(1) Monte Carlo simulation:
      This program is limited to simulation of events with a given probability
      distribution.

(2) Inventory simulation:
      This program is limited to finding the optimum order quantity and
      reorder point under uncertain demand rates and lead times.

(3) Queuing simulation:
      This program is limited to computation of the queue length, total cost
      (time), waiting time (cost), etc.
```

```
<<  BATCH INPUT DATA FORMAT  >>

Type in the values of the following input data requirements, after creating a
new file.  You may enter as many values as you want in a line, separating them
by commas for alphabetic characters and by commas or blank spaces for numeric
values.  However, the input data must be exactly in the following order:

1. Problem type
      1    : Monte Carlo simulation
      2    : Inventory simulation
      3    : Queuing simulation

For Monte Carlo simulation
   2. Number of categories
   3. For each category
        3.1.  Probability
        3.2.  Value
   4. Number of simulation runs

For Inventory simulation
   2. Holding cost per unit
   3. Shortage cost per unit
   4. Ordering cost per order
   5. Total annual working days
   6. Minimum order quantity
   7. Maximum order quantity
   8. Minimum reorder point
   9. Maximum reorder point
  10. Initial inventory
  11. Number of demand categories
  12. For each category
        12.1 Demand
        12.2 Probability
  13. Number of lead time categories
  14. For each category
        14.1 Lead time
        14.2 Probability
  15. Number of simulation runs

For Queuing simulation
   2. Number of arrival intervals
   3. Time and probability for each arrival interval
   4. Number of service times
   5. Time and probability of for each service time
   6. Number of simulation runs (arrivals)

** Sample Batch Input Data Set (Example 17.1) **

1      ; Monte Carlo simulation
5      ; five categories
.1,0   ; probability and value of category 1
.2,1   ; probability and value of category 2
.4,2   ; probability and value of category 3
.2,3   ; probability and value of category 4
.1,4   ; probability and value of category 5
500    ; five hundred simulation runs
```

```
PROGRAM: Simulation

Simulation Models

   1. Monte Carlo simulation
   2. Inventory   simulation
   3. Queuing     simulation

Enter a number (1 to 3): 1

** Monte Carlo simulation **

Enter number of categories: 5
Enter value and probability for category 1 : 0,.1
Enter value and probability for category 2 : 1,.2
Enter value and probability for category 3 : 2,.4
Enter value and probability for category 4 : 3,.2
Enter value and probability for category 5 : 4,.1

Enter number of simulation runs: 500

PROGRAM: Simulation << EXAMPLE 17.1-3 >>

***** INPUT DATA ENTERED *****

Monte Carlo simulation

      Category Distribution

--------------------------------------
      Value             Probability
--------------------------------------
       0.00               0.10
       1.00               0.20
       2.00               0.40
       3.00               0.20
       4.00               0.10
--------------------------------------


Number of simulation runs :   500

*****   PROGRAM OUTPUT   *****

Average value after  500  runs: 1.89
```

Summary

Many decision problems are often too complex and dynamic to apply simple optimization techniques. When all else fails, the only possible way to analyze the problem is to conduct an experiment. Simulation is such an experimental technique. Today, simulation refers to a computer-based simulation. Simulation has been applied to such problem areas as queuing, inventory control, network analysis, production scheduling, financial planning, and others. In this chapter we have discussed Monte Carlo, queuing, and inventory simulation models. Although microcomputers are not best suited for large-scale simulation, the *Micro Manager* is capable of handling simple simulation models.

References

Emshoff, J. R., and R. L. Sisson. 1970. *Design and use of computer simulation models.* New York: Macmillan.

Fishman, S. G. 1973. *Concepts and methods in discrete event digital simulation.* New York: John Wiley & Sons.

Forrester, J. W. 1961. *Industrial dynamics.* Cambridge, MA: MIT Press.

Frazer, J. 1978. *Introduction to business simulation.* Englewood Cliffs, NJ: Prentice-Hall.

Gordon, G. 1978. *System simulation.* Englewood Cliffs, NJ: Prentice-Hall.

Graybeal, W., and U. W. Pooch. 1980. *Simulation: Principles and methods.* Cambridge, MA: Winthrop.

House, W. C. 1977. *Business simulation for decision making.* New York: PBI.

Law, A. M., and W. D. Kelton. 1982. *Simulation modeling and analysis.* New York: McGraw-Hill.

Lee, S. M., L. J. Moore, and B. W. Taylor. 1985. *Management science.* 2d ed. Dubuque, IA: Wm. C. Brown Publishers.

Maisel, J., and G. Gnugnoli. 1972. *Simulation for discrete stochastic systems.* Chicago: SRA.

Naylor, T. H. 1971. *Computer simulation experiments with models of economic systems.* New York: John Wiley & Sons.

Reitman, J. 1971. *Computer simulation applications.* New York: John Wiley & Sons.

Roberts, N., D. Andersen, R. Deal, M. Garet, and W. Shaffer. 1983. *Introduction to computer simulation: A system dynamics modeling approach.* Reading, MA: Addison-Wesley.

Schmidt, J. W., and R. E. Taylor. 1970. *Simulation and analysis of industrial systems.* Homewood, IL: Irwin.

Shannon, R. E. 1975. *Systems simulation: The art and science.* Englewood Cliffs, NJ: Prentice-Hall.

Problems

1. Congress passed a bill and sent it to the White House. The president will either sign or veto it. If it is vetoed, the veto has no chance of being overridden in the Congress. The associated probabilities and anticipated returns are provided in the following table:

Event	Probability		Payoff
Sign	.5		$200,000
Veto	.5		−100,000
	1.0	EMV =	$ 50,000

The objective will be to measure the expected monetary return of the president's decision. An exact measure of the expected return is provided by the expected monetary value (EMV) in the above table. Instead of using an analytical method, however, this same measure of worth could be derived by using Monte Carlo simulation. Try 2,000 runs and then 4,000 runs of simulation by using the *Micro Manager* and compare these results with an analytical result.

2. Karen has the opportunity to invest $1,000 in a project for one year. She thinks that the return will depend on one of three possible future economic conditions: fast growth, normal growth, and slow growth. The following table summarizes information about the decision problem with the evaluating statistic (EMV = $90). Demonstrate the applicability of simulation to this general category of problems by running simulation 500 times.

Economic environment	Probability	Associated payoffs
Fast growth	.20	$400
Normal growth	.50	200
Slow growth	.30	−300

3. An investor has $10,000 to invest in common stocks. His selection is between companies *A* and *B*. He feels that each company's stock has a .4 probability of doubling his money and a .6 probability of losing half of his money. The investor's choices are: (a) Invest the entire amount in either *A* or *B;* (b) Invest $5,000 in one company and not invest the other $5,000; (c) invest $5,000 in *A* and $5,000 in *B;* or (d) not invest at all. Select the best choice by running simulation 50 times for each option.

4. The Metro Bus Company operates bus routes between Omaha and its home base in Lincoln. The company currently employs 10 drivers. The management keeps one driver in the reserve pool to cover for drivers calling in sick. The company reviewed personnel records and developed the following probability distribution for the number of drivers calling in sick on any given day:

No. of drivers sick	Probability
0	.25
1	.30
2	.25
3	.10
4	.10

Using simulation, estimate the use of the reserve driver and determine the probability that one or more trips will have to be canceled because of lack of drivers.

5. The port manager in the state of Washington would like to set up an effective port management policy. Since simulation appears to be the best method of analyzing this kind of problem, the port manager organized a management science group to conduct a feasibility study for this project. Most ships entering this port require about three days to unload, clean, and prepare for departure. Given the probability distribution for interarrival time between ships, determine by simulation the values for the random variables listed in the table.

Interarrival time between ships (days)	Probability
1	.15
2	.20
3	.25
4	.40

Ship number	Arrival interval	Waiting time	Ships in queue	Unloading time	Days in system
1					
2					
3					
.					
.					
.					
9					
10					

6. William Cooper, a warehouse manager, has been disturbed by what appears to be a larger-than-expected backlog of orders to be filled. He employs a clerk to fill orders. The orders are received according to the following empirically established distribution:

Interarrival time (in minutes)	Frequency
30	15
45	20
60	35
75	20
90	10

The distribution of service time necessary for a single clerk to fill orders is:

Service time (in minutes)	Frequency
60	10
90	30
120	30
150	20
180	10

The clerk works alone, taking orders from a single in-box. The manager wants you to simulate the required time for filling orders.

7. Gracias Car Wash is considering implementing another car-wash line. After reviewing historical data, the company established the following table for the probability of interarrival time of cars and service time.

Interarrival time (in minutes)	Probability	Service time	Probability
10	.15	15	.30
20	.30	20	.35
30	.30	30	.25
40	.15	35	.10
50	.10		

Simulate the car-washing process for 10 cars.

8. Livette Company's past records indicate the following demand patterns for its product and lead times as shown in the table below. Cost information for the item is:

Unit holding cost = \$8
Order cost per order = \$200
Stock-out cost per unit = \$10

Weekly demand	Probability	Lead time (week)	Probability
10	.15	2	.15
11	.30	3	.45
12	.20	4	.20
13	.20	5	.20
14	.15		

Assuming 30 weeks of total annual working time and twenty-five units of initial inventory, find the optimal order quantity and reorder point by using simulation.

9. A stockkeeping unit has the following probability distribution for daily demand and lead times:

Daily demand	Probability	Lead time	Probability
0	.05	2	.20
1	.15	3	.50
2	.30	4	.30
3	.30		
4	.20		

Find the optimal order quantity and reorder point by using simulation. The starting inventory level is 20. Cost information is provided below:

Carrying cost = \$6/unit
Ordering cost = \$50/order
Stock-out cost = \$10/unit

10. Stella Demsky is the inventory manager for Cherry Computer Company. Recently, the demand for Super-X has shown wide fluctuations. She wants to determine the expected demand for Super-X in stock during a reorder period, i.e., the time lapse from the stock reorder until the reordered goods are received. The most important information Stella is seeking to find is how far in advance she should order before the stock level is reduced to zero. On the basis of historical data about lead time and demand, Stella realizes that these two variables are random variables, described by the probability distribution shown below:

Lead time (days)	Probability	Demand per day	Probability
1	.5	1	.1
2	.3	2	.3
3	.2	3	.4
		4	.2

Simulate this problem to show the demand during lead time for 30 orders and to determine the expected demand during a lead time.

CHAPTER 18

Implementation of Management Science for Productivity Improvement

The basic objective of management science is to improve organizational effectiveness by helping people make good decisions. Thus, the true value of management science is realized only when management science models are actually implemented to real-world decision-making situations. Implementation of management science is of vital concern to practicing managers and management scientists alike. The purpose of this text has been to discuss how one can use the *Micro Manager* to actually implement management science decisions for improving productivity by using microcomputers.

Therefore, it is fitting to conclude this text with a discussion of a broad management perspective about the actual implementation of management science. In this chapter, we will first explore ways to improve organizational productivity and then discuss strategies for implementing management science.

Basics

Mary Parker Follet, over half a century ago, defined management as the process of "getting things done through people." We believe this is a very good definition of management because she emphasized the central importance of people in the management process. We also believe that only people can improve productivity in organizations. We may use computers, robots, or automated processes in organizations; however, we use such high technologies because people have the intelligence to use them. In other words, high technologies are embedded in people, and it is they who make it possible to use technologies in organizations.

In its purest form, productivity is the ratio of output over input in a given system. The output may include total revenue, production of goods, or services generated. The input may include such areas as money, people, equipment, time, effort, and so on. Basically, we have three ways to improve productivity. The first is to increase the output while maintaining the current level of input. The second is to decrease the input while maintaining the current level of output. The third way is to increase both the output and input while keeping the rate of increase in output greater than that of the input.

We have seen many instances where organizations exercise what we would like to call "neutron bomb mentality." At the first sign of a slight business difficulty, management zaps all human resources in sight to preserve buildings, equipment, and machines. Nothing wears out the motivational fabric faster than such a management approach. We believe that the best utilization of human resources, while exploring the ways to increase the output, should be the central theme of management.

Management science can be applied either to increase the output or decrease the input. Thus, the successful application of management science is important for improvement in productivity. However, ample evidence exists that shows the successful implementation of management science requires more than just a good knowledge of management science. The reason for this can be found in the requirements for improving productivity.

To improve productivity in any organization, we need four basic ingredients: a proper organizational climate; effective human resource management; application of modern technologies; and innovative management systems. We are beginning to realize the importance of management by ideology. We should have a prevailing organizational culture, management philosophy, or organizational values that actively encourage and advocate innovations through individual creativity. Such an organizational climate or culture is essential for sustained growth in productivity. Furthermore, management must continuously articulate what the organization cherishes, such as commitment, creativity, hard work, and the application of new technologies.

The second factor that is required for productivity improvement is creative human resource management. The most important resource that we have in any organization is the human resource. We must make long-term investments in people. Once we have productive people working for an organization, profits or other returns will be taken care of by themselves. It is essential that management recruit good people who share the same basic values as the organization does, train them to have effective work skills that they can use for the organization for the workers' entire lives, and then motivate them to use their creativity by providing them with a proper work environment.

The third requirement for improving productivity is the application of modern technologies. We are currently witnessing an intelligence revolution. Modern technologies such as computer-based telecommunication systems, optical scanning devices, voice recognition and storage, artificial intelligence, robotics, and laser technology are changing the way we live and work. Some of these technologies have profound implications for the development, production, delivery, and service of products. Organizations must continuously explore new ways to capture new technologies that will further improve productivity.

The final factor in improving productivity is that organizations must put things together in an effective way. Innovative management systems are required to integrate the organizational values, human resources, and technologies. Technologies do not run organizations, but human imagination does. The development of various computer-based technologies, such as manufacturing, information processing, decision support, and operation management systems, needs more than just state-of-the-art technologies. For example, the Japanese just-in-time production- and inventory-control system is an innovative management system that creatively integrates various positive inputs to improve productivity.

Management science has a unique role to play in improving productivity. It can be effectively applied to increase the output, decrease the input, or both simultaneously. Furthermore, with the advent of microcomputers and myriad new peripherals and software packages, we can integrate human resources, modern technologies, and scientific techniques for improving productivity. The *Micro Manager,* with its user-friendly features and comprehensive coverage, could serve as a vehicle to improve productivity in any organization.

The Implementation Problem

Many management science texts generally define implementation as a process or manner in which the manager actually uses the results of scientific effort. However, this traditional definition is no longer appropriate in many organizations, since the artificial distinction between the manager and scientist is increasingly nebulous.

In the past, many management scientists believed that their job was to perform their sanctified, scientific work and advise the managers how to improve their operations. However, many forward-looking organizations no longer create such a line of demarcation between the scientist and the manager. As a matter of fact, many organizations now have management scientists sprinkled throughout the organization as members of operating departments. Furthermore, many managers are as well trained in quantitative disciplines as the management scientists and some managers have come up through the management science, staff route. Thus, the traditional two-culture syndrome is no longer a major problem.

Today, we see a tremendous increase in computer literacy among managers, professionals, students, and children. The use of microcomputers to analyze information or data is no longer the exclusive domain of management scientists. As a matter of fact, many chief-executive officers have either a terminal or a microcomputer in their offices. The advent of microcomputers and user-friendly software has greatly blurred the remaining line of demarcation between the manager and the scientist.

The remaining, real problem of implementation is determining how or when various individuals should be included in the whole process of management science, including problem formulation, data analysis, model development and testing, model solution, solution implementation, and feedback analysis. In the next section, some implementation strategies are directed toward answering this question.

Implementation Strategies

We believe the role of management scientists is the same as for any other members of the organization. Their job is to work toward achieving organizational goals. Thus, we reject the notion that the management scientist's goal is different from the manager's goal. Furthermore, we strongly believe that it is the manager's responsibility to ensure that the management scientist work as a productive member of the organization. Therefore, the management scientist should be fully integrated into the functions of the department to which he or she belongs.

Numerous implementation strategies of management science have been proposed. Many of these come from studies that deal with the behavioral aspects of organizational change. Also, several studies have suggested simulation games. However, we believe the four factors we suggested for productivity improvement would be sufficient for creating the right type of environment for successful implementation of management science.

What is important for a successful implementation is a proper organizational environment where an effective two-way, top–down and bottom–up, communication system functions properly. The top–down system should be basically that of management by ideology. In this system, the broad superordinate organizational goals should be communicated downward. Hopefully, organizational values such as equity, dedication, long-term employment, hard work, and long-term growth of the organization would be filtered down throughout the organization.

The bottom–up system should be that of management by information. Based on the environment that management creates by ideology, the operating personnel and middle managers would develop explicit objectives and plans of action to achieve the broad organizational goals. Thus, the hunger for new information, data, technologies, methodologies, and innovative systems should be the basic characteristic at the lower levels of the organization. Many excellent American and Japanese organizations emphasize such dual-communication systems.

Figure 18.1 The Traditional Decision Making Steps in Organizations

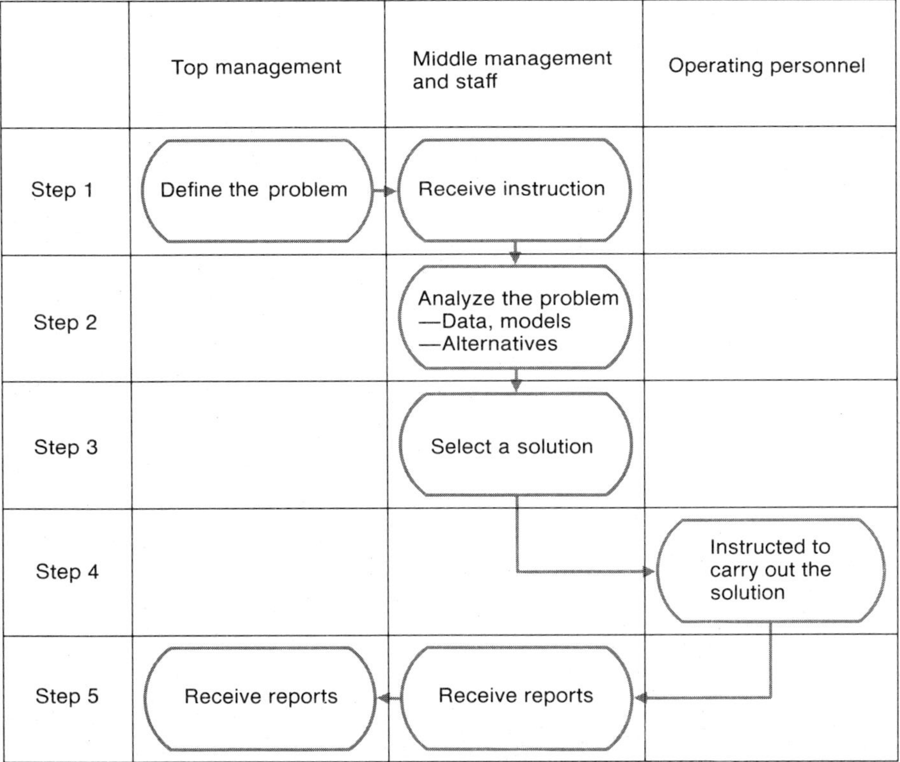

If the organization has management by ideology and information, the implementation of management science can be a relatively simple process. An effective decision-making process, which we discussed in chapter 1, can be used as the implementation strategy. For instance, contrast Fig. 18.1, which shows the traditional decision-making process, with Fig. 18.2, which presents an effective decision-making process in an organization that has the proper environment with the dual communication system.

We believe the availability of the *Micro Manager* will greatly enhance the probability of implementation. Managers typically would not implement management science results that they do not understand. Given the amount of ease and fun associated with the use of the *Micro Manager,* managers can play "games" with several simple examples that are provided in this text. The same reasoning can apply to the operating personnel as well.

Figure 18.2 The Effective Decision Making Steps in Organizations

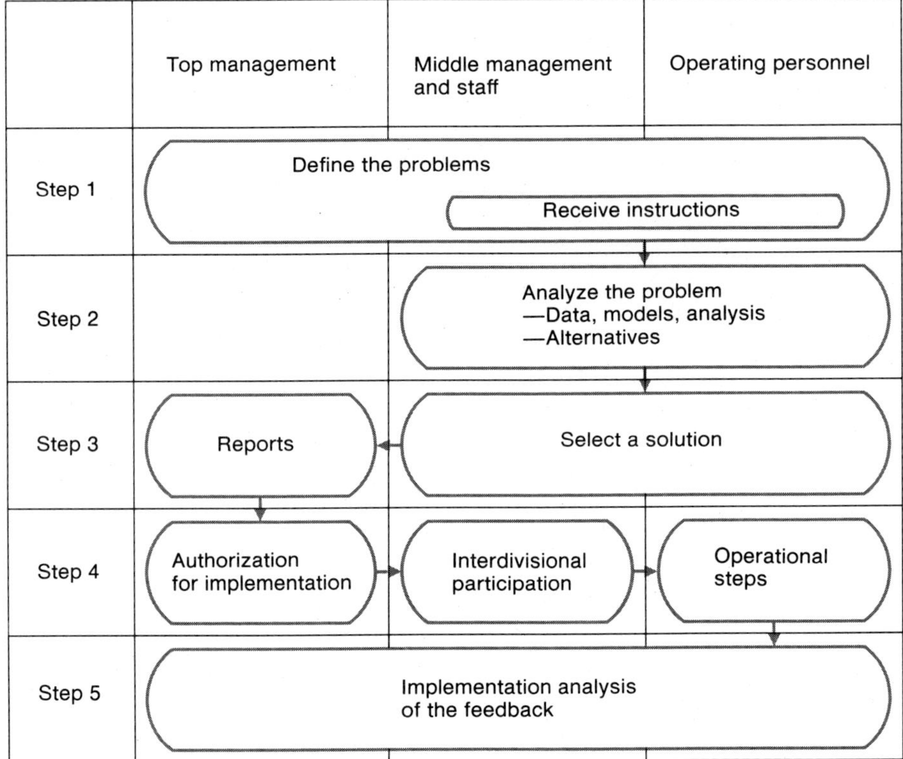

Summary

The true value of management science is realized when models are actually implemented to real-world situations. Thus, implementation of management science is of vital concern to both managers and management scientists. In this chapter, we have discussed philosophical issues concerning implementation of management science. Management science should be treated as an important means to improve productivity in an organization. The use of the *Micro Manager* will greatly enhance the probability of implementation.

References

Boulding, K. 1969. The specialist with a universal mind. *Management Science* 14:12, 647–653.

Churchman, C. W., R. L. Ackoff, and E. L. Arnoff. 1958. *Introduction to operations research.* New York: John Wiley & Sons.

Grayson, C. J., Jr. 1973. Management science and business practice. *Harvard Business Review* 51:4, 41–48.

Griener, L. 1967. Patterns of organizational change. *Harvard Business Review* 45, 119–30.

Gupta, J. N. D. 1977. Management science implementation: Experiences of a practicing O.R. manager. *Interface* 7:3, 84–90.

Hayes, R. H., and W. J. Abernathy. 1980. Managing our way to economic decline. *Harvard Business Review* 58, 67–77.

Lee, S. M. 1983. Japanese management and the 100 Yen Sushi House. *Operations Management Review* 1:2, 45–48.

Lee, S. M., L. J. Moore, and B. W. Taylor. 1985. *Management science.* 2d ed. Dubuque, IA: Wm. C. Brown Publishers.

Lee, S. M., and G. Schwendiman, eds. 1983. *Japanese management.* New York: Praeger.

———. 1983. *Management by Japanese systems.* New York: Praeger.

Lewin, K. 1947. Group decision and social change. In *Readings in Social Psychology,* eds. T. N. Newcomb and E. L. Hartley, 340–44. New York: Holt, Rinehart & Winston.

Ouchi, W. *Theory Z.* 1981. Reading, MA: Addison-Wesley.

Schultz, R. L., and D. P. Slevin, eds. 1975. *Implementation operations research/ management science.* New York: Elsevier.

Shakun, M. L. 1972. Management science and management: Implementing management science via situational normativism. *Management Science* 18, 367–77.

Watson, H. J., and P. G. Marett. 1979. A survey of management science implementation problems. *Interfaces* 9:4, 124–28.

Wysocki, R. K. 1979. OR/MS implementation research: A bibliography. *Interfaces* 9:2, 37–41.

APPENDIX A

Table A.1 Poisson probability values

r	λ 0.10	0.20	0.30	0.40	0.50	0.60	0.70	0.80	0.90	1.00
0	.9048	.8187	.7408	.6703	.6066	.5488	.4966	.4493	.4066	.3679
1	.0905	.1637	.2222	.2681	.3033	.3293	.3476	.3595	.3659	.3679
2	.0045	.0164	.0333	.0536	.0758	.0988	.1217	.1438	.1647	.1839
3	.0002	.0011	.0033	.0072	.0126	.0198	.0284	.0383	.0494	.0613
4	.0000	.0001	.0003	.0007	.0016	.0030	.0050	.0077	.0111	.0153
5	.0000	.0000	.0000	.0001	.0002	.0004	.0007	.0012	.0020	.0031
6	.0000	.0000	.0000	.0000	.0000	.0000	.0001	.0002	.0003	.0005
7	.0000	.0000	.0000	.0000	.0000	.0000	.0000	.0000	.0000	.0001

r	λ 1.10	1.20	1.30	1.40	1.50	1.60	1.70	1.80	1.90	2.00
0	.3329	.3012	.2725	.2466	.2231	.2019	.1827	.1653	.1496	.1353
1	.3662	.3614	.3543	.3452	.3347	.3230	.3106	.2975	.2842	.2707
2	.2014	.2169	.2303	.2417	.2510	.2584	.2640	.2678	.2700	.2707
3	.0738	.0867	.0998	.1128	.1255	.1378	.1496	.1607	.1710	.1804
4	.0203	.0260	.0324	.0395	.0471	.0551	.0636	.0723	.0812	.0902
5	.0045	.0062	.0084	.0111	.0141	.0176	.0216	.0260	.0309	.0361
6	.0008	.0012	.0018	.0026	.0035	.0047	.0061	.0078	.0098	.0120
7	.0001	.0002	.0003	.0005	.0008	.0011	.0015	.0020	.0027	.0034
8	.0000	.0000	.0001	.0001	.0001	.0002	.0003	.0005	.0006	.0009
9	.0000	.0000	.0000	.0000	.0000	.0000	.0001	.0001	.0001	.0002

r	λ 2.10	2.20	2.30	2.40	2.50	2.60	2.70	2.80	2.90	3.00
0	.1225	.1108	.1003	.0907	.0821	.0743	.0672	.0608	.0550	.0498
1	.2572	.2438	.2306	.2177	.2052	.1931	.1815	.1703	.1596	.1494
2	.2700	.2681	.2652	.2613	.2565	.2510	.2450	.2384	.2314	.2240
3	.1890	.1966	.2033	.2090	.2138	.2176	.2205	.2225	.2237	.2240
4	.0992	.1082	.1169	.1254	.1336	.1414	.1488	.1557	.1622	.1680
5	.0417	.0476	.0538	.0602	.0668	.0735	.0804	.0872	.0940	.1008
6	.0146	.0174	.0206	.0241	.0278	.0319	.0362	.0407	.0455	.0504
7	.0044	.0055	.0068	.0083	.0099	.0118	.0139	.0163	.0188	.0216
8	.0011	.0015	.0019	.0025	.0031	.0038	.0047	.0057	.0068	.0081
9	.0003	.0004	.0005	.0007	.0009	.0011	.0014	.0018	.0022	.0027
10	.0001	.0001	.0001	.0002	.0002	.0003	.0004	.0005	.0006	.0008
11	.0000	.0000	.0000	.0000	.0000	.0001	.0001	.0001	.0002	.0002
12	.0000	.0000	.0000	.0000	.0000	.0000	.0000	.0000	.0000	.0001

r	λ 3.10	3.20	3.30	3.40	3.50	3.60	3.70	3.80	3.90	4.00
0	.0450	.0408	.0369	.0334	.0302	.0273	.0247	.0224	.0202	.0183
1	.1397	.1304	.1217	.1135	.1057	.0984	.0915	.0850	.0789	.0733
2	.2165	.2087	.2008	.1929	.1850	.1771	.1692	.1615	.1539	.1465
3	.2237	.2226	.2209	.2186	.2158	.2125	.2087	.2046	.2001	.1954
4	.1733	.1781	.1823	.1858	.1888	.1912	.1931	.1944	.1951	.1954
5	.1075	.1140	.1203	.1264	.1322	.1377	.1429	.1477	.1522	.1563
6	.0555	.0608	.0662	.0716	.0771	.0826	.0881	.0936	.0989	.1042
7	.0246	.0278	.0312	.0348	.0385	.0425	.0466	.0508	.0551	.0595
8	.0095	.0111	.0129	.0148	.0169	.0191	.0215	.0241	.0269	.0298
9	.0033	.0040	.0047	.0056	.0066	.0076	.0089	.0102	.0116	.0132
10	.0010	.0013	.0016	.0019	.0023	.0028	.0033	.0039	.0045	.0053
11	.0003	.0004	.0005	.0006	.0007	.0009	.0011	.0013	.0016	.0019
12	.0001	.0001	.0001	.0002	.0002	.0003	.0003	.0004	.0005	.0006
13	.0000	.0000	.0000	.0000	.0001	.0001	.0001	.0001	.0002	.0002
14	.0000	.0000	.0000	.0000	.0000	.0000	.0000	.0000	.0000	.0001

r	λ 4.10	4.20	4.30	4.40	4.50	4.60	4.70	4.80	4.90	5.00
0	.0166	.0150	.0136	.0123	.0111	.0101	.0091	.0082	.0074	.0067
1	.0679	.0630	.0583	.0540	.0500	.0462	.0427	.0395	.0365	.0337
2	.1393	.1323	.1254	.1188	.1125	.1063	.1005	.0948	.0894	.0842
3	.1904	.1852	.1798	.1743	.1687	.1631	.1574	.1517	.1460	.1404
4	.1951	.1944	.1933	.1917	.1898	.1875	.1849	.1820	.1789	.1755
5	.1600	.1633	.1662	.1687	.1708	.1725	.1738	.1747	.1753	.1755
6	.1093	.1143	.1191	.1237	.1281	.1323	.1362	.1398	.1432	.1462
7	.0640	.0686	.0732	.0778	.0824	.0869	.0914	.0959	.1002	.1044
8	.0328	.0360	.0393	.0428	.0463	.0500	.0537	.0575	.0614	.0653
9	.0150	.0168	.0188	.0209	.0232	.0255	.0281	.0307	.0334	.0363
10	.0061	.0071	.0081	.0092	.0104	.0118	.0132	.0147	.0164	.0181
11	.0023	.0027	.0032	.0037	.0043	.0049	.0056	.0064	.0073	.0082
12	.0008	.0009	.0011	.0013	.0016	.0019	.0022	.0026	.0030	.0034
13	.0002	.0003	.0004	.0005	.0006	.0007	.0008	.0009	.0011	.0013
14	.0001	.0001	.0001	.0001	.0002	.0002	.0003	.0003	.0004	.0005
15	.0000	.0000	.0000	.0000	.0001	.0001	.0001	.0001	.0001	.0002

					λ					
r	5.10	5.20	5.30	5.40	5.50	5.60	5.70	5.80	5.90	6.00
0	.0061	.0055	.0050	.0045	.0041	.0037	.0033	.0030	.0027	.0025
1	.0311	.0287	.0265	.0244	.0225	.0207	.0191	.0176	.0162	.0149
2	.0793	.0746	.0701	.0659	.0618	.0580	.0544	.0509	.0477	.0446
3	.1348	.1293	.1239	.1185	.1133	.1082	.1033	.0985	.0938	.0892
4	.1719	.1681	.1641	.1600	.1558	.1515	.1472	.1428	.1383	.1339
5	.1753	.1748	.1740	.1728	.1714	.1697	.1678	.1656	.1632	.1606
6	.1490	.1515	.1537	.1555	.1571	.1584	.1594	.1601	.1605	.1606
7	.1086	.1125	.1163	.1200	.1234	.1267	.1298	.1326	.1353	.1377
8	.0692	.0731	.0771	.0810	.0849	.0887	.0925	.0962	.0998	.1033
9	.0392	.0423	.0454	.0486	.0519	.0552	.0586	.0620	.0654	.0688
10	.0200	.0220	.0241	.0262	.0285	.0309	.0334	.0359	.0386	.0413
11	.0093	.0104	.0116	.0129	.0143	.0157	.0173	.0190	.0207	.0225
12	.0039	.0045	.0051	.0058	.0065	.0073	.0082	.0092	.0102	.0113
13	.0015	.0018	.0021	.0024	.0028	.0032	.0036	.0041	.0046	.0052
14	.0006	.0007	.0008	.0009	.0011	.0013	.0015	.0017	.0019	.0022
15	.0002	.0002	.0003	.0003	.0004	.0005	.0006	.0007	.0008	.0009
16	.0001	.0001	.0001	.0001	.0001	.0002	.0002	.0002	.0003	.0003
17	.0000	.0000	.0000	.0000	.0000	.0001	.0001	.0001	.0001	.0001

					λ					
r	6.10	6.20	6.30	6.40	6.50	6.60	6.70	6.80	6.90	7.00
0	.0022	.0020	.0018	.0017	.0015	.0014	.0012	.0011	.0010	.0009
1	.0137	.0126	.0116	.0106	.0098	.0090	.0082	.0076	.0070	.0064
2	.0417	.0390	.0364	.0340	.0318	.0296	.0276	.0258	.0240	.0223
3	.0848	.0806	.0765	.0726	.0688	.0652	.0617	.0584	.0552	.0521
4	.1294	.1249	.1205	.1161	.1118	.1076	.1034	.0992	.0952	.0912
5	.1579	.1549	.1519	.1487	.1454	.1420	.1385	.1349	.1314	.1277
6	.1605	.1601	.1595	.1586	.1575	.1562	.1546	.1529	.1511	.1490
7	.1399	.1418	.1435	.1450	.1462	.1472	.1480	.1486	.1489	.1490
8	.1066	.1099	.1130	.1160	.1188	.1215	.1240	.1263	.1284	.1304
9	.0723	.0757	.0791	.0825	.0858	.0891	.0923	.0954	.0985	.1014
10	.0441	.0469	.0498	.0528	.0558	.0588	.0618	.0649	.0679	.0710
11	.0244	.0265	.0285	.0307	.0330	.0353	.0377	.0401	.0426	.0452
12	.0124	.0137	.0150	.0164	.0179	.0194	.0210	.0227	.0245	.0263
13	.0058	.0065	.0073	.0081	.0089	.0099	.0108	.0119	.0130	.0142
14	.0025	.0029	.0033	.0037	.0041	.0046	.0052	.0058	.0064	.0071
15	.0010	.0012	.0014	.0016	.0018	.0020	.0023	.0026	.0029	.0033
16	.0004	.0005	.0005	.0006	.0007	.0008	.0010	.0011	.0013	.0014
17	.0001	.0002	.0002	.0002	.0003	.0003	.0004	.0004	.0005	.0006
18	.0000	.0001	.0001	.0001	.0001	.0001	.0001	.0002	.0002	.0002
19	.0000	.0000	.0000	.0000	.0000	.0000	.0001	.0001	.0001	.0001

	λ									
r	8.10	8.20	8.30	8.40	8.50	8.60	8.70	8.80	8.90	9.00
0	.0003	.0003	.0002	.0002	.0002	.0002	.0002	.0002	.0001	.0001
1	.0025	.0023	.0021	.0019	.0017	.0016	.0014	.0013	.0012	.0011
2	.0100	.0092	.0086	.0079	.0074	.0068	.0063	.0058	.0054	.0050
3	.0269	.0252	.0237	.0222	.0208	.0195	.0183	.0171	.0160	.0150
4	.0544	.0517	.0491	.0466	.0443	.0420	.0398	.0377	.0357	.0337
5	.0882	.0849	.0816	.0784	.0752	.0722	.0692	.0663	.0635	.0607
6	.1191	.1160	.1128	.1097	.1066	.1034	.1003	.0972	.0941	.0911
7	.1378	.1358	.1338	.1317	.1294	.1271	.1247	.1222	.1197	.1171
8	.1395	.1392	.1388	.1382	.1375	.1366	.1356	.1344	.1332	.1318
9	.1256	.1269	.1280	.1290	.1299	.1306	.1311	.1315	.1317	.1318
10	.1017	.1040	.1063	.1084	.1104	.1123	.1140	.1157	.1172	.1186
11	.0749	.0776	.0802	.0828	.0853	.0878	.0902	.0925	.0948	.0970
12	.0505	.0530	.0555	.0579	.0604	.0629	.0654	.0679	.0703	.0728
13	.0315	.0334	.0354	.0374	.0395	.0416	.0438	.0459	.0481	.0504
14	.0182	.0196	.0210	.0225	.0240	.0256	.0272	.0289	.0306	.0324
15	.0098	.0107	.0116	.0126	.0136	.0147	.0158	.0169	.0182	.0194
16	.0050	.0055	.0060	.0066	.0072	.0079	.0086	.0093	.0101	.0109
17	.0024	.0026	.0029	.0033	.0036	.0040	.0044	.0048	.0053	.0058
18	.0011	.0012	.0014	.0015	.0017	.0019	.0021	.0024	.0026	.0029
19	.0005	.0005	.0006	.0007	.0008	.0009	.0010	.0011	.0012	.0014
20	.0002	.0002	.0002	.0003	.0003	.0004	.0004	.0005	.0005	.0006
21	.0001	.0001	.0001	.0001	.0001	.0002	.0002	.0002	.0002	.0003
22	.0000	.0000	.0000	.0000	.0001	.0001	.0001	.0001	.0001	.0001

r	7.10	7.20	7.30	7.40	λ 7.50	7.60	7.70	7.80	7.90	8.00
0	.0008	.0007	.0007	.0006	.0006	.0005	.0005	.0004	.0004	.0003
1	.0059	.0054	.0049	.0045	.0041	.0038	.0035	.0032	.0029	.0027
2	.0208	.0194	.0180	.0167	.0156	.0145	.0134	.0125	.0116	.0107
3	.0492	.0464	.0438	.0413	.0389	.0366	.0345	.0324	.0305	.0286
4	.0874	.0836	.0799	.0764	.0729	.0696	.0663	.0632	.0602	.0573
5	.1241	.1204	.1167	.1130	.1094	.1057	.1021	.0986	.0951	.0916
6	.1468	.1445	.1420	.1394	.1367	.1339	.1311	.1282	.1252	.1221
7	.1489	.1486	.1481	.1474	.1465	.1454	.1442	.1428	.1413	.1396
8	.1321	.1337	.1351	.1363	.1373	.1381	.1388	.1392	.1395	.1396
9	.1042	.1070	.1096	.1121	.1144	.1167	.1187	.1207	.1224	.1241
10	.0740	.0770	.0800	.0829	.0858	.0887	.0914	.0941	.0967	.0993
11	.0478	.0504	.0531	.0558	.0585	.0613	.0640	.0667	.0695	.0722
12	.0283	.0303	.0323	.0344	.0366	.0388	.0411	.0434	.0457	.0481
13	.0154	.0168	.0181	.0196	.0211	.0227	.0243	.0260	.0278	.0296
14	.0078	.0086	.0095	.0104	.0113	.0123	.0134	.0145	.0157	.0169
15	.0037	.0041	.0046	.0051	.0057	.0062	.0069	.0075	.0083	.0090
16	.0016	.0019	.0021	.0024	.0026	.0030	.0033	.0037	.0041	.0045
17	.0007	.0008	.0009	.0010	.0012	.0013	.0015	.0017	.0019	.0021
18	.0003	.0003	.0004	.0004	.0005	.0006	.0006	.0007	.0008	.0009
19	.0001	.0001	.0001	.0002	.0002	.0002	.0003	.0003	.0003	.0004
20	.0000	.0000	.0001	.0001	.0001	.0001	.0001	.0001	.0001	.0002
21	.0000	.0000	.0000	.0000	.0000	.0000	.0000	.0000	.0001	.0001

Table A.2 Values of e^x and e^{-x}

x	e^x	e^{-x}	x	e^x	e^{-x}
0.00	1.000	1.000	3.00	20.086	0.050
0.10	1.105	0.905	3.10	22.198	0.045
0.20	1.221	0.819	3.20	24.533	0.041
0.30	1.350	0.741	3.30	27.113	0.037
0.40	1.492	0.670	3.40	29.964	0.033
0.50	1.649	0.607	3.50	33.115	0.030
0.60	1.822	0.549	3.60	36.598	0.027
0.70	2.014	0.497	3.70	40.447	0.025
0.80	2.226	0.449	3.80	44.701	0.022
0.90	2.460	0.407	3.90	49.402	0.020
1.00	2.718	0.368	4.00	54.598	0.018
1.10	3.004	0.333	4.10	60.340	0.017
1.20	3.320	0.301	4.20	66.686	0.015
1.30	3.669	0.273	4.30	73.700	0.014
1.40	4.055	0.247	4.40	81.451	0.012
1.50	4.482	0.223	4.50	90.017	0.011
1.60	4.953	0.202	4.60	99.484	0.010
1.70	5.474	0.183	4.70	109.95	0.009
1.80	6.050	0.165	4.80	121.51	0.008
1.90	6.686	0.150	4.90	134.29	0.007
2.00	7.389	0.135	5.00	148.41	0.007
2.10	8.166	0.122	5.10	164.02	0.006
2.20	9.025	0.111	5.20	181.27	0.006
2.30	9.974	0.100	5.30	200.34	0.005
2.40	11.023	0.091	5.40	221.41	0.005
2.50	12.182	0.082	5.50	244.69	0.004
2.60	13.464	0.074	5.60	270.43	0.004
2.70	14.880	0.067	5.70	298.87	0.003
2.80	16.445	0.061	5.80	330.30	0.003
2.90	18.174	0.055	5.90	365.04	0.003
3.00	20.086	0.050	6.00	403.43	0.002

From Lee, Sang M., and Laurence J. Moore, and Bernard W. Taylor III, *Management Science*, 2d ed.

Table A.3 $P(0)$ for multichannel poisson/exponential queueing process: probability of zero in system

$R = \lambda/(S x \mu)$	Number of Channels: S								
R	2	3	4	5	6	7	8	9	10	15
0.02	0.96079	0.94177	0.92312	0.90484	0.88692	0.86936	0.85215	0.83527	0.81873	0.74082
0.04	0.92308	0.88692	0.85215	0.81873	0.78663	0.75578	0.72615	0.69768	0.67032	0.54881
0.06	0.88679	0.83526	0.78663	0.74082	0.69768	0.65705	0.61878	0.58275	0.54881	0.40657
0.08	0.85185	0.78659	0.72615	0.67032	0.61878	0.57121	0.52729	0.48675	0.44983	0.30119
0.10	0.81818	0.74074	0.67031	0.60653	0.54881	0.49659	0.44933	0.40657	0.36788	0.22313
0.12	0.78571	0.69753	0.61876	0.54881	0.48675	0.43171	0.38289	0.33960	0.30119	0.16530
0.14	0.75439	0.65679	0.57116	0.49657	0.43171	0.37531	0.72628	0.28365	0.24660	0.12246
0.16	0.72414	0.61838	0.52720	0.44931	0.38289	0.32628	0.27804	0.23693	0.20190	0.09072
0.18	0.69492	0.58214	0.48660	0.40653	0.33959	0.28365	0.23693	0.19790	0.16530	0.06721
0.20	0.66667	0.54795	0.44910	0.36782	0.30118	0.24659	0.20189	0.16530	0.13534	0.04979
0.22	0.63934	0.51567	0.41445	0.33277	0.26711	0.21437	0.17204	0.13807	0.11080	0.03688
0.24	0.61290	0.48519	0.38244	0.30105	0.23688	0.18636	0.14660	0.11532	0.09072	0.02732
0.26	0.58730	0.45640	0.35284	0.27233	0.21007	0.16200	0.12492	0.09632	0.07427	0.02024
0.28	0.56250	0.42918	0.32548	0.24633	0.18628	0.14082	0.10645	0.08045	0.06081	0.01500
0.30	0.53846	0.40346	0.30017	0.22277	0.16517	0.12241	0.09070	0.06720	0.04978	0.01111
0.32	0.51515	0.37913	0.27676	0.20144	0.14644	0.10639	0.07728	0.05612	0.04076	0.00823
0.34	0.49254	0.35610	0.25510	0.18211	0.12981	0.09247	0.06584	0.04687	0.03337	0.00610
0.36	0.47059	0.33431	0.23505	0.16460	0.11505	0.08035	0.05609	0.03915	0.02732	0.00452
0.38	0.44928	0.31367	0.21649	0.14872	0.10195	0.06981	0.04778	0.03269	0.02236	0.00335
0.40	0.42857	0.29412	0.19929	0.13433	0.09032	0.06065	0.04069	0.02729	0.01830	0.00248
0.42	0.40845	0.27559	0.18336	0.12128	0.07998	0.05267	0.03465	0.02279	0.01498	0.00184
0.44	0.38889	0.25802	0.16860	0.10944	0.07080	0.04573	0.02950	0.01902	0.01225	0.00136
0.46	0.36986	0.24135	0.15491	0.09870	0.06265	0.03968	0.02511	0.01587	0.01003	0.00101
0.48	0.35135	0.22554	0.14221	0.08895	0.05540	0.03442	0.02136	0.01324	0.00826	0.00075
0.50	0.33333	0.21053	0.13043	0.08010	0.04896	0.02984	0.01816	0.01104	0.00671	0.00055
0.52	0.31579	0.19627	0.11951	0.07207	0.04323	0.02586	0.01544	0.00920	0.00548	0.00041
0.54	0.29870	0.18273	0.10936	0.06477	0.03814	0.02239	0.01311	0.00767	0.00448	0.00030
0.56	0.28205	0.16986	0.09994	0.05814	0.03362	0.01936	0.01113	0.00638	0.00366	0.00022
0.58	0.26582	0.15762	0.09119	0.05212	0.02959	0.01673	0.00943	0.00531	0.00298	0.00017
0.60	0.25000	0.14599	0.08306	0.04665	0.02601	0.01443	0.00799	0.00441	0.00243	0.00012
0.62	0.23457	0.13491	0.07550	0.04167	0.02282	0.01243	0.00675	0.00366	0.00198	0.00009
0.64	0.21951	0.12438	0.06847	0.03715	0.01999	0.01069	0.00570	0.00303	0.00161	0.00007
0.66	0.20482	0.11435	0.06194	0.03304	0.01746	0.00918	0.00480	0.00251	0.00131	0.00005
0.68	0.19048	0.10479	0.05587	0.02930	0.01522	0.00786	0.00404	0.00207	0.00106	0.00004
0.70	0.17647	0.09569	0.05021	0.02590	0.01322	0.00670	0.00338	0.00170	0.00085	0.00003
0.72	0.16279	0.08702	0.04495	0.02280	0.01144	0.00570	0.00283	0.00140	0.00069	0.00002
0.74	0.14943	0.07875	0.04006	0.01999	0.00986	0.00483	0.00235	0.00114	0.00055	0.00001
0.76	0.13636	0.07087	0.03550	0.01743	0.00846	0.00407	0.00195	0.00093	0.00044	0.00001
0.78	0.12360	0.06335	0.03125	0.01510	0.00721	0.00341	0.00160	0.00075	0.00035	0.00001
0.80	0.11111	0.05618	0.02730	0.01299	0.00610	0.00284	0.00131	0.00060	0.00028	0.00001
0.82	0.09890	0.04933	0.02362	0.01106	0.00511	0.00234	0.00106	0.00048	0.00022	0.00000
0.84	0.08696	0.04280	0.02019	0.00931	0.00423	0.00190	0.00085	0.00038	0.00017	0.00000
0.86	0.07527	0.03656	0.01700	0.00772	0.00345	0.00153	0.00067	0.00029	0.00013	0.00000
0.88	0.06383	0.03060	0.01403	0.00627	0.00276	0.00120	0.00052	0.00022	0.00010	0.00000
0.90	0.05263	0.02491	0.01126	0.00496	0.00215	0.00092	0.00039	0.00017	0.00007	0.00000
0.92	0.04167	0.01947	0.00867	0.00377	0.00161	0.00068	0.00028	0.00012	0.00005	0.00000
0.94	0.03093	0.01427	0.00627	0.00268	0.00113	0.00047	0.00019	0.00008	0.00003	0.00000
0.96	0.02041	0.00930	0.00403	0.00170	0.00070	0.00029	0.00012	0.00005	0.00002	0.00000
0.98	0.01010	0.00454	0.00194	0.00081	0.00033	0.00013	0.00005	0.00002	0.00001	0.00000

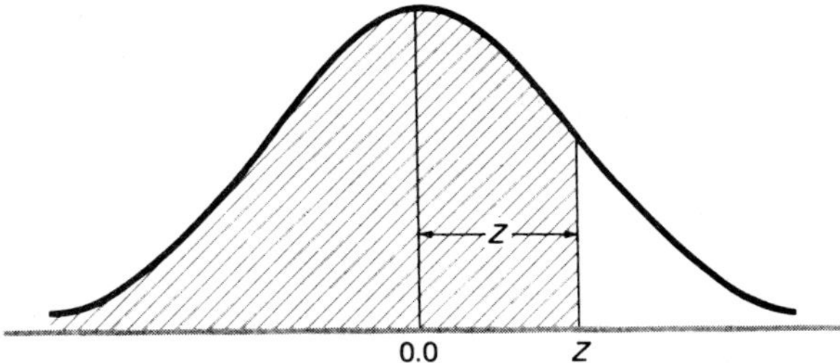

Table A.4 Normal probability values for values of Z

Z	.00	.01	.02	.03	.04	.05	.06	.07	.08	.09
0.0	.50000	.50399	.50798	.51197	.51595	.51994	.52392	.52790	.53188	.53586
0.1	.53983	.54380	.54776	.55172	.55567	.55962	.56356	.56749	.57142	.57535
0.2	.57926	.58317	.58706	.59095	.59483	.59871	.60257	.60642	.61026	.61409
0.3	.61791	.62172	.62552	.62930	.63307	.63683	.64058	.64431	.64803	.65173
0.4	.65542	.65910	.66276	.66640	.67003	.67364	.67724	.68082	.68439	.68793
0.5	.69146	.69497	.69847	.70194	.70540	.70884	.71226	.71566	.71904	.72240
0.6	.72575	.72907	.73237	.73536	.73891	.74215	.74537	.74857	.75175	.75490
0.7	.75804	.76115	.76424	.76730	.77035	.77337	.77637	.77935	.78230	.78524
0.8	.78814	.79103	.79389	.79673	.79955	.80234	.80511	.80785	.81057	.81327
0.9	.81594	.81859	.82121	.82381	.82639	.82894	.83147	.83398	.83646	.83891
1.0	.84134	.84375	.84614	.84849	.85083	.85314	.85543	.85769	.85993	.86214
1.1	.86433	.86650	.86864	.87076	.87286	.87493	.87698	.87900	.88100	.88298
1.2	.88493	.88686	.88877	.89065	.89251	.89435	.89617	.89796	.89973	.90147
1.3	.90320	.90490	.90658	.90824	.90988	.91149	.91309	.91466	.91621	.91774
1.4	.91924	.92073	.92220	.92364	.92507	.92647	.92785	.92922	.93056	.93189
1.5	.93319	.93448	.93574	.93699	.93822	.93943	.94062	.94179	.94295	.94408
1.6	.94520	.94630	.94738	.94845	.94950	.95053	.95154	.95254	.95352	.95449
1.7	.95543	.95637	.95728	.95818	.95907	.95994	.96080	.96164	.96246	.96327
1.8	.96407	.96485	.96562	.96638	.96712	.96784	.96856	.96926	.96995	.97062
1.9	.97128	.97193	.97257	.97320	.97381	.97441	.97500	.97558	.97615	.97670
2.0	.97725	.97784	.97831	.97882	.97932	.97982	.98030	.98077	.98124	.98169
2.1	.98214	.98257	.98300	.98341	.98382	.98422	.98461	.98500	.98537	.98574
2.2	.98610	.98645	.98679	.98713	.98745	.98778	.98809	.98840	.98870	.98899
2.3	.98928	.98956	.98983	.99010	.99036	.99061	.99086	.99111	.99134	.99158
2.4	.99180	.99202	.99224	.99245	.99266	.99286	.99305	.99324	.99343	.99361
2.5	.99379	.99396	.99413	.99430	.99446	.99461	.99477	.99492	.99506	.99520
2.6	.99534	.99547	.99560	.99573	.99585	.99598	.99609	.99621	.99632	.99643
2.7	.99653	.99664	.99674	.99683	.99693	.99702	.99711	.99720	.99728	.99736
2.8	.99744	.99752	.99760	.99767	.99774	.99781	.99788	.99795	.99801	.99807
2.9	.99813	.99819	.99825	.99831	.99836	.99841	.99846	.99851	.99856	.99861
3.0	.99865	.99869	.99874	.99878	.99882	.99886	.99899	.90893	.99896	.99900
3.1	.99903	.99906	.99910	.99913	.99916	.99918	.99921	.99924	.99926	.99929
3.2	.99931	.99934	.99936	.99938	.99940	.99942	.99944	.99946	.99948	.99950
3.3	.99952	.99953	.99955	.99957	.99958	.99960	.99961	.99962	.99964	.99965
3.4	.99966	.99968	.99969	.99970	.99971	.99972	.99973	.99974	.99975	.99976
3.5	.99977	.99978	.99978	.99979	.99980	.99981	.99981	.99982	.99983	.99983
3.6	.99984	.99985	.99985	.99986	.99986	.99987	.99987	.99988	.99988	.99989
3.7	.99989	.99990	.99990	.99990	.99991	.99991	.99992	.99992	.99992	.99992
3.8	.99993	.99993	.99993	.99994	.99994	.99994	.99994	.99995	.99995	.99995
3.9	.99995	.99995	.99996	.99996	.99996	.99996	.99996	.99996	.99997	.99997

INDEX

N

O

P

Q

R

S

T

U

V

W

Z